SCOTT COY

WHO
IS
GOD?

The Hebrew Names of God

A WHOLLY OWNED SUBSIDIARY OF TBN

PROFESSIONAL PUBLISHING MEETS POWERFUL PROMOTION

Trilogy Christian Publishers

A Wholly Owned Subsidiary of Trinity Broadcasting Network

2442 Michelle Drive

Tustin, CA 92780

For information, address Trilogy Christian Publishing

Rights Department, 2442 Michelle Drive, Tustin, Ca 92780.

Trilogy Christian Publishing/ TBN and colophon are trademarks of Trinity Broadcasting Network.

For information about special discounts for bulk purchases, please contact Trilogy Christian Publishing.

10 9 8 7 6 5 4 3 2 1

Library of Congress Cataloging-in-Publication Data is available.

ISBN 979-8-89041-891-3

ISBN 979-8-89041-892-0 (ebook)

DEDICATION

"We love Him because He first loved us" (John 4:19).

God is so generous in His love toward us that He graciously places people for special seasons in our lives to guide, encourage, and share the truths about Him and His undying love for each of us. My life is no different. When I was a young man, He placed my aunt Shireen Kreutz to demonstrate the quality of grace and love that made me believe Jesus was real. She was and is a true example of Jesus's love for us. Later, He gifted me a season of friendship with Charles Milstead, who told me the truth about Jesus Christ and led me to dedicate my life to my Lord and Savior; Charles testified to me without compromise about the Lord, and I have to say "that he was the right man at the right time." I am forever in debt to the bold witness of Christ.

My friend Ray Beadle accepted the Lord Jesus the same night I did. We became brothers at the altar, and he has never failed to pray for me. My other brother, Joe Randolph, pushes me to go further in the ministry, always encouraging me. My lifelong friend Jerome Peitz, who has since gone on to be with the Lord, was always there.

Foremost among those who have profoundly impacted my life is my cherished mother, Dorothy. Her enduring love, unwavering belief in me, and constant encouragement are blessings that make her the epitome of the best mother one could ask for.

He is: Elohim Ahavah

The God Who Loves

Blessings

TABLE OF CONTENTS

FOREWORD

It is with great pleasure that I recommend Scott Coy's new book for your reading pleasure. If it was a glass of water, I would tell you that it should be sipped, not gulped, and that it comes from a Higher Source—Living Water—and is pure and hydrating to your spirit man. Scott and I became colleagues and friends in 2016 when I had a divine appointment to set up Scott Coy Prophetic Ministries, his 501(c) (3) tax-exempt nonprofit. Since then, I have been privileged to hear about his Prayer Stop Ministry happenings, listen and participate in his radio shows, and read the devotions in this book one day at a time by email. He has supported my nonprofit, been a mentor, and was there with God's healing words when my husband passed away. One thing has been consistent all these years: Chaplain Scott Coy loves the Lord, has a heart for people and the Great Commission, and lives to share God's Word with all who will listen.

Enjoy! I did!

Blessings,

Kitty

—Dr. Kitty Bickford, DBS, MA, CPC
President, Pasture Valley Children Missions
Author, *Do Your Own Nonprofit* 51-book series

FALLOW

A MIRACLE IS SOMETHING YOU GO THROUGH

January 1

"Persecutions, afflictions, which came unto me at Antioch, at Iconium, at Lystra; what persecutions I endured: but out of them all the Lord delivered me."

2 Timothy 3:11

Not so long ago, while in prayer, the Lord told me this: "A miracle is something you go through."

Since then, I've given this much thought; I remember years ago, Oral Roberts wrote that someone once told him, "I don't believe in miracles!"

Oral replied, "That's because you haven't needed one yet." It's a simple answer, but true. Apostle Paul explains the hardships he suffered while he was in Antioch.

The Greek definition for *all* is: *Including all the forms of declension—all, every, any.*

Surprisingly, the description uses the word *declension*, which means a condition of decline or moral deterioration. We can undoubtedly witness this in our own time. All includes you—all your circumstances, all your hardships. I believe God can deliver you from them all. If you are going through a trial, give it *all* to God.

He is: Jehova-Palat
Deliverer
Blessings

A COUPLE FROM SWEDEN

January 2

"Like apples of gold in settings of silver is a word spoken at the right time."
Proverbs 25:11

One morning, I was out delivering food boxes to the homeless. When I returned, at Prayer Stop, a couple was waiting with another man in the parking lot. I overheard one man say, "That's him," in a thick Scandinavian type of accent, and he quickly said goodbye and left.

The couple said they needed prayer. We already had everything set up at Prayer Stop, so we sat down and began to minister to them. The tragic story they told me just left me quiet for a moment.

They were making their way back to Sweden, coming from California, where their twenty-three-year-old daughter had been tragically killed in a traffic accident—traversing the United States to recover her body. I would assume they stopped to mourn and heal with some friends in Murfreesboro. They were continuing on their way to catch a flight back to Sweden from Nashville. Prayer Stop was to be managed within their time constraints with faith and hope that the Lord would do something; they had heard of a man who prayed for people here.

And yet, there was one more thing that was very deep hurt to them. Twenty years ago, they helped a pastor begin a new church. Recently, while all this was happening, the pastor converted his Protestant church to another religious denomination. With no warning or indication, he had made this change. In a short period of weeks, it seemed as though everything most loved was gone.

I marveled within myself at the strength they had to go on. Imagine losing your daughter or child who was doing so well and so successful at a young age and finding that your church—your place of comfort—was gone at the most needed time.

They came looking for a miracle, and God didn't disappoint. As we prayed, I remember saying, "Because the enemy has done this to your child and your church, this will not be lost. You are to start your own church in your home. Because he has done this to your child, you will minister to young people of this age group."

As I looked up, I saw they were both crying, and then I looked to my right, and this young man was standing next to me with a backpack. I did not know he was next to me. I just said, "Hello, can we help you?" I had no idea he was there. He was just silently praying alongside us. He said, "I need prayer and a ride to Nashville."

I have learned when it's time to get out of the way and let the Holy Spirit do what He can only do. So, I said, "This is the couple to help you then!" I stood up and walked off. They spoke with the young man and prayed with him and offered to give him a ride. All three were smiling, and I noticed this look of awe on both faces of the couple as they looked at the young man; they knew God had intervened. The young man was their *first fruit*.

Afterward, I wondered how they came to find me. That part of the story is amazing as well. A Christian missionary to China had told them about me. In Detroit, I met Janice Bugg. She is a member of the church that they attended in Murfreesboro. Janice called me and said that she heard the couple say that our encounter had changed their lives.

One word from the Lord at just the right moment can change a life forever.

He is: Jehovah Rapha
The Lord Who Heals
Blessings

POWER UP

January 3   *"Do you not know that you are God's temple and that God's Spirit dwells in you?"*

1 Corinthians 3:16

Everyone is familiar with this Bible verse; even the most hardened criminals know it. You can be very assured that the devil knows it, and he fears it. The last thing he wants us to know is the power that comes with understanding the filling of the Holy Spirit.

I am amazed by the Holy Spirit; He holds back the enemy's evil in this world, and it is hard to believe, looking at current circumstances. But wait until after Jesus removes the Holy Spirit from the face of the earth during the tribulation. Then, you will see the true evil and what humankind is willing to do to one another.

The enemy fears the Holy Spirit, yet He is so very gentle with His children. I know He is with me. He does not condemn me, but He will convict me when I am wrong.

He will give me the courage to face the enemy, the understanding of how to pray. There have been times when every pore on my body could feel the presence of evil, but evil can't stand the name of Jesus. Please ask the Holy Spirit for understanding; I'm sure He'll give it to you.

> *"Wisdom is the principal thing; therefore, get wisdom; Yea, with all thy getting get understanding."*
>
> **Proverbs 4:7**

He is: Jehovah Ezrah
My Helper
Blessings

THE GAP

January 4

"I looked for someone among them who would build up the wall and stand before me in the gap on behalf of the land so I would not have to destroy it, but I found no one."

Ezekiel 22:30

Recently, I spoke with a lady who told me she studies the Bible and all religions. Years ago, she watched the movie *The Passion* and stated, "I'm really mad at God! Who could do such a thing to their own child?" She went on to relate her feelings to me about God (the abusive parent).

I had never thought of God this way, so I was careful with my response. I waited and then replied, "Have you ever worked for a boss who would tell you to go do something, but that same boss would never do that work himself?" she thought for a moment and nodded yes. I said, "How did it make you feel? Personally, I would resent it."

I went on to say, "Now, this is the hard part. Jesus was God. He came to do the job Himself. His eyes looked for a man to stand in the gap and found no one, so He came and stood for us. God is the greatest boss on earth."

It was a beautiful transformation that only a mother could have; I could see the anger melt off her face and turn to love. Jesus came to stand in the GAP on our behalf.

If God asks you to intercede for someone today, and I pray that He will, remember He dwells in you, and He will do it through you because He needs you to stand in the GAP for others.

He is: Entunchano
The God Who Intercedes
Blessings

GET YOUR MIND RIGHT

January 5

"And at the end of the days I, Nebuchadnezzar, lifted up mine eyes unto heaven, and mine understanding returned unto me, and I blessed the Most High, and I praised and honored him that liveth forever; for his dominion is an everlasting dominion, and his kingdom from generation to generation."

Daniel 4:34

King Nebuchadnezzar was filled with great pride and, by a loving God, brought down to insanity to save his soul; you can see that it worked.

Today, I drove by a homeless man who is often in a different state of mind. I prayed for him throughout the day, and I pray that he will be given "a right mind." Then, Daniel 4:34 came to my memory as I prayed for him.

I recalled the times in my life when I was given so much stress that I could not even think straight and of other people who have had their hearts and minds blinded by circumstance.

Notice the first thing King Nebuchadnezzar did when he regained his mind was to honor God and praise His name. You see, had he done this before, he would have never gone through his seven years of tribulation. When you get into a stressful situation, open your Bible to Psalm 91 and sing out loud to God, or do as I do, make your song of praise and feel the worship wash the stress away.

"Speaking to yourselves in psalms and hymns and spiritual songs, singing and making melody in your heart to the Lord."

Ephesians 5:19

He is: Jehovah-Rapha
The God Who Heals
Blessings

TEARING DOWN THE VEILS

January 6

"He hath blinded their eyes, he hardened their heart; Lest they should see with their eyes, and perceive with their heart, and should turn, and I should heal them."

John 12:40

A couple of days ago, I saw a man I had known for a while. I reached out and shook his hand. I noticed "the secret handshake" of a specific cult group.

I said, "Are you a _____ _____?" He sheepishly said, "Yes." Then, as they are all trained to do, he said he was not involved with it anymore. I laughed and said, "No, I caught you. You're in it."

He laughed, and I told him where it would lead him and that just because he had made a covenant with darkness did not mean that he would escape judgment (Isaiah 28:18). He agreed. He told me his son wanted to get into it as well. Now the darkness is trying to become generational.

I spoke with him some more and walked off and prayed silently to God. And then, direction came: "Ask if you can pray with him."

I went back and asked if I could pray for him, and he agreed. I asked God to remove the veil from his heart and to open the eyes of his understanding.

I think he does love Jesus, but the false promise of prosperity got him into the cult. Like a lost child thinking that the forest is easy to get out of until you are deep within.

As soon as I laid hands on him, I knew he would come back to the Lord because he gave the Holy Spirit permission to minister to him. When you pray for a lost loved one or a friend, remember:

"The eyes of your understanding being enlightened; that ye may know what is the hope of his calling, and what the riches of the glory of his inheritance in the saints."

Ephesians 1:18

He is: Jehovah-Go-el
Redeeming God
Blessings

COME ON IN;
YOU'RE WELCOME HERE!

January 7

*For we have not a high priest that cannot be touched with the feeling of our infirmities; but one that hath been in all points tempted like as we are, yet without sin.
Let us, therefore, draw near with boldness unto the throne of grace, that we may receive mercy, and may find grace to help us in time of need.*

Hebrews 4:15–16

This is one of my favorite verses in the Bible. Have you ever sinned and then felt bad about it? That remorse can keep you away from God. That's exactly what the enemy wants you to do: stay away from the Father and the Son. You hear a thought that tells you it will be easier to repent in a couple of weeks. Meanwhile, as time passes by, Satan keeps you under the bondage of self-guilt. Don't fall for that trap!

Jesus wants you to come boldly to the Throne of Grace and ask for forgiveness and mercy. If that's not enough, what else do you need while you're here? While you are here, *may you find grace.* Grace is a divine influence on your heart, which means He can heal your heart before you go. It's like going to an emergency room at a hospital where they fix your wounds and then give you the medicine to heal you on your way out. A loving God who always welcomes you will forgive.

He is: Elohay Selichot
The God Who Is Ready to Forgive
Blessings

WITH HIM TO THE END

January 8

"And they overcame him by the blood of the Lamb, and by the word of their testimony; and they loved not their lives unto the death."

Revelation 12:11

I have often thought that if I ever were to get a tattoo, this would have to be it. It would be a mark that would show the enemy that there is no turning back and a reminder to myself as well. The *blood of the Lamb* refers to Jesus on the cross, our *testimony* is our witness before the Lord, "…and they loved not their life unto their death." The time will come when we will face persecution unto the death. What this means is that we trust in the Lord and we love Him more than our life and we will pay the ultimate price by offering our life. The purpose of persecution is to get you to renounce Christ.

When I see this, it reminds me of a newspaper article I read about a Vietnamese man who moved to our community in the 1980s. After the war, he stayed with fellow soldiers to continue the fight against communism. All the men willing had a tattoo printed on their chest that identified them as soldiers fighting for freedom. Surrender would never be an option, and there was no turning back.

When life's stresses get you down and you feel like giving up, take a moment to have communion with the Lord. The new wine represents the blood, the bread represents Jesus's body, and Jesus is the Word of God—this is your testimony to the Lord.

Make your testimony say, "I'll never turn back. I'll never give up serving the Lord!"

He is: Jehovah Gibbor Milchamah
Mighty in Battle
Blessings

OUR LORD WHO SANCTIFIES

January 9

"I will bless the LORD at all times; His praise shall continually be in my mouth."

Psalm 34:1

"The angel of the LORD encamps around those who fear him, and delivers them."

Psalm 34:7

Years ago, I was driving along just singing praise songs to our God and really enjoying the fellowship. Then, I had this thought: "It's okay to say thank you to your angels as long as you don't praise them." I meditated about it for a second and simply said, "Thank you" to my guardian angel who watched over me. Then, suddenly, I realized and exclaimed out loud, "Oh my God! You see me in all my sin!" I didn't just cry; I bawled.

Then, I heard my angel's audible voice, and he said: "I only ever see you in your righteousness." The Lord allowed him to deliver me from my sorrows that day, and he did a good job. It is hard for us to understand that angels only see us in our righteousness. How is that possible? Because the blood of Jesus conceals our sin.

He is: Jehovah M'Kaddish
Lord Who Sanctifies
Blessings

HE'S YOUR HELPER

January 10

"Who has made us sufficient to be ministers of a new covenant, not of the letter but of the Spirit. For the letter kills, but the Spirit gives life."

2 Corinthians 3:6

Have you ever felt led to tell someone about Jesus but were just too scared to do it? I know I have, and I believe I have missed some great opportunities for the Holy Spirit to help someone. Sharing Jesus can be amazingly easy once you step out and talk about Him. When you have a relationship with the Holy Spirit, it's like talking about the greatest person you know, and that person happens to be your best friend. Trust that the Holy Spirit has made you sufficient to be a minister of the new covenant and that He is able to bring life into your conversation. People love to know Jesus cares.

He is: Jehovah Rohi
Lord, Our Shepherd and Friend
Blessings

GOD MOST HIGH

January 11

*"And having spoiled principalities and powers,
He made a show of them openly, triumphing over them in it."*

Colossians 2:15

This Scripture is referring to the descension of Jesus into hell immediately after His death on the cross. But did you know Jesus had the victory before He went to the depths of hell?

Jesus said this: "But no one can enter a strong man's house and plunder his goods, unless he first binds the strong man. Then indeed He may plunder his house" (Mark 3:27).

How bold was this? You know that the enemy was listening to every word Jesus was saying. God tells us what was in Satan's heart before his fall.

"You said in your heart, 'I will ascend to heaven, above the stars of God I will set my throne on high…I will make myself like the Most High'" (Isaiah 14:13–15).

But you are brought down to Sheol, to the far reaches of the pit.

While Satan keeps trying to ascend, God is the one who descended, who brought Himself down to mankind in order to lift us up, then went to the very depths of hell to save us.

As Jesus stood on Satan's neck, all the hordes of hell witnessed as the saints walked out of Abraham's bosom, making a show of him openly.

Next time you feel down because it feels like the devil is walking all over you, remember this:

"Behold, I have given you authority to tread on serpents and scorpions, and over all the power of the enemy, and nothing shall hurt you. Nevertheless, do not rejoice in this, that the spirits are subject to you, but rejoice that your names are written in heaven."

Luke 10:19–20

He is: El Elyon
God Most High
Blessings

AUTHORITY

January 12

But when the archangel Michael, contending with the devil, was disputing about the body of Moses, he did not presume to pronounce a blasphemous judgment, but said, 'The Lord rebuke you'."

Jude 1:9, ESV

Authority is something we all contend with at one time or another. This must have been a dramatic scene in heaven, Michael and Satan contending over the body of Moses.

Satan had an evil intent for Moses's body—he might have wanted to bury him in a large, expensive grave where people would have eventually turned Moses into a false god and fallen into idol worship, thereby misleading an entire nation.

God buried Moses Himself with His own hand, in a secret place, out of love and respect for Moses. And Michael did not blaspheme Satan, not because of who he is, but because of who he once was!

On one occasion, while I was talking to a man, he started going off about the devil. He railed against him as though the enemy was stupid. I remember thinking that this was foolish talk. He went on to say he completely had no fear of the devil. A couple of months went by. It was around 11:00 p.m. on a Saturday night, and I was completely exhausted. I received a call from this man, and he wanted me to come over to his house and pray with a group of men because he was under demonic attacks: clocks stopping, pictures falling off the walls, and his wife was in terrible fear.

I was so tired; I did not want to go. The Holy Spirit rose up in me and said: "Ask him if he is married to ____?" I had always assumed that they were married and had no cause to think otherwise. I asked him. His response was as though he fell over backward on the other end of the phone! He said, "Well, we intend to do the right thing one day."

I told him that there was no point in me going over there to pray because the enemy had legal authority to be in his home. Afterward, I thought back on what he had said a couple of months earlier, taunting the enemy yet knowingly living in sin.

The point of this is that that Michael and the angels operate under authority: God's authority, Jesus' authority.

"But it is not the spiritual that is first but the natural, and then the spiritual" (1 Corinthians 15:46).

If you don't respect the natural authority, you won't have authority in the spiritual.

> *"Submit yourselves therefore to God. Resist the devil, and he will flee from you."*

James 4:7

He is: Elohim
God of Might and Power
Blessings

RENEWER OF LIFE

January 13

"For you have heard of my former conduct in Judaism, how I persecuted the church of God beyond measure and tried to destroy it."

Galatians 1:13

This was the Apostle Paul explaining his call to the ministry of Jesus. Paul's name originally was Saul (Acts 13:9). Saul had a reputation. Notice how he did not say, "Maybe thou hast heard of my former days?" That is because he knew they had heard of him. Saul was a very brutal man when it came to the things of the church.

One day, Jesus gave me a vision of Saul from Tarsus. It was real and in real time. I was tied to a post that was like a T, with my arms and hands stretched out and tied to the top rail. Saul was standing there with a leather whip in his hands. He had reddish-brown hair and a full reddish-brown beard. He was wearing a long robe, and by the embroidery or design on it, I could tell he was not a poor man.

Saul looked intense, almost like he had a forced anger, when he gritted his teeth and took the whip. As he pulled the whip backward over his shoulder, he was not going to withhold from delivering pain. As the tail of the whip approached me, I came out of it. It was then that I realized how bad of a man Paul used to be. He had tortured Christians, and he was very good at getting Christians to renounce Christ.

But something happened on the road to Damascus (Acts 9). Jesus arrived! Not with what Saul deserved, but instead, with a new mission! People would have rejoiced had Jesus just struck Saul dead on that road. However, Jesus already knew what Paul would be: the author of much of the New Testament. Paul went on to write over half of the New Testament. He was whipped 195 times throughout his life. I can't help but think what he must have thought when every lash hit his back: "Is it payback?" No, Satan was trying to get Paul to become Saul again. Don't let your past sins whip you back into the former you.

He is: Shub Nephesh
Renewer of Life
Blessings

MIGHTY IN BATTLE

January 14

"He shall cover you with His feathers. And under His wings you shall take refuge;
His truth shall be your shield and your buckler."

Psalm 91:4

What does it mean for God to cover you with His feathers? Sounds weak, doesn't it? I have asked the Lord about this before, and He gave me a vision of a little chick snuggling under his mother's feathers: a lovely, precious, safe place to be.

I read a story about a farmer whose barn had burned to the ground, killing all the animals inside. As he walked through the debris, he saw a severely burned hen lying dead on the ground. When he kicked it over, little chicks ran out, still alive and unharmed. The mother had laid down her life to save her chicks. Doesn't this sound like Jesus?

Another thing I often wondered about was the use of a *buckler*. We all know what a shield does. It offers great protection from arrows and the enemies' other weapons. But a buckler? It's nothing more than a hardened pie plate—or so I thought.

While sitting at Prayer Stop a couple of years ago, I had an encounter. I looked over at the chair next to me, and there was this large man sitting there. He had black curly hair, no shirt, a large barrel chest, a leather girdle that was strapped over one arm, no pants, and a buckler. He sat half bent over with the buckler on his arm. Contemplating and a little angry, he sat up and then took the buckler with much force and a violent slicing thrust to my face!

Thank God it was a vision from the Lord! People driving by must have thought that I lost my mind when I jerked backward for no apparent reason. It was then that I realized that God will violently protect you with His buckler! It is an offensive and defensive weapon. Now, I read this scripture with a whole new understanding and appreciation for what God is willing to do to protect His children. And how does He protect you? With His Truth, and His Truth is Jesus.

"And Jesus saith unto him, I Am the Way, and the Truth, and the Life."

John 14:6

He is: Jehovah Gibbor Milchamah
Mighty in Battle
Blessings

LORD DELIVERER

January 15

"If that is the case, our God whom we serve is able to deliver us from the burning fiery furnace, and He will deliver us from your hand O king."
"But if not, let it be known to you, O king, that we do not serve your gods, nor will we worship the gold image which you have set up."

Daniel 3:17–18

As I typed this verse out and said it in my head, I kept putting, "If that be the case, our God whom we serve is able to deliver us from every need." I can't imagine a much greater need than to be delivered from a fiery furnace and an outraged king's hand. But we all will face our own furnace someday—whether it be bankruptcy, divorce, surgery, or homelessness—all are just words until you go through it.

But our God is able no matter what type of fiery furnace you are facing. God doesn't just deliver you before you get into the furnace. He meets you inside, in the midst of your trial. He communes with you! Imagine Shadrach, Meshach, and Abednego standing inside a roaring furnace that was so hot it killed the mighty men of valor who opened the doors. The men of valor, in their haste to obey the king's command, bound these three in their coats, trousers, their turbans, and their other garments. Why does the Bible give such detailed accounts of their outerwear? Notice when they came out of the furnace, they had all their stuff. The king sees them in the furnace with the Son of God and calls them out. All the princes, governors, and captains witnessed this great miracle of God!

When they came out, not a hair on their head was singed, nor were their garments affected. Not even the smell of fire was on them. But they had something else on them that no king or no furnace could ever take away! They had it recorded for all posterity, their victory in hand. They had the mantle of respect from the nation.

Maybe you are going through a trial. Find that place of communion with God, and you will be able to say, "Devil, you will respect me!" Now, that's the place to be.

He is: Jehovah-Palat
Lord Deliverer
Blessings

THE BELLS ARE ONE

January 16

"Evening, and morning, and at noon will I pray, and cry aloud: and He shall hear my voice."

Psalm 55:17

Have you ever wondered why churches use bells? It was a call to prayer three times a day: 6 a.m., 12 noon, and 6 p.m. It was and still is a reminder to many people around the world to take a moment and pray to our Lord. In Russia, the churches were built according to the distance in which you could hear the bells.

When making a bell at a foundry, the makers first pour molten metal into a mold and let it cool for a couple of days. After they remove it, a lathe cuts five different musical tones into the inner ring of the bell. Then, they take a tuning fork, and it has to be the right tuning fork, as there are several different tuning forks to choose from. The master bellmaker knows which fork to use. He takes the tuning fork and taps it, placing it to the side of the bell, and it energizes the tone of the bell because the tuning fork is the right pitch. The two together make a beautiful tone, and the tone is the same for the bell and the tuning fork.

God is the Master Bell Maker. When you come to Him in prayer, the Holy Spirit knows exactly what pitch you need to make a beautiful sound: the two sounds become one.

He is: Elohim Shama
The God Who Hears
Blessings

THE GOD WHO IS FAITHFUL

January 17

"This is a faithful saying: For if we died with Him, We shall also live with Him, If we endure, we shall also reign with Him, If we deny Him, He also will deny us. If we are faithless, He remains faithful; He cannot deny Himself."

2 Timothy 2:11–13

These verses really caught my attention this morning. It revealed to me that even when I don't feel like I have the faith to pray for someone, Jesus is faithful because He cannot deny Himself.

Let's look at one of the great patriarchs of the Bible, Samson. This was the promise given to his parents.

"…and he shall begin to deliver Israel out of the hand of the Philistines" (Judges 13:5).

We all know the story: When the Spirit of the Lord came upon Samson, he had great strength. Samson did some amazing feats in his lifetime. He was respected in his day as he sat at the gate of the city as a judge. But Samson had a rebellious nature about certain things. He was a Nazarene and had certain rules to follow: never drink strong wine, never touch a dead corpse, and never cut his hair. He would eventually break all three of these commandments. Then, Sampson met Delilah, who was bribed by the Philistines to betray him.

Samson wasn't always faithful toward God, but God was always faithful toward Samson.

This explains why some ministers can get into sin and remain there for years, but God doesn't revoke His call on their lives.

In the end, Samson pushed over the pillars, collapsing the building upon himself and killing three thousand Philistines—not ordinary citizens. These were the rich and political elite. When they died, it set the Philistines back for more than a hundred years! Imagine the anarchy that followed. Slaves had no masters, the government had no leaders, and the military had no commanders. This bought valuable time that allowed Israel to build strength that allowed Saul to become the first king of Israel.

Even in Samson's death, God honored him and placed him in the Hall of Faith, which is found in Hebrews 11. One day, you could be asked to pray for someone, and you may not feel like you have the faith to pray. Remember the character of God: He is ever faithful.

He is: El-HaNe'eman
The God Who Is Faithful
Blessings

RESTORE YOUR EYESIGHT

January 18

*"And why beholdest thou the mote that is in thy brother's eye,
but considerest not the beam that is in thine own eye?"*

Matthew 7:3

We all need to go to the Spiritual Eye Doctor on a regular basis to help us get our vision corrected. The word *mote* can also be translated as a twig or even a straw.

When I was in my early teens, one day, we were irrigating on the farm. As I was walking to the ditch, I went under some trees, and a twig caught me in the eye. I screamed from the immediate pain and instantly pulled it out. That also hurt. But after a few moments, the pain stopped, and I was all right. For symbolic effect, had I continued with that twig in my eye, I could have stumbled in the ditch.

Most people do not want to remove the twigs from their eyes because it can be painful. Leaving it in place might seem normal and even pleasant, but eventually, it will lead you straight into a ditch or a mote of your own demise.

Twigs represent different types of sins: the judgment of others, adultery, fornication, drugs, etc. It's easy for us to criticize the faults of others and even laugh at their failures.

If we refuse to remove our faults, the twig can become a beam so fixed in place that we need a surgeon to remove it. The best way to remove a twig is to renew your mind. How do you do that? Simple—read your Bible.

He is: Logos
The Word
Blessings

LOAD BEARER

January 19

"Do not be unequally yoked together with unbelievers. For what fellowship has righteousness with lawlessness? And what communion has light with darkness?"

2 Corinthians 6:14

Most Christians know what this scripture means. If you're a single Christian, I'm sure you've heard it before. But what is the definition of being unequally yoked?

Back in the day, before tractors were invented, people used oxen, mules, or horses to pull carts, plows, and whatever else needed to be pulled. Farmers had to make do with the animals on hand. Many times, the two animals were not the same size, so the larger animal carried the entire load or the burden of pulling the plow, while the smaller or lesser animal walked along beside and just kept the larger animal company.

In a relationship, being the burden carrier can be hard to bear. The Christian in the relationship will be the one to carry the burden, which reminds of the saying that there is no rest for the weary.

Well, here is the good news: That is not actually a verse in the Bible. Jesus will carry your burden for you.

Jesus said, "Come to Me, all you who labor and are heavy laden, and I will give you rest.

> *Take My yoke upon you and learn from Me, for I Am gentle and lowly in heart, and you will find rest for your souls."*

Matthew 11:28–29

Many times while praying for people, I have had a vision in which I see Jesus taking a yoke and placing it on His shoulders. What an awesome God we serve! When you feel so exhausted and at your wit's end with your spouse, family, or your job, ask Jesus to give you rest. Believe me, you will feel the weight lift off your shoulders.

He is: Jehovah Ezrah
My Helper
Blessings

THE WORD

January 20

And when the tempter came to Him, he said, if thou be the Son of God, command that these stones be made to bread. But He answered and said, it is written, Man shall not live by bread alone, but by every word that proceedeth out of the mouth of God.

St. Matthew 4:3–4

Have you ever wondered why this would have been a sin? I know I did for years. But here are some fascinating insights into the character of God.

> *In the beginning was the Word, and the Word was with God, and the Word was God.*
>
> *The same was in the beginning with God. All things were made by Him, and without Him was not anything made.*

St. John 1:1–3

Jesus is the Word, and the Word is God. Satan will never strategically outmaneuver God. Imagine the power of this statement. Jesus's name was originally the Word! God speaks the Word and creates the heavens and the earth. Satan cunningly deceived Eve with the spoken word by changing the context of the meaning of the word.

In Genesis 2:16–17, God tells Adam to tend to the tree of knowledge of good and evil.

In Genesis 3:3, Eve adds a couple of words to the commandment, "Neither shall you touch it lest you die." Where did this statement come from? You see, Satan had already been working on Adam and Eve's thoughts. It was never a commandment not to touch it. They had to touch it to tend to it.

"Ye shall not surely die: For God doth know that in the day ye eat thereof, then your eyes shall be opened and ye shall be as gods, knowing good and evil" (Genesis 3:4–5).

Here, we see how Satan deceives man with words. It was God's will for Adam and Eve to tend the tree. It was His will for Adam and Eve to touch the tree, but it was not His will for Adam and Eve to eat of the fruit from the tree of knowledge of good and evil. There are three wills on this earth: God's will, man's will, and Satan's will.

God created man with a free will. Satan deceived Eve into eating the fruit, first by thought and by adding a few words to a commandment and deceiving her with a lie of words. Now, because man followed Satan's will, they have gone out of God's will. And through sin, Adam and Eve gave all their authority over to Satan.

Satan deceived man by words, thus breaking God's will. It was God's will for Jesus to be on this fast for forty days, and Jesus was *never* out of God's will. Satan knew in order to defeat Jesus, he had to get Jesus out of the will of God.

But here is where God displays His master strategy, which Satan missed. In effect, God is saying that Satan stole man's free will by deceiving with the Word. Now, I have sent My Son, *the Word*, to take back My will for mankind!

Jesus defeated Satan with words, then gave this authority right back to man in Matthew 16:19 by giving the keys of the kingdom to Peter.

Just to let Satan know who has the authority, Jesus multiplied the seven loaves and fed thousands.

He is: Logos
The Word
Blessings

ADVERSITY BRINGS JOY

January 21

"In the day of Prosperity be joyful, But in the day of adversity consider: Surely God has appointed the one as well as the other, So that man can find out nothing that will come after him."

Ecclesiastes 7:14

It's easy to get excited about the first part of this sentence. Who wouldn't? I pray that you have many joyful days throughout your life.

I remember once I was driving down the road, and I prayed (paraphrased), "Lord, Theo's turning sixteen, and he needs a car." *Oh no! DawnMarie is turning eighteen, and she needs a car!* I went from one car to needing two cars in one single prayer. DawnMarie had returned to Louisiana to finish her senior year of high school and graduate with her friends while Theo was up here in Tennessee, separating us by 634 miles.

I had no idea what to do. But two or three nights later, some friends came to the house after work. They had bought a new car and felt that the Lord wanted them to give their old car to Theo and not to trade it in. At the same moment I was informed that a member from Louisiana called and wanted to give us a car as well! Theo's car was in our driveway, and DawnMarie's car was less than one mile from her house! I was so happy! I told several people at work, and they were amazed. I would say, "God can hit straight with a crooked stick!"

It was easy to be joyful that day. But another time, the weight of the world was on my shoulders. I needed money to cover the house note. I wasn't worried, but I was getting depressed from the length of this particular trial. I asked the Lord what to do. He said, "Listen to your Bible." I thought this was peculiar because I normally read my Bible. I remembered that I had some earbuds in my desk drawer. Even though I'm at my desk every day, I really don't open it much. When I opened my desk drawer, I saw a bank envelope, and there was $1,000.00 in it with a note that said, "God told me to give this to you." That's all. No telling how long it had been in my desk drawer. I made the house payment with a day to spare.

I was thankful and amazed at how God works. I knew the Lord would take care of me—He always has. But God sets the day of adversity next to the day of joy. Why is that? Because if you didn't have adversity, you would never know true joy. You can't have one without the other. And we never know what tomorrow may bring.

He is: El Shaddai
The All-Sufficient One
Blessings

THE GOD OF HEAVEN

January 22

"And He hath raised us up together, and made us sit together in heavenly places in Christ Jesus."

Ephesians 2:6

One day, while at a prayer meeting, I had a realization that we are to be seated on the right hand of Jesus and make supplications for our requests. Then, the light bulb went off! If I was seated with Jesus (*In the Spirit*), we are to pray down our needs. I have always prayed up for my needs.

You see, there are three heavens. The First Heaven is our atmosphere here around us where men live, with the sky above. The Second Heaven is outer space with the planets. This is also where the battle of spiritual warfare takes place.

"For we wrestle not against flesh and blood, but against principalities, against powers, against the rulers of darkness of this world, against spiritual wickedness in high places" (Ephesians 6:12).

The Third Heaven is God's throne, and Jesus sits on the right hand of God.

In World War II, the pilot's knew that having the higher altitude gave a great advantage in combat. The best advantage was to be able to look down on the enemy with the *sun* directly behind them, giving the pilots the element of surprise. With this tactical advantage, they could swoop down and do some damage.

Imagine the force we can do against a spiritual enemy when you attack them with the *Son* behind your back! And how do you get to this amazingly high altitude? On your knees, of course—through prayer.

He is: El Shamayim
The God of Heaven
Blessings

GOD MY ROCK

January 23

"The Lord Lives! Blessed be my Rock! Let the God of my salvation be exalted."

Psalm 18:46

When you look at this verse, it just explodes out of Psalm 18! In Psalm 17:3, David is pleading his case before the Lord: "You have tested my heart; You have visited me in the night; You have found nothing."

Next, in Psalm 18, David begins to remind himself of who God is and what He has done for him in the past. Suddenly, he shouts out with this:

"The Lord lives!"

"Blessed be my Rock!"

"Let the God of my salvation be exalted!"

It bursts out of his heart like the waters of Mount Horeb, the Rock that provided water for Moses and the Hebrew people in Exodus 17:6, which was the first time that the word *rock* was mentioned in the Bible. Jesus was the Rock and still is to this day.

"For they drank of that spiritual Rock that followed them, and that Rock was Christ" (1 Corinthians 10:4).

When going through the trials of life, remind yourself and God of what He has done for you in the past and thank Him. I have done this, and the presence of the Holy Spirit brought peace to me, knowing He wouldn't fail me. Remember, He is the God of your salvation, and salvation means victory.

He is: El Sela
God My Rock
Blessings

LIKE RIDING A BIKE

January 24

"Trust in the Lord with all your heart, and lean not on your own understanding; In all your ways acknowledge him, and He shall direct your paths."

Proverbs 3:5

Do you remember when you were a child trying to learn how to ride your bike for the first time? Your mom or your dad would stand behind you and hold your bike steady. You would get your balance and slowly start peddling while your parent ran along behind, encouraging you to keep peddling! Hold on tight! You're doing great! Then, their voice would start to seem faint, and you would look back and see that they had let you go on your own and that last wave and encouragement to look forward and keep going straight!

I hope this symbolism paints a picture in your mind of how God operates. When you first get filled with the Holy Spirit, you hear His directions so clearly, and His voice is right there. Then, as you learn how to walk in His steps, the voice becomes softer because now God is trusting you to walk in His paths. Our understanding would have God telling us everything, but He tells us not to lean on our understanding but *His*.

He is: Jehovah Shammah
The Lord is Here
Blessings

NEVER ALONE

January 25

"Though one may be overpowered by another, two can withstand him. And a threefold cord is not easily broken."

Ecclesiastes 14:12

I remember years ago watching a show in which a Navy fighter pilot gave his testimony about being shot down over Vietnam and then captured by the North Vietnamese army. He endured years of suffering and isolation. They tried hard to break him down and make him confess to war crimes. He was and hopefully still is a man filled with wisdom. I was captivated listening to his story. He said something which was his strength that no man could take away. He said, "When you're in isolation and you have the Lord, you are never alone." He was tapping into the power of a threefold cord: The Father, the Son, and the Holy Spirit. And he wasn't easily broken.

I've never had to endure pain and suffering like that, but I have had times of loneliness and loss in which the Lord was my friend and companion. I would just sit and pray, read my Bible, and put my hope in the Lord. To this day, He has never failed me. When the world turns against you, draw near to the Lord, and He will draw near to you. And remember: His cord won't break.

He is: Jehovah Rohi
Lord, Our Shepherd and Friend
Blessings

MORE THAN A CONQUEROR!

January 26

Nay, in all these things we are more than conquerors through him that loved us.
For I am persuaded, that neither death, nor life, nor angels, nor principalities,
nor things present, nor things to come, nor powers, nor height,
nor depth, nor any other creature, shall be able to separate us
from the love of God, which is in Christ Jesus our Lord.

Romans 8:37–39

I love this scripture! I used to attend a church pastored by Dr. Lee Lamury (Brother Lee), and he had a great analogy of this verse. He compared it to a champion prize fighter who trains very hard to win the heavyweight title. Think of all the hours of hard work and conditioning he must undergo to win this title: hours of brutal punishment and the mental preparation to endure the day of the big fight. He enters the ring and fights for the full twelve rounds, winning a triumphant victory! With hands raised in the air, they place the golden Heavyweight Champion of the World belt around his waist. He's done it! He has achieved the World Championship, and now he's the conqueror.

When he gets home, he shows his wife the belt, then opens that envelope with a check worth millions of dollars, smiles and signs the back of the check, and hands it over to his wife. Now, she has just become ***More than a Conqueror!***

That's how Christ Jesus sees us: more than conquerors. The fight is done, and the reward is ours.

He is: Elohim
God of Might and Power
Blessings

GOD OF GRACE

January 27

But whoso shall offend one of these little ones which believe in me, it were better
for him that a millstone were hanged about his neck, and that
he were drowned in the depth of the sea.
Woe unto the world because of offences! for it must needs be that
offences come; but woe to that man by whom the offence cometh!

Matthew 18:6–7

Do you remember one of the greatest players in the NFL, Barry Sanders, who played for the Detroit Lions as a running back? He always appeared to me to be a man of great moral character as well as a superior athlete. When he first began his NFL career, he fumbled the ball during a game. He became so angry at himself that he determined he would never fumble again. He went the rest of his career without ever fumbling the ball! Pretty amazing stat, considering he was a premier runner and carried the ball so much—just think about all the hits he took.

It's the same way with sin. We are going to drop the ball when it comes to offenses or getting offended, but don't just say, "Oh well," and go on about your day. Get angry at that sin! And determine in your heart not to do it again. Ask for forgiveness and forgive yourself as well, then move on, and if you repeat, repent.

What about when people offend you? Simple. Just forgive and move on. We read this scripture, but we always tend to miss the most important words in this verse: "must needs," or more easily translated to the word "necessary." Why would Jesus add this word? Because God allowed it when He gave us a free will. He set life and death before us, and then He gives us a hint: "Choose life" (Deuteronomy 39:19). But the choice is still ours to make. Every time we make the choice to offend someone, we have, in effect, chosen death over life.

Be a star running back for the Lord—choose life with your words.

He is: Yahweh-Channun
God of Grace
Blessings

THE GOD WHO HEARS

January 28

"The eyes of the Lord are upon the righteous, and His ears are open to their cry."

Psalm 34:15

When you first start off reading this, it sounds a little spooky if you don't know what He's talking about. We could have said, "The watchful, protective eyes of the Lord are upon us."

I've had a few encounters with demons over the years, and believe me, they are nothing that you want to look at. Fear is their biggest strength, as well as their biggest lie. One time, when I woke up in the middle of the night, there was a demon standing next to me. I was so scared I could not even say the name of Jesus. I just kept saying, "J! J!" trying to say Jesus. But while I was doing this, that demon took off around the end of my bed, and like a blur, it shot off out of the house! My wife woke up and shouted, "Jesus!"

What utterly amazed me was the fear the enemy had at the possibility of me saying "Jesus." I knew then that there is real power in the name of Jesus and that the devils fear it.

Many times over the years, I have read stories or listened to testimonies of the righteous who cried out to God for help, and He answered quickly! You will never get a busy signal when it comes to God. He is always ready to listen and show Himself strong on your behalf.

"For we wrestle not against flesh and blood, but against principalities, against powers, against the rulers of the darkness of this world, against spiritual wickedness in high places" (Ephesians 6:10).

He is: Elohim Shama
The God Who Hears
Blessings

HIS GLORY IS IN THE RAINBOW

January 29

"I do set my bow in the cloud, and it shall be for thee a token of a covenant between me and the earth."

Genesis 9:13

God created an amazing covenant with man. He flooded the earth and then made the "Noahic Covenant." These were some of the conditions of the new covenant:

- Re-populate the earth,
- Given rule over the animals,
- Capital Punishment,
- No more floods, and
- The Sign of the Bow.

The *bow*, or what we call the rainbow, was promised to all future generations as a sign that God would never again flood the whole earth. Here are some interesting facts and symbolisms about the rainbow:

It's a spectrum of seven colors, and seven represents God's number of completion.

- Red: Blood, bloodshed for sin;
- Orange: Warning, moving toward sin;
- Yellow: Welcoming, Spirit of God;
- Green: Righteousness, life, growth;
- Blue: Heavenly, Spiritual, Jesus;
- Indigo: Covering, clothing Bride of Christ;
- Violet: Justification.

A bow is a weapon, an instrument of judgment. It is quick judgment, especially if you're on the wrong end of an arrow. Notice how God positions the bow: If you are looking toward the skyline or horizon as the string (the treetops), the arch of the bow points upwards towards heaven. In effect, God is redirecting judgment back at Himself.

Red (which represents sin) is positioned on top, and violet at the bottom (which represents justification). It seems that God takes the judgment of sin and covers us with justification.

Now, from top to bottom, let's place the spiritual meaning of the colors into a symbolic sentence:

With the bloodshed for sin, after the warning has been given, with His Welcoming Spirit, He will bring righteousness, life, and growth from our Lord Jesus, who will cover the Bride of Christ and bring justification!

He is: El Hakkavod
The God of Glory
Blessings

HOLD YOUR HEAD UP

January 30

"Therefore, by Him let us continually offer the sacrifice of praise to God, that is the fruit of our lips, giving thanks to His name."

Hebrews 13:15

How or why could praise be a sacrifice? How do you eat the fruit of your lips? What is giving thanks to His name? And why not just thank Him? There are many questions behind this one verse if you meditate on it for a second, but let's break it down and find the fruit within.

Have you ever been so devastated by a sudden circumstance or tragedy that you didn't know what to say or even think? The loss of a loved one in which the hurt is so heavy that it felt like your soul had an anchor on it? You couldn't even talk, but you forced yourself to pray? To sing praise? This is your sacrifice of praise! It took all your strength to thank God, and this is the fruit of your lips.

But He said to me, "My grace is sufficient for you, for power is perfected in weakness." Therefore, I will most gladly boast all the more about my weaknesses, so that Christ's power may reside in me.

2 Corinthians 12:9

Whenever you feel as though you don't have the strength to move forward, remember that Christ is made strong through your weakness. I have noticed during the times that I had nothing left physically or emotionally, Jesus showed up. Now I realize that when I work to exhaustion, that is when Christ can be made strong. When you reach that point where you want to stop and rest, get excited and move on because now you will get to see a miracle-working God!

And what is giving thanks to His name? And why not Him? What are some of the names of God?

- Elohim (God of Might and Power)
- Jehovah Nissi (Lord of Victory and Miracles)
- Jehovah Rophe (or Jehovah-Rapha) (Lord of Health and Healing)

When you give thanks to His Name, He is proclaiming back to you who He is and who He wants to be in your life during this season.

He is: Rum Rosh
The One Who Lifts My Head
Blessings

HOW TO RECOGNIZE YOUR BLESSING

January 31

"And Abraham said unto his eldest servant of his house, that ruled over all that he had, Put, I pray thee, thy hand under my thigh."

Genesis 24:2

Abraham sent his loyal servant out to find a wife for his son Isaac. Abraham wanted a wife for his son, but he wanted her to be from his own country. He had the servant make a vow by placing his hand on Abraham's thigh.

The servant made the journey, and when he made it to Abraham's homeland, he prayed (paraphrased) that God would send Isaac's wife to meet him at the well, give him water, and offer to give drink to his animals. Before he finished the prayer, Rebekah arrived and did just that. The servant recognized his answered prayer,

"And the man bowed down his head, and worshipped the LORD" (Genesis 24:26).

I had an intoxicated man approach me at Prayer Stop. He started off by asking me for help with rehabilitation, and then we prayed for him. As we were ministering to him, my friend drove up. He is a manager for a men's rehabilitation program that helps men overcome addictions. My friend gave him his business card, telling him that he had to make the call. The man threw it down on the ground, saying that we didn't understand what he needed. He should have bowed his head and thanked God. When he wasn't looking, I stuck a Bible and the card in his bag. It was very evident that he did not recognize how quickly Jesus answered his prayer. Sometimes, we need help in understanding our answers so that we can be thankful.

He is: Di ou ta panta
My Everything
Blessings

FAITH THE FINAL FRONTIER

February 1

"And Abraham said, my son, God will provide for Himself the lamb for a burnt offering. So the two of them went together."

Genesis 22:8

Faith: The Final Frontier. Doesn't this sound like the opening of Star Trek? Do you know what the definition of frontier is? In part, it is the furthermost limits of knowledge or achievement in a particular subject.

Abraham had traveled for three days looking for just the right place to offer his son, Isaac, as the Lord had commanded him to do. Maybe Isaac figured out that something wasn't quite right about this trip. Isaac carried the wood on his back for the burnt offering, just like Jesus carried the cross.

In Hebrews 11:19, the Apostle Paul states that Abraham was fully persuaded that God would raise Isaac back from the dead, but Isaac was unaware of his father's intentions up until this point when maybe he started to figure it out. Isaac traveled the rest of the trip on his father's faith. He was willing to let his father bind him and lay him on the altar, trusting his father completely and suddenly. The Angel of the Lord showed up, then Abraham lifted up his eyes and saw that behind him, a ram was caught in the thicket. Abraham's faith carried both of them.

Sometimes, the hardships just seem to go on and on, and we keep trusting in our Father, but many times, people quit right before the breakthrough. Jesus will never ask you to do something without a plan to bless you. And if you make a mistake, God can fix that, too.

If you find yourself needing help with faith, ask Jesus. He will carry the wood for you.

"Cast your burden on the LORD, and he will sustain you; he will never permit the righteous to be moved" (Psalm 55:22, ESV).

He is: El-HaNe'eman
The God Who Is Faithful
Blessings

LOVE: IT HAS REWARDS

February 2

"Because he hath set his love upon me, therefore will I deliver him: I will set him on high, because he hath known my name."

Psalm 91:14

Have you ever faced a difficult situation that seemed to have no way out? We all have. Here's the formula you need to get through the situation: All you need is love (love for God, that is). Pretty simple, isn't it? If we amplify this verse:

"For upon Me he hoped, and I shall rescue him. I will shelter him for he knew My Name."

This is called "expectant hope" or faith. I once told a pastor, "I wish God would just tell me what to do." He smiled and said, "Now, that wouldn't be faith."

And he was right. Faith is just trusting the Creator of the universe and everything in it that He will help in our time of need. How do you get faith? By learning how to love God.

And how do you love God? By knowing His character and His personality. That's why I always list the names of God at the bottom of these devotionals. These are names that God has revealed to us about His character.

He is: Elohim Ahavah
The God Who Loves
Blessings

THE GREATEST COMMANDMENT!

February 3

"Jesus said unto him, Thou shalt love the Lord thy God with all thy heart, and with all thy soul, and with all thy mind."

Matthew 22:37

When I first became a Christian, I was a police officer in Louisiana. I read this verse, and it really distressed me. I thought to myself, *How can I love God with all my heart when I have never met Him?*

I went to my friend, the sergeant who led me to the Lord, Charles Milstead, and asked Him this question, "How do I love God with all my heart when I have never met Him? I met my aunt from far away once when I was a child, and I felt like I was just supposed to love her, but I didn't even know her."

Charles just looked at me with a blank stare and said, "I really can't answer that."

Now, I was in a real bind because my sergeant friend was always right and always had the right answers. In my mind, he knew everything. That day, as I drove my patrol car, I came up with a plan. I would go home and get on my knees and pray until I convinced myself that I loved God.

When I knelt down on my knees that evening, I began to pray, "Jesus, I love You," and the third time I said it, something began to happen to me. I felt the sensation of a cup of warm oil pour into my head, not onto it, but into me. When the oil reached my tongue, I could no longer speak. Suddenly, an audible voice said to me, "I love you too, Scott!" I whipped my head around to see who was standing behind me, but no one was there.

The voice of God had just spoken to me for the very first time! It was all-powerful, all-wise, and all-loving! And He knew my name! You would think that I would have been jumping up and down for joy! But I wasn't. All I could do was say, "Oh my God! Hell is real!" over and over again as the memories of all my near-death experiences began to flood my mind: the time I was stabbed in the chest, the time the cylinder fell out of a pistol when the man had the drop on me, the car wrecks! It was like they were flushing out my body! My sins! And God was there protecting me the whole time! And I despised Him and everything Christ stood for!

But He loved me! Hell is real, and a loving God has delivered me from it time and time again, and I despised Him, *but He loved me.*

God loves you, too, and He wants you to love Him.

He is: Jehovah Rohi
Lord our Shepherd and Friend
Blessings

FIRST LOVE

February 4

"We love him, because he first loved us."

1 John 4:19

This is one of my favorite verses in the Bible, not because it's short and easy to remember, but because it speaks of the goodness of God, that He loved us before we knew Him.

One day, while at Prayer Stop, a Muslim man came up to me and said, "What is this Prayer Stop?" I wish I could type in the beautiful accent he spoke with.

I explained that I pray to Jesus, and Jesus answers the prayers. Then, he mentioned something that most Muslims think, "I love God, but I don't know if He loves me. I hope He does."

In my mind, I went straight to this verse but did not say it. I said, "Do you have children?" His response was, "Yes." "And do you love them?" Again, he said, "Yes."

I said, "When your children were born, you loved them, didn't you? It was automatic, but your child had to learn to love you. It's the same way with God. He loves you because you're His child, and we learn to love Him because He's our Father."

Needless to say, he was incredibly happy when he walked off, and I could see that he was thinking. Love is what wins souls; I know His love won mine.

Please never underestimate the power of a seed sown.

He is: Elohim Ahavah
The God Who Loves
Blessings

HIS SAKE IS YOUR SAKE

February 5

"And be ye kind one to another, tenderhearted, forgiving one another, even as God for Christ's sake hath forgiven you."

Ephesians 4:32

Sometimes, I've thought that if I were ever stranded on a deserted island and only allowed one book out of the Bible, it would probably be the book of Ephesians. It can really provoke you to deep thoughts in the Lord.

This is such a beautiful verse in the Bible, pretty straightforward: be kind to one another, tenderhearted, forgiving…but then Paul says something very amazing, "Even as God for Christ's sake hath forgiven you."

The modern definition of the word *sake* is "out of consideration for" or "in order to help someone." But in the 1947 Webster's dictionary, it also meant fault, blame, guilt, blemish, and physical imperfection.

Did you know that because Jesus took all of your faults, all of your blame, all of your guilt, all of your hidden blemishes, and your physical imperfections (sickness), God the Father will accept you out of consideration for His Son?

One night, I had what is called a night vision. I was approaching Jesus and casting my crown before Him, then I stepped to the side of the platform and watched as others were casting their crowns before Jesus. Behind the platform was Father God sitting in a chair with His hands on His knees, watching and enjoying everything that was going on. I felt concerned, and I said, "Father God, this seems so unfair. What do you get out of this?"

God, our Father, is such a sweet being. He turned His head, smiled at me, and said, "I get you."

The sensation I had of this being an extremely poor trade was overwhelming. With all the people casting their crowns before Jesus, the trade was still not enough to cover the cost that Jesus paid for you and me.

Even in eternity, we may never know the true value of the trade. However, Jesus thinks you are worth every drop of His blood. He is the truth, so we can accept His opinion.

He is: Jehovah-Go'el
Redeeming God
Blessings

MAKE IT WELL FOR YOURSELF

February 6

*"Say ye to the righteous, that it shall be well with him:
for they shall eat the fruit of their doings."*

Isaiah 3:10

God's promises don't get much better than this. Often, in counseling with other people, I run across the sin of unforgiveness. But not in the way you think: It is mostly people having a hard time forgiving themselves, and they are even unwilling to do so.

> *Peter asked our Lord this question, thinking he was justified in forgiving someone seven times.*
>
> *Then came Peter to him, and said, Lord, how oft shall my brother sin against me, and I forgive him? till seven times?*
>
> *Jesus saith unto him, I say not unto thee, Until seven times: but, Until seventy times seven.*

Matthew 18:2–22

That's an incredible 490 times! But I have learned that this verse applies more to myself than to others. A past sin or failure comes to my mind over and over, like a broken record that just keeps playing the same line of music in my head. I have to forgive myself not once or twice but as many times as it takes.

What the Lord has called clean, let no man call unclean. When you ask Jesus for forgiveness, you are clean by the holiness of His blood, not by your works. When you accept Jesus as your Lord and Savior, you are made righteous through Him.

He is: Jehovah-Tzidkenu
The Lord our Righteousness
Blessings

WRESTLING FOR YOUR BLESSING

February 7

*"And Jacob was left alone; and there wrestled a man with him
until the breaking of the day."*

Genesis 32:24

This is the encounter Jacob had with God before crossing the Jabbok River. In my mind's eye, I can see Jacob looking at the stranger who approached him in his time of great fear. Jacob was fleeing Laban from behind and was about to face his brother Esau, who had sworn to murder him. Picture this: Jacob was left alone on the riverbank, staring down a stranger in the middle of the night.

Have you ever had such a huge problem in life that it felt like you were wrestling with God? Or worse yet, the opponent of God? Jacob was about to encounter his worst fear, Esau, and then God showed up in the form of a man? And now he has to wrestle until the break of day. Problem upon problem, and then this? But Jacob knew somehow that this was a divine encounter that he had to wrestle through, so they began to wrestle.

Have you ever wrestled with your children and let them win to build their confidence, and then bestowed a title on them like wrestling champion of the household? It's obvious that God let Jacob win because He reached down and dislocated Jacob's thigh. But Jacob still would not quit, and the reward was much greater than he could imagine. His name was no longer Jacob but Israel. And God blessed him there. Wow! A nation is born! His encounter with God meant God's favor, but it also meant being wounded.

Once, I had a man come up to me. He didn't say a word, and as he approached me, the Holy Spirit said, "He has been blessed with the trials of life!" Sometimes, you have to wrestle in prayer for your victory.

After Israel wrestled with God, something amazing happened! When Israel met big brother Esau, brotherly love kicked in instead of revenge.

Israel was never the same. He limped everywhere as a reminder of who he was. It's hard to do, but sometimes we have to say, "Thank You, Father, for this trial. I know it's for my blessing."

God believes you will win.

He is: Entunchano
The God Who Intercedes
Blessings

STUDY TO RELAX

February 8

The LORD is my shepherd; I shall not want. He maketh me to lie down in green pastures: he leadeth me beside the still waters. He restoreth my soul: he leadeth me in the paths of righteousness for his name's sake. Yea, though I walk through the valley of the shadow of death, I will fear no evil: for thou art with me; thy rod and thy staff they comfort me. Thou preparest a table before me in the presence of mine enemies: thou anointest my head with oil; my cup runneth over. Surely goodness and mercy shall follow me all the days of my life: and I will dwell in the house of the LORD forever.

Psalm 23:1–6

A couple of days ago, the Lord said, "Study to relax." Psalm 23 really puts that in perspective. In parenthesis, I wrote out the Hebrew definition of keywords.

- The LORD is my *shepherd* (He is to rule, associate with me as a friend. He wants to keep company with me. He will devour, eat up evil, feed me, use me as a friend. He is my keeper, my pastor).

- I shall not *want* (I shall not lack).

- He maketh me to *lie down* (to recline, make to rest, sit) in *green* (He places me in tender grass, green, tender herbs)

- *Pastures* (a house, a pleasant place):

- he leadeth me beside the *still* (comfortable, ease, quiet, resting) waters.

- He *restoreth* (He brings me back home again; He recalls to mind my recompense, recovers, refreshes, relieves, rescues, restores, retrieves, and rewards)

- my *soul* (my mind):

- He leadeth me in the paths of *righteousness* (the right natural, moral, or legal way) for His name's sake.

- Yea, though I walk through the valley of the shadow of *death* (shade of death, that is, the grave), I will fear no evil: for thou art with me;

- thy *rod* (Your weapon or punishing, fighting, ruling) and thy staff (Your support and Your sustenance), they comfort me.

- Thou *preparest* (You set everything in a row, You arrange and put in order in a very wide variety of applications. You set the battle in array, You direct, furnish, handle, join in the battle, ordain the outcome) a table before me in the presence of mine enemies:

- thou *anointest* (You satisfy, accept, fatten, and take away the ashes from sacrifice)
- my head with *oil* (With pure perfumed oil), my cup runneth over.
- Surely goodness and mercy shall *follow* (You run after me, chase me, and even pursue) me all the days of my life: and I will dwell in the house of the LORD forever.

Amen!

He is: Jehovah Shalom
The Lord is Peace
Blessings

IT TAKES TIME

February 9

"But strong meat belongeth to them that are of full age, even those who by reason of use have their senses exercised to discern both good and evil."

Hebrews 5:14

What is strong meat? Is it like a steak that lifts weights? Actually, it comes from the Greek word *ster-eh-os'*, which means solid, stable, steadfast, or sure. In addition to this, Paul adds the word *meat*, which also originated from the Greek word *trof-ay'*, which is defined as nourishment, rations, wages, or food.

We are encouraged to pursue strong meat (a solid and stable lifestyle). How do we get this strong meat? Find a good church with a good pastor, an anointed minister who can teach you the uncompromising Word of God. It takes a lot of courage to get up in front of people and speak the truth about sin, especially when someone walks in that you know is in this sin. Your first thought is, "How did they end up here today?" The Holy Spirit, that's how! He knew that person needed to hear the truth.

But in the prophetic arena, you need to be able to recognize when the enemy is trying to fool you into making a prophetic word that could mislead someone from Christ. This is how you exercise your senses to know both good and evil. Does the word match up to the Bible? Does it edify the hearer?

A Navy Admiral once said, "You can't be a good leader until you have learned how to be a good follower." Love to follow so that you can be loved when you get to lead.

He is: El Roi
The God Who Sees Me
Blessings

WHY GO TO CHURCH?

February 10

"And let us consider one another to provoke unto love and to good works:
Not forsaking the assembling of ourselves together, as the manner of some is; but
exhorting one another: and so much the more, as ye see the day approaching."

Hebrews 10:24–25

Over the years, I have run across many people who think that they really don't need to go to church. But this verse clearly states that you should attend a church. A church body should be a place of encouragement and exhortation, a place that encourages members to do great works for God.

I remember a letter sent by a man to the editor of a newspaper. The letter said that the man could find no good reason for going to church anymore and that after 20-plus years, he couldn't see where it had helped him. He couldn't remember all the sermons and thought it was pointless to continue on.

Someone took the time to reply and wrote something like: He had been married for over twenty years. He couldn't remember every meal his wife had cooked for him, but he knew he had eaten them and that they had nourished him and sustained him long enough to get to the next meal.

He explained that this is what your pastor does for you. He prepares a sermon and then feeds you the Word of God so that you can be prepared for what the world throws at you.

I'm sure the sermons will sustain you, nourish you, encourage you enough to continue on in your pilgrimage. In turn, maybe you will be able to encourage others, lay hands on the sick, and watch them recover, comfort those who mourn, or be the peacemaker. If you are not part of a church body, ask Jesus where you can go to help encourage others. Your gifts are needed, too.

He is: Shub Nephesh
Renewer of Life
Blessings

WHY, GOD, WHY?

February 11

"And not only so, but we glory in tribulations also: knowing that tribulation worketh patience; And patience, experience; and experience, hope: And hope maketh not ashamed; because the love of God is shed abroad in our hearts by the Holy Ghost which is given unto us."

Romans 5:3–5

Have you ever wondered why bad things just keep happening to you? Years ago, a prophetess told me, "The reason God allows you to go through so much trouble is that when you pray for someone, you won't have to say, 'I think God can deliver you.' You can say, 'I know God will deliver you!'"

The following week, I ran into people who started telling me their problems. I smiled and said, "I know God can deliver you because He delivered me from the exact same thing." This is how you can glory in tribulations by giving your testimony of how God delivered you. You will see it after the trial is through. You will have a little more understanding and more experience, and with that experience, you will have hope for the trial you are currently going through. Being able to say, "I know God has delivered me before. I'm sure He will do it again," is possible because, with each trial, you gain a little more trust in God.

If you put your hope in God, you will never be put to shame. And remember *love*—that's a gift the Holy Spirit brings when He moves into your heart. But love requires exercise—exercise it by showing love to someone who you consider unlovable. Pretty soon, you will see them in the same way that God sees them.

He is: Jehovah Jireh
The Lord Who Provides
Blessings

NAME SIX

February 12

"For this, Thou shalt not commit adultery, Thou shalt not kill, Thou shalt not steal, Thou shalt not bear false witness, Thou shalt not covet; and if there be any other commandment, it is briefly comprehended in this saying, namely, Thou shalt love thy neighbor as thyself."

Romans 13:9

While in prayer one day, the Lord asked me a question, "Scott, can you name six of the Ten Commandments?" Needless to say, I was surprised by the question, so like an overweight athlete trying to do a fifty-meter hurdle for the first time, I managed to do it. I'm quite sure Jesus was not impressed.

But this really got me thinking. Why would He just ask me to name only six? Why not all ten?

What about the other four commandments?

- Thou shalt have no other God besides me.
- Thou shalt not make any graven image.
- Thou shalt not take the name of the Lord thy God in vain.
- Remember the Sabbath day and keep it Holy.

Why were these not included? The simple answer can be found in one word: *love.*

You see, if you love your neighbor as you love yourself, you won't harm anyone. Love fulfills all the law. With love, you would never want to do anything that would harm someone else, you would love God with all your heart, you would never dream of having another god before Him, and you would want to spend every day with Him. If you love God with all your heart, you will detest sin.

Think about this: Love is what kept Jesus on the cross.

"Love worketh no ill to his neighbor: therefore, love is the fulfilling of the law" (Romans 13:10).

What manner of love can you bestow on someone today?

He is: Elohim Ahavah
The God Who Loves
Blessings

THE GOD WHO SEES ME

February 13

"Do not remove the ancient landmark, Nor enter the fields of the fatherless."

Proverbs 23:10

Landmarks were boundaries set up by the property owners to mark their territories. They define the outer edges of your property lines, and it is still the system we use today, except we now have modern lasers and marker posts to make the job easier.

It's a sin to remove a boundary line, and sin is pretty easy to do. For example, you are building a fence between you and your neighbor. He'll never notice that your fence is a foot farther onto his property line, but God will.

What about other boundaries? Boundaries concerning someone's reputation, their spouse's reputation, or their children? It's easy to whisper a comment that starts a spark that starts a fire that can ruin a reputation that has been hard-earned. No one will notice, but God will, and God is just. Something as simple as cutting a joke to your friend about his wife can create a spark of jealousy in a marriage.

One time, my pastor was eating lunch at a restaurant. When he left, he forgot to pay his bill. The waitress asked my neighbor if she knew that man and told him that he had forgotten to pay his bill when he left. My neighbor said, "Oh, that's Pastor So-and-So. I know he just forgot. He's very honest. Let me pay it for him."

You see, that's how you protect someone's landmark—in this case, the pastor's reputation. He could have just as easily told the lady the name of the church and let her call. But by paying for the pastor's lunch, he reinforced the pastor's good reputation by showing that he was worth picking up his tab.

Don't break down landmarks. Instead, be a landmark in someone else's life.

He is: El Roi
The God Who Sees Me
Blessings

ALL-SUFFICIENT GOD

February 14

*"When the righteous cry for help, the Lord hears,
and rescues them from all their troubles."*

Psalm 34:17

What a great scripture to know when things have gotten out of control. Hopefully, that will never happen to you, but if it does, you can rest assured that God hears and He answers.

We can all relate to this verse when seemingly insurmountable circumstances hit our lives. But have you ever given a thought to the little things? We have this false sense of belief that tells us that God is too busy to be bothered with our *little* problems. Let me share this story that a friend of mine told me years ago:

He was a manager of a jewelry store. He worked hard to make sure that all the details were handled. So basically, that's management talk. Translated, it means that he worked long hours. One night, he was working on a precision wristwatch. The store was closed, and it was about 11:00 p.m. He was repairing a man's wristwatch, trying to replace a tiny little gear back onto the post. It was so small that he was using tweezers and a magnifying glass to position the gear over the post. He was very tired and getting frustrated because he could not get it back on the post. He told me that he had been trying for over twenty minutes to get just this one piece back into position.

Out of frustration, he just said, "Jesus, would You help me?" Suddenly, the gear popped out of the tweezers onto the post, and he heard the Lord say this to him: "I care about the smallest detail of your life." He sat there in awe, looking at how small that gear was, and astounded that God cared about something so trivial.

Sometimes, the trivial can make your life miserable. Trivial matters matter, and so do your prayers. Don't ever think that your problem is too small for God to be willing to show His magnitude on your behalf.

He is: El Shaddai
All Sufficient God
Blessings

POWER OVER HELL

February 15

*"And I also say to you that you are Peter, and on this rock,
I will build My church, and the gates of Hades shall not prevail against it.
And I will give you the keys of the kingdom of heaven, and whatever you bind on
earth will be bound in heaven, and whatever you loose on e
arth will be loosed in heaven"*

Matthew 16 18–19

This saying took place at a specific cave in Caesarea Philippi, which is at the base of Mount Hermon. The cave is actually called *The Gate of Hades*, as well as *The Grotto of Pan*, named after a pagan god. People would throw their sacrifices into the inner part of the cave that had deep-flowing springs. If no blood came out of the spring in front of the cave, the sacrifice was accepted.

Jesus deliberately brought His disciples to this location and made this statement of faith. With the powerful image as His backdrop, He gave Peter, you, and I the power over hell. Then, He said the gates of Hades (hell) would not prevail against us.

How can a gate prevail? The only way a gate can prevail is if it is open and something comes pouring out. Since the devil is a liar, I would suspect that you can expect lies to come pouring out, flowing like a foul spring.

If the devil is a master of lies, what other gates should we be concerned about? How about your ear gate?

Have you ever heard about the pearly gates? This comes from:

"And the twelve gates were twelve pearls" (Revelation 21:21).

I've been told that your eardrum is so white that it looks like a pearl. When I was told this, I immediately thought about this scripture and how amazing it is that sound must pass through your pearly white ear gate to get to your mind.

Sometimes, those aren't just your negative thoughts popping into your head. When you get a negative thought, such as you will never get through the situation you are facing, you can counterattack with this: "We live by faith, not by sight" (2 Corinthians 5:7).

Do you remember the part about the deep-flowing springs and the blood after the sacrifice? If you go back to: "Be of good cheer daughter, your faith hath made you well" (Matthew 9:22).

This was about the woman with the issue of blood that wouldn't stop flowing, and Jesus healed her. She was from Caesarea Philippi, too. Jesus was proving a point, telling the enemy that its blood had no power and its gates would not prevail.

He is: Jehova-Uzzi
The Lord My Strength
Blessings

WE ARE CONFIDENT

February 16

"O Death, where is your sting? O Hades, where is your victory?"
The sting of death is sin, and the strength of sin is the law.
But thanks be to God, who gives us the victory through our Lord Jesus Christ.

2 Corinthians 15:55–57

Death: it doesn't get much more serious. I'm pretty confident in saying that Jesus's victory on the cross is the complete answer to this topic. Death couldn't kill Him, and the grave couldn't hold Him, simple as that.

I've read and heard testimonies of Christians who have died, came back to life, and said things like, "Don't fear death because I didn't feel a thing!"

"We are confident, yes, well pleased rather to be absent from the body and to be present with the Lord" (2 Corinthians 5:8).

The word *absent* in Greek means to emigrate, to vacate, or be absent.

I love the word emigrate; it means to leave one's own country to migrate to another. In this case, it would be your own body or a tent, which is your tabernacle. A tabernacle is a movable place of worship, and as Christians, we are temporarily stationed here on earth until we get to go home to the ultimate place of worship, the throne room of God!

When Christians leave this plain, the Holy Spirit just now told me this, "Be blessed in the loss of a loved one." He will welcome them into His sanctuary.

He is: Maon
Dwelling Place
Blessings

THE FIRST AND THE LAST

February 17

Therefore, we also, since we are surrounded by so great a cloud of witnesses, let us lay aside every weight, and the sin which so easily ensnares us, and let us run with endurance the race that is set before us, looking unto Jesus, the author and finisher of our faith.

Hebrews 1:1–2

People love to watch a great athletic performance, to watch the greatest athletes perform at the highest levels. Today, I remembered a video I saw a few years ago of a track race, which made me think about this scripture. It was probably a fifty-meter hurdle men's competition. The gun sounded, and all the men took off. One man was particularly heavy, not because of fat but because he had so much muscle. Every time he jumped, his last foot couldn't clear the hurdle. The next one came, he knocked it down, and the next, and the next. The other contestants left him behind and completed the race. Finally, I was just hoping that he could make one clean hurdle, and on the last one, he tripped and fell, got up, and finished the race.

I've noticed that some Christians have a more difficult time running their race. To be truthful, most Christians won't make a clean race, clearing every hurdle placed before them. You lose a job, get back up, and run for the next hurdle. Another calamity awaits you, and another.

Sometimes, the hurdles are by our own doing, but sometimes, we have an enemy that changes the height of the jump. But Jesus knows how strong you are in the Spirit:

And not only that, but we also glory in tribulations, knowing that tribulations produce perseverance, and perseverance, character, and character, hope.

Now hope does not disappoint because the love of God has been poured out in our hearts by the Holy Spirit who was given to us.

Romans 5:3–5

Has life knocked you down? Always trying to clear a hurdle, thinking about giving up on the Lord? Place your hope in the Lord because hope in the Lord pins medals.

Years after the event, I only remember the man who struggled so hard to finish his race. Ironically, he struggled because he was so strong. Everyone in the stadium watched and pulled for him to finish, and very few noticed the flawless victory of the winner. The great cloud of witnesses is watching you run your race, pulling for you, with the Holy Spirit encouraging you. He won't leave you behind.

He is: Alpha and Omega
The First and the Last
Blessings

THE GOD WHO INTERCEDES

February 18

No weapon formed against you shall prosper, and every tongue which rises against you in judgment, you shall condemn. This is the heritage of the servants of the LORD and their righteousness is from Me Says the LORD.

Isaiah 54:17

These are good words to know when people are speaking all manner of evil against you. It's hard to take sometimes, especially when you have just been kind to someone and they cuss you, but there is another enemy that places Jesus in tough spots—it's our own tongues. Notice it says every tongue; this includes your own tongue. The enemy uses your own words against you whenever he can.

One night not long ago, I had a very vivid dream, a night vision. As I was standing, storm clouds rolled in. They were very threatening with lightning and thunder. I saw Jesus standing on a cliff that was jetting out. He was silent and just looked at the storm clouds approaching Him. The clouds stopped, and out of them came an enormous blowfish! It was larger than a blimp by three times the size, and it was angry. It approached Jesus, reached down and picked Him up, brought Him to his face, and spoke to Him. Jesus was tiny in comparison, but He absolutely showed no fear, no emotions. The blowfish angrily spoke to Him and then placed Him back on the cliff and left. I knew the conversation was about something I had said earlier in the day.

"'And I will rebuke the devourer for your sakes. So that he will not destroy the fruit for you in the field,' says the Lord of hosts" (Malachi 3:11).

You have the right to repent for your own words when they slip out. In some translations, the words "you shall condemn" have been translated into "you shall vanquish," which means to overcome. Be glad you can overcome your own words and forgive the words of others.

He is: Entunchano
The God Who Intercedes
Blessings

LION TAMER

February 19

"Break their teeth, O God, in their mouth;
break out the great teeth of the young lions, O LORD."

Psalm 58:6

When you first read this scripture, it makes you think, "Whoa, dude, you have some issues here!" Maybe King David really did mean it that way. However, he was the king, and it's never a good idea to upset a king. David could have just sent his army to shut some enemies up.

Recently, while in California, I was praying outside at an incredibly beautiful farm owned by a friend. As I stood on the top of the hill looking down into the countryside, I said, "Lord, please bless this land."

No sooner had the words come out of my mouth than I clearly heard the enemy say very angrily, "I promise you!"

I grew up in the country, and I know a threat when I hear one. Instead of cringing in fear, I laughed with joy and raised my hands and said joyfully, "Oh, Lord! Break my enemy's teeth so that he can lie to me no more!"

Instantly, I felt this inner joy, a gentle peace over me. It was so gentle, so pleasant. We don't need to get scared or violently angry to defeat the works of the enemy. Praise is the weapon of choice. I think that King David was talking about demonic spirits.

"Be temperate and vigilant because your adversary the devil, as a roaring lion, walks about, seeking whom he may devour" (1 Peter 5:8).

Yes, Lord! Break the teeth of the young lions that they lie to me no more! Say it with joy because praise confuses the enemy! If people are speaking against you, pray against the spirit that is governing them (your enemy, not the person).

He is: Jehovah Gibbor Milchamah
Mighty in Battle
Blessings

LABELS

February 20

"Neither repented they of their murders, nor of their sorceries, nor of their fornication, nor of their thefts."

Revelation 9:21

I know that this verse relates to the last days. Many believe that we are well into the very last days. This verse explains what people are doing and their refusal to change. Let's take a look at a brief definition of some of these words from the original Greek:

Sorceries: Pharmakeia, medication (this is where we get the term pharmacy from, drug use), sorcery, witchcraft. *Fornication*: Poneia, harlotry (including adultery, incest), idolatry

Here is the definition of the word *label*: a name or a title, and affixed to a thing, it describes clothing. Labels that are attached to others and even to some of us in the past. How do you remove a label? On a jacket? I guess you could just cut it off, but what about when it's stuck to your reputation?

"No man putteth a piece of new cloth upon an old garment, for that which is put in to fill it up taketh from the garment, and the rent is made worse" (Matthew 9:16–17).

Jesus knows how to remove old labels. He doesn't just rip the tag off; He gives you a whole new coat! What He is talking about is forgiving your sins so that you can receive the Baptism of the Holy Spirit. He cleans your reputation from the inside label out, but changing is your choice. People don't believe it is that easy; they feel that they can never be forgiven for the sins of their past, even Christians. Not forgiving yourself can be a very tormenting sin. Forgive yourself, repent while there is still time, for today is the day of your salvation.

He is: Jehovah Tzidkenu
The Lord Our Righteousness
Blessings

HE'S YOUR POTTER

February 21

"Therefore, if any man be in Christ, he is a new creature: old things are passed away; behold, all things are become new."

2 Corinthians 5:17

All things are become new. This includes your faith. It should be refreshed daily through prayer. But what hinders faith? Pride.

"Pride before destruction, and a haughty spirit before a fall" (Proverbs 16:18).

Many times while praying for people, I have seen a vision of myself stepping back and pointing up towards God and saying, "Give God the glory!" or "To God be the glory!" The Holy Spirit does this for me so that I won't fall into pride, a snare the enemy sets to steal my anointing. When tempted to take credit for God's work, just cast the thought out quickly and tell the person to God be the glory!

I asked the Lord, "What stops people from praying for others?" I believe He replied, "Steamboat repercussion." I had to think about this answer for a while. Your prayers flame the fires that heat up the boilers in hell. Steam represents power, a force that is built up within the inner bowels of the ship until it can start moving the vessel, a boat, or a locomotive. In your case, it would love to move the vessel in the wrong direction, and you are the vessel. But the amazing thing about steam is that it can be controlled. And with all its force, it makes the weakest-sounding noise of all the horns. Have you ever noticed that? It will make you laugh when you see a huge boat make a toot or a person complaining. We call that letting off steam. This would be a spirit of condemnation that creates self-doubt.

The definition of *repercussion* is an unintended consequence occurring after an event or action, especially an unwelcome one. There's also another peculiar thing about this word: *Repercussion* is a noun, which is a person, place, or thing. It has the ability to come back at you. Sounds almost like the name of a demon, doesn't it?

Years ago, I watched "To Hell and Back," a war movie about the most decorated war hero in WWII, Audie Murphy. His platoon was ordered to take a home that was set on the highest hill, which was strategic for both sides because it was the high ground and essential for observation. Once the Americans would take it, the Germans would regroup and make a counterattack and retake the same high ground. That high ground was lost and won several times before it was held for good.

I've noticed that sometimes you have to fight the same spiritual battle over and over again. One day, you will hold the high ground if you keep on fighting in prayer and faith. Clay is molded by faith, and it can take more than one attempt to make it into a perfect vessel. You are clay in His hands.

He is: Yotzerenu
Potter
Blessings

JUDE'S PRAYER

February 22

Now to Him who is able to keep you from stumbling. And to present you faultless before the presence of His glory with exceeding joy, To God the Savior, Who alone is wise, Be glory and majesty, dominion, and power, Both now and forever, Amen.

Jude 1:24–25

This scripture resonates with the essence of the Lord's Prayer. Jude, the half-brother of Jesus, is a significant reminder of its profound significance. I'm sure you have heard these one-liners before:

- "Place your trust in God to see you through."
- "A prayer in time saves nine." (Actually, I just made that last one up, but it's probably true.)
- How does the Holy Spirit keep you from stumbling? Here are a couple of simple examples:
- You get too much change back at the cash register, and that little conviction causes you to correct the mistake,
- Someone makes a thoughtless comment. On the inside, you're fuming, but you hold your peace because you know that's what Jesus would want you to do.

Why would Jesus do this for us? After all, He has already paid the ultimate price. Jesus has a burning desire in His heart to please the Father. One day, He will escort you to the throne room of the Father and announce your name and present you faultless before Him! And Jesus will do this with exceeding joy!

Just like in the Lord's Prayer, Jude starts off by positioning who God is and finishing it with praise. It is quite all right to personalize the following prayer for yourself, but you can also personalize it for your children. Just insert your child's name in the place where I have typed "me." You don't have to quote it exactly because the Holy Spirit knows your heart's intent. He judges the heart, and His intent is to judge it pure.

Lord Jesus, please keep me from stumbling today and present me faultless. Let me enter the presence of His (Your) glory with exceeding joy. To God the Savior, who alone is wise, be glory and majesty, dominion, and power, Both now and forever, Amen.

He is: Jehovah Qadash
The Lord Who Sanctifies
Blessings

FOUNTAIN OF LIVING WATERS, ORCHESTRATED

February 23

*"And I will put my Spirit in you and move you to follow
My decrees and be careful to keep My laws."*

Ezekiel 36:27

Recently, I attended a prophetic conference, and I received a beautiful revelation of the meaning of this verse and the beautiful dance between the Father, the Son, the Holy Spirit, and you.

During praise and worship service, for some reason, I decided to go sit in the back of our church, in the sound booth. While sitting there, I observed Pastor Ray coaching our drummer, a beautiful young lady, Miss Randi, with the most precious smile. Pastor Ray used to be a professional drummer who toured with famous bands. Miss Randi, a talented and aspiring musician, wanted to learn how to play the drums, so Pastor Ray took her under his wing.

As the music was being played, I sat next to Pastor Ray and watched him give Miss Randi hand signals, letting her know what to do. He would hold his hands out and flutter his fingers, and she would respond by gently fluttering the symbols with her drumsticks. He would hold his right hand higher and flutter his fingers, and she would move to the right symbol, point both hands with one finger, and make a tapping motion. She would go to the snare and hit the rhythm to match the rest of the band. All the while, both were smiling in complete enjoyment of the matching orchestration.

It was very pleasing to watch, and at the end, you could tell Pastor Ray was pleased with her performance. He smiled and nodded with approval, and Miss Randi responded with a smile that let you know she was pleased that she had pleased the master drummer. Then, Pastor Ray told me that they had never rehearsed the signals. He said, "She just understands what I'm trying to say; it's like the Holy Spirit guides us."

It was then that I saw the similarity of how the Trinity works. The Father positioned next to the Son, Jesus signaling the Holy Spirit what to do, and we respond hoping to get the Father's approval. It's like the Master Puppeteer orchestrating the most elaborate show on earth, except the puppet has a choice to please the Father.

When you receive the Holy Spirit, He works with you, guiding your steps, nudging you to please the Son, and this pleases the Father. It is for your benefit. How beautiful is that?

He is: Maqowr Chay Mayim
Fountain of Living Waters
Blessings

A JOY RIDE

February 24

"So, I sought for a man among them who would make a wall, and stand in the gap before Me on behalf of the land, that I should not destroy it; but I found no one."

Ezekiel 22:30

Have you ever had someone say to you that they were standing in the gap for someone? This is the Bible verse they are referring to, and what they are talking about is praying for someone, or a country, political leaders, or maybe a need that someone has.

What God really needs you to do is pray for their salvation so that their name would be found in the Lamb's Book of Life. I love this saying: "Your prayers matter!" Because they do.

A few years ago, I had an elderly neighbor lady who didn't much care for me. When I would come home after work, she would be sitting outside smoking a cigarette, put the cigarette out, and go back inside the house every time I pulled in my driveway. She was never rude to me, but it was obvious she didn't care to be around me.

One day, I went outside, and the ambulance was next door. All those years of smoking had caught up with her, and like a domino effect, other health problems crashed down on her, and soon she was in a nursing home.

While praying one morning, I thought about this verse and realized she had no one to stand in the gap for her. I started praying that the Lord would heal her. I spent considerable time praying and really believed for several months that she would recover. However, she died. To be honest, I was shocked.

Just being honest, I said to the Lord, "What did it matter, God? I spent all those hours praying for her, and she died." When you think your prayers have no effect, it can really hurt and be very discouraging. That is exactly how the devil wants you to think and feel. That night, I had a very vivid dream. I was driving my bus, and my neighbor lady stepped onto the bus. I was excited to see her! As I drove, you could feel all the bumps in the road and hear the engine noises. It felt very real.

I said, "Hi, Miss Cathy! How are you?" As she sat down on my bus, she turned into a nurse, a completely different person sitting in the chair. And that was the end of my dream or, in this case, a night vision.

When I woke up, I knew exactly what the dream meant. My prayers had allowed a nurse to lead her to the Lord in her last moments of life. The bus represented my ministry, and they had both gotten on because of my prayers and the great effectiveness of the Blood of Jesus Christ.

"Everyone who trusts in Him will never be put to shame" (Romans 10:11).

Your prayers matter. Even though you may not see anything happening, trust in Him.

He is: Elohim Shama
The God Who Hears
Blessings

JUDGE

February 25

"But solid food belongs to those who are of full age, that is, those who by reason of use have their senses exercised to discern both good and evil."

Hebrews 6:14

The beginning of this sentence is actually a metaphor relating to food in the spirit. For years, I have thought about this scripture. I thought it meant knowing the difference between right and wrong. But how could that require you to be *of full age*? A young child knows the difference between right and wrong. It's taught, but it is also inherent. So, this scripture means more than just right and wrong. That's what I love about the Bible—it's alive! The living Word just gets deeper the more you study. That is, those who, by reason of use, have their senses exercised.

Tonight, I had the fortune of serving on a ministry team for another ministry. They asked me to pray for people at the service. I saw a young man in the crowd. I asked him to come forward for prayer. He was approximately twenty years old and had been studying about speaking in tongues. He is very intelligent, but reasoning was his block to actually receiving the gift of tongues.

But the Lord told me this young man was chosen to be a prophet. He liked that, but then I told him it takes fifteen to twenty years to be promoted to the office of prophet. To him, this was a lifetime. I said, "You have to understand that in order to become a good leader, you first must become a good follower." I said some other things to him, and that is what brought his understanding into place with what God is calling him to do. "You can't give a loaded M-16 to an infant," I said. Then, he understood that this promotion would take learning.

For a few weeks, I was getting really mixed words. It was confusing, and it felt like the Lord would say something, then a couple of days later, change what He had said. (I must note that these were personal words to me and not with other people.) I was beginning to get depressed and wanted to stop with prophecy. But instead of quitting, I called my friend Joe. I explained what was going on, and he just laughed and said, "New levels, new devils!"

I felt such a sense of relief come over me. Now I knew I was dealing with a demon. After looking into it further, I learned that this is called a religious spirit that tries to imitate the Holy Spirit. Well, we cast that out really quickly.

This is how you discern good and evil in the spirit. When you pray in the Holy Spirit, you exercise your senses. Three areas you need to discern:

- Is this your thought?
- Is this the Holy Spirit?
- Is this of God, and does it line up with the Scripture?

"In this know ye the Spirit of God: Every Spirit that confesses that Jesus is Christ, is come in the flesh is of God" (1 John 4:2).

If it sidesteps the question, cast it out. There are many ways that the Holy Spirit can speak with you, but be assured the conversation will always hold up to Scripture—that's your baseline.

"Do not quench the Spirit. Do not despise the prophecies. Test all things; hold fast to that which is good. Abstain from every form of evil" (1 Thessalonians 5:19–22).

I encourage people to check my prophetic words and look up the scriptures I use to ensure that I am telling you the truth. Test all things and hold on to that which is good.

He is: Shaphat
Judge
Blessings

FASTING

February 26

"As they ministered to the Lord and fasted, the Holy Spirit said, 'Set apart for Me Barnabas and Saul for the work to which I have called them'."

Acts 13:2

Have you ever wondered why fasting is so important? I have, and I have fasted often in my life, not really knowing why. When I was a young Christian, I listened to a pastor explain that fasting was just starving yourself in order to get God to speak to you. Well, he was a good pastor, but this was wrong, and it really was a stumbling block for me in regard to the importance of fasting and prayer.

The start of this verse bears some looking into *as they ministered to the Lord.*

I checked twenty-five different Bible versions on this. The consensus would be that they prayed to the Lord in this instance or worshiped the Lord. Some suggest the performance of religious duties and ministry work, but that would just be out of place for what they were trying to accomplish. What they were seeking was sure direction from the Lord, and we see that the Holy Spirit gave the answer. Here is the importance of this fast: It gave us thirteen books of the New Testament that Paul later wrote.

When we fast, it crucifies the flesh by placing it under the subjection of our spirits. We put our desires behind the desire of the spirit.

I have a little dog named Chance, and we are best buds. One night, as I was going to bed, I realized that I had forgotten to feed Chance, so I turned around and went back to the kitchen and fed him. Now, if you have ever owned a dog, you know that the biggest thing in their lives is food. After I gave him his dinner, and it was late, he looked at me as I walked off to go to bed. Then, he looked back at his bowl of food and left his food to come to bed with me. But the look on his face was like he was happy to leave the food just to be with me. I thought, *Man, that's really sweet. He would rather be with me than eat.*

A couple of days later, I was sitting on the couch watching TV, and as dogs do, without me noticing, he was sitting in my lap with his head resting against my chest, laying on my heart, and I was petting him. My first thought was, *How did you get here?* As I looked at him, I remembered that he had sacrificed a meal in order to be with me, and as he laid his head against my heart, I had a sense of appreciation and love for him. Then, the Lord spoke to me and said, "This is how I feel when you fast for Me."

You see, what can you possibly give God? He knows what food is to us. He created it. When you fast, offer it up as a sacrifice of praise combined with your prayers. It touches the Father's heart, and He will guide your direction.

He is: Elohim Ahavah
The God Who Loves
Blessings

THE WAY

February 27

"And it came to pass, that, as they went in the way, a certain man said unto Him, Lord I will follow thee whithersoever thou goest."

Luke 9:57

The Holy Spirit uses His words very carefully here in this text. Notice it says *the way.*

We get the word *way* from the Greek word, *hod-os'*, which means a road, act, or distance, a journey, (high-) way. It occurs 120 times in the Bible in various uses. Here, you can see that they are walking down a road, taking a journey in the natural. But did you know that the early church was actually referred to as *the Way*? We can see Apostle Paul referring to this in,

"But this I confess to you, that according to the Way which they call a sect" (Acts 24:14).

And again in Acts 24:22, "But when Felix heard these things, having more accurate knowledge of the Way, he adjourned the proceedings."

Jesus and the disciples were walking on a road, but the road was a journey—a spiritual journey that everyone can walk—every nation, every people, every individual. Every person is really on his own way, one way or another. The Bible says in Proverbs 21:2, "Every way of a man is right in his own eyes: but the LORD weighs the hearts."

We weigh spiritual matters in our minds, but God weighs them in our hearts. Your heart is what God is after because He has already given you His heart. Only you can allow Him *the Way* into your heart. Then, He can show you His Way, which is a much better road to travel.

He is: El Roi
The God Who Sees Me
Blessings

TRUE GOD

February 28

And these signs shall follow them that believe; In my name shall they cast out devils, they shall speak with new tongues, They shall take up serpents, and if they drink any deadly thing, it shall not hurt them, they shall lay hands on the sick and they shall recover.

Mark 16:16–17

Recently, I had two different people ask me this same question, "How do you get so much faith?" Frankly, it's a hard question to answer on the spot. For a long time, I would just take the attitude that once I prayed, it was now God's problem, not mine, because I would worry about whether or not God would answer. But by giving it over to God, it turned into trust, and trust equals faith.

You have the same Holy Spirit; just pray for others and ask the Lord to use you. I think faith comes in stages throughout your life, but to put it simply for the sake of time...

1. 1. Blind Faith. When I first became a Christian, I was really on fire for the Lord and only knew this one Scripture on the last page of the book of Mark 16:15–18: "They shall lay hands on the sick, and they shall recover."

2. 2. Learned Faith. We get this by observation and from following a good pastor with sound teaching. Paul said in Acts 22:3, "I studied under Gamaliel and was thoroughly trained in the law of our ancestors."

3. 3. Faith by Experience. This is by what you've been through in life, the experiences you have with your own prayers being answered. Seeing the results when you pray for others, you'll start to get excited.

"For the kingdom of God is not in word, but in power" (1 Corinthians 4:20).

"…and I will shew thee my faith by my works" (James 2:18).

Go ahead and ask God to use you today to bless someone with a prayer. I know He will give you an opportunity to pray for someone. If you need the courage to pray, ask Jesus, and He will supply that, too.

He is: Elethinos Theos
True God
Blessings

SEEDTIME

VICTORY IN REST

March 1

"For the Lord, The Holy One of Israel, said, "In quiet and rest is your salvation: Peace and hope are your strength."

Isaiah 30:15

God is so amazing! He operates contrary to what the world tells us. Rest soothes the soul—the battle-torn soul. Sometimes, I think our spirit is wrapped in a body that looks more like a Band-Aid, in mummy-type layers of cloth holding our spirit in. I have ministered to counselors who have pushed themselves so hard that they have reached burnout syndrome. They reach a place where it only takes one more little thing to push them into quitting. They begin by taking the burdens of others onto themselves. Instead of casting their cares over to Christ, they carry the worry in their mental toolbox. We were never created to be the burden bearers.

If you counsel or advise people, when they leave, their problems go, too. Don't let them linger in your mind. I don't stay up at night worrying about them (well, I try not to) because I'm not God, and neither are you. I've seen devout Christians leave the church because they picked up someone else's offense. When it comes to offenses, you need to stay on the defensive, with peace and hope as your strength.

He is: Shub Nephesh
Renewer of Life
Blessings

THE ONE WHO LIFTS MY HEAD

March 2

"Why, my soul, are you downcast? Why so disturbed within me? Put your hope in God, for I will yet praise him, my Savior, and my God."

Psalm 42:11

Have you ever been depressed? A depression that is so deep within you that all your physical pores feel depressed? It can be hard to lift your arm or even your head to give a polite smile.

"But thou O LORD art a shield for me, my glory, and the lifter up of mine head" (Psalm 3:3).

Did you notice that "O LORD" is in all caps? Because the Jewish people considered the name of God very sacred, they would not spell out the vowels. "O LORD" was written YHWH in this instance, and this is where we derive the word Jehovah as well. It shows God to be eternal. It also stresses His redemptive nature towards Israel. But I want to take it one step backward to look at:

"Many are saying about me, 'Even with God on his side, he won't be victorious'" (Psalm 3:2).

Selah. Get excited! This Psalm is not directed towards the nation of Israel; it is directed toward you! "Many are saying about me," and me is you! Father God is saying that *all* of His redemptive nature is focused on you! He is your shield, your shield of faith:

"Above all, taking the shield of faith, wherewith ye shall be able to quench all the fiery darts of the wicked" (Ephesians 6:16).

Back in the day, the Romans dipped their shields in water before the battle in order to quench the flaming arrows the enemies would shoot towards them.

While praying one time, I had a vision of a shield catching on fire, and it was on fire quickly. It looked like someone had dipped it in lighter fluid. The Holy Spirit let me know that these were the words that people said against themselves and their situations, and those words take away the effectiveness of the shield. Please don't say negative things about yourself. You were made in the image of God, and every time you belittle yourself, you are belittling the image of God. So do not fear:

"So do not fear, for I am with you; do not be dismayed, for I am your God. I will strengthen you and help you; I will uphold you with my righteous right hand" (Isaiah 41:10).

How do you turn this depression around? With a joyful heart. I realized some time ago that happiness is the gift you give yourself. Place no evil before your eyes, listen to no bad thing, watch a clean comedy, and if you still can't laugh, fake a laugh until you laugh. I promise it won't take long if you ask Jesus to help you. Once you do that, you have this promise:

"A merry heart doeth good like a medicine: but a broken Spirit drieth the bones" (Proverbs 17:22).

He is: Rum Rosh
The One Who Lifts My Head
Blessings

THE HEALING OF A GRIEVING SPIRIT

March 3

"The righteous cry, and the Lord heareth, and delivereth them out of all their troubles. The Lord is nigh unto them that are of a broken heart; and saveth such as be of a contrite spirit."

Psalm 34:17–18

I asked the Lord, "What do You want me to teach on today?"

He responded, "The healing of a grieving spirit." Have you ever heard of the term, Broken Heart Syndrome? The Bible nailed it centuries before modern science did. Take a look.

"For this cause the cords of my heart are sounding for Moab, and I am full of sorrow for Kir-heres" (Isaiah 16:11, BBE)

Simply put, your heart has tendons that look like strings. When sudden trauma hits, such as the loss of a loved one, a breakup in a serious relationship, or a divorce, these strings can break, causing a broken heart.

Isaiah is referring to how much his heart is hurting for the loss of Moab, who was the descendant of Lot, Abraham's nephew. They had turned away from God, only to become His enemy. Kir-here is a city in Moab. When the king of Judah, Jehoram, invaded Moab because of their great sin, the king of Moab in the city of Kir-here offered his oldest son as a burnt sacrifice on top of the city wall. This was how far they had strayed from the Lord (2 Kings 3:27).

Truly a righteous man, Isaiah may have suffered from Broken Heart Syndrome, maybe even felt the heart of God, for a lost nation. After the sacrifice, the children of Israel gave up the attack in utter disgust and turned and left the battle. God will never give up the fight for you.

Jesus took our suffering on the cross two thousand years ago. Everyone is aware of the physical sufferings Jesus endured on the cross, but have you given thought to the "Seven Emotional Sufferings" Jesus experienced?

- Stress: Sweated blood in the garden.
- Betrayal: Judas, a loved disciple and friend, betrayed Him.
- Abandonment: The other disciples all fled.
- Rejection: His own people rejected Him.
- Humiliation: He was stripped naked in public for all to see.
- Persecution: Hostility and ill-treatment because of who He was.
- Injustice: Judged innocent by Pilot but sentenced to death.

- Separation from God: "My God, My God, why hast thou forsaken Me?"

Because of His emotional sufferings, we have been given these verses:

> *"For we have not a high priest who is not able to be touched by the feelings of our feeble flesh; but we have one who has been tested in all points as we ourselves are tested, but without sin. Then let us come near to the seat of grace without fear, so that mercy may be given to us, and we may get grace for our help in time of need."*

Hebrews 4:15–16

What is a contrite spirit? Feeling or expressing remorse, affected by guilt. Isaiah certainly hadn't done anything wrong. The war took place over a century earlier, yet he had a contrite heart for the loss of a bloodline relative to Israel and Judah. Forgiveness is the first step to mending those heartstrings, and God will do the rest. God is good.

He is: Jehovah-Rapha
The Lord Who Heals
Blessings

GOD'S PERFECT KNOWLEDGE OF MAN

March 4

For You formed my inward parts; You covered me in my mother's womb. I will praise You, for I am fearfully and wonderfully made; Marvelous are your works, And that my soul knows very well.
My frame was not hidden from You, When I was made in secret, And skillfully wrought in the lowest parts of the earth. Your eyes saw my substance, being yet unformed. And in your book, they were all written, the days fashioned for me. When as yet there were none of them.
How precious also are Your thoughts to me, O God! How great is the sum of them! If I should count them, they would be more than the numbers of the sand; When I awake, I am still with You.

Psalm 139:13–18

A Christian scientist once said, "Everyone knows about the magnitude of God and His greatness, but when you get down to the cellular level, you realize how great God is."

God created you in your mother's womb. God, You formed my inward parts. I will praise You, for I am fearfully and wonderfully made.

Fearfully is translated from Hebrew yârê' (yaw-ray'). It is defined as morally to revere. God reveres His creation!

Have you ever looked into the eyes of someone you deeply loved and just marveled at their beauty? When God looks at you, He marvels at His creation. The pupil of His eye, the very center of His universe, is you. Imagine this from God's perspective: He has been from the beginning, and there is no end with God. But He has awaited your existence for all eternity and now is your time on this earth and He wants you to love Him as much as He loves you.

My frame was not hidden from You. God knows your strengths, and your times are in God's hands. He has a plan for you. He controls the innermost parts of the earth and the highest achievements of any man.

"For I know the plans I have for you, declares the LORD, plans for welfare and not for evil, to give you a future and a hope" (Jeremiah 29:11).

His thoughts for your future with Him are all good.

And in your book, they were all written, the days fashioned for me. When as yet there were none of them. Your name is in a book, and it has been there for an exceedingly long time. He chose your days on this earth, and God would have never placed you in a time where you couldn't succeed and overcome the obstacle of sin in your life.

How precious also are Your thoughts to me, O God! God loves you. Yes, you! Look at your hand or another body part and marvel at how much work God has already done on you. You are quite a project—His masterpiece, His most precious work. This is easy for me to type because I know it's true: you are His favorite.

He is: Elohim Ahavah
The God Who Loves
Blessings

GOD OF GRACE

March 5

"No longer drink only water, but use a little wine for your stomach's sake and your frequent infirmities."

1 Timothy 5:23

Alcohol: As a Christian, this topic has come up many times over the years. And it's a tough one to answer, but I do have a couple of experiences to share.

I used to smoke cigarettes and truthfully enjoyed smoking. Didn't really want to quit, but I knew I needed to. I would quit for a year or two and then pick them back up, quit again no problem.

One day, the Holy Spirit led me to quit smoking. I didn't want to, but I tried to please God.

Then, a few weeks later, the Holy Spirit told me, "There's that whiskey settlement."

Whiskey settlement? Am I going to get hit by a liquor truck crossing the street or something? I couldn't figure out what He was talking about.

He's so patient with us. A couple of weeks later, I remembered someone had given me a bottle of whiskey for a Christmas present that I had never opened. When I took it out of the closet, I had a vision of me pouring the whiskey down the drain. That's what He meant about the whiskey settlement. It was expensive, but I knew what the Lord meant, so I obeyed.

"All things are lawful for me, but not all things are expedient. All things are lawful for me, but not all things edify" (1 Corinthians 10:23).

All things are lawful. You can have a drink and not feel condemned about it unless the Lord has told you differently. In my case, if I were to drink in public, it could cause someone to have doubts about the Lord or make them think that it's okay to drink as much as you want. This would not edify someone else or build them up into a better person.

A nice lady told me this story a few days ago, and I felt it answered a lot of questions. She said that her mother, a Christian lady, went to a restaurant and ordered a glass of wine. Before the waiter returned, she prayed this prayer, "Lord, if it's not okay for me to have this glass of wine, I want You to cause the waiter to spill the glass on my lap." When the waiter returned, he placed the wine in front of her, cleared some items off her table, and even reached around her wine glass. As he left her table to serve the table next to her, she remained focused on the waiter. When the waiter reached for something on the other table, he knocked over a glass of wine into the man's lap!

She said the Lord spoke to her very clearly, "What's allowable for some is not allowable for others."

I couldn't agree more. Some people have a low tolerance for alcohol or gambling or numerous other things. Ask the Holy Spirit if it is allowable for you to have a drink. He may say, "Please, skip it this time." You may be surprised who walks into the room. It could be the person you've been talking to the Lord about for years.

He is: Yahweh-Channun
God of Grace
Blessings

NOW GOD CAN USE YOU

March 6

*Brethren, I do not reckon to have laid hold of it yet, but this one thing I do,
forgetting those things which are behind and extending
myself unto those things which are ahead,
I press toward the mark for the prize of the high calling of God in Christ Jesus.*

Philippians 3:13

Have you ever made a mistake? Something that you wish you had never said or done? Does it keep coming back to you every day? Relax. It's just the devil trying to keep you in that place of poor self-worth. It amazes me how the human mind works, and believe me, Satan knows how to use tragedy and mistakes to keep you down.

Have you ever been to a circus and looked at the massive elephants standing there, swaying their trunks back and forth? I'm sure you noticed that the elephants just had small, quarter-inch ropes around their ankles, and the rope was staked to the ground. We all know that there is absolutely no way that little piece of thread could hold such an enormous beast. But it doesn't start out that way.

When the circus trainers first get the baby elephant, they shackle a large chain around the infant elephant's ankle and place a very strong stake in the ground. As the baby elephant pulls and pulls to no avail, it finally gives up trying to escape. Eventually, the trainer can take the chain off and replace it with a small rope. This smaller rope is much easier for the trainer to handle than that large chain. When the full-grown 15,000-pound male elephant pulls on the rope, it feels the resistance to his ankle and stops pulling, standing there only chained in his mind and the memory of the sensation of restraint.

Satan uses this same tactic with people, too. He gets you thinking that you can't fulfill your dream because you have failed so many times before. That's called condemnation; you can tell it's the enemy because it never forgives, and it pushes you to more hurting thoughts, even thoughts of suicide.

"Submit yourselves therefore to God. Resist the devil, and he will flee from you" (James 4:7).

That's why we need to put the past behind us and step into the future—daily. So, how do you know when it's God correcting you?

"Now no chastening for the present seemeth to be joyous, but grievous: nevertheless, afterward it yieldeth the peaceable fruit of righteousness unto them which are exercised thereby" (Hebrews 12:11).

When God corrects, it is for your benefit. Sure, it hurts—two words from God can send you looking for a place to hide. But afterward, it brings joy because, like a champion boxer, you faced your opponent head-on, confronted your sin, and won a fight with repentance by putting your pride aside and asking Jesus for forgiveness. Now, God can use you.

He is: Shub Nephesh
Renewer of Life
Blessings

GOD WITH US

March 7

"And it came to pass, that after three days they found Him in the temple, sitting in the midst of the doctors, both hearing them and asking them questions."

Luke 2:46

The word "doctors" is referring to the teachers and instructors of the oracles of God. In this instance, they had found Christ and were astonished at His answers! We will sit around God and be astonished for all eternity learning from the Greatest Instructor.

"Love never fails. But if there are prophecies, they will be caused to cease; if tongues, they shall cease, if knowledge, it will be caused to cease" (1 Corinthians 13:8).

In this passage, Paul expresses that a time will come when prophecy, tongues, and knowledge will no longer be necessary. Why? Because, in that future state, we will be in the presence of Jesus in all His glory. There will be no need for prophetic insights into the future, no necessity for speaking in tongues, and no requirement for words of knowledge because we will be directly in the presence of the ultimate source of all knowledge.

And His love for you will never cease. Looking back on your life, have you ever gone through a trial and thought, "How will I ever get through this?" And somehow, you did. Maybe God gave you a miraculous miracle, or maybe things just smoothed over. You overcame an obstacle in your life that you thought impossible, and maybe you even thought that it would never end, and it came to pass.

One day, while talking to a troubled man who was about to go to jail for a lengthy stay, he asked me a very sincere question based on a deep love for his wife. "How am I going to make it that long without my wife? I can't be away from her for so long." He went on to tell me how much he would worry about her.

I thought for a moment and remembered this old saying: My Bible never said, "It came to stay." It always says, "It came to pass!" He's out now, back with his wife, and it came to pass.

The King James Bible quotes this saying approximately 120 times for different reasons— some good and some not so good. But if you think about it, they all came to pass.

It's easy to see that Jesus' parents sought Him for three days and found Him at the temple, the church. If you're seeking Jesus, trust me, you will find Him because He already knows where you are.

He is: Immanuel
God with Us
Blessings

NAIL IN A FIRM PLACE

March 8

When He had come down from the mountain, great multitudes followed Him.
And behold a leper came and worshiped Him, saying,
"Lord, if You are willing, You can make me clean."
Then Jesus put out His hand and touched him, saying,
"I am willing; be cleansed." Immediately his leprosy was cleansed.
And Jesus said to him, "See that you tell no one; but go your way, show yourself to
the priest, and offer the gift that Moses commanded, as a testimony to them."

Matthew 8:1–4

This was immediately after Jesus came down from giving the greatest speech ever given, known as the *Sermon on the Mount*, or *The Beatitudes*, which means *supreme blessedness*. You receive this same blessedness when you read *The Beatitudes*. Just like the leper, you receive faith. Take note that he waited for Jesus to come down from the mountain.

> *And all the people saw the thunderings, and the lightnings, and the noise of the trumpet, and the mountain smoking: and when the people saw it, they removed, and stood afar off.*
>
> *And they said unto Moses, speak thou with us, and we will hear: but let not God speak with us, lest we die.*

Exodus 20:18–19

The New Testament is a mirror of the Old Testament. God gave Moses a Sermon on the Mount; God gave Jesus a Sermon on the Mount. But here is the greatness of Jesus. God could not come into contact with mankind, but Jesus (God in the flesh) was able to come down from the mountain and come into contact with mankind.

And when Jesus came down, He came into contact with the most rejected person of society: a leper. Imagine all the crowds would have scattered away. If we had a bird's eye view, we would have seen a large bubble pattern form around Jesus and the leper. People would have given him a very wide space. Imagine the rejection with all the disdain that came with it. People always scurrying away from him, giving him ugly looks, shouts, and insults. Some people might have even thrown rocks. None of us have ever faced rejection like that before.

One time, a young lady came up to me and told me that she had been diagnosed with HIV and wanted prayer. As we sat there, I asked her, "May I hold your hand while we pray?"

Then, I heard a broken little child's voice, that sounded so hurt, say, "You want to touch me?!"

Immediately, I was out of my body and into Jesus' body. I saw a vision of the leper approaching Jesus on his knees, asking if He would heal him. I was in the body of Christ! I saw His arm reach out to that man. With the long sleeve of His robe, I felt the love in His heart and heard His thoughts: *"Not only do I want to heal you, but I want to die for you!"* It was overwhelming. I looked up, and the young lady was crying, and I was astonished. Jesus came wanting to die for us so that we could be with Him.

Then, Jesus sent the now-healed leper to fulfill the Levitical Law in accordance with Leviticus 14 by going to the priest and making his offering. This was accomplished by sacrificing one bird on a cedar plank under running water and dipping hyssop in the blood and sprinkling the blood on the live bird and setting the live bird free.

The blood and the water represented Jesus, the hyssop represented the whip, and the wood represented the cross. The bird represents us being set free from sin. But this also would have been a testimony to the priest after the crucifixion. Jesus was willing to die for the priests, too.

His love for you prevailed over His sufferings for you. He's so good.

He is: Yated Aman Maqom
Nail in a Firm Place
Blessings

THE GOD OF MY SALVATION

March 9

Thou art my hiding place; thou shalt preserve me from trouble;
thou shalt compass me about with songs of deliverance. Selah
I will instruct thee and teach thee in the way which thou shalt go:
I will guide thee with mine eye.

Psalm 32:7–8

This Psalm was written by King David, and it really is a masterpiece of praise. David had learned to trust the Lord in his hard circumstances.

When I was a young child, I remember being chased by bullies, and believe me, they meant to do me harm. As I ran down an alleyway, I found a round pipe culvert to hide in at an abandoned factory. They came down the alley and walked past me; I even think one looked in the pipe but didn't see me.

That memory came to mind as I was typing this. I think that is like Father God when someone is out to do harm and they walk past you to the next person. A lady friend of mine told me that she was in a parking garage walking to the elevator. A man came out to rob her. When the door of the elevator opened up, a mouse came running. She screamed and had so much fear of the mouse that the mugger helped get rid of the mouse and forgot to rob her! Unfortunately, he robbed the next person who came through. God can hide you from evil and preserve you from trouble.

He is: Jehovah Ezrah
My Helper
Blessings

SONGS OF DELIVERANCE

March 10

"And David spoke unto the Lord the words of this song in the day that the Lord had delivered him out of the hand of all his enemies, and out of the hand of Saul."

2 Samuel 22:1

It's pretty straightforward: David is thanking God for his deliverance. But if we look at Psalm 32:7…"Thou art my hiding place; thou shalt preserve me from trouble; thou shalt compass me about with songs of deliverance. Selah."

This scripture implies that God is singing songs of deliverance over us.

One night, I had a very vivid dream. I was in the Olympics, in the middle of the ice-skating rink, sitting on a stool. I could see crowds of people. Their silhouettes were gray, and I couldn't see their faces, but I knew that they were the cloud of witnesses that watched us. Camera flashes were going off. I had a thin veil over my face. I could see the judges looking at me. As I sat there, a beautiful lady came out and started to sing to me and walked slowly around me singing. Then, suddenly, we were directly behind the judge's stand, and the crowd was going wild. I knew we had done very well and that we had won! An angel of the Lord had performed all the work—she won my race for me. I've seen this angel before, and she has spoken to me in other dreams and in prayer once. His angels sing songs of deliverance for our salvation.

Notice in this next verse it switches from David to God:

"I will instruct thee and teach thee in the way which thou shalt go: I will guide thee with mine eye" (Psalm 32:8).

He has delivered you unto His salvation. He can start to instruct you on how to walk before Him into your own victory—victory over sin. Once you have victory, you can sing your songs of deliverance, and joyful they will be.

He is: El Yeshuati
The God of My Salvation
Blessings

THE ONE WHO LIFTS MY HEAD

March 11

*Now Jabez was more honorable than his brothers, and his mother
called his name Jabez, saying, Because I bore him in pain.
And Jabez called on the God of Israel saying, "Oh that you would bless me indeed,
and enlarge my territory, that your hand would be with me, and that You would
keep me from evil, that I may not cause pain!"
So, God granted him what he requested.*

1 Chronicles 4:9–10

Many people will recognize this verse known as the Prayer of Jabez. *Jabez* in Hebrew means to grieve, or sorrow. Imagine the stigma that goes along with being named Jabez. Every time someone called your name, you would be reminded that you caused your mother to grieve with pain. You can see the emotional grief it caused him and his low self-image by the end of his prayer, "*...that I may not cause pain.*" A lifetime of verbal bullying had beaten his self-image out of his belief system. An elderly friend of ours stated that she despised bullying because it beat the identity out of a person's character.

"Now Jabez was more honorable than all his brothers." Notice in the scripture that they beat his self-image next to nothing, but they could never beat down his honor. He knew what pain felt like, and he did not like it, and he did not want to cause pain to others. This is what made his prayer so selfless. He wanted his borders increased so that he wouldn't have to engage in battle and cause more pain.

Character is built in suffering. I don't think Jabez noticed it, but others did, and most importantly, God did. Jabez was established by God. How grateful he must have been when he noticed his prayers had been answered. Remember, God is on your side.

He is: Rum Rosh
The One Who Lifts My Head
Blessings

THE GOD OF ALL COMFORT

March 12

And a certain scribe came, and said unto him, Master, I will follow thee withersoever thou goest.
Jesus saith unto him, the foxes have holes, and the birds of the air have nests, but the son of man hath nowhere to lay his head.

Matthew 8:19–20

This scripture is unique. I know from speaking with people throughout the years that it really has caused quite a bit of misunderstanding in the body of Christ. You could preach this in ten different ways. But let me give you a different take on it. Jesus stated that He only spoke what He was told by the Father (John 12:49–50). For the sake of time, Jesus was never poor. He was born poor in a stable. He left His first estate in heaven to become a man—to be with us in our poor state.

"And going into the house they saw Mary his mother, and they fell down and worshiped Him. Then opening their treasures, they offered Him gifts, gold, frankincense, and myrrh" (Matthew 2:11).

The Magi delivered the gifts. They were welcomed into kings' courts because of their great knowledge. That's how they were invited into King Herod's court so rapidly.

Herod was paranoid, constantly worried about being murdered, acted like a maniac, exhibited a psychopathic demeanor, demonstrated a tendency towards violent behavior, and was a mass murderer. At one point, he even had his own children executed based on a rumor generated by his palace servants. However, he was also one of the world's greatest architects.

Herod built the second temple, and it was impressive. After that accomplishment, he installed his own Pharisees, Sadducees, and Scribes. This is why some were referred to as Herodians. They were loyal to Herod for their own personal gain.

Matthew 8:19 said that a certain scribe came, and Jesus gave him an unusual answer with some hidden meaning. Foxes, in that part of the world, had unusual characteristics. They liked to dig holes (especially in grape vineyards), they ate the grapes and were a great nuisance to the landowners.

Remember, Jesus called Herod a fox. Symbolically, grapes represent the blood of Christ.

Birds are divided by Mosaic Law into two categories: *clean* and *unclean*. Unclean were not divided, but the clean birds were divided for a sacrifice.

Here's the scenario: Herod sent a scribe to follow Jesus around and report on everything Jesus said and did. But Jesus was not buying it! "But the Son of Man hath nowhere to lay His head." Basically, Jesus said that He had no part in worldly desires and that He didn't need Herod's personal gain.

The Holy Spirit will reveal to you when the enemy has set a trap, and He will steer you in the right direction to avoid a pitfall if you trust Him.

He is: Theos Pas Paraklesis
The God of All Comfort
Blessings

STRENGTH MADE PERFECT

March 13

"And the devil that deceived them was cast into the lake of fire and brimstone, where the beast and the false prophet are, and shall be tormented day and night for ever and ever."

Revelation 20:10

Sometimes, as Christians, we will suffer setbacks: the tragic loss of a loved one, getting behind on bills, losing a job, getting divorced, and any number of other trials. We're never really defeated when it *seems like* we have suffered defeat. I believe in good sportsmanship, but after a spiritual loss or a failure, I'm not going to shake the devil's hand, tell him good game, and give him a pat on the back. No, I'm going to remind him and his demons about Revelation 20:10. He needs reminding of his ultimate defeat. When Jesus was nailed to the cross, Satan's eternity was sealed forever.

There is only one way the enemy can defeat you: It is called *choice*. It's your choice to decide to remain in Christ or to quit and walk away. Every trial and hardship a Christian endures has one sole intended purpose: to get you to stop serving Jesus Christ. Only you can walk away. It's your choice. When you get so beat down by the enemy and all you have left is weakness, congratulations, you've made it to… "My grace is sufficient for thee: for my strength is made perfect in weakness" (2 Corinthians 12:9).

Praise God! Do you see the cycle? This is how we always walk in victory.

He is: El Nathan Neqamah
The God Who Avenges Me
Blessings

REDEEMING GOD

March 14

And when thy days are fulfilled and thou shalt sleep with thy fathers,
I will set up thy seed after thee, which shall proceed out of thy bowels,
and I will establish his kingdom. He shall build a house for My Name, and I will
establish the throne of his kingdom forever.

2 Samuel 7:12–13

This was the Word of the Lord to His faithful servant, King David. It was in David's heart to build a temple for God. On the previous day, the prophet Nathan had told David that it would be a good thing for David to do. But Nathan had not checked with the Lord before he gave David his own thoughts, and now the Lord was sending Nathan back to David to correct some bad advice.

David had many great qualities, but two of his greatest attributes were his understanding of the character of God and his deep love for the Father. But God said that David had been a man of war and had shed blood, and because of that, he could not build the temple. Imagine how devastated David must have felt when Nathan came back with the true word of God.

Have you ever had a lifetime desire that you just couldn't accomplish? Maybe family and a career just wouldn't allow it, or maybe your own lack of self-worth became an invisible barrier that only you could see. But when you get older, you may look back and wish you had done it.

Years ago, I wanted to go to Mexico and be a missionary for the Lord. As I sat in church, I felt that the Lord told me, "I haven't called you to that." As I sat alone in the congregation, tears began to flow. I tried hard to keep my composure. Friends walked by and patted me on the back, saying, "It'll be okay, Scott," not even knowing what was going on inside my battle-torn mind. Then, what David did, and this verse came to my mind:

"Now for the House of God I have prepared with all my might" (1 Chronicles 29:2).

David didn't just sit back and give up on his vision. He knew it was the task of his son Solomon to build the temple, and David knew the tremendous task that it would be for a young man to undertake. So, David prepared all the architectural plans for the temple, all the vessel designs, instrument designs, and weights and measures to the smallest details! He saved and donated in today's money upwards of $20 billion toward the future construction of the temple!

I thought, *If David could do that, I could give a week's pay to Mexico missions, and it would be as though I actually spent a week in Mexico doing the work of a missionary! I could stay at home, keep my remote control, and get credit for their hard work. It's a win-win!*

If you've missed an opportunity in life, just ask God to give you an understanding of how you can still get credit for the call. He will guide you.

He is: Jehovah—Go-el
Redeeming God
Blessings

UNLIMITED CALLING

March 15

"And call upon me in the day of trouble:
I will deliver thee, and thou shalt glorify me."

Psalm 50:15

We all know that God is the beginning and the end; He knows everything. Somehow, I don't think He knew how much I would have to call upon Him, how many days of trouble I have had. I've told Father God that it's such an unfair trade—I accepted Jesus, and He gave me eternal life, which is worth more than anything, and yet, He helps me through all my troubles. Surely, He gets tired out by me.

I once had a beautiful dog named Sootie, and she followed me everywhere. She was always on my heels. One day, while doing some carpentry work in the house, I was running in and out of the shop often. Every time, I had to stop and wait for Sootie to follow me out and then back in. Sootie was standing next to me as I was about to make another trip back outside, and I just got angry and said, "Sootie, would you just leave me alone!"

Then, I thought to myself, *What if God gets tired of me?* I felt guilty for saying that to my best friend; she just wanted to be with me. Then, I became worried that maybe God was getting tired of me with all my problems. I carried this worry for a few days. At the next Sunday service, the pastor was preaching, and he said, "God never gets tired of you coming to Him with your problems!"

I was so relieved! Sometimes, our lives feel like a thousand-piece jigsaw puzzle all scrambled up in a box with the picture side down. But somehow, He can put it all together right side up.

He is: El Kanna
Jealous God
Blessings

DON'T LET GO

March 16

"And after him was Eleazar the son of Dodo, the Ahohite, one of the three mighty men with David when they defied the Philistines who were gathered there for battle, and the men of Israel had retreated.
He arose and attacked the Philistines until his hand was weary, and his hand stuck to the sword. The Lord brought about a great victory that day, and the people returned after him only to plunder."

2 Samuel 23:9–10

This is an account of David's three mighty men of valor. One man's name was Eleazar. I love all things God! Especially men and women who are willing to sacrifice it all to serve the Lord.

There were many men who served under King David, but only three were called "The Mighty Men." These three men did unheard-of exploits for the king and the nation of Israel. But did you ever realize that we would have never heard of them if it wasn't for the great faith of King David? When David, as a young man, went up against Goliath, the entire military of Israel was watching. When Goliath's head came off, Israel's faith rose up.

Notice in the scripture that it said, *"Eleazar's hand was weary, and his hand stuck to the sword."* He had fought so hard and for so long that he was exhausted, and his hand froze to the sword. I see it as though he couldn't let go with pain so intense that his fingers locked to the handle. But somehow, he kept fighting because that's what he knew to do. I don't believe he went out to gain a reputation. He went out for the people, and I think that because he let them have the plunder.

There are many pastors like that: When things are difficult, they won't let go of the sword, except nowadays, the sword is found in:

"And the sword of the Spirit which is the Word of God" (Ephesians 6:17).

Their words of faith make the congregations rise up for the week ahead. They push through the sermons on Sundays when the enemy has battled against them all week long, turn the other cheek when they have been wronged, and endure hardships silently to protect the call.

Next time you see your pastor, thank them for sticking to their calling.

He is: Elohim
God of Might and Power
Blessings

MY LIGHT

March 17

*Then shall thy light break forth as the morning, and thine health shall
spring forth speedily: and thy righteousness shall go before thee;
the glory of the LORD shall be thy rereward.
Then shalt thou call, and the LORD shall answer; thou shalt cry, and he shall say,
Here I am. If thou take away from the midst of thee the yoke,
the putting forth of the finger, and speaking vanity.*

Isaiah 58:8–9

Sounds like a great promise, and it is, but the seven preceding verses explain how you can obtain this promise. Isaiah talks about all the sacrifices people place on themselves to obtain the favor of God, and yet they never seem to get anywhere.

"and to let the oppressed go free, and that ye break every yoke?" (Isaiah 58:6)

Oppressed is defined as mental pressure or distress or prolonged abuse or control.

There are many ways to place yourself under oppression. By using drugs, you can give yourself over to mental distress or mental control of a demon. Some Christians have an unspoken belief that if they have a medical prescription for it, then it is okay. It may be legal, but that does not make it okay to use some drugs for pleasure. If you are in pain and you need medication, it is acceptable.

We also tend to dwell on offenses such as things done to us years ago. Instead of letting them go, we pick the thoughts up like favorite pets and try to cuddle them in our minds. The misery of being wronged and self-pity can feel like a toy poodle, but it is actually an angry viper trying to choke the light out of your destiny.

Stop judging others! Doing so allows the enemy a stronghold in your life. This includes politicians, athletes, school teachers, police officers, and any other person. (Yes, I'm guilty, but it's only because I'm right.)

When I first began to preach, I noticed that when I pointed my index finger to illustrate something, three of my fingers were pointing back at me! If you have a particular sin in your life that you struggle with, renew your mind by reading your Bible often, praying for His help, and watch His Word deliver you.

Then you shall call, and the Lord will answer.

He is: Ori
My Light
Blessings

DREAMS

March 18

Now when they had departed, behold, an angel of the Lord appeared to Joseph in a dream, saying, "Arise, take the young Child and His mother, flee to Egypt, and stay there until I bring you word; for Herod will seek the young Child to destroy Him."

Matthew 2:13

While asleep, Joseph received a night vision with instructions to flee to Egypt and wait. Some ministers say as much as one-third of the Bible is related to dreams. That would make sense, observing that we sleep approximately one-third of the day.

When I was a young Christian, people would tell me that God only spoke to you in a still small voice, based on 1 Kings 19:11–13. But there is another scripture that says God chooses how He will speak to you. Needless to say, this caused me much spiritual trouble and many hours of prayer. Then, one day, the Lord revealed to me that He had been speaking to me all along through images, visions, and dreams.

> *"For God may speak in one way, or in another. Yet man does not perceive it.*
>
> *In a dream, in a vision of the night, when deep sleep falls upon men, while slumbering in their beds, Then He opens the ears of men and seals their instruction.*

Job 33:14–16

Yes, the Lord will speak to you through dreams and visions. This is often the way Muslims accept Jesus as their Savior (through night visions) because they believe that God can speak to you through dreams.

How do you know if a dream is from God, you, or the devil? A dream from God is always in color, and the color has meaning. For example, a person wearing yellow might mean that the person is seeking self-glory. Multi-colors would represent the Holy Spirit.

I had a dream once that my dad was standing by a door wearing a wide-brimmed hat with a pheasant feather sticking out and a funky multi-colored sports coat. I said, "Dad! Where are you going?"

He straightened his coat and said, "I'm going to Chattanooga," and walked out the door.

My dad represented the Holy Spirit, and He was letting me know that a revival was going to break out in Chattanooga, Tennessee. Two weeks later, I saw on television that a revival had started at a truck stop, and I believe it is still going on today.

The enemy cannot create; he can only replicate, so he cannot create color. One night, I had a dream, and in the dream, a voice said, "You're a liar." I thought, *Wait a minute! I'm not a liar!*

I woke up, and a demon without a face had its hands and arms up to its elbows inside my head. The face was flat like a plate and white without any noticeable markings. Red hair down to the shoulders and a white gown. This thing was trying to replicate the Holy Spirit.

A soulish dream is more like a file download of the day's events, and your mind is sorting things out. You can also force yourself to have a specific dream. False prophets would do that back in the Old Testament, as seen in Jeremiah 29:8.

God is grand, and He loves to use symbolism in dreams. While studying Christian dream symbolism, I noticed that, often, the Holy Spirit gives me symbols in visions that are the same as dreams. Knowing this really helps me to prophetically explain the vision to the person I'm praying for. This is called understanding.

I recommend getting the book *The Divinity Code to Understanding Your Dreams and Visions* by Adam F. Thompson (Destiny Image, 2011). It's an excellent primer on dream symbolism. Be quick to pray and ask the Lord to give you an understanding of your dreams, visions, and symbols.

He is: Gelah Raz
Revealer of Mysteries
Blessings

THE LORD IS THERE

March 19

"And whatsoever ye ask in My name, that will I do. That the Father may be glorified in the Son."

John 14:13

"Follow after charity and desire spiritual gifts, but rather that ye may prophecy" (1 Corinthians 14:1).

Have you ever been to church and listened to someone prophesy? Have you ever wondered if this is still available to the body of Christ? Good news—it is! And you can have this gift, too. Some people believe that the gifts of the Spirit died out with the apostles, but nowhere in the Bible does it say they have stopped, and to support this belief, they quote:

"Love never ends. But as for prophecies, they will come to an end, as for languages (tongues), they will cease, as, for knowledge, it will come to an end" (1 Corinthians 13:8).

In sales, we call this an open-ended statement. There is no time frame attached to it in this context. If it must come to pass, why would God keep it as an open-ended statement? Let us look at:

"But of that day and hour knoweth no man, no, not the angels of heaven, but My Father only" (Matthew 24:36).

God keeps the timeframe open because after the church is taken up, or the millennial reign of Christ begins, there will be no need to prophesy, to speak in tongues, no need for words of knowledge.

Here and now, the gifts are needed. Speaking in tongues is coded messaging between you and God that the enemy cannot decipher. A word of knowledge is the Lord letting you in on someone's personal problem for you to get them help from above. Prophesying edifies, builds others up, and encourages.

Now, anyone (that's saved) can prophesy, but speaking as a prophet is another office. A prophet will be given future insights into what will happen, and that will help people prepare. Typically, a person will start off prophesying, and God may promote them to the office of prophet.

Years ago, I had a vision of myself picking up a rusted sword. I didn't know what to make of it at the time; it perplexed me. Years went by.

One day, while at my desk, my wife walked in and said, "Your mother sent you this." My mother sent me a Bible from my great-grandmother. It was dated around the 1850s. As my wife handed me the Bible, the vision came back! The Bible turned into that sword! It was a fast glimpse of the old vision that I had wondered about for years.

When I read it, I was awed by the reverence in the *good* book. There were no personal study notes written in the margins or underlined scriptures. She had locks of hair tucked between the pages, little paper notes from others, one newspaper article, and everything saved seemed to be a precious memory.

As I was studying to learn how to prophesy, I thought, *I'll look in the old family Bible and see how it reads compared to nowadays.* To my amazement, she had underlined with a pencil the very same scriptures that I was studying! Scripture for scripture, I guess I had just never noticed it before. You see, she believed prophecy was still available. Wouldn't you like to leave that gift to your children?

"A good man leaves an inheritance for his children's children: and the wealth of a sinner is laid up for the just" (Proverbs 13:22).

Laid up for the just: maybe he's talking about a gift that an unsaved person let fall to the ground—a spiritual gift that was never used. Take up your sword and grab hold of your gift. Spend time in prayer and ask the Son if you can have a gift that will glorify the Father. We all love presents, and God gives the best gifts. Selah.

He is: Jehovah Shammah
The Lord Is There
Blessings

THE GOD OF PRESENCE

March 20

"Thou preparest table before me in the presence of mine enemies: thou anointest my head with oil; my cup runneth over."

Psalm 23:5

In Exodus, the Israelites were given exact instructions on how to prepare the Tabernacle for the Lord. The furnishings of the Tabernacle were a tent or movable structure, which later became the Holy Temple. We see further instructions from Yahweh in:

"And thou shall put pure frankincense upon each row, that it may be a bread of memorial, even an offering made by fire unto the LORD" (Leviticus 24:7).

The symbolism of these words is beautiful and is continued through the New Testament. The Table of Shewbread was just a small table overlaid with gold about three feet long and two feet tall. The bread was placed on the table weekly in the Presence of the Lord and was called the Bread of Presence.

"And Jesus said unto them, 'I Am the bread of life: he that cometh to me shall never hunger, and he that believeth on me shall never thirst'" (John 6:35). Frankincense is olive oil combined with certain spices that we call anointing oil; this oil symbolizes the Holy Spirit.

"But the wise took the oil in their vessels with their lamps" (Matthew 25:4).

Cup refers to our bodies. Jesus used a cup to describe the scribes and the Pharisees in Matthew 23:25:

"Woe unto you scribes and Pharisees, hypocrites! For ye make clean the outside cup and of the platter, but within they are full of extortion and excess."

Be wise and fill your cup with the Holy Spirit, and ask God to overflow you with His presence because these are your enemies:

"For we wrestle not against flesh and blood, but against principalities, against powers, against the rulers of the darkness of this world, against spiritual wickedness in high places.

Selah" (Ephesians 6:12).

He is: Theos Pas Paraklesis
The God of All Comfort
Blessings

UNCHANGING

March 21

"Children obey your parents in the Lord for this is right. Honor thy father and mother; (which is the first commandment with promise;) That it may be well with thee, and thou mayest live long on the earth."

Ephesians 6:1–3

Every parent knows this verse. You may not be able to quote much scripture, but this is the one scripture you can remember for your kids. Our kids referred to it as "the Bible threat," maybe because it proceeded the possibility of a short, miserable life. I guess the glass is either half full or half empty, depending on which half you want.

I spoke with a person who travels around the country in all-white clothing and self-proclaims herself as an apostle/prophet of the Lord. She told me that God told her, "This verse is related to the Father and the Holy Spirit, not your parents." I tried to gently explain that it does refer to your parents.

The word "father" comes from the Greek word *pater*, which literally means father or parent. But to clarify for all future generations, *pater* is used in the very next verse:

"And fathers provoke not your children to wrath: but bring them up in the nurture and admonition of the Lord" (Ephesians 6:4).

We know God is not going to provoke your children to wrath. Instead, He wants you to train them and educate them in the ways of the Lord. I have dealt with people like this lady more than once. I have noticed that there is a common thread: unwillingness to submit to the authority of others. What she has is called *a religious spirit*. This type of spirit is a placebo of the Holy Spirit, and people with this spirit are out of covenant with the body of Christ, going from community to community.

"Even though they make a show of being religious, their religion won't be real. Don't have anything to do with such people" (2 Timothy 3:5).

Pretty strong words, but well-meaning Christians take them into their homes, despite what the Bible says. Eventually, they get enough, and in this woman's own words, "they can't take the truth about getting rid of all the idols in their homes, and changing their lives, after about a week, they kick me out."

It's not the kicking out that worries me. It's what she leaves behind in the Spirit. Another thing I've noticed is that people with a religious spirit often say that you can get baptized by yourself. This philosophy rejects the authority placed over you by Christ—even Jesus was baptized by John.

Another phrase you will hear them say is, "The Word of God has been written incorrectly, mistranslated by man." This would mean that God is not able to protect His written Word.

The Dead Sea Scrolls were discovered in 1947 by an Arab shepherd boy. Written by the Essenes, most are leather, some on parchment, containing about 200 scrolls.

Just to be clear, the Dead Sea Scrolls contained every book of the Old Testament except the book of Esther. These manuscripts were over one thousand years older than our previous manuscripts. They were written in Hebrew, Aramaic, and Greek.

By saying that the Bible has been mistranslated, they can say and do say, "God told me!" You will hear this often in their conversations. The religious spirit, by imitating God's authority, tries to take away your free choice.

This woman with the religious spirit told me that she is often brought to church services, and she takes notes, then proceeds to rebuke the pastors afterward. I explained that the Bible says:

"Do not rebuke an elder" (1 Timothy 5:1).

But according to her, "This does not apply to the office of a prophet!"

When you explain what the Bible has to say, people with religious spirits will often retort that the Bible is inaccurate. By pressing them, in some cases, they will admit that they have never actually read the Bible.

But in the end, you just have to hold your peace because they love the pleasures of this world more than the truth of God. Hold up their names before God in prayer and ask the Lord to reveal to them His truth.

He is: Lo Shanah
Unchanging
Blessings

MY HELPER

March 22

But that ye may know my affairs, and how I do, Tychicus, a beloved brother and faithful minister in the Lord, shall make known to you all things
Whom I have sent unto you for the same purpose, that ye might know our affairs, and that he might comfort your hearts.
Peace be to the brethren, and love with faith, from God the Father and the Lord Jesus Christ.

Ephesians 6:21–23

Tychicus is mentioned five times in the Bible, and he is always mentioned with great qualities. He was beloved, a faithful minister in the Lord, a fellow servant with Paul, and a reliable source. His name comes from the Greek word *Tuchikos*, which means fortuitous or fortunate, and it derives from other Greek words that mean bring to pass, make ready, enjoy, or refresh.

Tychicus' purpose in this visit to the church at Ephesus was "that you might know our affairs." Paul sent him to encourage the church with what Paul had accomplished. These testimonies were meant to comfort their hearts.

Then Paul closes this beautiful description of Tychicus with these words, *"from God the Father and the Lord Jesus Christ."* Notice Paul did not say, *"and the Holy Spirit."* This is because the Holy Spirit dwelt in Tychicus, and Tychicus carried all the qualities of the Holy Spirit with him wherever he went, bringing the testimonies of Christ and how Paul, in bonds, represented the gospel in hardship!

Tychicus had the gift and call of an evangelist. He saw the greatness in hardships, hard times, hard economies, and these encouraged and exhorted him. To him, hardships blow in and build you up with faith, bringing you comfort. They encourage you to endure. The testimonies are sure. They bring love and faith, ambassadors for Christ.

Tychicus not only brought the letter to the Ephesians for Paul, but he also wrote it for Paul, a Father in Christ, not knowing that two millennia later, we would still be reading it.

You can have the same Holy Spirit living inside you, and you can write a letter for the Father with the pen of your life and give it to the Son. Not only will Jesus read it, but He will help you to re-write the ending.

"That if thou shalt confess with thy mouth the Lord Jesus, and shalt believe in thine heart that God hath raised Him from the dead, thou shalt be saved" (Romans 10:9).

He is: Jehovah Ezrah
My Helper
Blessings

A NAIL IN A FIRM PLACE

March 23

For the preaching of the cross is to them that perish foolishness,
but unto us which are saved it is the power of God. For after that in the wisdom
of God the world by wisdom knew not God, it pleased God by the foolishness of
preaching to save them. Because the foolishness of God is wiser than men,
and the weakness of God stronger than men.

1 Corinthians 1:18, 21,25

Have you ever been called a fool for Christ? Maybe you knowingly did something good for someone who had wronged you in the past. Your friends and family members perceived it as you are being taken advantage of. Even the person, as they took your last bit of money, chuckled to themselves, thinking, "What an idiot!" Pure foolishness in the world's eyes, but in reality, it is the power of the cross.

Nails did not hang Jesus on the cross; it was His love for us that kept Him there while the criminal next to Him taunted Him, saying, "If you be the Christ, get us down from here!" It was foolishness to him that our Savior would hang on that tree so that the blessings of Abraham would be ours.

But in all the pain and suffering, the power of God was being displayed, and we knew it not. How much strength did it take to endure? All Jesus would have had to do was cry out, then a thousand legions of angels would come to save Him, but He endured.

The wisest theologians stood and watched their Messiah die on a tree but could not see the wisdom of God because the foolishness of God is wiser than men. People think it's crazy to see someone standing on a soap box preaching the gospel, enduring insults and laughter. But God, in all His wisdom, chose this method to spread the gospel: preaching was God's idea.

I've thought about this verse (1 Corinthians 1:25) many times over the years. What other ways could God have chosen? Once, I heard a story about some missionaries in the Middle East who were going to play the Jesus movie. Muslims came from all around because Jesus had appeared to them in the sky and said, "Go to this village to learn about Me." How else could He have done it? He's pretty smart. I'm sure He could have come up with many other ways. But I think He made the right choice.

You see, the power of the cross was not in the nail; it was in the love. Love has made fools out of us all, and God is foolishly in love with you, and His foolishness is wiser than men.

Are you having troubles? Maybe in your marriage? Look at your wedding ring and view it like the cross—no nails, keep it there.

He is: Yated Aman Maqom
A Nail in a Firm Place
Blessings

THE FIRST DISCIPLES

March 24

*Now when he had left speaking, he said unto Simon,
Launch out into the deep, and let down your nets for a draught.
And Simon answering said unto him, Master, we have toiled all the night,
and have taken nothing: nevertheless at thy word I will let down the net.
And when they had this done, they enclosed a great multitude of fishes:
and their net brake.
And they beckoned unto their partners, which were in the other ship, that they
should come and help them. And they came, and filled both the ships,
so that they began to sink.
When Simon Peter saw it, he fell down at Jesus' knees, saying,
Depart from me; for I am a sinful man, O Lord.
For he was astonished, and all that were with him,
at the draught of the fishes which they had taken:
And so was also James, and John, the sons of Zebedee, which were partners with
Simon. And Jesus said unto Simon, Fear not; from henceforth thou shalt catch men.
And when they had brought their ships to land, they forsook all, and followed him.*

Luke 5:4–11

Jesus traveled down to the Sea of Galilee, where Peter and his crew were. The crowds were so huge that Jesus got into Peter's boat and gave His sermon. Imagine the quiet hush of a large crowd so intent on hearing the spoken word of God and the crystal-clear water lapping against the shore.

Jesus must have been excited knowing that, today, Peter would join His ministry. Many people can relate to listening to a life-changing sermon—the one that turns their world upside down and changes the course of their eternity. The Holy Spirit orchestrates this with every person that comes to the Lord: a comment here, an act of kindness there, a miracle from God, and you're in! The whole time, Jesus knows that today is your day! And suddenly, out of conviction, you fall before His knees in the realization that He is so good and you are not.

Jesus started off preaching a commanding sermon, captivating everyone. When He finished, He told Peter to launch out into the deep waters and let the net down. Peter, by listening to the spoken word, had a certain knowledge of the Lord and a level of respect. Many people live at this level, going to church, following the rules, which are kind of a sacrifice to the Lord.

Here is how we can tell that Peter had respect. Peter used the word *master*, which means teacher. Peter had respect for Jesus, but at that point, he didn't not know who Jesus was.

But Peter did know fishing. The maximum depth of the Sea of Galilee was about 141 feet. The water was truly clear, and during the day, the fish went deep. That is one of the reasons they fished at night.

Pulling in a net from a hundred feet of water is a lot of work. It's like the first time you pray for someone—you do it out of service to God, not thinking you're worthy to be used by God. But then God shows up! God had a greater purpose for them not catching any fish that night.

Peter didn't fall down until after the fish were caught and, in the boat, Peter's worldly way of work was done. Two miracles took place at that moment: the fish and Peter's conversion. Peter's respect went from teacher to Lord, which means *supreme authority*! The first words Jesus said at that moment of Peter's conversion were, *"Don't be afraid."* In effect, He was saying, "I can use you." God can still use you, and it is never too late to do something for the Lord.

He is: Or Goyim
Light of the Nations
Blessings

THE HOOK

March 25

When they had come to Capernaum, those who received the temple tax came to Peter and said, "Does your Teacher not pay the temple tax?"
He said "Yes." And when he had come into the house, Jesus anticipated him saying, "What do
you think, Simon? From whom do the kings of the earth take customs or taxes, from their sons or from strangers?"
"Nevertheless, lest we offend them, go to the sea, cast a hook, and take the fish that comes up first, and when you have opened its mouth, you will find a piece of money: take that and give it to them for Me and you."

Matthew 17:24–27

Capernaum was a small fishing village located on the Sea of Galilee. Jesus had established His headquarters there for several months during His ministry. It was a small village of about 1,500 people.

Notice the men approached Peter and not Jesus. What's up with that? Satan wanted to intimidate, causing Peter to back down. Maybe Satan wanted to test his leadership. Peter answered "Yes" and said nothing else. It was a tough question for a new convert to answer.

Once you have given your life to Christ, the enemy will bring the tough questions your way, and like all of us, more than likely, you will get them wrong in the beginning. This is by Satan's design to destroy your confidence in the Lord.

Why didn't they just ask Jesus themselves? They called Him teacher by saying *your teacher*. This shows that they did not recognize Jesus, even though He has turned their town upside down with revival. Tradition and position were more important to them than God.

Earlier, Jesus had pronounced a woe against Capernaum in Matthew 11:23, and that was probably the cause for them not liking Jesus too much. If they had believed in a living God, they would have sought out repentance instead of fault through tax.

Then, we see that Jesus referred to Peter as Simon; the name Peter means *rock*. Jesus had given that name to Peter as a new identity, and by calling him Simon, he was implying that Peter had slipped back into his old ways. Remember the very first thing He said to Peter? *"Don't be afraid!"*

When the temple tax collectors asked Peter, Peter could have said, "Ask Him yourself."

Nevertheless, Jesus was going to teach Simon a lesson about who He was. How many thousands of fish do you think Simon caught in his lifetime? I bet he never caught a fish with a coin in its mouth.

Simon had to walk all the way down to the seashore thinking about this whole ordeal, astonished in disbelief that he had been dragged into this, and he might have thought, "Why me?" The answer was simple: Peter was promoted in leadership, and the devil despises authority, especially if it threatens his.

One time, I talked about someone, and the Lord told me, "You need to receive correction."

I knew what I had said was wrong, and I just said, "Father, I'll take it like a son."

I really thought that He would place me on probation in the ministry or something similar. Instead, He said, "I want you to take a spoon and give it in the offering bucket." You know it sounds silly, doesn't it? But I had to explain to my wife why I needed to place a spoon in the offering bucket and wait until the next church service to place it there. Nevertheless, it gave me a lot of time to think about my mistake and the words that came out of my mouth.

Simon went through the same process because we are the fish, and only precious words of gold should come out of our mouths, not a painful hook.

He is: Lo Shanah
Unchanging
Blessings

I'M GOING FISHING

March 26

But when the morning had now come, Jesus stood on the shore,
yet the disciples did not know that it was Jesus.
Then Jesus said to them, "Cast the net on the right side of the boat, and you will
find some." So they cast, and now they were not able to draw
it in because of the multitude of fish.
Therefore, that disciple whom Jesus loved said to Peter, "It is the Lord!" Now
when Simon Peter heard that it was the Lord, he put on his outer garment (for he
had removed it) and plunged into the sea.

John 21:4–7

And after Jesus's resurrection in John 21:3, Simon Peter said to them, "I'm going fishing."

Peter had been commissioned to be a leader, and he had led in the wrong direction by returning to his old ways, hence the reference to Simon Peter. He was trying to return to the world he knew before he was converted, but he had a new anointing, a gift from God that he did not understand yet. When Peter said these words, six other disciples followed him.

I have a very good friend who used to be one of the roughest dealer rappers around. Now, he is a successful businessman, evangelist, and promoter. One day, I said, "You know, Joe, you used to be successful when you were bad, and now you're successful when you're good. There's good success, and there's bad success."

Jesus gave Peter a choice at that moment by loading him up with fish and blessing him. Simon could have opted to go back to his old lifestyle, a place of comfort.

Mentioning of his garment was not a coincidence. Look at the symbolism: He had removed his garment. When I go swimming, I usually take my clothes off, but Simon Peter put his garment back on. The symbolism is Peter picking up the mantle that he was about to leave behind. Before, he was terrified to walk on the water, but then he plunged into the water for Jesus! Before, he wanted to get as far away from the Lord as possible, but then he wanted to be as close as possible. Unlike in the beginning, he didn't wait for all the fish to be pulled into the boat. He left his worldly work behind. The other disciples were so excited they didn't even pull the net in. They dragged the net behind them with the same effect. We'll leave the world behind for Jesus!

"Bring some of the fish you have just caught." Simon Peter went up and dragged the net to land, full of large fish, one hundred and fifty-three; and although there were so many, the net was not broken.

John 21:10–11

Here, again, is the symbolism of the work Peter would do. He turned back to the world and brought fish to the Lord. The fish represent the people, the nations.

Long ago, I heard of a British officer who was stationed somewhere in Africa in the 1800s. He must have spent a considerable amount of time doing research on this subject. But he discovered that at that time, there were one hundred and fifty-three nations on the earth—a fish for every culture. Peter really was "going fishing."

Peter helped to establish the church, the foundational rock for the Lord that has lasted and endured. Of course, he had a little help along *the Way*, but you have the same Holy Spirit inside of you.

God can use you too: one word to the right person, one act of kindness, and you may have just brought the next Mother Teresa into the kingdom, the next TD Jakes, or just someone who will be grateful for your words for all eternity. I know those who are my personal heroes: my aunt Shireen, my friend Charles, who led me to the Lord, my mentors, and the list goes on and on.

Please get on someone's list. The Holy Spirit will give you opportunities if you just ask.

He is: Jehovah Ezrah
My Helper
Blessings

A PRAYER FOR RELIEF

March 27

"You number my wanderings; Put my tears into your bottle; Are they not in Your book? When I cry out to You, then my enemies will turn back; This I know, because God is for me."

Psalm 56:8–9

What precious words written by King David as he reflected back on being captured by the Philistines and taken in the city of Gath. He instructed the chief musician to set this psalm to the music, "The Silent Dove in Distant Lands," "A Michtam of David," which means poem, and this one was a prayer for relief from tormentors.

The thing is, David walked into the city of Gath; he was on the run from King Saul, who wanted to kill him. David had wandered around in the desert for so long with the threat of death on his heels every day that stress got to him. God truly was numbering his wanderings and watching his decisions. David sought refuge in the worst place he could have picked. He went to Gath carrying the sword of Goliath, the same city Goliath the Giant was from!

Yes, they well knew who David was, their enemy, and they were perplexed at his presence. David realized what he had gotten himself into and faked insanity in order to escape the presence of his enemies. At that moment, what if he had remembered the promise from God? I don't know, but if a dude walked into my palace alone, carrying the sword from my biggest giant and the greatest warrior in my kingdom that he had killed, then I might have given him whatever he asked for.

Have you ever been so stressed out that you went to someone for advice that you know didn't like you? I have, still to this day, and I know it was not the best decision I ever made. The heading of this Psalm, the Silent Dove, suggests David was not seeking to hurt anyone, neither the Philistines nor King Saul. But most people don't think that way.

While David was out on the lam, he must have cried considerably. Reflecting back on his sufferings, he realized that he had never been alone. When you are so hurt by whatever circumstance, God takes your tears and places them in a bottle. Just like you would if someone you loved gave you the most precious gift ever, God puts your tears in a place of honor on a shelf in heaven, and they are precious to Him. On the day of judgment, He will bring them down before those who caused you the hurt, and the tormentors (demons) who caused the tears will cry for eternity.

After David had escaped Gath, he went to a place called Ziklag, a place in the Philistine Kingdom of Gath. David was rescued from his enemies to be "put in a place of uncertainty." David remained there for about sixteen months, resting and conquering. You see, God needed a king, and a king must be tested. What looks like a failed test to us is a victory in God's eyes because no matter what, David loved God.

"No matter what, God is for me. No matter what, I still love God." Sometimes, you just have to say that to yourself, the enemy, and to God. That drives the tormentors crazy! It's fun to get even in the Spirit! Jump up and down and praise Him! You can't help but laugh, and laughter is the best medicine (Proverbs 17:22).

He is: El Nathan Neqamah
The God Who Avenges Me
Blessings

PLEASE PREPARE FOR TOMORROW

March 28

Then Moses returned to the LORD and said, "Oh, these people have committed a great sin, and have made for themselves a god of gold! Yet now, if You will forgive their sin-but if not, I pray, blot me out of Your book which you have written. And the LORD said to Moses, "Whoever has sinned against Me, I will blot him out of My book."

Exodus 32:31–33

While Moses was on Mount Sinai, the people made a golden calf and called it God. Moses told everyone who was on the Lord's side to come to him, and then he had the priests go and kill everyone who didn't cross the line, about three thousand men. It's one way to get sin out of your camp.

But then Moses approached Yahweh (God) and confessed the sins for his people, asking Yahweh for His forgiveness. Some put the estimate at about two million people who came out of Egypt. Moses realized the magnitude of their transgressions. He stood in the gap and asked Yahweh to take his life for the people and then to remove his name from the Lamb's Book of Life.

I have read this history lesson many times over the years, and one day, it hit me—the enormous humility and love that Moses had for his people. He was willing, as a leader, to be a sacrifice to save a nation. When this astonishment impacted me, I went to my knees before the Lord, and I said, "God, Moses is a far greater man than me! I'm not willing to go to hell for anybody!"

I was being very sincere. I was astonished. Then, the Holy Spirit came and just loved me. I've never known why I felt His presence like that until just now. I believe He just said, "It was your sincerity."

God will not ask us to be accountable for another person's sins. But He will hold us accountable for our sins. In the book of Leviticus, there was an offering for unintentional sins but no offering for intentional sins. If you play the Grace card too much in the belief that you can be forgiven for your intentional sin after you have become a born-again Christian, one day, you will flip that card only to see a joker—you've been fooled.

He is: Elohay Selichot
The God Who Is Ready to Forgive
Blessings

BECOME AN OLIVE TREE

March 29

"And now thy two sons, Ephraim, and Manasseh, which were born unto thee in the land of Egypt before I came unto thee into Egypt, are mine; as Reuben and Simeon, they shall be mine."

Genesis 48:5

The patriarch Jacob is speaking to his son Joseph about Joseph's two sons, Ephraim and Manasseh. When Joseph was promoted out of prison by God, the Pharaoh of Egypt gave Joseph authority over all Egypt, answering to no one but Pharaoh. Pharaoh also gave Joseph an Egyptian wife, Asenath, and she gave birth to two sons, Manasseh, the firstborn, and Ephraim, the second.

Reuben and Simeon were the first two sons of Leah, Jacob's first wife. Jacob is using his spiritual authority as Israel to graft Ephraim and Manasseh into the nation of Israel, making them two prominent tribes in Israel and giving them the full promise of Abraham, his grandfather. If you noticed, Israel named the second son first in the blessing; this is because God judges the heart, and Ephraim was special to God.

When you accept Jesus Christ as your Lord and Savior, just like Ephraim and Manasseh, you are grafted into the kingdom of God with the promise of Abraham's blessing.

"a wild olive tree, were grafted in. So now you, too, receive the blessing God has promised Abraham and his children, sharing in God's rich nourishment of his own special olive tree" (Romans 11:17).

Just like Ephraim, you become His own special olive tree.

He is: Georgos
The Gardener
Blessings

RUN FOR YOUR LIFE!

March 30

"Then the Lord knows how to deliver the godly out of temptations and to reserve the unjust under punishment for the day of judgment."

2 Peter 2:9

You know, that Scripture is a contract between you and God. Let's break it down some:

1. The word *Lord* comes from the Greek word *Kurios*, which means *supreme in authority*. (Judge)

2. Next, we have the word *godly*, which is rooted in the Greek word *Eusebes*, defined as devout, pious, or reverent. (Defendant)

3. Temptations come from the Greek word *Peirasmos*, putting to proof by an experiment of good or of evil. (Prosecutor)

Sounds like a courtroom, doesn't it? You have a judge, a defendant, and a prosecutor. The difference is the prosecutor in this court creates the situations for the crime scene. To this day, it amazes me how the enemy sets up Christians. It seems as though he will plan a situation of deception long in advance.

"But every man is tempted, when he is drawn away of his own lust, and enticed" (James 1:14).

The word "lust" means desire, especially for what is forbidden.

"Then when lust (desire) has conceived, it gives birth to sin; and sin, when it is full-grown, brings forth death" (James 1:15).

Notice that word "lust" (desire) again? Here, James is using it more in the context of a thought. He's taking this from the tenth commandment: *Thou shalt not covet.*

And how does the enemy get in? It all starts with the first thought. I have noticed that the thought is often laid up through unforgiveness or judgment.

"Brethren if any man be overtaken in a fault, ye which are spiritual restore such a one in a spirit of meekness, considering thyself, lest thou also be tempted" (Galatians 6:1).

I remember a famous minister who was very judgmental against the gay community, only to be caught in a relationship with another man. He didn't understand how he had fallen into such a lifestyle. This verse explains it: the spirit of the action that he judged came back on him, causing him to fall into the same temptation.

How do you forgive when someone has deeply hurt you? First, pray and ask Jesus to help you with a desire to forgive that person and begin to intercede for them. I know it's hard, but you must do it for your own sake.

I've been in many instances over the years in which the enemy had set a trap for me to step into sin. I've asked God to give me a way out. Sometimes, I've had to whisper it under my breath, the door opened, and I ran. Don't stick around and play with the thought because the thought is designed to bring you to death. Personally, in God's courtroom, I think your best plea is, "I plead the blood of the Lamb!" And God will open a way of escape.

Always be quick to forgive and sometimes quick to flee.

He is: Jehovah- Palat
Deliverer
Blessings

BECOME ALL THINGS

March 31

For though I be free from all men, yet have I made myself servant unto all, that I might gain the more.
And unto the Jews I became as a Jew, that I might gain the Jews; to them that are under the law, as under the law, that I might gain them that are under the law;
To them that are without law, as without law, (being not without law to God, but under the law to Christ,) that I might gain them that are without law.
To the weak became I as weak, that I might gain the weak: I am made all things to all men, that I might by all means save some.
And this I do for the gospel's sake, that I might be partaker thereof with you.

1 Corinthians 9:19–23

Paul was teaching how to evangelize. He started off by saying, "*I have made myself a slave, a servant to all people.*" Notice he didn't say, "When I went, I expected to be served." He did the serving.

While attending school, I told the Lord I was getting tired of always being the one to do the cleaning after class. Seems like in every church I go to, I end up being the one to do the cleaning or the dishes afterward. That night, I finished class and started to clean the bathrooms.

While in there, a lady came in, and she was so happy to see me cleaning. She said, "I know you're a rich man! And it just does my heart so good to see a rich man humble himself for the Lord!"

I was so tired I just said, "Thank you," thinking if I had to be a rich man to help her, I'd bear the burden of being rich. Maybe not the best example, but close enough. *I have made myself a slave to everyone.*

Another time, a relative's close friend died. They were a different crowd, and they all met at a bar in town. All the deceased's friends were gathered together. I went over there because I knew my relatives would be hurting deeply. When I walked in, everyone knew who I was, "the Holy Roller," but they appreciated my presence. I spoke with people while they drank. It didn't bother me, but I could tell that the fact that a Christian had come to pay respects made them feel better. I didn't lead anyone to the Lord that night, but a seed was planted that Christians do care. *To those who are without (outside) the Law, [I became] as one without the Law,*

I was at a Full Gospel businessmen's event, and the evangelist made an altar call for the unsaved to come forward. My friend Ray was standing there, and the man said, "I see you standing. Come on up!" Ray had accepted the Lord two months before me; I knew he was saved. Ray just bowed his head and walked up reverently. Then I noticed several other men get up out of their chairs and go forward to accept the Lord.

I asked Ray about that afterward, and he said, "You know that has happened to me a few times before. I guess the Lord just uses me to prime the pump for others." Maybe it's because Ray worked on pumps for a living? But Ray became as though he were unsaved to get others to be saved. *And I do all this for the sake of the gospel, so that I may share in its blessings along with you.* Ray gets to share in the blessings of others, and so can you.

He is: El Moshaah
The God Who Saves
Blessings

THE REASON FOR DEATH

April 1

And the eyes of them both were opened, and they were naked, and they sewed fig leaves together, and made themselves aprons.
Unto Adam also and to his wife did the Lord God make coats of skins, and clothed them.

Genesis 3:7 and 3:21

Back to the beginning. After the fall of man, Adam and Eve sewed fig leaves together and made aprons. At that particular moment, we didn't see any gender bias when it came to sewing. They were both in a hurry to get dressed; they sewed fig leaves as an act of self-righteousness in trying to cover their sin.

It wasn't just that they knew that they were naked. Think about all the other emotions that rushed into their being: shock, fear, embarrassment, condemnation. Then God showed up, and both Adam and Eve were afraid. Notice the serpent remained silent. He had already been cast out of heaven; at that point, he knew his limits. However, God, in His wisdom, gave them a new covering, one made of skins. Some theologians suggest that God did not actually kill anything in the garden but that He made skins, just like He created everything else, maybe.

Imagine how emotionally hard it must have been for God to kill the animals before Adam and Eve. God does have emotions: love, patience, kindness, and long-suffering. God, by killing the animals, reinforced death. Adam, Eve, and the devil saw how death was. Satan gets a firsthand lesson in how to kill. Not realizing that death, which he craves so much, would be his defeat: Christ's death on the cross.

"So He drove out the man; and He placed at the east of the garden of Eden cherubims, and a flaming sword which turned every way, to keep the way of the tree of life" (Genesis 3:24).

Hebrew tradition speculates that the first part of this sentence, "So He drove out the man," was left incomplete due to the haste in which God had to get them out of the Garden and away from the Tree of Life.

He is: Alpha and Omega
The First and The Last
Blessings

WHITE STONE

April 2

He that hath an ear, let him hear what the Spirit saith unto the churches; To him that overcometh will I give to eat of the hidden manna, and will give him a white stone, and in the stone a new name written, which no man knoweth saving he that receiveth it.

Revelations 2:17

"He that hath an ear" is letting you know this is for everyone. John wrote this letter to the seven churches. This portion of the letter pertains to the church at Pergamum—the worldly church. Pergamum is the throne room of Satan, literally the seat where Satan dwells.

They were in the heat of the battle. They were surrounded by temples made to Zeus, Apollo, and Athena. The cults worshiped Caesar along with idolatry and demon worship. They taught the doctrine of Balaam. Balaam was none other than the false prophet in Numbers 31 who taught King Balak to corrupt God's people.

Jesus urges the Christians to persevere. "A white stone with your new name on it." What does this symbolize? The Roman gladiators had that as a retirement incentive. If they made it to retirement, they would receive a white stone. They could take this stone into any shop in Rome and obtain what they wanted free of charge (I'm sure the taxpayers covered the cost).

This stone will be very precious to you. Jesus will give you the name that is the real you, the inner you. Whether or not we get to tell others our new identity, I'm not sure. But if we are allowed to say to others our name, I'm sure it will be quite the conversation starter.

The church at Pergamum knew the value of this stone.

Once, I had a vision of someone entering into heaven. He grew younger as he entered. I could see heaven in the background, and it was colorful and beautiful. I also know a lady who told me she had an experience and saw heaven. She told me she wanted to go there every day; she longed to be there. We need to remind ourselves daily that perseverance is the key to overcoming.

He is: Gelah Raz
Revealer of Mysteries
Blessings

THE STORY OF LIFE

April 3

Do not remember the former things. Nor consider the things of old. Behold I will do a new thing. Now it shall spring forth: Shall you not know it? I will even make a road in the wilderness. And rivers in the desert.

Isaiah 43:18

People were set in their ways back in the day, and many churches refused to make the change. My old pastor used to say, "The message never changes, but the method of delivery does." With this technical culture that we live in, you can see the change.

Today, a lady asked me to pray for her. As we prayed, the Lord told me that she was in chagrin. I told her what the Lord said. Then, I received these blank stares back at me. I explained that I'd heard this word years ago but didn't really know what it meant. Her daughter Googled it. It meant distress or embarrassment at having failed or been humiliated. She told me that was exactly the right explanation of what she was dealing with. This in the Bible is called a word of knowledge. The word of knowledge goes right to the core of the problem. I asked the Lord what to pray, and the Holy Spirit gave me this verse:

"There is therefore now no condemnation to them which are in Christ Jesus, who walk not after the flesh, but after the Spirit" (Romans 8:1).

Please, put your past behind you and move on, leave the former things, the regrets of past failures. We've all failed multiple times.

Babe Ruth, the greatest home run hitter for the New York Yankees, had more strikeouts than home runs. Sometimes, it's just a matter of getting up to the plate one more time.

My friend Jerome used to always tell me, "Your opponent is just as tired as you. Give the effort one more time than him, and you'll win." Don't allow the enemy to stop you one prayer away from your victory.

Are you under attack from the enemy? Whatever your enemy is, it will not outlast the written word of God. *Behold I will do a new thing. Now it shall spring forth: Shall you not know it?*

A *new thing* springs forth, and you will know it! Take encouragement! The things you call failures, God calls "utterances" that will spring forth into someone else's life for encouragement. He can use you to create a river in a dry place and a new road of hope for someone in the wilderness. Let your hope spring forth.

He is: Maqowr Chay Mayim
Fountain of Living Waters
Blessings

PURE RELIGION

April 4

"But had some questions against him about their own religion and about a certain Jesus, who had died, whom Paul affirmed to be alive."

Acts 25:19

Religion, when mentioned, seems to some to be good. But religion comes from the Greek word *deisidaimonia* (dice-ee-dahee-mon-ee'-ah). It is only found seven times in the scriptures, and in this instance, it means superstition, superstitious, reverencing the gods, in a bad sense.

If you keep researching, you will find that this word is based on other Greek words that just decline in definition, and by this, I mean they get worse. When you boil this word down, it actually ends up being described as demon worship! Wow, I did not know that, and I certainly didn't see that one coming. The base word, *daimon* (dah'ee-mown), means to distribute fortunes, or a demon or supernatural spirit (of bad nature), or devil.

I read a true story about a false god in India called Lord Ganesh, the elephant-headed Hindu god of wealth and power. This elephant obtained wealth and power by drinking milk through its trunk.

In 1995, a Hindu man had a dream that the god was thirsty (point to remember, not all dreams come from God). The next day, he went and placed a teaspoon of milk to the trunk of the statue as an offering to the god. The porous stone soaked up the milk from the teaspoon. Needless to say, this supposed miracle went all across India, and hysteria caused a milk shortage. In my opinion, the true identity of Lord Ganesh was availed. Milk supplies were so short that shopkeepers raised their prices by more than twenty times. In today's value, that would roughly be $34.00 per gallon of milk. Yes, the shopkeepers made money, and the poor remained poor. This is what religion will do for you—it breaks you every way it can.

"Pure and undefiled religion before God and the Father is this: to visit orphans and widows in their trouble, and to keep oneself unspotted from the world" (James 1:17).

Amazingly, the word *religion* does not fall into the same category as above. It comes from the Greek word *threskeia* (thrace-ki-ah). It means ceremonial worship. Did you know that when you help the widows and orphans, you are worshipping God? James combined the words God and the Father, and by connecting these words together, he is showing the degree of importance in helping widows and orphans. And also, there is no object of worship, no idolatry.

Once, while sitting in a church service, our pastor preached on helping widows and orphans. This beautiful widow was sitting in front of me, so I gave her $20. I really was blessed that day, not even knowing it at the time. The lovely lady turned out to be my future wife, and the $20 bill that I gave to her meant so much to her at that moment that she kept it in her wallet until after we were married. As my pastor used to say, "You can't out-give God."

He is: Elohim Ahavah
The God Who Loves
Blessings

THE GOOD WILL SUFFER

April 5

"When the enemy comes in like a flood, The Spirit of the LORD will lift up a standard against him."

Isaiah 59:19

Have you ever felt like a demonic attack is going on all around you? For different people, it is different things. Some people go through hard financial struggles, others sickness or mental torment, and on and on it goes. So many bad things happen that you know there is a force behind it.

Notice that the word LORD is in all caps here, transliterated. It indicates they wrote the actual name in Hebrew here. They use the name RAUCH YAHUAH, which means Holy Spirit. When you're in a spiritual trial that is being deployed in the physical, imagine the Holy Spirit rushing around you and above you, raising a standard—a signal flag that lets all the heavenly forces see that this is the point of battle where the forces need to gather.

As children, we used to watch those old cowboy westerns. The battles would be going on, and then we would hear a bugle blowing off in the distance, and we would get all excited! The Cavalry was coming, and the bad guys would always take off.

He is: Jehovah Gibbor Milchamah
Mighty in Battle
Blessings

TAMAR

April 6

"Judah begat Pharez and Zara of Tamar: Pharez begat Hezron: Hezron begat Ram."

Matthew 1:3

This scripture is about the lineage of Jesus Christ. I was really fascinated with Tamar and how it came to be that she was named in the line of Christ. Abraham received the promise of the Messiah that it would come down through his family line. Abraham, Isaac, Jacob, Judah. Judah had a firstborn son named Er. Judah took Tamar as a wife for Er. Apparently, Er was a pretty bad guy, and God slew him, leaving Tamar a widow. By custom, she married the other brother, and he had the same fate. God slew him also (Genesis 38:7–10).

Tamar has now been widowed twice. By custom, the third son, Shelah, was to be given to her for a husband by the father, Judah, in order to raise up seed for both the other sons who had died. Judah told Tamar to wait for his youngest son to come of age and marry him. Years went by; the third son, Shelah, was a grown man, and Judah had not kept his word. Tamar decided to take matters into her own hands.

She took off her widow's garments and dressed as a harlot, deceived Judah, and slept with him. Judah did not know it was Tamar. She took his ring, his bracelets, and his staff as a pledge for future payment. Three months later, Tamar was with child. Judah heard of this and commanded her to be brought forth and burned for being a harlot. Tamar presented the pledged items and asked Judah, "To whom do these belong?" Judah immediately realized what had happened.

"And Judah acknowledged them, and said, She hath been more righteous than I; because that I gave her not to Shelah my son. And he knew her again no more" (Genesis 38:26).

Pastors have really preached some ugly things about Tamar over the years. How could

she have devised such a wicked scheme? But God saw it differently. Tamar married Er, Judah's son. The Messiah was to come out of the tribe of Judah. While Tamar was married to Er, he told her of this promise. Er didn't really believe the promise just by the way he lived.

Judah appeared to have taken the promise lightly as well by sleeping with a harlot. Out of this whole story, there is one magnificent lady who believed the Word of God to be true. She waited for the promise. She embraced God even though her culture and family had other gods. She waited for years. She endured. Even Judah said, *"She hath been more righteous than I."*

Tamar is in the line of Judah and is mentioned in the lineage of Jesus Christ. One of only four ladies mentioned in the lineage: Tamar, Rahab, Ruth, and Mary—all of whom had a special kind of faith and love for God. Tamar had faith. She simply believed God's promise. In the end, all that matters is what God thinks about you.

He is: El Roi
The God Who Sees Me
Blessings

RAHAB

April 7

*"And Salmon begat Boaz of Rachab, and Boaz
begat Obed of Ruth, and Obed begat Jesse."*

Matthew 1:5

Rahab is an interesting lady named in the lineage of Jesus Christ. Let's take a look at this "Lady of Faith." Joshua 2:1 says, "And Joshua the son of Nun sent two men secretly from Shittim as spies, saying, 'Go view the land especially Jericho.' And they went and came into the house of a prostitute whose name was Rahab and lodged there."

It's obvious that God is being true to His character by guiding the steps of these young men to a place of safety. How did they end up there? They more than likely asked someone where they could lodge for the night. Rahab had rooms to rent, and she lived inside the walls of Jericho, and she also happened to be a prostitute. The two spies needed a room, and this sounded like a good cover story, a place to hide. Immediately, whoever they asked told the king, and the king sent his men to deal with them. The king's men arrive at Rahab's house, and she tells them that the men came to her. She did not know who they were but left before the city gate closed, saying, "Pursue them quickly, for you will overtake them" (Joshua 2:6). But she had brought them up to the roof and hid them with the stalks of flax that she had laid in order on the roof. Spinning of flax. It shows us that Rahab was making clothes for her family and possibly selling them to others. She was an entrepreneur. By laying them in order, she kept her house clean, and by hiding them under stalks of flax, we can tell a little bit about Rahab's identity. Flax stalks were used to make clothing, and women did the spinning of the flax. Rahab sounded like a Proverbs 31 woman. After the troops left, she went to the roof and had a conversation with the men. Basically, she said that all the people of the lands had heard how the Lord had parted the Red Sea for the Hebrews to cross, and everyone's heart melted with fear. Then, she made her confession of faith before the two men, her Romans 10:10.

Joshua 2:11 says, "For the Lord your God, He is the God of heavens above and the earth beneath."

She provides the men a way of escape by letting them down using a cord through a window. She ties the scarlet cord in the window as a sign of redemption (scarlet represents the blood of the Lamb), a thin red line of salvation, not knowing that she would be grafted into the very bloodline of the Messiah. She had been redeemed; her life circumstances didn't represent the change at that very moment. She was still living in the same brothel. When Rahab and her family came out of their stone prison, they were slaves to sin no more.

Even so faith, if it hath not works, is dead, being alone. And in like manner was not also Rahab the harlot justified by works, in that she received the messengers, and sent them out another way?

James 2:17–25

Rahab displayed her faith in God through her works of faith. Your faith can work, too.

He is: Jehovah-Palat
Deliverer
Blessings

RUTH

April 8

"The book of the generation of Jesus Christ, son of David, son of Abraham.
Abraham begat Isaac; Isaac begat Jacob.
Salmon begat Boaz of Rachab; Boaz begat Obed of Ruth."

Matthew 1:1–2,5

Ruth was the third "Lady of Faith" mentioned in the bloodline of Jesus. Let's take a look and see how she managed to get in line. Ruth was not Hebrew; she was a Moabite. Those of Moab were descendants of Lot, Abraham's nephew. Jewish tradition states that she was the daughter of Eglon, the King of Moab. First, we have to start with how this came into being.

> *Now it came to pass, in the days when the judges ruled, that there was a famine in the land. And a certain man of Bethlehem Judah, went to dwell in the country of Moab, he and his wife and his two sons.*

Ruth 1:1–2

The name of the man was Elimelech, his wife was Naomi, and his two sons were Mahlon and Chilion. Mahlon married Ruth; Chilion married Orpah. Elimelech, Mahlon, and Chilion all died in Moab. No account is given as to why or how, but possibly because they were sickly from childhood. Mahlon meant sickness, and Chilion meant failing.

So, Naomi, Orpah, and Ruth were widows. Tradition would have Ruth and Orpah marry the next of kin, but Naomi had no more children. Naomi, at that point, had lost all confidence in God, and she really believed that she was cursed, and for good reason.

Naomi, Orpah, and Ruth have a very emotional and dire situation. Out of love, Naomi asks Orpah and Ruth to leave and go back to their own families so that they can live. But Ruth cleaves to Naomi and decides she will go with Naomi and suffer whatever fate Naomi encounters. Remember, tradition states that Ruth was the daughter of a king, but instead of going home, out of deep love, she made this confession of faith:

"Wherever you go I will go, and wherever you lodge I will lodge, Your people shall be my people, And your God my God" (Ruth 1:16).

Ruth had already accepted the God of the Hebrews as her God. She had a lifestyle worth going back to, but she chose to go with God. At that point, she has only heard about His reputation: how He parted the Red Sea and fed the Hebrews in the desert for forty years, conquered Jericho, and how Salmon married Rahab.

But she was ready and was going to encounter God on a personal level, going from a God of Possibility to a God of Provision. The amazing thing about this whole story is how God just seemed to be silent. They had lost everything and then walked through the dry land back to the beginning, the place where Naomi started, and for Ruth, a place she had only been told about: Bethlehem—Judah.

When they arrived, it was obvious that Naomi was too old to work, so Ruth decided to be a provider for her mother-in-law. Ruth goes looking for work as a gleaner. By God's law, when the harvesters worked the fields, if they dropped the grain, it was to be left for the poor to pick up. They did not go back and harvest the second crop; this was left for the poor to gather. They also left the corners of the fields unharvested for the same reason.

Ruth (by chance?) ended up in Boaz's field, and she worked so hard that when Boaz arrived, he noticed her working. He asked his employees who this young lady was. The men bragged about her to Boaz. By that time, the men all knew who Ruth was. Boaz was deeply impressed with this hard-working lady, willing to take care of her family at all costs. She sounded just like his mother, Rahab. She was exceptionally beautiful and hard-working.

Back to Elimelech. If you look at Matthew 1:5, Elimelech was also a son of Salmon, and Naomi was his niece. This would have made Boaz their near kinsmen. Boaz was rich, but what strikes me most about this man is his character and integrity. He spoke with Ruth and asked her to work with his men for her own safety, told her to drink from his water, and gave her to eat from his table. Then, Boaz told his men to leave grain behind on purpose for Ruth to gather and to leave her alone and not to touch her. Ruth went home that day with a whole sack of grain and dinner left over for her mother-in-law. Naomi got her first glimmer of hope. You can imagine the joy coming back to her face when she exclaimed, "*Blessed be he of the LORD, who has not forsaken His Kindness, to the living and the dead!*"

Naomi realized that Boaz was near kinsmen. Just like the two spies that landed at Rahab's door in Jericho and she hid them under stalks of flax, Ruth ended up in the only field that could save her. God's mercy followed this family. Silently, God had positioned them in the same field of harvest. But unknown to them, God had placed them in the family line of the *great harvest*.

Naomi instructed Ruth on the customs of the land, and Ruth followed the instructions on how to approach Boaz. He, in his integrity, falls in love with Ruth's integrity. He realized that she followed God by her actions. He stated that she did not go after young men, rich or poor. But he saw that she was fulfilling the law of God by seeking him to be her husband. Boaz might have been excited at finally finding his Proverbs 31 wife! The book of Proverbs hadn't been written yet, but Ruth was a lot like Boaz's mother, Rahab. Double win.

Boaz goes to the elders as the redeemer-kinsmen and redeems Ruth, all of Elimelech's former properties, and promises to raise an inheritance to Mahlon. Now, in covenant, together because they honored and trusted God above all else, God honored them. They married, and Ruth gave birth to Obed. Naomi was the best grandmother; she loved and cared for Obed so much that the people of the town jokingly said, "There is a son born to Naomi."

What set Ruth apart was her character. We do not know when in her heart she decided that God was her God. But I believe it was long before she left Moab. Maybe one day, as a single young lady in a foreign land walking in a field, she said a prayer asking God, "Who are you?" and then, Mahlon showed up. Selah.

He is: Jehovah Jireh
God My Provider
Blessings

ACCEPTABLE WORDS

April 9

"The preacher sought to find acceptable words:
and what was written was upright words of Truth."

Ecclesiastes 12:10

These words were written by King Solomon. I've read them many times over the years, and for some reason, I always think about preaching in front of King Solomon. No pressure there; he was only the wisest man in all of the earth's history. He said the preacher searched for his words carefully. But in truth, Solomon was talking about himself. Solomon was the preacher in this story.

Solomon wanted his words to be acceptable and upright before the Lord. Solomon was letting us know the importance of choosing our words carefully and speaking wisely. In this book, he tried to paint a picture of the truth in your mind.

"The words of the wise are like goads, and the words of scholars are like well driven nails, given by one shepherd" (Ecclesiastes 12:11).

Goads were sharp sticks used to drive cattle. In spoken terms, they are meant to provoke someone to thought. Well-driven nails mean they stick with your thoughts. The shepherd represents your pastor.

Have you ever been in church, and your pastor preached something that angered you? More than likely, what he or she has just done is uncovered an area of your life that needs adjustment.

I remember when I was a young Christian during the church service, turning to my wife and saying, "Have you been talking to Him about me?" Now, years later, I realize it was the Holy Spirit revealing to me some areas I needed to change.

"And further, my son, be admonished by these. Of making of many books there is no end, and much study is wearisome to the flesh" (Ecclesiastes 12:12).

When you feel like you have had your toes stepped on by the pastor, take a moment and reflect: *admonish* means to warn, reprimand, or reprove; it's like a yellow caution sign that lets you know to slow down before you reach the curve and wreck.

> *Let us hear the conclusion of the whole matter: Fear God and keep*
> *His commandments. For this is man's all.*
> *For God will bring every work into judgment, including every secret thing.*
> *Whether Good or evil.*

Ecclesiastes 12:13–14

Ask Jesus to reveal to you the matter in more detail. How do I correct this? So that He can bring the matter to a conclusion. Keeping God's commandments is *all*; this means "whole," as in your whole life.

He is: Elohay Selichot
The God Who is Ready to Forgive
Blessings

THE POWER OF NUMBERS

April 10

"Though one may be overpowered by another, two can withstand him. And a threefold cord is not quickly broken."

Ecclesiastes 4:12

When the Romans invaded Britain, the British noted the formation of the Roman legions and reportedly said, "When they fight in detached parties, they sacrifice the general cause." They understood the necessity to break the lines of formation and get the individuals scattered. They recognized the power of teamwork and knew the value of two people working together instead of one person working alone. With two people working together, the work output more than doubles.

I have a friend who is an electrician. He has an apprentice who works for him. Many times, he will be several rungs up on a ladder and ask his apprentice to grab a tool. The man is quick to bring it; the apprentice is a support to him. Imagine how much time and energy it would consume if my friend had to climb down the ladder and get the tool, then back up and restart where he left off. That is why their work productivity increases from two to four.

If the apprentice can see the need before it arises, he can have the tool ready. Many times in your job, someone has said, "You need to do this." It is because they can see a need that you are not aware of.

Some theologians say this Scripture doesn't apply to marriage, but it certainly does. While lying in bed one night, the Holy Spirit woke me up to pray for someone. I was very tired. I prayed and then woke my wife and asked her to join me in prayer because:

"Where two or three are gathered together in my name, there I am in the midst of them" (Matthew 18:20).

We created a threefold cord that couldn't easily be broken. We experienced power through prayer and the promise that Jesus would be there. Take time to pray with your spouse, even if it is just for a moment, knowing that Jesus will be standing there next to you. What a great way to start the day!

He is: Jehovah Shammah
The Lord Is There
Blessings

FAITH BRINGS FEAR

April 11

"Do not rejoice over me, my enemy: When I fall, I will arise: When I sit in darkness, The Lord will be a light to me."

Micah 7:8

This is such a beautiful Scripture, and I think if you are going through struggles in life, it really brings the meaning out. I used to go hunting in the bayous of southern Louisiana. At the end of the day at the camp, we would make something to eat. It didn't matter what we made. It always tasted better than the best restaurant.

The fictional character Don Quixote said, "Hunger is the best sauce in the world." That's what this verse sounds like when you're going through one of life's trials. Hunger is the best flavor enhancer. I've noticed over the years that hunger brings out different characteristics in people. Some people get nice—it even seems as though they soften. Others get angry or agitated. Some get faint, and when you fast, it can make you feel better.

Our pets get very loving when they are hungry. I once had a friend who had a pet Boa constrictor. When it was hungry, it became people-friendly.

When you are going through a trial, this verse sounds so much better, has so much more meaning, and so much more authority. Say it out loud with faith, and you will feel the circumstances lift. The enemy tries to bring fear into your life. That's why Jesus said:

"Therefore do not be anxious about tomorrow, for tomorrow will be anxious for itself. Sufficient for the day is its own trouble" (Matthew 6:34).

When you start worrying about tomorrow, it brings fear into your thoughts. Fear is the opposite of faith. But when you read this Scripture out loud, it builds your faith. Turn it around in your mind and spirit today. *Faith brings fear to the enemy.*

He is: El-Moshaah
The God Who Saves
Blessings

FAITHFUL IN THE LEAST

April 12

"He that is faithful in that which is least is faithful also in much: and he that is unjust in the least is unjust also in much."

Luke 16:10

Many people always equate this scripture to ministry, and it certainly does apply to ministry, but its application should be considered in many other areas of life.

I remember a true story about the vice president of a very prestigious corporation. He was about to receive a promotion to president. He and the president went out to lunch at the company cafeteria to discuss business. While in line, the president noticed that the vice president hid a 3-cent piece of butter underneath a slice of bread. When they reached the cashier to check out, the man did not reveal the butter to her.

The next day, when all the board members were present and ready to vote for the new president, the existing president told them the story of what he had witnessed in the checkout line. He told the board members that he did not want this man to succeed him and stated, "If he can't be trusted in the small things, he can't be trusted with the big things!" The board listened to him and went on to vote for another person for the position.

Do not despise small beginnings; you never know where they may take you. I used to tell my salespeople all the time. A small sale to a little house could be the grandmother to an owner of a huge business.

Sin has the same impact—play around with a little sin, and it will lead to something a little bigger until you're caught up in something that took you farther than you thought possible and left you wondering how you ever got there.

If the Lord asks you to do something that seems trivial, jump on it with all your gusto because He wants to see you faithful in much! God is for your success!

He is: El-HaNe'eman
The God Who Is Faithful
Blessings

THE SECRET TO HAVING A GREAT DAY!

April 13

"Cause me to hear thy loving kindness in the morning; for in thee do I trust: cause me to know the way wherein I should walk; for I lift up my soul unto thee."

Psalm 143:8

What a great way to start your day! Ask God to set the conditions for you to hear His loving kindness in the morning.

It's a very interesting choice of words to say *cause*. Cause means to produce an effect or set a condition. Imagine waking up in the morning and asking God to set your conditions so that He can show His loving kindness to you. Sounds really selfish, doesn't it?

But God can do it. He's never too busy to help you understand who He is. But you can help Him with setting the conditions by reading your Bible first thing in the morning, even if it is just a chapter or two. This gives the Holy Spirit something to draw on for you throughout the day.

One time, we were babysitting a small child, and we took her to the park to play. There were several children, and I was enjoying watching them all play. When one child fell and started to cry, my wife said, "Watch this." As the parent attended the crying child, all the other children in the playground gathered around in a circle, observing the other child, making sure the child was going to be okay. Looks of concern filled all those little faces; it was so precious. When the child stopped crying, all the children went back to playing.

You see, little children do that when another child gets hurt. To me, it was innocent compassion. Somehow, I saw how God intended for man to be, and by this little demonstration, I saw His loving kindness.

His loving kindness will produce and affect the way in which you walk. During the course of the day, you may have to decide about doing the right thing. Maybe someone gives you too much money back at the checkout line. You return the extra money because you know that honesty is the way you should walk.

King David wrote this Psalm. David was above most everyone else when it came to lifting up his soul to God. How did David lift up his soul to God? By praise and worship of the Most High and remembering all the times God had saved him before. When you start singing to God, you will lift up your soul.

Have a blessed day, a day filled with His loving kindness!

He is: Jehovah- Ra'ah
The Lord Is My Shepherd
Blessings

THE GOD WHO SEES ME

April 14

And Jesus stood still, and commanded him to be called. And they call the blind man (Bartimaeus), saying unto him be of good comfort, rise; He calleth thee.
And he, casting away his garment, rose, and came to Jesus.
And Jesus said unto him, "What wilt thou that I should do unto thee?" The blind man said unto Him, Lord, that I might receive my sight.
And Jesus said unto him, Go thy way; thy faith hath made thee whole. And immediately he received his sight, and followed Jesus in the way.

St. Mark 10:49–52

Have you ever wanted something so badly that you were willing to give up everything to get it? Bartimaeus did. This man acted in faith that Jesus would change his life. The Hebrews waited until a ceremony called *Bris* before they named their children. Bris is the seventh day after birth when the child is circumcised. When the young child was circumcised on the eighth day, the name was given. Bartimaeus: *Bar-* means son of, *Timaeus* means foul, in a religious sense, defiled, polluted, unclean, infamous.

Bartimaeus was the son of Timaeus, and apparently, this disease ran through the family. Oral tradition said that he was born in sin because a curse was upon him; he was cursed. People told Bartimaeus to shut up, but he cried louder still. Jesus took notice, stopped, and commanded him to be brought forth.

And here is the second act of faith: *And he, casting away his garment, rose, and came to Jesus.* Bartimaeus cast his garment. Why would he throw his coat down? This garment represented his identity. It was known as a beggar's garment. He had previously gone to the priests, and it was certified that he was blind and unable to make a living. Priests gave him that garment to beg as a way of life and survival.

By faith, Bartimaeus was leaving his past behind, his old identity. He was no longer going to be the blind beggar—no longer foul, defiled, polluted, unclean, infamous. But wait, he was still blind when he threw off his garment. He showed that he was willing to go one step further and trust Jesus Christ to heal him.

There are times when you must take the first step toward God, and then He will answer your prayer. I can see Jesus smiling at Bartimaeus and saying, "Go thy way; thy faith hath made thee whole." Imagine Bartimaeus's first sight in the world was to look straight into the eyes of his creator, Jesus.

"And immediately he received his sight and followed Jesus in the way."

He followed Jesus in the way. This does not mean the road they were walking on. It refers to the *way of Christ*. Before they coined us as *Christians*, it was called *the Way*.

The word *whole* is a remarkably interesting choice of words by Jesus. Whole means to heal, deliver, protect, or do well. Bartimaeus received a new name that day, a new identity. Jesus changed Simon's name to Peter, which means *Rock*. Bartimaeus had a new name, too. He was whole, a Son of God, doing well, and famous for his faith. Only Jesus can change your life like this.

He is: El Roi
The God Who Sees Me
Blessings

FAITH TO FORGIVE

April 15

Take heed to yourselves, if thy brother trespass against thee seven times in a day,
and seven times in a day turn again to thee, saying, I repent, thou shalt forgive him.
And the apostles said unto the Lord, Increase our faith.
And the Lord said, If ye had faith as a grain of mustard seed, ye might say unto this
sycamine tree, be thou plucked up by the root, and be thou
planted in the sea, and it should obey you.

Luke 17:4–6

Jesus had much power when He spoke. He often used metaphors (objects) so that we could relate to the power of His words. Jesus was talking about forgiveness and let us know that it is not optional.

The apostles understood what Jesus said and replied by saying, *"Increase our faith."* By no mere chance was this conversation happening there with the sycamine tree as a backdrop, or maybe they were even sitting under the shade of the sycamine tree.

The sycamine represented unforgiveness, but why would He use the sycamine tree? Many scholars think that it is just a mulberry tree or a sycamore tree. But there is a sycamine tree that bears fruit like a fig tree. The fruit is not as sweet as the fig, and I've read that it is a little bitter, too. The sycamine was also used to make burial caskets. It has a huge trunk with a root system that is twice as deep as the tree, and it is a beautiful tree on the outside.

Growing up on a small farm in Northern California, I remember having to help my dad and brother dig up a stump that had to come out. The roots were tapping into our septic tank. It took days to get that stump out of the ground. The hole around the stump just kept getting bigger and bigger. We would have to take an axe to chop the roots. Then, we attacked the tap root (the main root going down into the ground), and that was the hardest root to cut. We hooked a big chain to a tractor and pulled and pulled. The front wheels on the tractor would come up in the air, and the stump wouldn't move. However, eventually it came out.

Unforgiveness can take root in your heart the same way. When people make mention of unforgiveness, remember the root is twice as deep as the outer appearance. That root is going down, tapping into your heart, drawing life, and depositing death.

There was a lady I talked with who wanted so much to speak in tongues. For years, she had prayed and prayed, but for some reason, it never happened. I prayed with her, and nothing happened. I asked the Lord to make me aware of the problem. The Holy Spirit impressed upon me that it was unforgiveness. I told her this, and she just nodded her head and said, "Yes, that is the problem." It was rooted deep. She used to be a millionaire, and as a widow, people had taken all her money and thrown her out on the streets, and she was homeless. It took her months to forgive after that conversation, but one day, she told me that she had started to pray in tongues. When she reached the place of forgiveness, the Lord could bless her.

But Jesus said all you need is faith the size of a mustard seed. He's not asking you for much to work with. He will throw that unforgiveness into the sea of forgetfulness.

He is: El-Nahsah
Forgiving God
Blessings

THE POWER OF AND

April 16

*And it came to pass, that as He was come nigh unto
Jericho, a certain blind man sat by the way begging:
And hearing the multitude pass by, he asked what it meant.
And they told him, that Jesus of Nazareth passeth by
And he cried, saying, Jesus, thou son of David, have mercy on me.
And they which went before rebuked him, that he should hold his peace: but he
cried so much the more, thou son of David have mercy on me.
And Jesus stood, and commanded him to brought unto Him: and
when he was come near He asked him,
Saying what wilt thou that I shall do unto thee? And he said, Lord,
that I may receive my sight,
And Jesus said unto him, receive thy sight: thy faith hath saved thee.
And immediately he received his sight, and followed him, glorifying God: and all
the people, when they saw it, gave praise to God.*

Luke 18:35–43

The first thing I notice when reading this piece of history is how many times Luke used the word *and*. Thirteen times in all!

The word *and* means to join together in sequence or joining elements. It almost seems like the word *and* can be a hurdle of its own in this story.

How many *and*s did this blind man have to overcome to actually get his miracle? The first *and* relates to time. When you're going through a trial, time is always the first hurdle to overcome. We want this burden to end today. However, Jesus knows what He is doing. The next step to overcoming is hearing. He heard the multitudes passing by, and what were the multitudes following? They were following the Word of God.

"And the Word was made flesh and dwelt among us" (John 1:14). When the blind man found the Word, he knew that was the answer to his prayer. He, not being able to see, recognized the answer to his needs, and the answer always points back to Jesus!

Next, he had to overcome the opinions of man. I don't know why people always try to stop others from coming to the Lord, but they do. Through his own desire to have his life changed forever, he caused Jesus to stand still and take notice. When you cry out in prayer to the Lord, He will take notice. The next three *and*s:

"And Jesus stood, and commanded him to brought unto Him: and when he was come near He asked him, saying what wilt thou that I shall do unto thee?"

It is as though Jesus stood as the Father, the Son, and the Holy Spirit. Come before the throne, petition the Son. His faith saved him, his eyes were opened, his life changed, and he received.

Now the final *and* is ready—he gave praise and thanks to Jesus! He followed Him, always giving thanks.

He is: Logos
The Word
Blessings

BA'AL-PERAZIM—THE LORD BREAKING FORTH

April 17

*The Philistines also came and spread themselves in the valley of Rephaim.
And David enquired of the LORD, saying, Shall I go up to the Philistines?
Wilt thou deliver them into mine hand?
And the LORD said unto David, "Go up: for I will doubtless
deliver the Philistines into thine hand."
And David came to Baalperazim, and David smote them there, and said, The
LORD hath broken forth upon mine enemies before me, as the breach of waters.
Therefore, he called the name of that place Baalperazim.*

2 Samuel 5:18–20

So here are the representations of these places and names: *Valley of Rephaim* means Valley of the Giants. *LORD:* LORD is in all caps; the actual name used here is YAHUAH, which means, "I AM HE WHO BREATHES LIFE!"

"Go up: for I will doubtless deliver the Philistines into thine hand." Keywords: *Into thine hand.*

David had to do his part. I have seen this several times over the years: A Christian receives a word and then just sits back, waiting for God to do it. Guess what? It just doesn't happen. The word falls to the ground. Sometimes, you must get your hand into it.

Ba-al Perazim: The Lord Breaking Forth.

David entered Baalperazim and then named it Baalperazim after the victory. How can this be? Because in order to gain victory, you must first see the victory. David didn't go into battle wishing he could gain a victory; he came in knowing he had a victory. Don't let your circumstances name themselves! We all face giants at one point or another in our lives, such as circumstances that are beyond our control or obstacles that are just too big to overcome.

I once asked the Lord what the Leviathan was in the book of Job, and He answered me. He said something like this: "Any obstacle in life that is too big for you to conquer without My help."

After David won, he named the place *Baalperazim*, "The Lord/Breaking Forth." David knew, without a shadow of a doubt, that God was on his side, and he was going forth for the win. He had weakened his enemies before him, and then David knew his authority.

He is: Jehovah Gibbor Milchamah
Mighty in Battle
Blessings

CORRECT YOUR PATH

April 18

*"O Lord, I know that the Way of man is not in himself:
it is not in man that walketh to direct his steps."*

Jeremiah 10:23

When reading this scripture, it is easy to make a simple thought: God directs my steps. But here are a couple of words that slip by *the Way*. Initially, in the New Testament, people who followed our Lord Jesus were referred to as the people of *the Way*, as we can read in Paul's defense before Felix: "But this I confess to you, that according to the Way which they call a sect, so I worship the God of my fathers, believing all things which are written in the law and in the prophets" (Acts 24:14).

The Way comes from the Greek word, *hod-os'*, which means a road or the route. It amazes me how often, when a bad situation comes about, that my first thought is usually not so good. Easy for your mind to go to the gutter, or your reaction can have you jump into a ditch. Our flesh gets in the Way of *the Way*. Romans 12:2 explains how to overcome this problem:

"And be not conformed to this world: but be ye transformed by the renewing of your mind, that ye may prove what is good, and acceptable, and perfect, will of God."

Simply put, read your Bible and read it often. Proverbs has thirty-one chapters, one for every day of the month. Many times, one of the scriptures will pop into my head when a situation comes about. For example:

"A soft answer turns away wrath," and "Correction is grievous unto him that forsaketh the Way" (Proverbs 15:1 and 15:10).

Don't get on the wrong side of the Lord and need His correction—iron things out in your own heart and mind first.

"A man's heart devises his ways, but the Lord directs his steps" (Proverbs 16:9).

He is: Jehovah-Rapha
The Lord Is my Shepherd
Blessings

RECIPE FOR A GOOD LIFE

April 19

*But this thing commanded I them, saying, Obey My voice, and I will be your
God, and ye shall be my people: and walk ye in all the ways that
I have commanded you, that it may be well unto you.*

Jeremiah 7:23

If Betty Crocker had a recipe for living a good life, this would be it—Bible promises from God extended to everyone. I can see someone going through hardship reading this verse and the scripture lifting his or her head with hope. Hope is to desire with the expectation of obtainment or fulfillment.

Once, many years ago, while I was praying, I was thinking about how fleeting life is. It is short, and I felt like, by the time I learned all this, there wouldn't be time to accomplish what needs to get done. Then, the Holy Spirit spoke to me and said: "I can do a lot in a lifetime, Scott."

It doesn't matter where your starting point is with God; He can do a lot with your life. Why not let Him start today?

He is: Shub Nephesh
Renewer of Life
Blessings

TAKE A LEAP OF FAITH

April 20

"Now faith is being sure of what we hope for and certain of what we do not see."

Hebrews 11:1

By faith, we believed in Jesus. Jesus was the one who gave us faith. "Looking unto Jesus the author and finisher of our faith."

Hebrews 12:2

Many of us start on fire for the Lord, wanting to do everything so that we can give back to the one who gave so much for us. But the world has a way of keeping you down.

I recently watched a video of two lions—male and female. They were at a safari park, but instead of a fence, a twelve to fifteen-foot-deep trench surrounded the lions. The lions were lying on the grass, watching the tourists pass by. As the tourists traveled by, the instincts of the female lioness kicked in, and she wanted to hunt. She crouched and looked at the tourists as they rolled slowly by, then she poorly leaped off the grass and didn't even come close to clearing the mote. She landed down inside the pit; at first, the tourists gasped as the lion began its leap, then began to laugh at her fall. I'm confident the lion hit bottom hard. Then, you could hear the people laugh and talk about the lion's leap. They thought it was crazy for the lion to make a failed attempt.

I noticed the huge male lion lying down on the green grass, calmly watching everything and not caring that the other lion had fallen into a pit. As I listened, I observed that no one talked about the male lion. He was a strong male encircled by an empty trench, all the power any animal could have and the ability to clear the empty mote, but no desire to try.

Then, I thought that they wouldn't have laughed if that female had made it across the trench. Their laughter would have been shouts of fear, angry words, and pounding the side of the vehicle to scare her off. That probably would have scared her off, too, but maybe not; after all, they would have been her prize. For some reason, I think if she tries hard enough and learns what mistakes she made on her previous attempts, she will clear the moat one day.

Faith: The lioness doesn't even know what that is, but she has it. Don't let your failed attempts make you sit in the church pew. That's the way the enemy would have it. Jesus is the Finisher of your faith, and that's the way He would have it. People will always put you down and even mock you, mainly because they fear anyone who tries to jump the trench and succeed for the Lord.

He is: Alpha and Omega
The First and the Last
Blessings

SEASONS

April 21

"To everything, there is a season and a time to every purpose under the heaven: A time to be born, and a time to die; a time to plant, and a time to pluck up that which is planted."

Ecclesiastes 3:1–2

Seasons: times we go through—some are short, some are long. In the natural, some are cold, and some are hot. Knowing what season you are going through would be a big help sometimes.

One of the most challenging seasons in life is after you part from a close friend or a loved one goes on to be with the Lord. Over the years, the Lord has placed people into my life just at the right moment. Friends who knew how to say the right thing at the right time to make everything much better.

Maybe it was your mother or your father, brother or sister, or someone else with that gift. They didn't always say things that were too sensitive, but after a while, you looked back and thought, 'How'd they know?' The Holy Spirit positioned them there, a battle plan that didn't stop after you became saved. He still places people around you to grow you.

When people move on with their lives one way or another, we need to learn to say, "Thank You, Lord, for my time spent with them." The gift of time is one that only God can grant.

Sometimes, you're the one positioned to do the planting in someone else's life. You may think you need a huge tractor with a large disc to get your seed planted, but often, it's a simple act of love that matters most: one little, tiny seed and your season is served.

He is: Georgos
The Gardener
Blessings

THE LORD MY FATHER

April 22

"The Lord is like a Father to His children, tender and compassionate to those who fear Him."

Psalm 103:13

Many times over the past few years, the Lord has graciously applied this scripture to me. There have been times while praying for someone that I have missed it, prophetically, that is. Sometimes, when I make a mistake, I see a vision of a child twelve or thirteen months old, a toddler. The child has fallen, and with his upstretched arms, he shuffles back to his Father; that is all there is to it, and I know what it means. The Father never scolds the child for falling; instead, He comforts him and then encourages him to walk again and praises him for his next little accomplishment, no matter how small.

He doesn't remind the child of his past failures but instead looks forward to the days when the child can run independently. In the back of our minds, we miss the toddler days because they were so sweet and precious, but we're proud of what and who they have become as adults.

If the Lord leads you to pray for someone and you should stumble in prayer, don't think that God is mad at you, and don't give up for good. Know that God the Father can make it right, ask Him to correct your steps, and then pray some more.

He is: Abba
Father
Blessings

FINDING HIS PLACE

April 23

*"He who dwells in the shelter of the Most High
will rest in the shadow of the Almighty."*

Psalm 91:1

This Psalm plants a vivid image in our imaginations, but what kind of image should we imagine? Some people would think of a home, others the shade of a tree. But let's look at this from God's perspective.

The word *dwells* could imply a few things, oddly enough it can mean 'to judge', which implies that we consider our actions and thoughts through God's standard, or to sit or even marry into God's ways.

Shelter. Where would God have shelter? Somewhere above, as we see, He is positioned here by calling Himself *The Most High.* This shelter is set above us—above our thoughts and limitations of the flesh. We see this in:

"And hath raised us up together and made us sit together in heavenly places in Christ Jesus" (Ephesians 2:6).

Rest in the shadow of the Almighty. That shade tree you're resting under happens to be God. Have you ever been talking with someone, and their back is to the sun? Politely, they raise their hand to block the sun out of your eyes so that you can see.

When you're in God's presence, He will open your eyes so you can see clearly. A stressful situation suddenly doesn't look quite so bad. It can be a tough place to reach when you're so stressed out that you can hardly pray, but learn to pray under stress and sing a song of praise.

He is: Jehovah-Machsi
The Lord My Refuge
Blessings

EASTER

April 24

"And if a man smites his slave or his maid with a rod and he dies under his hand, he shall be surely punished. Not with-standing, if he continues a day or two, he shall not be punished, for he is his money."

Exodus 21:20–21

A couple of years ago, a Muslim man posted this verse on Facebook. In the comments, he asked how I could possibly serve a God like this, a God who permits people to be treated in this way.

I thought about the question he asked, and to be honest, it is a very fair question. After I gave this some thought, I realized that this doesn't condone slavery or slave brutality, but instead, it points us to today, to the resurrection of Jesus Christ. The very understanding is that the same people who crucified Jesus Christ could receive forgiveness after His resurrection on the third day!

Jesus was betrayed for the price of a slave when Judas took thirty pieces of silver. Remember, Judas was the treasurer for Jesus's ministry. Because of this, Jesus qualified this verse, but it goes beyond that. If we look to the Old Testament, we begin to see the picture that God bought Jesus centuries before, around 538 BC, in the book of Zechariah:

I told them, "If it's alright with you, pay me what I've earned. But if it isn't, don't." So, they paid out what I had earned—30 shekels of silver.

Then the LORD told me, "Throw the money into the treasury—that magnificent value they placed on me!" So, I took the 30 shekels of silver and threw them into the treasury of the Temple of the LORD.

Zechariah 11:12–13

In Exodus, we see the price of a slave was thirty pieces of silver:

"If the ox shall push a manservant or a maidservant, he shall give unto their master thirty shekels of silver, and the ox shall be stoned" (Exodus 21:32).

Judas sold Jesus for a price, a price previously paid for by God over 500 years before when Zechariah cast the thirty pieces of silver into the treasury. God could have set the price at any amount he wanted, so why thirty pieces? Symbolically, the number thirty represents the right timing or the right moment to reign or minister.

Three by ten equals thirty, which carries the meaning of perfection or fullness.

Three is divine order.

Ten marks the right moment.

Three also represents the Godhead, completion. With this completion, we see that Jesus's betrayal was completed in:

"Then one of the Twelve, who was called Judas Iscariot, went to the high priests and inquired, 'What are you willing to give me if I betray Jesus to you?' They offered him thirty pieces of silver" (Matthew 26:14–15).

The first betrayal was committed by Adam, and the last betrayal was committed by Judas:

> *Then Judas, who had betrayed him, regretted what had happened when he saw that Jesus was condemned. He brought the thirty pieces of silver back to the high priests and elders,*
>
> *saying, "I have sinned by betraying innocent blood." But they replied, "What do we care? Attend to that yourself."*
>
> *Then he flung the pieces of silver into the sanctuary and went outside. Then he went away and hanged himself.*
>
> *The high priests picked up the pieces of silver and said, "It is not lawful to put this into the Temple treasury because it is blood money."*
>
> *So they decided to use the money to buy the Potter's Field as a burial ground for foreigners.*
>
> *That is why that field has been called the Field of Blood to this day.*
>
> *Then what had been declared through the prophet Jeremiah was fulfilled when he said, "They took the thirty pieces of silver, the value of the man on whom a price had been set by the Israelis,*
>
> *and they gave them for the potter's field, as the Lord commanded me."*
>
> **Matthew 27:3–10**

We serve a living God who sold Himself into slavery so that you could be made free.

He is: El Chai
The Living God
Blessings

HOPE

April 25

Brothers and sisters, I do not consider myself yet to have taken hold of it. But one thing I do: Forgetting what is behind and straining toward what is ahead, I press on toward the goal to win the prize for which God has called me heavenward in Christ Jesus.

Philippians 3:13–14

I met a lady who quoted this scripture to me, but in a natural way; it was sort of her philosophy on life. She said, "Don't think about the past and all the bad things that have happened to you over the years. They make you just want to give up. Instead, find something good to hang onto—something that you want to achieve—and that will cause you to go on."

I knew she was quoting this scripture, but she was doing it wisely by not confronting me with Scripture or beating me over the head with the Word. It's an excellent approach when witnessing to someone.

She was constantly smiling and seemed to care about me genuinely. She did not know who I was, and this was the first time we had ever met. I spoke with her about the Lord and life, and then the Lord gave me a prophetic word for her. She was so excited; it seemed as though the Lord was thanking her for speaking His word, but the word He gave her was about her future and how He would use her to counsel others because of her wisdom.

She was correct; we should put the hurts of the past behind us and look forward to the future set before us. Hope brings life, and hope means to expect an outcome.

He is: Rum Rosh
The One Who Lifts My Head
Blessings

BE YE THANKFUL

April 26

And let the peace of YAHUAH rule in your hearts, to the which also ye are called in one body; and be ye thankful. Let the word of HAMASHICH dwell in you richly in all wisdom; teaching and admonishing one another in psalms and hymns and spiritual songs, singing with grace in your hearts to YAHUAH.
Paul knew what he was saying when he wrote, "Be ye thankful."

Colossians 3:15–16

It's hard to focus on your problems when you start giving thanks for what you have. Problems bring you down, but thankfulness lifts you.

You know God is awesome. How can you ever pay Him back? He has provided everything you have, and in return, He asks for a simple payment: a thank you. When you're thankful, you will be well-favored. Thankfulness goes up, but it comes back down. I've never thought of it this way until now.

Thankfulness will cause the Word to rise in you and dwell richly. Now that's worth being thankful for!

He is: Adonai Yahusha Hamashiach
The Lord: I Am He, The Anointed Messiah
Blessings

PROFITING FROM TRIALS

April 27

My brethren, count it all joy when you fall into various trials, knowing that the testing of your faith produces patience. But let patience have its perfect work, that you may be perfect and complete, lacking nothing. If any of you lacks wisdom, let him ask of God, who gives to all liberally and without reproach, and it will be given to him.

James 1:2–8

James starts this letter out like a boxer throwing a punch, and he gets straight to the point. These Christians were going through intense persecution because of Roman rule.

"My brethren, count it all joy when you fall into various trials."

I'd be a liar if I told you that I didn't struggle with this very issue myself. How do you get happy when your world is falling apart? Well, emotions are your personal choice in life. You can choose to walk around mad all the time and angry at others. You can choose to be depressed because of your situation.

Years ago, I used to look at people who were always happy, always smiling, and it just seemed like God gave them the gift of happiness. Then I realized that happiness is the gift you give yourself. You're the only one who can decide for yourself to be happy or any other emotion you choose to follow.

Every trial is for one purpose—to test your faith. Do you think trials get easier as you get older in the Lord? Well, they don't. Things that would have made me crumble years ago don't even seem to matter that much anymore. You come to a place where you know God is just going to handle it. But then the devil changes strategies on you, and guess what? You get more opportunities for joy.

Now, James tells us that to have joy, we need to understand this: "Knowing that the testing of your faith produces patience."

Trials test your faith, and faith brings patience. Now, what's so good about patience? Patience is the quality of enduring, working through to the end. When a person loses their patience, what happens? They usually blow up in anger or shortcut a project at work and don't do the job correctly.

What happens when you do a job incorrectly? More than likely, you will have to go back and do it over again. My old pastor used to say that just like the Israelites, you get to take another lap around in the wilderness.

"But let patience have its perfect work, that you may be perfect and complete, lacking nothing."

How is the work made perfect? By your joy in the matter, you can only have joy if you believe God is on your side and you know that He can save you. But we lose our patience when we get mad at God for not pulling us through. But here's the kicker: If you get angry at God for not pulling you through, ironically, that means you have faith in God! But the enemy has perverted your faith into anger. I, for one, am guilty of this. So, if you are going to get mad at God, that's probably a good time to count it all joy and laugh at the enemy.

"If any of you lacks wisdom, let him ask of God, who gives to all liberally and without reproach, and it will be given to him."

I think this is another place where we tend to get off base with the Lord. This wisdom is for the trial that you are going through. You can ask God this question, "Father God, what do I need to do, or what am I doing that is causing this? Lord, I know You want to show me something and teach me something. Otherwise, You would not allow this in my life. What do You want to be for me during this season?" One time, I asked the Lord this, and I immediately saw a vision of Jesus holding me and caressing the back of my head, comforting me.

He never left me, nor will He leave you.

He is: Jehovah Tzidkenu
The Lord Our Righteousness
Blessings

TRUST HIM

April 28

"As for God, His way is perfect: the Word of the Lord is tried: He is a buckler to all those that trust in Him."

Psalm 18:30

When I first read this scripture years ago, I thought, *What good is a buckler? It's just a little shield that looks like a plate out of the kitchen cabinet.* Sometimes, you can spend years thinking about a Bible verse off and on and foolishly never think to ask Jesus what it means.

A couple of years ago, while I was sitting at Prayer Stop, I had a genuine vision. I happened to look over to my right, and in the chair next to me sat a man wearing only a leather loincloth. He had curly dark brown hair, a huge burly chest, and he was holding a buckler, and I think it was on his left arm. He was studying it, and admiring it.

This man was serious, and I could tell he had fought before. Then suddenly, he lifted his arm and crossed his chest and, in a side thrust, took that buckler and violently swung it towards my face! The edge would have come straight into my head, but before it hit me, the Lord pulled me out of the vision, and the man was gone.

I learned how seriously violent a buckler was; not only is it made for defense against a sword, but it can be a lethal offensive weapon, too.

As I read this just now, and for the very first time, I saw how Jesus was hidden multiple times in this verse.

"Jesus said: 'I Am the way the truth and the life. No one comes to the Father except through Me'" (John 14:6).

Jesus was perfect—the sacrificial lamb. Jesus was inspected for fault, and no fault was found.

"That ye may know that I find no fault in Him" (John 19:4).

Jesus was the Word:

"In the beginning, was the Word, and the Word was with God, and the Word was God" (John 1:1).

We can see that Jesus is a buckler to all those who trust Him, and Jesus is God.

"…Which He hath purchased with His own blood" (Acts 20:28).

Jesus won't just block the enemy from attacking you; He will violently defend you with the same shield He uses to guard you.

He is: El Nathan Neqamah
The God Who Avenges Me
Blessings

SUFFERING

April 29

And it came to pass, when Joseph was come unto his brethren, that they stripped Joseph of his coat, the coat of many colors that was on him; and they took him, and cast him into the pit: and the pit was empty, there was no water in it.

Genesis 37:23–24

Rejection doesn't get much more profound than Joeseph being thrown down into a pit by his own family and, a couple of hours later, sold into slavery. Rejection can have significant spiritual, emotional, and psychological impacts on a person. How it affects an individual can vary greatly depending on their beliefs, coping mechanisms, and support system.

You may suffer from rejection as we all have, and you may not know how to turn. It gets to the point where we beg God instead of thanking God. However, some possible good consequences come from rejection; you can ask any famous country singer, and songs about rejection have made many gold records. But in Joseph's case, his brothers were about to murder him, and then Reuben stepped in and saved his life by having him thrown into the pit, intending to save him later. What would Reuben have been able to do if he had returned and rescued Joseph later that day? Hand him a flask of water and a morsel of bread, and like Moses, send him out into the wilderness. My point is the trial would happen no matter which way Joseph turned.

Some signs that you are suffering from rejection are loss of self-worth, low self-esteem, feeling inadequate, self-doubt, questing God, your belief in Christ, and anger. We have an enemy, and these are emotions that he will employ to bring you to a place of rejection, rejection of Jesus Christ as your Lord and Savior, as your deliverer. The whole purpose of any trial is to get you to renounce God, get angry, quit, and give up. It's like Satan is filling your cup, a cup of wrath.

I have been fortunate to have suffered through these types of trials. I asked Jesus with a broken heart a couple of times, "Why?" I heard the same answer, "They didn't reject you; they rejected Me." Jesus is well acquainted with rejection; Joeseph was a prototype of Christ's suffering and His rejection. Every time someone walks away from Jesus, it's that type of rejection that He suffers once again. It is like a form of worship to the enemy, but to Christ, it is an opportunity for Him to display His grace and His love towards you.

He knows what you have been through and chooses to fill your cup with His blood, the communion of Christ. No matter which way you turn, Jesus has a plan. It may not look or feel like it now, but I know "you will overcome." The actions of others do not determine your value. Jesus Christ determines your value; He laid down His life for you because He determines your worth.

He is: Hesed ( )
O give thanks unto the LORD; for he is good: for his mercy endureth forever.
Blessings

PEACE TO YOU!

April 30

Jesus said to them again, "Peace to you!
As the Father has sent Me I also send you."
And when He said this He breathed on them, and said to them,
"Receive the Holy Spirit."
"If you forgive the sins of any, they are forgiven them;
If you retain the sins of any, they are retained."

John 20:21–23

Imagine being huddled in fear for your life, astonished at the wild trial that you have suddenly been thrust into, a furnace of circumstances the enemy has planned and implemented. Suddenly, Jesus steps into the room and says, "Peace to you!"

The word "peace" comes from the Greek word *Eirene (i-rah'-nay).* It means prosperity, quietness, rest, set at one again.

There have been times in prayer when I have felt the presence of Jesus come into the room; some people refer to it as a breakthrough in prayer. Either way, it feels good. You can sense the peace of the Lord, and you don't want to leave.

Once, while in prayer in the presence of the Lord, I had to leave for work. I felt guilty for having to go. Like a father patting a little child on the head before sending the child off to school, the Holy Spirit said to me in a lovely tone, "Okay, let's go about your day."

I never noticed it until just now; He used the word "let's," which is the abbreviation for "*let us* go about your day." Even though I was leaving my place of prayer, the Holy Spirit was packing His lunch and going with me. He had no intention of letting me go alone! Though I was going to work, He was going with me, just as He commissioned the disciples to go out before us.

You may not be going to a pulpit today, but you're still going out for Jesus. Chances are there will be someone you have to forgive, and for their sake, forgive them of their sin so that the Lord won't have to hold them to it. The choice is yours.

He is: Jehovah Shalom
The Lord Is Peace
Blessings

OUT OF DESOLATION

May 1

And king Solomon sent and fetched Hiram out of Tyre.
He was a widow's son of the tribe of Naphtali, and his father was a man of Tyre, a
worker in brass: and he was filled with wisdom, and understanding and cunning to
work all works in brass. And he came to King Solomon and wrought all his work.

1 Kings 7:13–14

This simple verse in the Bible seems to be just a note of who worked on the temple. But it symbolizes the character and wisdom of the Father, the Son, and the Holy Spirit.

Hiram, interpreted from Hebrew, means whiteness or noble.

And he was a widow's son from the tribe of Naphtali, which means "rock."

A widow's son is a lonely place. And his father was a man of Tyre, which also means "rock."

And he was filled with wisdom and understanding and cunning to work all works in brass. Brass is a metal made of copper and zinc, and the proportions can be varied to create a range of different types of brass with differing properties and abilities.

Brass symbolizes judgment and justice in the Bible.

Maybe one day you will find yourself in a place of desolation, a place where you need to petition the Son (the Rock) for the whiteness of your sins. After you have been forgiven, you then become a son of God the Father, which brings *nobility*. Jesus knows how to get the right proportions to your situation. He can rebuild your Temple if you allow the Holy Spirit to come into your heart.

Jesus can make you be what He intended for you to be.

He is: El Sela
God My Rock
Blessings

A TIME TO WIN

May 2

"And the God of peace shall bruise Satan under your feet shortly,
The grace of our Lord Jesus Christ be with you. Amen."

Romans 16:2

When you're going through some stuff, this is the scripture you want to flip your Bible open to accidentally! It's powerful, but the depth of the meaning is explosive. How can peace prevail over evil? Without a fight? When transliterated, this verse would read:

"And YAHUAH SHALOM shall bruise Satan under your feet shortly, The grace of our ADONAI YAHUSHA HAMASHIACH be with you. Amen."

YAHUAH: The Lord, the Supreme Authority, the Supreme Divinity. Shalom. Peace.

Shalom's definition is peace or a state of affairs. Peace is the opposite of war. How can this be? How can a God of Peace prevail over the god of war? Where does trouble come from? Where does it start? The book of James answers this:

"But each one is tempted, when they are drawn away of their own lust and enticed" (James 1:14).

Lust comes from the Greek word *epithumia*, which means a longing for things forbidden. Every war has happened because someone wanted something that belonged to someone else. It began with a thought. How do we win the battle over thoughts?

"Commit thy works unto the LORD, and thy thoughts shall be established" (Proverbs 16:3).

ADONAI YAHUSHA HAMASHIACH: Let's write this out in a complete translation.

The LORD, MASTER, OWNER, I AM HE who avenges, defends, delivers, helps, preserves, rescues, saves, brings salvation, your Savior, who brings you to victory, THE ANOINTED MESSIAH!

ADONAI didn't just earn these titles. He also created them. He said that He would bruise Satan under your feet. He is saying He will crush him completely!

Wow! Just like Jesus walked on water, you can walk over your problems.

He is: Jehovah Nissi
Lord of Victory and Miracles
Blessings

THE SUPREME AUTHORITY

May 3

"The Name of the YAHUAH is a strong tower;
the righteous runs into it, and is safe."

Proverbs 18:10

Most translations read: "The name of the Lord is a strong tower; the righteous run to it and is safe."

YAHUAH is the Hebrew name of God, the Supreme Authority. This translation can bring this scripture to life, depending on how you translate it—the words from Greek or Hebrew—or whatever Bible you choose to study. Here are some other translations:

"[is of great strength The name of the lord]; to it and running up the just are raised up high]" (Proverbs 18:10, ABP).

"The Name of the Lorde is a strong tower: the righteous runneth unto it, and is exalted" (Proverbs 18:10). (1587 Geneva)

"The name of the LORD is a strong tower: the righteous shall run into it, and be raised up" (Proverbs 18:10). (Jubilee)

"The name of the LORD is like a strong tower. Those who do what is right can run to him for protection" (Proverbs 18:10, ERV).

In your day of trouble, there is only one supreme being that can deliver you. You should give thanks for Him being your Deliverer before the day of trouble ever comes near. Many people put their trust in finances, insurance, or pensions, but the very next verse lets you know where not to put your trust.

"The rich think their wealth will protect them. They think it is a strong fortress" (Proverbs 18:10).

Your security will never be in finances because your wealth is in Him.

He is: Yahuah Yireh
The Lord Who Provides
Blessings

LET ME YIELD

May 4

Then cometh Jesus from Galilee to Jordan unto John, to be baptized of him.
But John forbad him, saying, I have need to be baptized of thee,
and comest thou to me? And Jesus answering said unto him, Suffer it to be so now:
for thus it becometh us to fulfill all righteousness. Then he suffered him.

Matthew 3:13–15

The Apostle Paul would not be persuaded to follow the will of the Lord. Christians read this and view the Apostle Paul as the one person who knows all things and was obedient to the Lord in all things. Looking at it from my perspective, Paul thought everyone else was wrong, including the Holy Spirit.

Really, what we are reading is what many Christians are doing today: following their own will and justifying their decision as it being God's will. I've seen people waste their lives waiting on a false belief that they were doing God's will. Paul was clearly forewarned concerning the danger. Likewise, he was warned not to go. Paul was suffering from a thing called pride.

In the previous verse, 21:4, "They told Paul through the Spirit not to go up to Jerusalem." However, fortunately for us, the Holy Spirit works for us through our mistakes. While imprisoned by his own choice, Paul wrote four books of the New Testament: Philippians, Colossians, Ephesians, and Philemon. Hypothetically, let's juxtapose another possible scenario:

Paul is obedient to the warning, and during the four years, he visits the churches, and he further increases the congregations and the new regions the Holy Spirit would have sent him to. And during his free time, he writes even more letters to the churches. I don't know, but I know Paul stepped out of God's perfect will into His permissive will. Until we get to heaven, we won't know the trillions of scenarios that could have come forth. New regions getting saved, next-generation Christians could have made the impact, Genesis 5 may have avoided the plague of Islam.

We can get entrenched in our faith even when we are wrong. I am guilty of holding onto false promises for far too long. Usually, it worked out to my shame. "Here counsel, and receive instruction, that thou mayest be wise and thy latter end. There are many devices in a man's heart; nevertheless the council of the Lord, that shall stand" (Proverbs 19:20–21).

Paul refused counsel, and he sat in "time out for a while," I noticed that his letters became softer and filled with more love than previously before. Paul wrote the epistles, but the epistles wrote Paul.

He is: Kurios
Supreme in Authority &
He is: El-HaNe'eman
The God Who Is Faithful
Blessings

YOU CAN'T OUTGIVE GOD

May 5

"Pure and undefiled religion before our God and Father is this: to care for orphans and widows in their distress, and to keep oneself unstained by the world."

James 1:27

When I see the word pure, it reminds me of a glass of cool, clean water—something that you can see through without any undissolved solids or silt. After all, who would want to drink unclean water?

I find it interesting that the word *undefiled* comes from the Greek word *am-ee'-an-tos,* which comes from another Greek word *al'-fah.* Alpha is the first letter of the Greek alphabet. I think it is no coincidence that God chose this to be a representation of pure religion. The first order is to keep yourself from being undefiled. Then He gives us some straightforward instructions: to care for orphans and widows.

Keep yourself out of trouble; today, the opportunity to get into sin is around every ____. Well, you can fill in the blank.

He is: Yahweh-Channun
God of Grace
Blessings

THANKFULNESS

May 6

"Therefore, by Him let us continually offer the sacrifice of praise to God that is, the fruit of our lips, giving thanks to His name."

Hebrews 13:15

Thankfulness is a word to live by. The other day, I went to get some hot water from my kitchen faucet, and for some reason, the hot water ran slowly out of that faucet. My first instinct was to complain about the faucet running so slowly, but instead, I caught myself before I said anything, and I thought, *There are people in other countries that don't even have water.*

The opposite occurred. I became grateful for what I had. I said, "Thank You, Lord, that we have running hot water."

Now, when I use the faucet, I don't get bothered about the slowness of the water. I think about how fortunate I am to have the things that I have and how blessed I am to have a slow faucet. It reminds me of how good I have it in life. Every time I go to use it, I feel a sense of joy because what the enemy intended to use to make me angry, God used to teach me how to understand the joy of *thankfulness.*

Thankfulness will produce fruit that you can live by, even share the gospel with others that can help them yield fruit.

Lord Jesus, I thank You and ask You to bless all those who read this.

He is: El Deah, The God of All Knowledge Blessings

WHOSE WILL BE DONE?

May 7

*"So, when he would not be persuaded, we ceased, saying,
'The will of the Lord be done'."*

Acts 21:14

It's a beautiful relief to know that God has placed a bodyguard at your side, helping you to walk according to God's will for your life. How many times have you thought not to do something, and you did, then it didn't work out so well? Maybe that was your angel giving you a warning.

Years ago, while I was driving and worshiping God, I thought that I would take a moment to thank my angels for all the work they have done for me. I wasn't praying to them or worshiping them. I just wanted to say "thank you."

As I said, "Thank you," a thought struck me like a ton of bricks, and I cried out, "I'm so sorry! You see me in all of my sins!" I began to cry, and I wept very hard and loud. A moment later, I heard an audible voice speak to me. It wasn't God or the Holy Spirit; it was my guardian angel, and he said, "I only ever see you in your righteousness!"

Wow! What a profound statement. How can this be? How would this even be possible? Through the blood of Jesus.

"He made the One who knew no sin to become a sin offering on our behalf so that in Him we might become the righteousness of God" (2 Corinthians 5:21).

He is: Yahweh-Channun
God of Grace
Blessings

SING YOUR WAY OUT

May 8

Ye shall not need to fight in this battle: set yourselves, stand ye still, and see the salvation of the LORD with you, O Judah and Jerusalem: fear not, nor be dismayed; tomorrow go out against them: for the LORD will be with you.

2 Chronicles 20:17

Have you ever been up against a situation so big that there isn't any way to overcome it?

King Jehoshaphat was up against an army of three different nations that had placed Jerusalem under siege. They were facing total annihilation.

At the most challenging times of my life and in the loneliest moments when there has been nothing, I could still sing His praise. When you have no hope, everything you do becomes so very hard. Doing a load of laundry, and every shirt feels like it weighs ten pounds; the lawnmower is like trying to push a plow.

But what I noticed was that God never left me. Jesus would give me prophetic words for others, reveal mysteries to me in the Bible. At times, the Holy Spirit would feel like a blanket covering my back and head.

Sometimes, singing praise to God in all your troubles can be the most brutal warfare on earth. That's what Jehoshaphat did. He consulted with the people and appointed singers to go out before the army. Here's what they sang; "Praise the LORD, for His mercy endures forever."

If you're down and facing a situation beyond your control, God made it simple. One sentence to your victory.

The armies that were trying to conquer Jehoshaphat ended up slaying one another down to the last man. For three days, the kingdom of Judah stripped the jewelry and carried back the wealth to Jerusalem, and that was their reward for operating in faith and obedience. Now you know what Jesus did for three days after the crucifixion, bringing the saints from paradise before the Father.

You see, you're His reward.

He is: El Moshaah
The God Who Saves
Blessings

FIND HIM IN HIS WORD

May 9

*"Thou shalt fear the LORD thy God; him shalt thou serve,
and to him shalt thou cleave, and swear by his name."*

Deuteronomy 10:20

At first read, this looks like a contradiction in principles. Let's dig a little deeper into the meaning of this compelling statement. Thou shalt *fear*; in this case, the word fear means to morally revere God. Causatively, it would be a very frightening experience to be in God's presence. Also, the LORD's name is in all caps, rendering this back to the original Hebrew, reads את eth-YAHUAH ELOHAYKA.

את eth are the first and last letters of the Hebrew Aleph-Bet (their alphabet).

Aleph, which symbolizes the Ox Head, a symbol of strength, as well as the symbol of the crown.

א Tav is the last letter and represents the cross, the mark of the covenant.

YAHUAH: THE LORD

ELOHAYKA: Your GOD (singular meaning the only God).

Him shalt thou *serve*. Serve in Hebrew is *aw-bad*, to place yourself under bondage with an unusual implication in meaning, and that is to be a "worshiper."

And to him shalt thou cleave. Cleave comes from the Hebrew word *daw-bak*, which means "to cling to, to pursue, to overtake, to be joined together."

And *swear* by his name. Swear comes from the Hebrew word *shaw-bah*.

And wow! Does this word have meaning? It means to "seven oneself."

To "seven oneself" comes from the Seven Cardinal Virtues: prudence, justice, temperance, fortitude, faith, hope, and charity, or to take an oath.

Now, let's sum up the compelling statement in this verse:

"Thou shalt morally revere as if you are in his presence, the Alpha and Omega Jesus Christ, the beginning and the end, the only God."

Indebt yourself to worship Him, pursue after Him, overtake Him.

Be joined together with Him in virtues: prudence, justice, temperance, fortitude, faith, hope, and charity by His name.

You can overtake Him in worship and find Him in prayer. It's like when you were a small child, and you would chase after your dad, and your dad would always let you catch Him.

He is: El Elyon
God Most High
Blessings

THE UNJUST STEWARD EXPLAINED

May 10

And he said also unto his disciples, There was a certain rich man, which had a steward; and the same was accused unto him that he had wasted his goods. And he called him, and said unto him, How is it that I hear this of thee? give an account of thy stewardship; for thou mayest be no longer steward. Then the steward said within himself, What shall I do? for my lord taketh away from me the stewardship: I cannot dig; to beg I am ashamed. I am resolved what to do, that, when I am put out of the stewardship, they may receive me into their houses. So he called every one of his lord's debtors unto him, and said unto the first, How much owest thou unto my lord? And he said, An hundred measures of oil. And he said unto him, Take thy bill, and sit down quickly, and write fifty. Then said he to another, And how much owest thou? And he said, An hundred measures of wheat. And he said unto him, Take thy bill, and write fourscore. And the lord commended the unjust steward because he had done wisely: for the children of this world are in their generation wiser than the children of light. And I say unto you, Make to yourselves friends of the mammon of unrighteousness; that, when ye fail, they may receive you into everlasting habitations.

Luke 16:1–9

Have you ever wondered about this parable? It looks like the servant is destroying the master's wealth, and then the master commends him for his actions. But back in that day and time, the steward was in charge of collecting debts owed to his master. The way a steward made his money was on a commission basis, and he charged whatever he thought he could get. He was setting a very high percentage, double the debt.

When the master demanded accountability, he decided that he had better gain some favor with these other business people, hoping that he might be able to get another job. He took and wrote off his commissions and charged a low-interest loan if they paid it off right away.

The master was pleased to get his money back with his interest, making the steward profitable in his eyes. So, I guess the moral of the story is: Be good to your company's customers, just in case you need another job someday.

He is: El Roi
The God Who Sees Me
Blessings

HARD TIMES

May 11

*"Many are the afflictions of the righteous: but the LORD
delivereth him out of them all" (Psalm 34:19, KJV).
"Adonai is close to the brokenhearted and saves those crushed in spirit."*

Psalm 34:19, TLV

Let's break down some of these words to get a complete understanding of this promise and what this life insurance policy covers.

Many: The word "many" really covers all types of hardships. Abundant (in quantity, size, age, number, rank, quality).

Afflictions: Bad or evil, adversity, calamity, displeasure, distress, exceedingly grievous, harm, heavy hurt, misery, noisome, sore, sorrow, trouble, vex, wicked, wretchedness, wronged.

Righteous: Just, lawful, honest (person).

Delivereth: To snatch away, to defend, escape, without fail, part, pluck, preserve, recover, rescue, save, surely, take (out).

All: Simply put, it covers everything.

"But without faith it is impossible to please him: for he that cometh to God must believe that he is, and that he is a rewarder of them that diligently seek him" (Hebrews 11:6).

Hebrews 11 is called the "Chapter of Faith" or "The Hall of Faith." This chapter is meant to encourage you when you're going through hard times because you can see what others endured for a promise.

Regardless of what you do for God, without faith, it is impossible to please Him. You will face situations where you must practice faith to please Him.

I know the WWQ approach; I've done it before: The Wimpy, Whiny, and Quit. I probably had a gold belt in it. I am not proud of it.

I know when problems hit, sometimes you think, "Again? Really?" But you'll never take a mountain top for Christ until you have learned to conquer the hills, and in all of my years, I have never seen a sword with a rearview mirror on it.

"He delivers the poor in their affliction" (Job 36:15).

He is: Elohim Yare
God Most Awesome
Blessings

YOU'VE GOT A FRIEND

May 12

"ז This poor man cried out, and the LORD heard him and saved him out of all his troubles."

Psalm 34:6

I have the honor of working with some impoverished people. One day, I had a lady ask me to pray for her. She had recently chosen to dedicate her life to the Lord. I asked the Lord what He wanted me to tell her, and He said, "Tell her everything will be alright, and expect an increase suddenly."

Wow! What a great word to lean on when things are going rough. But because she has dedicated her life to the Lord, she has this to stand on as well,

"פ The righteous cried out, and the LORD heard and delivered them out of all their troubles" (Psalm 34:17).

One of the cool things about a Scripture like this is that you can place your name inside this Scripture. By doing this, you add a level of intimacy between you and the Lord and create your personalized prayer.

"פ The righteous cried out, and the LORD heard and delivered _____ out of all their troubles" (Psalm 34:17).

I decided to leave the word "their" the same because I don't want them to be my troubles.

Recently, I wanted to bring a problem I had to the Lord. I asked Him if I could talk about some issues I was having. Immediately, I saw the Holy Spirit, and He was sitting at a table. He was relaxed, but when I asked Him the question, He sat up intently, looked at me, and said, "Sure,

bring it to me."

I was so shocked I didn't know what to say. He truly was concerned about my problem.

"ק Many are the afflictions of the righteous, but the LORD shall deliver him out of them all" (Psalm 34:19).

God knows that life will sometimes be hard in this world, and He especially knows that it will be harder for His people because we have an unseen enemy. But we have His Word, a promise He won't ever forget because it's hard to forget someone you love, and He loves you.

He is: El-Moshaah
The God Who Saves
Blessings

WILLING AND OBEDIENT

May 13

"If ye be willing and obedient, ye shall eat the good of the land."

Isaiah 1:19

You've probably read this verse before. I know it seems so simple, and yet it takes the Holy Spirit to reveal the meaning behind it. You see, this verse is totally about the Holy Spirit and you. Two key words, *willing* and *obedient*, but how? My life has taken a drastic change since I started following this life success scripture.

Be willing, but willing for what? Be ready to allow the Holy Spirit to speak to you and through you. The Holy Spirit has asked me to give a prophetic word to someone or do something for Him. Truthfully, every time, it takes a step of faith to follow through with the request. Often, it makes no sense to me as to why.

The words are sometimes meaningless to me, but to the person receiving, they make a lot of sense, and occasionally, they make no sense to that person. When that happens, ask for understanding.

Once, I prayed for a young man, and I saw a picture of him sitting at a loom spinning. I told him what I saw, and then I said, "You're spinning the Fruit of the Loom." Everyone laughed at me, including him. But a few minutes later, the Spirit of Prophecy landed on that young man, and he started to prophesy and couldn't stop. Everyone who came near him was getting a word from God! It was incredible. They even announced it from the pulpit. I had never seen that before; it was like being in the Old Testament.

Being obedient to relay the message is critical; it allows you to be trusted more by the Holy Spirit and builds your trust in Him. If you mess up, it is okay. Learn from your mistakes and pray some more.

He is: Yahweh-Channun
God of Grace
Blessings

READY TO FORGIVE

May 14

"Put up with each other, and forgive anyone who does you wrong, just as Christ has forgiven you."

Colossians 3:13

Having a choice is such a great thing, but notice there is no choice not to forgiveness. We seem to think that Jesus will understand why we didn't forgive someone. The sin of unforgiveness is a weight that so easily entangles us, like a bird in the fowler's net. A few times over the years, I have had people say something like, "I'll forgive them just as soon as they apologize."

I prayed with someone the other day, and the Holy Spirit said, "First comes forgiveness, then the apology." People who do not forgive have flown into the fowler's trap of unforgiveness—a plan set up by the enemy to snare them. Why?

Once, I had two ladies pull up to me at Prayer Stop. The driver had terrible allergies. Her mouth, ears, and eyes itched all the time, and she said it had started within the last year. She had to carry a handkerchief to wipe her eyes because they watered and teared up all the time due to the itching. The Holy Spirit told me, "Ingested nightmares." So, I asked her if she had changed her diet.

She said, "No, all that's been checked. They did an allergy test and couldn't find anything wrong."

I asked, "How do you sleep? Do you have nightmares?"

She said, "No, I sleep great!"

Then, I told her what the Holy Spirit told me, and it made no sense to either of us. At this moment, I saw the Holy Spirit standing by a boulder. He reached down and, with His hand, flipped it over. I knew this meant to dig a little deeper. Then, it hit me, so I asked: "Did you pick up somebody else's offense?"

She burst into tears and confessed that someone had wronged her mother. The passenger was aggressively nodding her head up and down. I told her that because she had seen the offense

with her eyes, heard it with her ears, and had spoken against them with her mouth, she was having these problems. I prayed a prayer of forgiveness with her, and she forgave them.

It turned out that the passenger was deaf, so I prayed with her, too, and she screamed out, "I can hear him!" They left happy.

"…and forgive anyone who does you wrong, just as Christ has forgiven you."

I know better than most about having to forgive people. It's hard sometimes, and sometimes it can take days to put my selfish pride down, but I do, and so should you. Please take my advice and do it now.

He is: Elohay Selichot
The God Who Is Ready to Forgive
Blessings

THE BEAUTY OF GOD

May 15

"And let the beauty of the Lord our God be upon us; and establish the work of our hands upon us; yea, the work of our hands establish thou it."

Psalm 90:17

Gosh, all you can think when you read this verse is that it is pleasant and comforting. The word "beauty" originates from the Hebrew word *no-am*, which means "agreeableness, delight, suitableness, splendor, grace, beauty, or pleasantness."

I spoke with my supervisor recently, and she told me how thankful she was for her job and that she knew that the Lord had placed her there so that she could support her family. She was letting God's beauty, His pleasantness, be upon her and her job, the work of her hands, and it made me realize that I needed to be thankful as well.

By reading this verse, we learn that it is up to us to let God's grace be upon us. By doing this, we allow God to establish the work of our hands. A pleasant work environment that's all most of us want, and now we know the secret.

He is: Yahweh-Channun
God of Grace
Blessings

ALL CREATION

May 16

For we know that even the things of nature, like animals and plants, suffer in sickness and death as they await this great event. All around us we observe a pregnant creation. The difficult times of pain throughout the world are simply birth pangs. But it's not only around us; it's within us. The Spirit of God is arousing us…

Romans 8:22

While I was out at a homeless camp, a Pitbull dog came up and greeted me. He was very friendly and a loyal companion to his homeless owners. I thought about this verse while petting this animal and talking to the people. It's not his fault that this world is such a mess. How have the animals taken the brunt of the fall? But this animal will remain loyal and continue to be a best friend to his owners, and it's his calling.

If only I could be as good a person as my pets think that I am! Oh, wretched saint that I am! But there's hope yet!

"And like wise also the Spirit helps our weakness; for we know not how to pray as we ought, but the Spirit itself makes entreaty for us with groaning's which cannot be uttered" (Romans 8:26).

With the power of the Holy Spirit, we don't always know what to pray for. How can we? Who knows what's going to happen within the next hour or the following year, for that matter? It's so easy for everything to crash and for you to find yourself living under a bridge. I pray that it will never happen to you. When you pray in the Holy Spirit, He knows what to pray for and what lies ahead and the possible destruction that He intercedes for on your behalf. What a wonderful God we serve!

He is: Entunchano
The God Who Intercedes
Blessings

WHAT DO YOU SEE IN ME?

May 17

Blessed are the poor in spirit, for theirs is the kingdom of the heavens.
Blessed are those that mourn, for they shall be comforted.
Blessed are the meek, for they shall inherit the earth.
Blessed are those who hunger and thirst for righteousness,
for they shall be satisfied.
Blessed are the merciful, for they shall obtain mercy.
Blessed are the pure in heart, for they shall see God.
Blessed are the peacemakers, for they shall be called the sons of God.
Blessed are those who suffer persecution for righteousness' sake,
for theirs is the kingdom of the heavens.
Blessed are ye when men shall revile you and persecute you and shall say all
manner of evil against you falsely for my sake.

Matthew 5:3–11

Recently, the Lord asked me, "What do you see in Me?"

I didn't know how to respond, so I said, "Thou knowest Lord."

The Lord showed me an image of myself passing out rice to the very poor and praying with them. Then, He said, "What you see in Me is what you become."

What do you see in Jesus? Do you see a harsh judge who will judge the sins of the world?

Do you see Jesus as the one who overcomes temptations and defeats the devil? Do you see Him as your protector, your provider, your Savior, or the one who blesses?

So why would I ask so many questions? Because if you believe these things, you will become the one who blesses the poor in spirit and assures them that the kingdom of heaven is theirs.

You will bless those who mourn, and you will comfort them. You will be gentle, and you will inherit the earth. You will bless those who hunger and thirst for righteousness because they will be filled by your words.

You will bless others by being merciful. You will become pure in heart, and you will see God.

You will become the peacemaker and be called the son of God.

You will be persecuted, but the kingdom of heaven will be called yours.

He is: El Roi
The God Who Sees Me
Blessings

THE MIRACLE OF PROPHECY

May 18

"And God wrought special miracles by the hands of Paul."

Acts 19:11

While in Haiti, I was invited to speak at a Christian university. At first, they asked me to speak words of encouragement. Then, the day before I arrived, they asked me to tell them about miracles I had seen.

For some reason, I could not remember any miracles. Maybe it was due to stage fright. I've witnessed so many miracles over the years that I have probably forgotten half of them. The following day, before I went to speak, I asked the Lord to help me remember some of the miracles I had seen. He spoke to me and said, "It's not about the miracles you've seen; it's about the miracles you possess!"

What an awesome God we serve! You see, God is not about yesterday. He is about today. If you don't ask for a miracle, you probably won't see it. If you're a born-again believer and baptized in the Holy Spirit, you possess miracle-working power. Miracle-working power: You can't buy it, that's for sure, but you can readily have it.

So, I asked Him what He wanted me to say to the students. He said, "Impart to some and prophesy to the others."

"And when Paul had laid his hands upon them, the Holy Spirit came on them, and they spoke in tongues and prophesied" (Acts 19:6).

It was truly marvelous! I prayed for every student in the chemistry class that day, and every student received a prophetic word from God.

He is: Lo Shanah
Unchanging
Blessings

RETURN TO ME

May 19

"Therefore, say thou unto them, Thus saith the LORD of hosts: Return unto Me, saith the LORD of hosts, and I will return unto you, saith the LORD of hosts."

Zechariah 1:3

Zechariah opens with a compelling invitation which God still offers today: "Return unto Me, saith the LORD of hosts, and I will return unto you, saith the LORD of hosts." I've had people come to me in the past and tell me basically that they have given up on going to church.

Hosea shows this beautiful character of God and His willingness for you to return to Him:

"I will heal their backsliding, I will love them freely: for mine anger is turned away from him" (Hosea 14:4).

This verse takes away the guilt, and once you've been out for a while, you start to have subtle thoughts of disbelief. Will God forgive me? People will think I'm a hypocrite, and so on. Whatever your negative thinking, God says He will heal you and love you freely.

When you find yourself in a place of exhaustion, you need to stir up the gifts within you. I've recommended to people in the past to take little steps of faith. Say to yourself, "I will read two chapters in my Bible today, and I will spend five minutes in prayer."

The Lord will help you break through, and this gives Him something to work with on your behalf.

Remember this: God is for you if your heart is for Him.

He is: Adonai Tzidkenu
The LORD Our Righteousness
Blessings

BE YOUR FUTURE

May 20

"Cast out the scorner, and contention shall go out;
yea, strife and reproach shall cease."

Proverbs 22:10

While driving, I was speaking with a man in the back seat. As we spoke, I occasionally looked at him in the rear-view mirror to make eye contact. He told me about his relationship problems with his girlfriend, and he revealed that she was extremely jealous, volatile, and that she had gotten physical with him and gave him a black eye with a severe cut.

Cut seemed to be the appropriate word at that point; he needed to cut all ties with that relationship before it was too late, but he was in love. He told me it was over, and he knew it.

I realized that as we were talking, I was looking in the rear-view mirror. A mirror works by reflecting light, and light travels at about 186,000 miles per hour. The distance between us of about three feet meant that everything I was seeing was from the past. I saw a past perspective on his current situation!

Sometimes, we must put relationships in the past, and that can be extremely painful. Some friends come into our lives for a season and then move on. Hopefully, we are better for the encounter.

My advice to this man was to start confessing that he makes the right choices in his life and repeat it over and over until the right choices begin to happen. Deep down, we know the right choice. We just don't always want to make it. The greatest man who still lives once said:

"Peace I leave with you, my peace I give unto you: not as the world giveth, give I unto you. Let not your heart be troubled, neither let it be afraid" (John 14:27).

He is: Jehovah Shalom
The Lord Is Peace
Blessings

NO COLLECT CALLS

May 21

"And the LORD called Samuel again the third time. And he arose and went to Eli, and said, Here am I; for thou didst call me. And Eli perceived that the LORD had called the child."

1 Samuel 3:8

Samuel, one of my favorite prophets. He just seemed like a caring man who did things right. Here, we have young Samuel in the temple, and when he hears the voice of God for the third time, he gets up and runs to the head priest, Eli, who was probably in his 80s or 90s at that point. He realized what was transpiring and instructed Samuel on what to say.

I love how God approached the youthful Samuel with patience. Four times, He called out to Samuel, and on the fourth call, Samuel got it right. You see, when God calls, He does it person-to-person. He did not tell Eli what He was doing, and He wanted to speak with Samuel.

Before they laid down to sleep, the Bible states that *the lamp of God was put out*. That is symbolic of the light of Eli's ministry coming to an end. There is no more mention of God speaking with Eli. From then on, He spoke through Samuel.

Every person on earth gets a call from God, but few people answer.

When you hear Jesus call your name, be sure and say: "I'm here LORD."

He is: Jehovah-Shammah
The Lord Is There
Blessings

POWERFUL MINDSET

May 22

*"For God hath not given us the spirit of fear; but of power,
and of love, and of a sound mind."*

2 Timothy 1:7

This Bible verse is one of my favorite scriptures. Sometimes, we can get into situations in which we need to settle ourselves down. For example, past-due bills can bring us into a place of fear, and fear is a type of bondage that the enemy uses for control. But God wants us to operate in a spirit of power, love, and a sound mind.

Recently, I was in the hospital with COVID and COVID-19 double pneumonia. I had been running a fever for days. The most challenging thing was that I could not remember any Bible scriptures. I later found out that when your oxygen level gets too low, it causes memory loss.

It was looking like I was going to have to be placed on a ventilator. I cannot take the thought of something in my throat; even typing this out is making me squirm. I was scared, and then someone texted me this scripture.

I was so grateful, and I immediately started to quote it to myself. The fear lessened, and I did not have to go on the machine. Faith replaced fear, and with faith restored, it gave me confidence that I would recover.

Fear starts in your mind, and faith starts in the heart.

He is: Theos Pas Paraklesis
The God of All Comfort
Blessings

HOT TOPIC

May 23

"Be ye angry, and sin not: let not the sun go down upon your wrath:
Neither give place to the devil."

Ephesians 4:26–27

Anger is a hot topic. I used to have anger issues, mainly stemming from frustration, stress, and the mailbox; it just wouldn't stop sending me bills.

Then, one day, I just said to myself, "You're the only one who controls this."

I started controlling my anger; the more I tried, the easier it became. But there are times when righteous anger swells up inside me. I was at Prayer Stop one Saturday, ministering to people. A man sat with me and started talking about revivals going on overseas, the great miracles of healing, etc. Then, he began to talk about how little faith there is in the United States. Mind you, I'm sitting on side one of the busiest roads in the Boro with signs that state, "Do You Need a *Miracle?*"

He went on to say Americans don't have the faith to get healed. Like a kettle of boiling water, the Holy Spirit rose inside me, and I said, "That's because they don't have people always telling them they don't have faith!"

One is spiritual anger, and the other is fleshly anger. I read a quote, "Anger is punishing yourself for what someone else did." Don't punish your flesh for what someone else has done.

When you let anger pass you by, those words that get you into trouble will stay unspoken, and that gives *no place for the devil.*

He is: Sar-Shalom
Prince of Peace
Blessings

NAME THAT FAITH

May 24

Christ hath redeemed us from the curse of the law, being made a curse for us: for it is written, Cursed is everyone that hangeth on a tree:
That the blessing of Abraham might come on the Gentiles through Jesus Christ; that we might receive the promise of the Spirit through faith.

Galatians 3:13–14

The Apostle Paul wrote this epistle to the Galatians. The Galatians were trying to combine Judaism with Christianity, believing that they would have to be circumcised to be saved.

The Galatians were falling into the trap that so many modern-day Christians live by, which creates the tangled web of works. People still believe that they have to do works to be saved.

I saw a festival for the Lord on television years ago. Men were on their knees, whipping their backs as a sign of repentance. I thought to myself, *They have made the cross to no effect.*

That means that they did not believe that the blood of Jesus was enough for their salvation.

When Jesus died on the cross, He was cursed so that we could receive the blessing of Abraham and that the blessing of the Spirit of Faith would be ours. Faith that Jesus Christ is our salvation and faith for our circumstances. You can have faith in His name, and faith has many names.

"The just shall live by faith."

He is: El Yeshuati
The God of My Salvation
Blessings

THE CALLING

May 25

And Abram went up out of Egypt, he, and his wife, and all that he had, and Lot with him, into the south.
And Abram was very rich in cattle, in silver, and in gold.
And he went on his journeys from the south even to Bethel, unto the place where his tent had been at the beginning, between Bethel and Hai;
Unto the place of the altar, which he had made there at the first: and there Abram called on the name of the LORD. And Lot also, which went with Abram, had flocks, and herds, and tents.

Genesis 13:1–5

It is by no accident the author chose these words: *up out of Egypt.* Egypt is symbolically a material place, a place of bondage and enslavement. Occasionally, in the Old Testament, when times got hard, the Hebrews would head towards Egypt to escape and try and make a better life for themselves through material gain. We tend to do the same by chasing material things for fulfillment.

Abram came up out of Egypt extraordinarily rich. The Hebrew word for rich is *kabed*, which means "heavy." Notice in the last verse that Lot went with him. Lot had flocks, herds, and tents, but the author does not describe him as rich. That is because Abram carried a heavy burden that Lot did not have: *the calling*.

The calling can become heavy burdens or the richness of caring for others, family, work, illnesses, and possessions. Too much stuff can make us feel like millionaires of burden.

Just like Abram returned to his first encounter with God at Bethel (which means "The House of God"), sometimes we need to return to the place of our own Bethel or that place where we first called upon the name of the Lord, which is that place in our hearts called sincerity.

He is: Shub Nephesh
Renewer of Life
Blessings

TAP INTO THE LORD

May 26

*"Blessed is the man who trusts in the LORD, whose trust is the LORD.
He is like a tree planted by water, that sends out its roots by the stream, and does not fear when heat comes, for its leaves remain green, and is not anxious in the year of drought, for it does not cease to bear fruit.*

Jeremiah 17:7

This is such a beautiful verse and promise given to us by God, and it reflects God's love towards us. In the six preceding verses, God is talking about the people in the land of Judah worshiping the goddess Asherah. It was a form of tree worship. In 2 Kings 18, we see that King Hezekiah removed all the high places and cut down the groves, destroying the works of the enemy.

The irony is, using the analogy of a tree, God offers to make you strong! Symbolically, the tree represents a nation or a person. The symbolism of root equals tapping into God's Word, and the stream represents the Holy Spirit.

The Holy Spirit is not afraid of any heat the enemy may bring. When hard times come, you will not be afraid, and you will still bear fruit: *reward*. Rewards can be monetary, possessions, family, or, more importantly, your treasure in heaven.

He is: El Roi
The God Who Sees Me
Blessings

LESSON ONE

May 27

Thus says the Lord, your Redeemer,
The holy one of Israel:
"I am the Lord your God,
Who teaches you to profit,
Who leads you by the way you should go."

Isaiah 48:17

I read this scripture the other day, and I thought about it for a moment and said, "Hmm, I've never actually asked God to teach me how to prosper?"

As I went to pray, it just sort of popped out, "Lord, teach me how to prosper!" Then, I prayed and commanded the enemy to restore a hundred-fold what he had stolen from me!

Then, I wondered what a hundred-fold was and how much that was exactly. I grabbed a tissue and folded it. One fold makes two, but two folds make four! Fold three makes eight, fold four makes sixteen, fold five makes thirty-two, fold six makes sixty-four, and fold seven makes one hundred and twenty-eight! Needless to say, if you do the math all the way, you end up with a huge number. I thought I might have misinterpreted a hundred-fold, but the Lord told me, "Your formula is sure."

Then, He said, "Indemnity." That means security or protection against a loss. Or it could mean, "A sum of money paid as compensation, especially a sum exacted by a victor in war as a condition of peace!"

"For we wrestle not against flesh and blood, but against principalities, against powers, against the rulers of the darkness of this world, against spiritual wickedness in high places" (Ephesians 6:12).

Know who your enemy is and take your victory!

Next, He told me, "You cannot pay back that which you cannot afford to pay."

Basically put, don't go buy that new rifle on a credit card, save up, and just pay cash. I asked the Lord what all this means, and He said, "Lesson one."

It was then that I remembered the words to the prayer: He teaches you to profit. I had simply asked God a question, and He gave me my first lesson.

He is: El Deah
The God of All Knowledge
Blessings

BIBLE SCRIPTURES FOR SELF-DEFENSE

May 28

*"If a thief be found breaking in, and be smitten so that he dieth,
there shall be no bloodguiltiness for him."*

Exodus 22:2

If someone breaks into your home and you're in fear for your life or the safety of your family, you have the right to defend yourself and your family. This Bible verse is saying that you will have no guilt before God.

"If the sun be risen upon him, there shall be bloodguiltiness for him—he shall make restitution; if he have nothing, then he shall be sold for his theft" (Exodus 22:3).

If the person surrenders or turns and flees, you shall not kill him (*if the sun be risen upon him*), meaning that if the perpetrator lives until the next day, they need to pay back what they stole or damaged. If they didn't have the ability to pay, they were to be sold into slavery for compensation. Now they go to prison, and the court collects the fines.

> *For he is a minister of God for thy good. But if thou do that which is evil, be afraid; for he does not bear the sword in vain, for he is a minister of God, a revenger to execute wrath upon him that does evil.*

Romans 13:4

This instruction is about authority figures such as police, judges, district attorneys, and other people in authority. Ministers for good, if you're the head of your household, you are the High Priest of your home and a minister for good unto your family. This Bible verse places the sword on you to defend your family.

"Then he said unto them, but now, he that has a purse, let him take it and likewise his provision bag; and he that has no sword, let him sell his garment and buy one" (Luke 22:36).

Jesus knew that His time on earth was coming to an end and that people would need to defend themselves from evil, so the Lord was letting them know that this would be necessary as He would no longer be there.

The term "sword" comes from the Greek word *Machaira* (MAX-A-RA), *makh'-ahee-rah* for dagger; a knife, that is, dirk; figuratively war, judicial punishment: sword.

The dagger was a defensive weapon men carried openly in their belts. It was curved and had an ornamental look to it. It was a necessity when traveling for self-defense.

In comparison, if you go to Revelations 19:15, you will see that God is referring to the sword as the Word of God:

> *And out of his mouth goeth a sharp sword, that with it he should smite the nations: and He shall rule them with a rod of iron: and he treadeth the winepress of the fierceness and wrath of Almighty God.*

Revelations 19:15

Sabre is a long and broad cutlass (any weapon of the kind); sword.

The Lord is referring to a battle sword because He is engaged in battle, but this sword represents the Word of God.

"A righteous man falling down before the wicked is as a murky spring and a polluted well" (Proverbs 25:36).

As Christians, we are to defend the weak, the widows, the orphans, especially against violent people. How can you defend them if you're not armed?

> *Those that built on the wall and those that bore burdens and those that laded wrought with one hand in the work and with the other held a weapon.*
>
> *For the builders, each one had his sword girded by his side, and so they built. And he that sounded the shofar was by me.*

Nehemiah 4:17–18

God blessed these men in their work while they took up arms to defend themselves.

"Deliver the poor and destitute; deliver them out of the hand of the wicked" (Psalm 82:4).

How can you defend the poor and needy from the wicked if you're not armed? I learned long ago that I can't physically take every person out there.

"Not defending yourselves, dearly beloved; but rather give place unto the wrath of God, for it is written, Vengeance is mine; I will repay, saith the Lord" (Romans 12:19).

Paul is referring to the verse found in Deuteronomy 32:35:

"Vengeance and recompense are mine, in the time when their foot shall slide; for the day of their calamity is at hand and that which is determined upon them makes haste."

This means Christians should not be going after someone to get revenge or hunting down someone who has wronged us. Trust God to let the police handle that.

He is: Jehovah Uzzi
The Lord My Strength!
Blessings

A FATHER'S HEART

May 29

*"Teach me thy way, O LORD; I will walk in thy truth;
firm up my heart that I might fear thy name."*

Psalm 86:11

Psalm 86 was a Prayer of David. Sometimes, I wonder if David even knew the depths of his writings and how far they would go to help us all. There is one simple little line in this sentence that can be so easily overlooked: "Teach me Thy way, O LORD."

It's a hidden gem lying right out in the open. We never stop to realize that God is a great teacher. God ordained teachers and established ministers to teach His Word for generation after generation. But did you ever stop to think that God loves to teach us?

I listened to a lady named Kat Kerr talk about a vision she had in heaven. She said Father God was sitting on His throne, teaching thousands of people. They were sitting on the ground, intently listening to every word God taught, every eye just entirely captivated by the wisdom and

knowledge being taught. She said God loved teaching them. Maybe somehow, we've failed to notice that people who aspire to be teachers have been given a character trait of God in their hearts. If you find yourself in a situation where you do not know what to do, that would be an excellent start to your prayer with

"Teach me Thy way, O LORD."

He is: El Deah
The God of All Knowledge
Blessings

LOST AT SEA

May 30

*Who is a God like unto thee, that pardoneth iniquity, and passeth by the
transgression of the remnant of his heritage? he retaineth not his anger forever,
because he delighteth in mercy.
He will turn again, he will have compassion upon us; he will subdue our iniquities;
and thou wilt cast all their sins into the depths of the sea.
I am glad that we serve a forgiving God.*

Micah 7:18–19

Have you ever had someone you loved do you wrong? I have, and it hurts deeply. I struggle with the spirit of unforgiveness. The enemy takes delight in reminding me daily what they did to me, like a hammer that bangs into my consciousness, trying to drive the nail of unforgiveness deep into my heart.

When we sin, the accuser is quick to rush to God and point out our sins, banging at Jesus, too, to provoke Him to anger.

Father God wrote His Word for people, but He governs by His words. This scripture reminds God of His willingness to forgive. The Word reminds Him of who He is, a merciful God.

Since the Garden of Eden, people have tried to attain god-like status. If you want to be more like Jesus (I heard these words), "Suffer the grief no more."

"…and thou wilt cast all their sins into the depths of the sea."

Jewish tradition calls this the Sea of Forgetfulness. If God can forget our sins, we need to learn how to forget the sins of others and forget the worst sin of all—the sin we have done to others. I say this because it is what Satan uses to torment believers day and night.

If you are having trouble forgiving someone or forgiving yourself, ask Jesus for help to cast the sin into the Sea of Forgetfulness before you cast the sin into your heart.

I've been very far out in the Deep Blue, and believe me, the ocean is a big place. Once you lose something out there, it's gone forever.

He is: El Nahsah
The Forgiving God
Blessings

IT DOESN'T ALWAYS GO THE WAY YOU THINK

May 31

Rather, "If your enemy is hungry, feed him; if he is thirsty, give him a drink. For by doing so you will heap coals of fire upon his head."

Romans 12:20

Do not be overcome by evil, but overcome evil with good.

I always chuckle to myself when I hear someone who is having issues with someone else. Inevitably, this scripture will come up as advice on how to handle the situation. They'll say something like, "You know what the Scripture says? If your enemy is hungry, feed him."

I have had an encounter with this scripture before. Years ago, my family and I came home from church one Sunday afternoon, and inexplicably, my two neighbors just started shouting at us. They made no sense as to why they were so angry at us, and it was just this wild barrage. In hindsight, maybe they were arguing with each other, and when we said hello, the anger was directed towards us for no reason.

So, I thought about this scripture; I went to the store and bought an angel food cake, came home, and walked over to see if I could make amends for whatever had caused them to be so angry. I thought wrong.

To put it kindly, they yelled at me some more, saying they would never eat my cake! So, I went home, sat at my dining room table, and ate my angel food cake; it was tough to swallow. I sat there and thought that I had done no wrong, but they refused my peace offering. It had made them angrier. I thought that they could stay mad, and I would eat my angel food cake. It still didn't feel delicious. I still didn't understand. I expected them to smile and say, "Thank you, we didn't mean what we said. Please forgive us."

"With all thy getting, get understanding" (Proverbs 4:7).

Without knowing it, I had heaped coals of fire on their heads; what was I thinking? When hot coals hit your conscience, you're going to yell at whoever threw them. Eventually, they forgave us, and when it came time to move, they were sorry that I was leaving; we had become friends.

I'll never forget the day I sat by myself at my table and ate angel food cake that tasted like lumps of humiliation. Obeying Scripture isn't always easy, but maybe, somehow, they saw Christ in me, or perhaps I saw what Christ had seen in me before I accepted Him as my Lord and Saviour.

He is: El Nahsah
Forgiving God
Blessings

HARVEST

HOW DEEP ARE YOUR HURTS?

June 1

"Jesus saith unto her, I that speak unto thee am he."

John 4:26

Most of us are familiar with the story of the woman at the well. What causes me to marvel about it is that she was the first person to whom Jesus revealed His identity.

Once, while in Haiti, I watched a young orphan girl throw a bucket into the well and draw water. The well looked deep and somehow had a lonely feeling about it. When you look down into that shallow, dark abyss, it can cause you to reflect on things.

I'm sure this woman at the well reflected many times when she cast her bucket into the deep well. Her hurts went deeper than the water level. People tend to throw her into a role when they read this story. She probably had five husbands because of her horrible attitude. More than likely, some had passed away from illnesses or age; others just left.

At the time of the scripture, she was living with a man, but they were not married. No, there was too much hurt connected with that commitment. Many preachers say that she went to the well at midday because of her shame. I say she went because she had enough of people: their judgmental looks, the whispered gossip that could only come from others who had never empathized with her deep hurts.

But that day, the Father, the Holy Spirit, and the Son had another reflection for her, and it was called *grace*. When you read the whole story, notice how Jesus persuades the conversation. He confronts the legalism of her view. Coincidently, legalism places people into bondage. Her reaction was curiosity, but how? How could He get her out of this bondage? Then, Jesus positioned a test of truthfulness, and she passed! Praise God, and she didn't lie. She skirted around her most profound hurt. Then, the Lord revealed to her that He knew her deepest pain, but He did it gracefully. He's not out to condemn, and He's there to edify.

In a picturesque way, we can see what was in her heart and what she had been holding. She didn't know where to worship. Perhaps she was thinking that she and her people were not good enough to worship in Jerusalem or good enough for God to love them. She might have wondered where to go to worship and where to find God. Others were doing the act of worship, but she was seeking who to worship by finding the true place of worship. Then, Jesus revealed to her that it was not a place, that she was to worship *"in spirit and in truth."*

Suddenly, you can see the wheels turning in her mind. As she asked about the Messiah, the Christ, Jesus responds, *"I that speak unto thee am he."*

The lady at the well left, leaving her waterpot behind because she was coming back and she was going to bring a crowd with her! It would be Jesus' first revival. She went straight to the men of the city and told them that she had found the Messiah. They came out and believed, and not wanting to give her any credit, they told her it was not because of her testimony. It was because they heard for themselves.

My thoughts on what the men of the city said to her? Well, welcome to the ministry, sister. Some things will never change. But I'm sure that there are many Samaritans in heaven who are grateful for her testimony.

Do you have something to share when it comes to Christ?

He is: Maqowr Chay Mayim
Fountain of Living Waters
Blessings

YOUR ROAD

June 2

"And he came and dwelt in a city called Nazareth, that it might be fulfilled which was spoken by the prophets, He shall be called a Nazarene."

Matthew 2:23

Here, we have the record of Joseph, Mary, and Jesus in their guided travels. Sometimes, we think we have a destination where we're supposed to go, and then God changes our direction. In this case, He warned Joseph in a dream to go another way.

Joseph had good reason to be afraid of the change of direction, fearful because he was going back to Judea, but later found out that Herod's son Archelaus now reigned that region. Joseph wanted to return to Judea because it was familiar; Jesus was born in Bethlehem. Maybe Joseph thought that's where he was supposed to raise Jesus. Instead, God sent him to Nazareth. Phillip, the son of King Herod, the brother of Archelaus, was a much more peaceful ruler and reigned over this region.

God let Joseph travel this road until the right time to change his course. Sometimes, we can start in the direction we think God wants us to travel, only to be re-routed to face our fears and test our faith. New beginnings can be very stressful, but, in the end, they bring increased faith and bring you into a place of peace called Shalom.

"The Shalom of God, which surpasses all understanding, will guard your hearts and your minds in Messiah Yeshua" (Philippians 4:7).

He is: Jehovah-Ra'ah
The Lord Is My Shepherd
Blessings

THE DAY GOD LISTENS

June 3

I CRIED out to God with my voice- even unto God with my voice; and He gave ear to me. In the day of trouble, I sought the Lord; My hand was stretched out in the night without ceasing; My soul refused to be comforted. I remembered God, and was troubled; I complained, and my spirit was overwhelmed.
Selah

Psalm 77:1–3

Notice the words "I CRIED" are in caps. Asaph, the writer, wants you to know the depths of his anguish from the first two words. But first, let's see who Asaph was and why he would be grieving to despair. Asaph was a Levite appointed by King David as the chief priest to help carry the ark of the covenant back to Jerusalem. He was known as a prophet who wrote Psalms 50, 73–83. Psalm 83 is called an imprecatory prayer. A Holy Spirit-filled prayer invokes a prophetic curse against Israel's enemies. The Hebrews, to this day, are waiting for the prophecy's fulfillment.

So why was Asaph so troubled? No one knows why, but be of good cheer! By not knowing Asaph's troubles, we cannot apply this to one problem; this is an open blank for your benefit, somewhat like Paul's thorn in his side. "My Grace is sufficient for thee" (2 Corinthians 12:9).

Asaph prayed throughout the night, his hands stretched toward the heavens, seeking an answer, and then he wrote, "I remembered God and was troubled." How can you remember God and be troubled? The Lord will often remain silent during these times. e.g., when a student takes a test, the teacher remains silent.

But now he makes a mistake and has God's ear, but instead of praise and thankfulness, he complains to God, and suddenly, his spirit is overwhelmed; we tend to use the term "quenched the Spirit." Being humble, he writes, Selah, which means "pause and think about that." He recalls God from the former days, all the days of victory, the wonders of old, how God parted the Red Sea so His children could cross over!

When you start thanking God and remembering the many times He has saved you from disaster, it's your turn to win.

Selah.

He is: Entunchano
The God Who Intercedes
Blessings

THE BURNING BUSH

June 4

And the angel of the LORD appeared unto him in a flame of fire out of the midst of
a bush: and he looked, and, behold, the bush burned with fire,
and the bush was not consumed.
And Moses said, I will now turn aside, and see this great sight,
why the bush is not burnt.
And when the LORD saw that he turned aside to see, God called unto him out of
the midst of the bush, and said, Moses, Moses. And he said, Here am I.

Exodus 3:2–4

God does not do anything without a purpose. Look at the word bush, which comes from the Hebrew word *sen-eh*. It means "to prick; a bramble: bush." Why did God pick a thornbush? And why did God appear out of it with a flame of fire and not consume it?

When Adam sinned, the thorn bush became part of the curse; before the curse, thorns were non-existent. But now, they represent the fallen state of humanity and how God dwelt with humankind in our fallen state. God is an all-consuming fire, yet in His multitude of grace, He allows man to remain in our fallen state without consuming us in flames.

The second time Moses returns to Mount Sinai, God comes down from heaven to the top of Mount Sinai, and He rests as a consuming fire. Moses brings all the children of Israel and, like an imperfect bride standing before a throne, the general population cannot approach His presence. Thankfully, God had a plan in Deuteronomy 18:18:

"I will raise up for them a prophet like you from among their fellow Israelites and I will put my words in his mouth. He will tell them everything I command him."

Jesus is that prophet, the Lamb of God, the Bridegroom: "Let us be glad and rejoice and give Him glory, for the marriage of the Lamb has come, and His wife has made herself ready" (Revelations 19:7).

Be ready.

He is: Akal Esh
The Consuming Fire
Blessings

STRONG TOWER

June 5

*"The Name of the Lord is a strong tower;
the righteous run into it and are safe."*

Proverbs 18:10

This verse is one of my favorites. In times of trouble, you can run to the name of the Lord, but what if you don't know his name?

"How then shall they call on the one they have not trusted? And how shall they trust in the one they have not heard of? And how shall they hear without someone proclaiming?" (Romans 10:14, TLV)

His Hebrew name is YAHUSHA HAMASHIACH. However, we say, "Jesus the Christ." In the day of trouble, you can run to His name and be safe.

Years ago, I delivered bottled water for a living. One day, I was delivering bottled water to a residence, and halfway between the house and the water truck, a German Shepard aggressively came towards me. I'm not afraid of dogs; however, this one had mange. The animal stopped and began to circle me, growling, trying to gain a position to attack. Standing there with a bottle of water on my shoulder, I couldn't get to the house or the truck. I thought, *Lord, it's one thing to get bit by a dog, but it's another thing to get bit by a dog with mange!*

Suddenly, out of nowhere came this mockingbird, and it started attacking the dog! I was able to get back to my truck the whole time, listening to the dog whelp because the bird was putting it on him! The dog ran off, and I thanked God! I knew the Lord heard my thoughts. I never said it out loud, but innocently, I had run to the name of the Lord.

There are times in your life when you will be confronted with temptations, dangers, and snares. In your mind, you can run to the name of Jesus, a strong tower. You can find such personal meaning and comfort in Romans 10:14 and the power of Jesus' name. This verse speaks to faith's importance and sharing the gospel message with others. To trust in and call upon the name of Jesus, one must first hear about Him and believe in Him. And this can only happen through the proclamation of the gospel by believers. In times of trouble, it is natural to turn to God for help and protection. And as I experienced, God can work miraculously to provide for our needs and protect us. The name of Jesus is a powerful source of strength and refuge; by calling upon it in faith, we can trust that we will be saved and protected.

He is: Migdal Oz
Strong Tower
Blessings

THINGS TO REMEMBER

June 6

"Wherefore I put thee in remembrance that thou stir up the gift of God, which is in thee by the putting on of my hands."

2 Timothy 1:6

Sometimes, it's easy to forget who we are in Christ. Lethargy is a state of feeling very tired, inactive, and sluggish, often to the point of having difficulty functioning. It can be caused by a variety of factors, such as lack of sleep, physical illness, certain medications, depression, or unhealthy lifestyle habits.

For months, I struggled with exhaustion. I went to the doctors, the cardiologist, and the hospital for medical tests, and they all gave me a clean bill of health, saying everything was fine. It made no sense as to why I was always so exhausted. I thought my time had come, and then, one morning, I sat down for prayer. The Lord said, "Rebuke a spirit of lethargy." As soon as I said those words, I felt a cloud lift off every part of my body, and I felt great!

I don't know why the Lord let me go through all that; no telling how many times He had spoken to me about things and given prophetic words for others. But the enemy was trying to quench the Spirit within me. Jesus renewed my strength. Please remember when your pastor lays hands on you and prays, those prayers, like a chain of hands throughout history, go back to the very hands of Jesus. And Jesus is where we get our strength.

He is: Jehovah Uzzi
The Lord My Strength
Blessings

BLACKSTONE'S MEMORIAL

June 7

*"The pride of thine heart deceive thee, thou that dwellest in the clefts of the rock,
whose habitation is high; that saith in his heart,
Who shall bring me down to the ground?"*

Obadiah 1:3

This prophecy is against the Edomites/Nabateans, a tribe that initially caused Israel much trouble. They were direct descendants of Esau, the older brother of Jacob, who later was named Israel. When the Hebrews left Egypt, the Edomites refused passage to Moses, and throughout history, they assisted other countries in attacking and plundering Israel. After their deployments, they would return to their capital city, Petra.

Petra is a city carved out of rock capable of holding thousands of people. Many believe that at the battle of Armageddon, the Jewish would flee to Petra for their safety.

In the 1940s, evangelist W.E. Blackstone printed Bibles (in Hebrew) and buried them in Petra for the Jewish people when this time came. He invested $8000.00, more than 140,000.00 in today's money! He did this before Israel even became a nation! Blackstone referred to himself as "God's little errand boy."

He is also considered the father of Christian Zionism and paved the way for the nation of Israel with his petition called the Blackstone Memorial (1891). The Petition is the influential document that generated the historical Balfour Act, which re-created the modern-day Nation of Israel.

On the other hand, King Herod was called 'The King of The Jews' and was a descendant of the Nabateans; he's known for his great architectural works and for trying to kill the newborn Christ.

Whose works will stand longer? Herod's or Blackstone's? One man crucified a King, and the other built the nation for the coming King. You can be a builder, too, by building your faith for the coming King.

He is: Tsur-Yisrael
Rock of Israel
Blessings

THE PROMISE

June 8

"And I will put enmity between thee and the woman, and between thy seed and her seed; it shall bruise thy head, and thou shalt bruise His heel."

Genesis 3:15

After Adam's fall, Father God promised a Messiah, but how did they get so much revelation out of this verse? Enmity is the state or feeling of being actively opposed or hostile to someone or something. Just moments before, Adam and Eve were in God's perfect will. Suddenly, there is a shift, and now, a separation exists between man and God.

When God speaks to them, they are in hiding and notice who is still present: Satan. God immediately prophesies that hostility will be between Satan and the seed of women, not between God and humankind. God loves His creation and reveals His plan to redeem us. *Thy seed and her seed*: Satan's seed is sin and death. Adam named the woman Eve because she was the mother of all living beings. It's the only time in the Bible when the *seed* is attributed to a woman. Every other time, it is attributed to a man, e.g., Abraham, the father of all nations, and the lineage of King David. Hence, this is where we start to understand the virgin birth of Christ.

In Genesis 4:1, Eve gives birth to Cain and exclaims, *"I have gotten a man from the Lord."*

Many texts do not use the word "from," and some scholars say that this is one word that is not in the text. If so, what Eve exclaimed would be more like this: *"I have gotten a man, the Lord."* Eve thought she had given birth to the Messiah. Unfortunately, it was going to take a lot more work and sacrifice. Over the centuries, God continued to reveal His plan. The first seven men named in the lineage of Christ began to show that the cost of redemption would be the highest price ever paid in the history of creation. These are their names: Adam, Seth, Enos, Cainan, Mahalaleel, Jared, Enoch, Methuselah, Lamech, and Noah. When we transliterate the seven names, we see God's plan unfolding:

"The man appointed mortal sorrow; The Blessed God shall come down teaching, His death shall bring the despairing rest. By His life, could He teach us? By sacrificing His life, God defeats death. Only in righteousness could He defeat sin."

God continued to reveal His plan through prophecy.

"Therefore, the Lord Himself will give you a sign; The virgin will conceive and give birth to a son, and will call Him Immanuel" (Isaiah 7:14).

There were 414 prophecies in the Old Testament concerning Jesus, and He fulfilled them all.

" ...it shall bruise thy head, and thou shalt bruise His heel."

Bruising Satan's head, Jesus overwhelmed him by giving him a defeating blow on the cross. Satan still retaliates against humankind, whom he hates, attacking the heel, the rear of God's army. When you strike at the heel, you slow the forward progress, but we have two heels and can always make one more step toward victory. And if you can't take another step, I'm pretty sure He will carry you.

He is: El Yeshuati
The God of My Salvation (Victory)
Blessings

SOURCE OF MY STRENGTH

June 9

"In the day of my trouble I will call upon thee: for thou wilt answer me."

Psalm 86:7

How's your day going so far? No matter who you are, you can be assured in life that you will have trouble. When I was a child, we used to have this red rotary dial telephone with a long cord to the wall. I remember laying on the bed looking at it, hoping God would call me on it; no matter how long I looked at it, it never rang. When it did ring, it was always for my brother or sister.

It's not that God didn't know how to use a rotary phone. God is always willing to listen. I did not know how to dial the correct number to reach Him. You see, many years before there was this thing called email, there was knee mail.

We got on our knees and talked to God, and we have His promise that He will listen. But when your time of trouble comes, you want Him to answer, and God will answer.

His answer may or may not be with words. He may answer with a response or supply the need. He could send someone by that says just the right thing at just the right moment, and somehow it makes everything better, and yes, that was God, and be sure to say "thank you."

It's good to have Him on your speed dial.

He is: Jehovah-Jireh
God My Provider
Blessings

FOOD FOR THOUGH

June 10

"You prepare a table before me in the presence of my enemies; You anoint my head with oil, my cup overflows."

Psalm 23:5

This verse is a beautiful picture of God's provision and protection, even in difficulties.

Similarly, Romans 12:20–21 says, "If your enemy is hungry, feed him; if he is thirsty, give him something to drink. In doing this, you will heap burning coals on his head. Do not be overcome by evil, but overcome evil with good."

These verses remind us to show kindness and love to those who may not offer it in return. By serving them and sharing God's blessings, we shine a light in the darkness and overcome evil with good.

Think about times when you've been in the company of people who didn't like you. How did you respond? Did you reach out in kindness and love, offering the fruits of the Spirit (love, joy, peace, patience, kindness, goodness, faithfulness, gentleness, and self-control)? Doing so can be difficult but can also have a powerful impact.

Finally, the idea of the Lord anointing our heads with oil symbolizes His protection and peace. Just as a shepherd would anoint his sheep to keep away irritating insects, we can ask God to anoint us with His peace and security, even in the midst of difficulties. And when we do, our cups will surely overflow with His blessings.

He is: YAHUSHA HAMASHIACH
Jesus Christ (Salvation in the Messiah)
Blessings

THE GREAT RACE

June 11

"The eyes of the Lord are everywhere, keeping watch on the wicked and the good."

Proverbs 15:3

It's easy to think that if we don't get caught, there's no harm done. But the truth is, God is always watching, constantly aware of our actions and motives.

As we go about our daily lives, let's strive for excellence in everything we do, including the small details that others may not see. For example, giving back a mistakenly overpaid dollar, letting go of a minor annoyance in traffic, or giving credit where credit is due, even if it means someone else takes the credit for our work.

It's also important to remember that what we do impacts others. We can all recall moments when we've spoken words that hurt someone. That's why being kind and compassionate in all our interactions is so important.

The story of the man in heaven who saw a picture of himself helping a young boy train for a track meet reminds us that the things that matter most to God are not our victories or accomplishments but our acts of kindness and love.

Ultimately, the race of life is not about winning first place but about being a faithful servant of God. So let's strive to be kind, compassionate, and faithful in all we do, and trust that God will reward us with the words, "Well done, good and faithful servant."

He is: The Alpha and Omega
The First and the Last
Blessings

GOD'S BANKING SYSTEM

June 12

"And I will give you pastors according to mine heart, which shall feed you with knowledge and understanding."

Jeremiah 3:15

Jeremiah's passage refers to the ultimate reign of Christ, where God recognizes the need for pastors to lead His church.

Pastors and belonging to a church community are virtual gifts from God. He chooses pastors to care for and guide His people; their importance should not be taken for granted. Your pastor may not be the most gifted speaker, but they have a purpose and something that God wants to impart to you.

I once heard a story about a pastor feeling discouraged and wanting to leave his church. On his trip home, he stopped at a rest area and discovered a group of abandoned kittens. Feeling sorry for them, he fed them with the food he had. The Lord spoke to him and said, "You have fed the kittens; now feed my sheep." Despite his initial reluctance, the pastor stayed and cared for the church, only to eventually pass the mantle to another.

The role of a pastor is a weighty one, and you need to be an encouragement to them. One day, they will stand before the Lord and be held accountable for their actions, including their care for the people in their charge.

So, make good deposits into your "spiritual account" with your pastor as the teller.

He is: El Roi
The God Who Sees Me
Blessings

YOUR HEART THE DEEP SEA

June 13

"Deep calls to deep in the roar of your waterfalls; all your breakers and waves have swept over me."

Psalm 42:7

Psalm 42 brings to mind a time when I worked offshore in the Gulf of Mexico on an oil platform. It was one of my first trips into the deep blue waters, and I saw three magnificent waterspouts towering toward the sky. A seasoned veteran I was with told me not to worry; they were just waterspouts. But to me, they looked like tornadoes.

This verse reminds me of the sight of those waterspouts. They appeared like an old phonograph, with the horn reaching towards the heavens and the waves and breakers appearing like ridges on a vinyl record. The deep calling to the deep. What would God hear?

The metaphor of this verse is about what God looks for when He examines your heart and inner being. Sadly, He can only hear the authentic sound of your heart during trials. What sounds does God want to hear from within you? The sounds of future praise, the sounds of His victory in your life.

David proclaimed his faith in God, saying, "For I shall yet praise Him." No matter how difficult life gets, let the Lord hear these words from your heart, "For I will praise Him!" The deep is calling out to the deep, and He's calling out to your heart.

He is: El Chay
The God of My Life
Blessing

STORE YOUR HEART

June 14

"Offer the sacrifices of righteousness, and put your trust in the Lord."

Psalm 4:5

What are sacrifices of righteousness? As I pondered this verse, I heard these words from the Holy Spirit: "What you're doing right now." Studying His Word, the Bible, you're taking valuable time to learn God's word, His ways. Spending time searching out God by reading the Bible, getting up and going to church, singing His praises, and kneeling in prayer are sacrifices of righteousness. Little by little, these sacrifices add up. I don't know if Jesus uses compound interest, but I know He pays well, and the retirement benefits are fantastic. These sacrifices bring the words of Jesus to life.

> *But lay up for yourselves treasure in heaven, where neither moth nor rust doth corrupt, and where thieves do not break through and steal:*
>
> *For where your treasure is, there will your heart be also.*

Matthew 6:20–21

Your sacrifices of righteousness build treasure, and the treasure positions your heart, and by positioning your heart, you complete this verse: *"And put your trust in the Lord."* Now you know where your heart is; it's trusting in the Lord.

He is: Jehovah-Tzidkenu
The Lord Our Righteousness
Blessings

HIS WORD IS ETERNAL

June 15

"The words of the Lord are pure and tried, like silver refined seven times in a furnace of earth. You, Lord, will keep them safe, preserving them for all generations."

Psalm 12:6

It's incredible to think about how well God has preserved His word for thousands of years. There was a period when many people thought the Bible was outdated and inaccurate, but in 1947, a discovery was made that would change everything. An Arab shepherd boy found ancient scrolls in a cave near the Dead Sea, and after traveling to Bethlehem and then to Jerusalem, the scrolls were sold to buyers. Symbolically like a resurrection, a shepherd boy looking for a lost goat finds the scrolls and brings them to Bethlehem, the birthplace of Christ, and now they are on display in Jerusalem.

The discovery of these scrolls, which included every book of the Old Testament except for the book of Esther, proved God's word had never changed! The fact that the scrolls were found just when people were starting to question the accuracy of the Bible is almost as if God planned it. It's a testament to the power and durability of God's words, which remain just as relevant today as they were thousands of years ago.

He is: Jehovah
Eternal
Blessings

GOD THE FINISHER

June 16

"But if I drive out demons with the finger of God, then the kingdom of God has come upon you".

Luke 11:20

This verse highlights the power of Jesus' words and actions and His close relationship with God the Father. By saying that He drives out demons with the "finger of God," Jesus emphasizes that the power behind His miracles is not His own but from God. The Greek word for "finger" in this verse is *daktulos*, which is related to the Greek word *deka*, meaning "ten." Ten is the number of completeness, and it's interesting to note that ten plagues were cast upon the Egyptians in the story of Exodus. The plagues were considered the "finger of God" in their own right, demonstrating His power and control over the natural world.

Similarly, Moses delivered the Jewish people through the power of God, and God wrote the Ten Commandments with his finger. These events all point to God's complete control and management over the world and His people. With these associations in mind, when Jesus says He drives out demons with the "finger of God," He emphasizes the source of His power and the completeness and finality of His actions. He is letting people know that when God puts His finger towards their healing, He completes the work He began in them. Not only were people healed, but they also believed in Jesus as the Messiah. So, when we say, "Jesus, You complete me," we acknowledge the power and completeness of His love, grace, and salvation in our lives.

He is: El Racham
The Compassionate God
Blessings

LIFE'S TRAILS

June 17

"But He answered and said, 'It is written, "Man shall not live by bread alone, but by every word that proceeds out of the mouth of God".'"

Matthew 4:4

The great temptation of Christ by Satan himself was his best effort to defeat Jesus. At this moment in history, Jesus had just fasted for forty days and forty nights in the wilderness and was now starving. Satan said, "If you be the Son of God, command that these stones be made bread." This verse is one of the most perplexing temptations ever and is quite a brilliant tactic on the enemy's part. But why was it a sin?

Would it have been a proud display of showmanship and power? There is no sin that I can see; Jesus had already turned water into wine before this, and this is where Satan came up with the idea.

Here's what Satan was trying to do: the same thing he does to all of us. Jesus was always in God's perfect will and all the time. It was God's will for Jesus to be on this fast. The fast was done, but yet not complete.

Jesus had not received the okay from God to eat, and being moments away from victory, He would have stepped out of God's perfect will.

There are times when the enemy tries to pull you out of God's perfect will, and it could be a better job offer in another town that would pull you out of the church body God placed you. If you make the change, things probably won't go as smoothly, but the God of all grace will be with you in His "permissive will." Because just like Adam and Eve, you always have a choice.

Before making a life-changing move, get with God to pray. You can say this: "Lord Jesus, if this is within Your perfect will for my life, please open the door. If not, please close the door for this opportunity." He will either open it or close it, but either way, be thankful.

He is: Yahweh-Channun
God of Grace
Blessings

ENCOURAGE YOURSELF IN THE LORD

June 18

"For your Maker is your Husband; the Lord of Hosts is His name, and your Redeemer, the Holy One of Israel. The God of the whole earth shall He be called."

Isaiah 54:5

This verse refers to the return of the exiles from Babylon back to Israel, but it also provides a powerful description of the character and identity of God. As a Christian, when everything seems to be coming after you, this verse can be used in prayer as a reminder of who God is and who He is on your behalf.

God uses six different names to identify himself in this verse:

- Maker: This means that God is your creator and accomplisher.
- Husband: God is married to you and your needs, and when you are married to God, the two of you become one.
- Lord of Hosts: God is in charge of a massive army of organized angels waiting to fight on your behalf.
- Redeemer: God is ready to repurchase you and to assume your debt, paying it in full and canceling your sin.
- Holy One of Israel: This is the line of Abraham and the God of the Gentiles, as stated in Romans 3:29.
- The God of the Whole Earth Shall He be Called: God is confident in His immutable victory, as sure as your last breath. God has won.

It is okay to remind God of who He is according to His word, especially when things are tough. As stated in:

"Put me in remembrance; let us plead together; declare thou, that thou mayest be justified" (Isaiah 43:26).

He is: Jehovah–Sabaoth
Lord of Hosts
Blessings

FATHER'S DAY

June 19

Sing unto God, sing praises to his name: extol him that rideth upon the heavens by his name JAH, and rejoice before him.
A Father of the fatherless and a judge of the widows is God in his holy habitation. 6 God setteth the solitary in families: he bringeth out those bound with chains: but the rebellious dwell in a dry land.

Psalm 68:4–6

I thank God that we can live in a country where we can praise His name, JAH. JAH comes from the Hebrew word *YAW*, which means "The Lord Most Vehement." The definition of Vehement is "forceful, passionate, or intense, with great feeling." This title declares God's intense and passionate love for us and His desire to see us overcome all obstacles.

In these verses, we can find comfort and promise that God will deliver us from what we are going through. If you are a widow, praise God, for He is a judge on your behalf and will look out for you and take care of you. If you are lonely, God will set you up in a family. The chains represent sin, addictions, and challenging obstacles we can't overcome without His help.

He is: Jah
The Lord Most Vehement!
Blessings

FREE FROM FEAR

June 20

"And when Herod would have brought him forth, the same night Peter was sleeping between two soldiers, bound with two chains: and the keepers before the door kept the prison."

Acts 12:6

King Herod was on a killing spree and had already executed the apostle James. His sights are now set on killing Peter. Despite his evil intentions, the church was praying for Peter's release. Their prayers were so powerful that Jesus sent one of His angels to rescue Peter from the prison.

When Peter arrived at the front gate, a young girl named Rhoda recognized him and ran back to the house to tell the praying people. They didn't believe her, thinking she was either mistaken or crazy. They even suggested it might be Peter's angel, as if Peter had already passed away.

This lack of faith raises the question, who had faith in this situation? The answer is Peter did! He was facing certain death, with sixteen guards charged with keeping him in prison and two soldiers bound to him with chains on either side. Yet, he was sound asleep. This peace and confidence could only come from faith in God.

The angel had to kick Peter in the side to wake him up! When Peter came to the gate, he was greeted by a young girl, a girl of nobility who recognized him. A stark contrast to his earlier denial of Christ to a servant girl when he was filled with fear. Now, Peter was a changed man, no longer afraid of death. He had become the Apostle that Jesus called him to be.

Jehovah-Palat, the Deliverer, had set Peter free from the chains of sin and fear. And just as Peter was set free, so can we all be set free through our faith in Jesus Christ.

He is: Jehovah-Palat
Deliverer
Blessings

JESUS IS THE CAPTAIN

June 21

*"Thou rulest the raging of the sea: when the waves
thereof arise, thou stillest them."*

Psalm 89:9

Psalm 89 speaks to the authority and power of Jesus over the ocean. Jesus's command is beautifully demonstrated in Mark 4:39, *where Jesus stills a raging storm on the sea with just a word.*

It's interesting to note that most of us would have rebuked the waves instead of the wind when faced with tumultuous waves. However, Jesus always knows the root of the problem; in this case, it was the wind.

I heard about a sixth-grade teacher who took his students to see the movie Titanic to find a solution to save the passengers. Their solution was simple yet practical—they suggested turning the ship around in a circular motion, throwing everything that could float into the inner circle between the ship and the iceberg, then mooring alongside the iceberg and anchoring to it. This solution would have changed the outcome if only the captain had thought to pray and ask God for an answer.

The enemy often tries to convince us that there is only one downbeat ending to our problems. But as Christians, we have Jesus as the author and finisher of our faith, and He is the one who writes the best-selling book in world history. Just like Jesus anchored His body to the cross, which many saw as death, to produce everlasting life, we, too, can anchor ourselves to Jesus when our problems seem insurmountable.

He is: Qeren Yesha'
Horn of My Salvation
Blessings

GET IN SHAPE

June 22

"But now, oh Lord, thou art our Father; we are the clay, and thou our potter; and we all are the work of thy hand."

Isaiah 64:8

Christians may feel nervous when they read this verse, and that's understandable. Being molded is a complex and painful process. However, we should view this process from Jesus' perspective. Jesus has likely pursued us, planned our lives, and positioned the right people to speak or act at the right moments. When we finally accept Jesus as our Lord and Savior, it's time to get serious about our gospel growth. And so, Jesus starts from scratch, molding us like a potter and his clay.

When I first accepted Jesus as my Lord and Savior, I asked for a word from God, and He gave me: "Perseverance." At the time, I was surprised and wanted miracles and an easy life, but the difficulties continued. However, my faith and fortitude grew with each trial, and I learned to trust that God would see me through.

God molds us into the vessels He desires, some for honor and some for dishonor. To become a vessel of honor, we must avoid immorality. Then, like an object in a furnace, we will reveal our beauty during the most challenging seasons of our lives through acts of kindness and love. And this is what God is looking for.

He is: Yaw-Tsar
Potter
Blessings

STAND STILL AND FIND YOUR ANSWER

June 23

"And Moses said unto them, stand still, and I will hear what the Lord will command concerning you."

Numbers 9:8

Have you ever found yourself in a situation where you don't know what to do? Moses learned this approach: stand still and listen to God's words. It can be challenging to remain calm when all the world's stresses are hitting you simultaneously, like when every customer wants the same product now, and you can't seem to deliver. But take a moment and ask God how to get the job done. You will be amazed at what He can suggest. More often than not, the solution is already in your possession, and stress hinders you from seeing it.

I once had to change the brakes on my car, but the new brake pads wouldn't fit. I prayed for a solution but still couldn't figure it out. Finally, I took a break and had a ham sandwich. And then it came to me: the cylinder must not be completely depressed. I had the idea to use a clamp I had in the shop for woodworking and a piece of wood, and it worked.

It was a good sandwich, but I wonder if the idea came from between the two slices of bread. I had taken a moment to relax, allowing God to give me the idea.

So, take a moment to ask God, get quiet with Him, and He will answer.

He is: Gelah Raz
Revealer of Mysteries
Blessings

SPIRITUAL HOUSE CLEANING

June 24

"Neither shalt thou bring an abomination into thine house, lest thou be a cursed thing like it: but thou shalt utterly detest it, and thou shalt utterly abhor it; for it is a cursed thing."

Deuteronomy 7:26

Deuteronomy is known as the "Book of Obedience." Delivered to and written by Moses, it outlines principles for a blessed life. What classifies as an abomination? An abomination is morally disgusting, such as pornography, but more importantly, something God hates. Certain cultures will practice abominable religions and then give you an artifact that appears harmless, but is it? No.

At a yard sale once, I saw a picture with a beautiful Indian lady on it. It was round and had lovely feathers hanging off it. I thought, *I know someone who has things like this in their home. I'll get it for them.* I hung it from a hook on the ceiling in my den.

Shortly after this, I felt my prayers were not going anywhere, as if they were not going past my ceiling (my den was where I always prayed and studied). One of my son's friends came into the house and noticed the picture, and he told me it was called a dream catcher.

One morning, I sat down to read my Bible. I quickly fanned the pages from the back to the front and read the words in perfect order: "You have a demon!" I was shocked. I looked at the dream catcher and thought, *I need to call someone.* I called a lady that I knew and asked her about it. She said, "Scott, you need to get that out of your house right now because they pray evil spirits into those objects!"

Enough said. I started praying, took it down from the ceiling, and carried it to the trash. As I walked, I saw the lady's countenance change into complete anger! I said, "I'm not giving you a chance to get into somebody else's home!" I broke it over my knee and immediately felt the atmosphere *break*! Instantly, peace entered my home.

An evil spirit was no longer hindering my prayers. If you feel your prayers are blocked, it may be time you do some spiritual house cleaning. Objects like horoscopes and certain types of music can usher them in. They are keys that the enemy uses to gain entrance into your home or your life. It can be challenging because, possibly, a friend or family member gave it to you.

He is: Sar-Shalom
Prince of Peace
Blessings

WALKING YOUR PERSONAL ROAD

June 25

Delivering thee from the people, and from the gentiles, unto whom now I send thee. To open their eyes, and to turn them from darkness to light, and from the power of Satan unto God, that they may receive forgiveness of sins, and inheritance among them which are sanctified by faith that is in Me.

Acts 26:17–18

Jesus commissioned Saul on the road to Damascus and is now being sent out to the Gentiles to preach the gospel. If you look at Saul's conversion, you will notice that most of his trouble came from his native people.

The number one fear of people is public speaking, but when we peel back this fear, we can see the real worry is not public speaking but the fear of what is called ostracization, of being excluded from society. It is especially true for Muslims who convert to Christianity. They can lose everything: family, friends, and even their life. Satan uses ostracization to build his empire and will use it against you, too.

When Christians are first born again, they face adversity from their well-meaning family members who don't understand the transfer of power. Satan's power is hate-based, while God's power is love-centered and centered on you. What does Jesus mean when He says, "and to turn them from darkness…"?

The word "darkness" comes from the Greek *skotos*, which means obscurity, the state of being unknown, inconspicuous, or unimportant. Obscurity is where the enemy wants you to be, but God wants you to be a light that all can see.

"Neither do men light a candle, and put it under a bushel, but on a candlestick; and it giveth light unto all that are in the house" (Matthew 5:15).

You are now the light in the room, and your life may be the only light in your room, so let yourself shine.

He is: El Yeshuati
The God of My Salvation
Blessings

"I AM" YOUR CIRCUMSTANCE

June 26

"Ah, Lord God! Behold, thou hast made the heaven and the earth by thy great power and stretched out arm, and there is nothing too hard for thee."

Jeremiah 32:17

I always seem to limit God to my understanding of how things work. For some reason, He doesn't have a problem handling my problems. I recently read this, "If God is leading you into troubled waters, it's because your enemy can't swim."

In 1869, John Wesley Powell conducted the first expedition down the Colorado River inside the Grand Canyon. Powell had grown up on the Mississippi River and was well experienced with dangerous waters.

However, the rapids of the Colorado River were unnerving to some of his crew. Three of his men decided the rapids ahead were too rough to navigate. The men decided to hike out of the canyon and make the rest of the journey on foot.

Powell and the rest of his team forged ahead. The rapids that looked so rough weren't as fierce as they appeared; they had been through worse, and after this, the sailing was much easier than before. They went on to complete their expedition and won the journey.

As for the three men that hiked out, sad to say, they were never seen again, more than likely killed by hostiles. Ironically, safety was in the rapids. Sometimes, the boat ride can be challenging.

If God has brought you into a situation or allowed you to get there, it is for a reason, and remember this verse: "For with God Nothing shall be impossible..." (Luke 1:37)

He is: YAH
"I AM"
Blessings

WRITE YOUR OWN BOOK

June 27

And I heard a voice from heaven saying unto me, Write, Blessed are the dead which die in the Lord from henceforth: Yea, saith the Spirit, that they may rest from their labors; and their works do follow them.

Revelation 14:13

The Holy Spirit is directing the Apostle John to write these words, which offer assurance and the order of the blessing. It is noted that rest comes immediately upon a saint's death; their labor is over, and their works follow them. Works done for the Lord are recorded in the "Book of Life" or "Book of Acts."

I once had a vision of a hand fanning through pages in a ringed binder. The Lord asked, "Do you know what this is, Scott?" My reply was, "No, Sir." Then, the Lord said, "This is the Book of Life, your life, Scott." I wish there had been a couple hundred more pages in the book, but perhaps they use a smaller font in heaven? Now that I think about it, they must use a tiny font, microfilm. In that case, it was undoubtedly a novel.

Revelation 20:12 states,

"And I saw the dead, great and small, stand before God; and the books were opened: and another book was opened; which is the book of life; and the dead were judged by those things which were written in the books, according to their works."

Works follow a person into heaven, like cars behind a train. However, it's important to remember that you can do nothing of value unless through Christ, which will be a testament to a person's faith in Christ.

The Holy Spirit once told me, "Acts of audacity in faith are recorded for posterity." Bold acts of faith are recorded for future generations.

He is: Basileus Hagios
King of Saints
Blessings

FOR HIS NAME

June 28

And he sent and beheaded John in the prison.
And his head was brought in a charger, and given to the damsel:
and she brought it to her mother.
And his disciples came, and took up the body, and buried it,
and went and told Jesus.
There was only one greater prophet than John the Baptist, and that was Jesus.
The devil could not stand him, or is it that the devil could not withstand him? John
created a wave of revival, so the devil made a wave of retaliation. Opposition
was so significant that it cost him his life. Not surprisingly, he used the
one thing that he could to kill John with, and that was his integrity.
The character of this great prophet is second to none.

Matthew 14:10–12

When John stood before King Herod concerning his brother Philip's wife, he sternly told him, "It is not lawful for you to have her!" Herod was an adulterer, and the truth was standing before him in his way.

John was cast into prison, and King Herod would come and talk to John about the law. The anointing of the Holy Spirit was with John, which attracted King Herod. But to keep his oath, he still had John beheaded. King Herod had a worldly sense of integrity, while John had holy integrity.

People tend to read over the last verse in Matthew 14:12: "And his disciples came, and took up the body, and buried it, and went and told Jesus." It was no small thing for them to pick up John's body and bury him. By Mosaic law, they were required to ceremonially wash and remain outside the city walls for seven days until considered clean. Seven days passed, and they asked, "Now, what do we do? Where do we go?" They had followed John's revival and helped him in his ministry of repentance.

It would be best if you did the same thing should tragedy strike. John's disciples turned to Jesus and unknowingly began a new ministry. Although not much is known about them in the Bible, we can observe that these men were not seeking fame. They wanted to serve. Scholars believe that they were among the seventy sent out later in Jesus's ministry to witness the gospel and, in a way, resurrected. Indeed, they were men of honor and sacrifice.

He is: Jehovah-Go'el
My Redeemer
Blessings

BLENDER LIKE FAITH

June 29

"Therefore, I remind you to stir up the gift of God that is within you, which was given to you through the laying on of my hands."

2 Timothy 1:6

The Apostle Paul had trained Timothy to be a missionary and pastor. I can imagine the day Paul placed his hands on Timothy and prayed for him, imparting a spiritual gift. Then, he sent him out on the Great Commission. Part of Paul's heart must have gone with Timothy that day.

I have had great men of God pray for me in the past, and it is humbling to think that someone from a previous generation placed their hand on me and prayed, just like the generations before them, going back to the hands of Paul or even Jesus.

The churches in Asia were departing from the true gospel and leaving behind the gospel of grace for a false gospel of legalism. Timothy must have been exhausted from all his hard labor, only to have it thwarted by people who could not accept the gospel of Jesus.

Paul encouraged Timothy to use the gifts placed within him and to stir them up. He reminded Timothy that his mother and grandmother had great faith and passed it down to him. Can you think of a relative who may have prayed for you and passed the faith on to you, a friend, or a pastor?

When you are exhausted and feel like you have nothing more to give, stir up the Holy Spirit within you through praise and prayer. You have a miracle within you, and someone needs it.

He is: YAHWEH YIREH
The Lord Will Provide
Blessings

THE LORD HATH NEED OF YOU

June 30

Saying, Go ye into the village over against you; in the which at your entering ye shall find a colt tied, whereon yet never a man sat: loose him, and bring him hither. And if any man ask you, Why do ye loose him? thus shall ye say unto him, Because the Lord hath need of him.

Luke 19:30–31

I noticed that the disciples didn't ask any questions or doubt that the colt would be there. They just did it, followed his instructions, saying nothing more, nothing less, and the owners let them take it.

Yesterday, I was praying for a man, and the Holy Spirit said, "Protect him in his night runs." When I prayed, I added three more words, the Holy Spirit quickly corrected me, "I said, 'Protect him in his night runs.'"

I asked the man if that meant anything to him, and he was very excited and said, "Yes, it did." Three more words, and it would have meant nothing to him. The meaning would have been changed and worthless. It's important to be obedient to the word given. We can see that the disciples followed His instructions and learned obedience.

Here is a brief timeline of the events before, during, and after in the book of Luke.

Jesus spoke in parables, comparing life to heaven, the kingdom of God. He gave a directive, loosed a bound colt, cleaned house (the temple), and tested.

Bound by our circumstances, and like the colt tied to the fence, the Lord sends the Holy Spirit to us as a witness. His words can set you free and loosen the knots of sin the enemy has used to bind you. Jesus releases you from your bondage and cleanses your past. Initially, it's a joyful ride, and everything seems new and wonderful. Then comes the cleaning process, followed by testing. This little donkey teaches us how to be led to our destiny, and suddenly, things begin to change.

He is: Adonai
Sovereign, Lord, Master, Owner
Blessings

TAKE YOUR REAL ESTATE

July 1

"But that which ye have, hold fast till I come. And he that overcometh, and keepeth my works unto the end, to him will I give power over the nations."

Revelation 2:25–26

General Patton said, "I don't like to pay twice for the same real estate!" I know more than anyone what it's like to want to quit and give up when it comes to serving the Lord, throw in the towel, and ride the pew until the rapture. Hebrews 10:38 says, "If they shrink back, God will have no pleasure in them." This verse alone should motivate us to strive to be better Christians.

The word "power" in this verse comes from the Greek word *exousia*, which means "a sense of ability, delegated authority, potentate, a monarch, or a ruler." But what does the term "nations" mean? "Our struggle is not against flesh and blood but against the rulers, authorities, powers of this dark world, and spiritual forces of evil in the heavenly realms" (Ephesians 6:12).

When we pray, we take the fight to the heavenlies and overcome, holding our spiritual ground. If the enemy tells us that we're not making a difference, it's because we are. If we weren't, he wouldn't waste his time trying to discourage us. So, let's keep up the good work and hold fast to what we have.

He is: El Yeshuati
The God of My Salvation (Victory)
Blessings

PASSING GRADE

July 2

"For though you might have ten thousand instructors in Christ, yet you do not have many fathers; for in Christ Jesus, I have begotten you through the gospel. Therefore, I urge you, imitate me."

1 Corinthians 4:15–16

I listened to an evangelist tell a story about two men playing pool. One man was an excellent pool player. As they played together, the man was amazed at how good his friend was, and he remarked: "You're really good! You should go pro." His friend replied, "Oh, I'm not good enough to be a pro; I'm a B-level player at best."

The man said, "I don't know, you look like an A-level player to me." His friend replied, "That's because you have never seen an A-level pool player."

This message stuck with me for days and struck a core in my heart. I knew I was a C-level Christian at best. I would think about this message while I worked. I had never won any awards, always on the losing sports teams. During the same period of time, I set out to win my company's Employee of the Month award. For six or seven months straight, I performed, I led the company in new sales every month, but someone else always received the award, no matter how hard I worked. It was frustrating, then one day, as I was about to leave, I overheard another salesman congratulate my friend and fellow salesman, Don, for winning the Employee of the Month award. Don was so gracious he whispered to the man, "Shhh! I don't want Scott to know it would hurt his feelings. He tried so hard to win this." He hadn't even placed it on his desk out of consideration for my feelings. In the first month, someone beat me in new sales and only by a margin of two new customers.

I silently slunk out of the office on a Friday afternoon to head home. Sometime during the week before this, when my mind wasn't thinking about polishing the coveted award. I had prayed and asked God if I could spend a day with an A-level Christian. The only man I knew who filled this category was my pastor, Brother Lee Lamury, a man of great faith and accomplishment. I asked God if I could spend a day with Brother Lee. I remember thinking it was a wasted prayer because Brother Lee was so busy, and who was I?

Sunday prior, Brother Lee announced that he needed several men from the church to come in on Saturday and help with some much-needed work. We had the best men of Christ I had ever known, and this body of men enjoyed stepping up to do work for the Lord whenever the opportunity arose, without fail.

I arrived on Saturday morning, Brother Jerry Harvey, Brother Lee, and no one else. We waited awhile, and Brother Harvey had things he had to do, so Brother Lee wanted me to work with him that day. As we worked together, I knew the Lord had answered my prayer. I noticed Brother Lee was a man of deep thought and little talk. I could tell he was deeply bothered that no one arrived to help out, but he never said anything, and I could sense it somehow. As we worked together, he shared success principles with me governing work ethics, "Five minutes of preparation for a job can save you forty-five minutes of work" and more. He spoke with me about leadership.

I was afraid to tell him about my selfish prayer. While driving, I told him about not getting the award, how deeply it hurt, and how hard I had tried.

He thought momentarily and said, "Sometimes God will test you to see how you will handle defeat so that He can reward you more in the future."

As we were about to leave for the day, I could tell he was very concerned about why no one had come. He excused himself for a moment, went to a backroom in the church, and prayed. Moments later, he came out of the room, and his face was brilliantly shining, brimming with a smile from ear to ear. He walked up to me, shook my hand, and said: "I'm glad I was able to spend the day with you!"

The Lord had told him my prayer and answered mine. The following Monday, I walked into work and congratulated my friend Don for the award and how happy I was for him to receive it.

I never did receive that award as a salesman, but two years later, I was promoted to branch manager. My branch won twelve awards at the company banquet that year, almost a clean sweep of every award the company had to offer, and it was my honor to stand in the grand ballroom of the Hilton Hotel and present my friend Don with the "Employee of the Year Award."

Oh, and by the way, I won Branch Manager of the Year.

I encourage you to find a real Father in the Lord and imitate Him; the principles are for your success in life and success in Christ.

He is: El Deah
The God of All Knowledge
Blessings

JESUS NEVER FAILS

July 3

"Beareth all things, believeth all things, hopeth all things, endureth all things. Charity (Love) never faileth."

1 Corinthians 13:7–8

Years ago, while living in Louisiana, I stopped at the Sears store to pick up something I had ordered. As I was waiting for the item to be delivered, I started a conversation with a young man from Pakistan. He was missing an arm from the shoulder. He told me that he was going to college and was excited about his new bike since he walked a couple of miles to campus every day.

I thought about it for a moment and then asked him, "How are you going to get the bike home?" He said, "I'll just ride it from here; it's not that far." I explained that I didn't think that this bike came put entirely together because it was being shipped to this location.

Almost as if on cue, a few moments later, the bike came out in a huge box. The shocked look said it all: the young man was stranded, and there was no way he could carry that box home having just one arm. I told him not to worry; I would be glad to give him a ride, so we loaded the bike in the trunk of my car and drove him to his apartment.

Along the way, he told me he was working his way through college, hoping for a better future back home. I was struck most by his determination, self-independence, and polite personality. When I dropped him off at his apartment, I asked him how he would put the bike together and if he would like me to come to help him assemble it.

He declined, said he would be able to do it, and sincerely thanked me for my help. As tears welled up in my eyes, I thought, *No, thank you.*

I learned a lesson in humility and determination from him that I have never forgotten.

Jesus Christ is love (charity). He bears all things, He believeth all things (this means He believes in you, He knows what you can be and what you can be), He created all things, and He will never fail you!

Because despite what the world has to say about you, *love never fails*, and Jesus Christ is love.

He is: Elohim Ahavah
The God Who Loves
Blessings

GOD'S CAMPAIGN PROMISE

July 4

If my people, which are called by my name, shall humble themselves, and pray, and seek my face, and turn from their wicked ways; then will I hear from heaven, and will forgive their sin, and will heal their land.

2 Chronicles 7:14

If I were to ever run for president, this would be the first line in my national economic plan. My strategy to get elected.

One president yells, "Change!" another "Make America Great Again!" I would yell: "Second Chronicles 7:14."

You see, it's not up to the president to change our country. It's up to the people. We the people need to change our hearts. Fortunately, God has brought this down to a personal level, giving everyone the ability to ask for His help in their time of need.

For several years, I set up signs on the side of the road and prayed for people. My pastor, Paul, said it best, "How much hurt can a person be going through that they would drive up to a stranger and ask for prayer? The answer is a lot."

He understood what the Lord was doing. I witnessed it first-hand time and time again: people completely broken, with no way out, receive a miracle from God.

Why? Because, at a certain point, they humbled themselves, putting away their pride, asking God for help. He's a God of second chances.

He is: El-Moshaah
The God Who Saves
Blessings

QUIET HOPE

July 5

This I recall to my mind, therefore have I hope. It is of the LORD'S mercies that we are not consumed, because his compassions fail not. They are new every morning: great is thy faithfulness. The LORD is my portion, saith my soul; therefore will I hope in him. The LORD is good unto them that wait for him, to the soul that seeketh him. It is good that a man should both hope and quietly wait for the salvation of the LORD.

Lamentations 3:21–26

Jeremiah penned the book of Lamentations around 586 B.C. Jeremiah, the prophet in his grief, sought a place to mourn as he watched the army of the Chaldeans destroy Jerusalem and the Temple Mount.

He landed here at this place, a rock formation that had a long history. When approaching from a distance, it looks like a human skull, and its original name was Golgotha.

On this day, it took on another name, "Jeremiah's Grotto," meaning a small picturesque cave.

I wonder if he knew it was the same place that Abraham offered Isaac, his only son, some 1260 years earlier? (Genesis 22)

Abraham traveled for three days before he came upon this strange-looking grotto, where Isaac carried the wood on his back, just like Jesus did when He arrived at the same spot 616 years later, the place we call *Calvary*.

Sometimes, we suffer and don't understand why, but somehow, Jeremiah, a man who suffered more than almost any other prophet, wandered here, the final place of salvation. As his tears fell to the ground, he wrote this:

"It is good that a man should both hope and quietly wait for the salvation of the LORD" (Lamentations 3:26).

At the time, you probably don't understand why you're going through this, or your friend or family member is suffering. It could be that their tears may fall on an altar, a holy place where God Himself will bring someone you love to the foot of the cross.

"Thou tellest my wanderings: put thou my tears into thy bottle: are they not in thy book?" (Psalm 56:8)

Hope in God. One day, He will turn the page in Thy Book and remember your tears.

He is: El Yeshuati: God of My Salvation Blessings

BRUISED REEDS

July 6

"A bruised reed shall he not break, and the smoking flax shall he not quench: he shall bring forth judgment unto truth."

Isaiah 42:3

What exactly is a *bruised reed*? Reeds are found in the Middle East, and they grow three to five feet tall. They are hollow in the middle and are related to sugar cane. Egyptians considered reeds to be a symbol of grace. When the temperatures climb, they slump over, and as the day cools off, they rise back up. I've read that it's pleasant to sit and watch this in the afternoons.

This type of hollow reed makes a good flute, flutes that lasted for generations. A shepherd boy could have a flute made by his grandfather and passed down to him, and they cherished it. Sometimes, a reed would get dropped to the ground and possibly broken. The reed was called a *bruised reed*.

You can almost visualize a young shepherd boy breaking his flute, bringing it home to his mother, and asking her to fix it. The mother would not cast it out. She would fix it with a string and some wax. Maybe it would sound a little different, have a different tone, but it could still play. It could perhaps even sound better. Times come in life when circumstances have beaten us down, and the enemy will constantly try and tell you that you are a failure, remind you of all your past mistakes.

"All that the Father giveth me shall come to me; and him that cometh to me I will in no wise cast out" (John 6:37).

At this point, you can start to feel burned out, just like smoking flax, a smoldering candlewick, and the smoking flax shall he not quench:

The breath of life, sometimes we need Jesus to breathe the *"breath of life"* back into us and re-light the fire.

"…he shall bring forth judgment unto truth."

Judgment means a favorable or unfavorable verdict on our behalf

Truth comes from the Hebrew word *emeth*, which means "certainty, assured, faithful, and true."

"For his anger endureth but a moment; in his favour is life: weeping may endure for a night, but joy cometh in the morning" (Psalm 30:5).

Believe me; God knows all the circumstances.

He is: Yahweh Channum
God of Grace
Blessings

THE PRAYER OF FAITH

July 7

*Is any among you afflicted? let him pray. Is any merry? let him sing psalms.
Is any sick among you? let him call for the elders of the church; and let them pray
over him, anointing him with oil in the name of the Lord:
And the prayer of faith shall save the sick, and the Lord shall raise him up; and if
he have committed sins, they shall be forgiven him.
Confess your faults one to another, and pray one for another, that ye may be
healed—the effectual fervent prayer of a righteous man availeth much.*

James 5:13–16

These verses are called "The Prayer of Faith." It's like the formula for Christians when it comes to prayer.

1. Having a bad day: Pray.

2. Having a good day: Sing.

3. Having sickness: Get oil, have the elder pray.

4. Having sinned: Confess.

"And the prayer of faith shall save the sick." The prayer of faith is much simpler than you think. When I first started stepping out and praying for people, I was consumed with having enough faith for my prayers to get answered for others. What would people think if I prayed for them and nothing happened? Well, I know the answer now: if nothing happened, nothing would have happened.

Then, one day, I just decided, "God, this is on You. If I pray for someone, there's nothing I can do to make it happen; only You can make it happen." My attitude was that it was God's problem now. Unknowingly, I stumbled into faith, and you see, I had placed my faith in God simply by giving it over to Him.

"The effectual fervent prayer of a righteous man availeth much."

Another time I was having a particular problem with sin, I spoke with some elders in the church, and they pointed out that my problem wasn't with sin; it was with something else. It was like they stood back from the forest, and they could see the trees, and I was in the middle of the woods. The sense of relief was immediate, and I was set free from guilt. Because they prayed effectually and in faith, the Lord revealed the truth. If your elders are filled with The Holy Spirit, you will get your healing.

"If the Son, therefore, shall set you free, ye shall be free indeed" (John 8:36).

He is: Jehovah-Rapha
The Lord Who Heals
Blessings

A WORD TO RUN WITH TODAY

July 8

And Jesus answering saith unto them, Have faith in God.

For verily I say unto you, That whosoever shall say unto this mountain, Be thou removed, and be thou cast into the sea; and shall not doubt in his heart, but shall believe that those things which he saith shall come to pass; he shall have whatsoever he saith.

> *Therefore I say unto you, What things so ever ye desire, when ye pray, believe that ye receive them, and ye shall have them.*
>
> *And when ye stand praying, forgive, if ye have ought against any : that your Father also which is in heaven may forgive you your trespasses.*
>
> *But if ye do not forgive, neither will your Father which is in heaven forgive your trespasses.*

Mark 11:22–26

If I were a baker, this recipe would be in my files, with a list of ingredients:

1. Faith in God—As much as possible.
2. Mountain—The bigger, the better.
3. No doubt in your heart—See rule 1.
4. Believe—Expect a "suddenly."
5. Forgiveness—Lay it aside, yield it up.
6. *Ought* against *Any*—Past tense, see rule 5.

Miracle instructions:

Use a mixing bowl that equals the size of your heart and mind combined.

Step One: Have faith in God, pray a lot, believe a lot.

Step Two: Discard Mountain. It is from the Greek word *Or'-os;* this word is obsolete, and God already considers it gone.

Step Three: Remove all doubt, use as needed: "Trust in The Lord with all your heart, and lean not unto your own understanding" (Proverbs 3:5).

Step Four: Add more belief. Note: you cannot over-saturate. Use John 14:1. "Let not your heart be troubled: ye believe in God, believe also in me."

Step Five: Forgiveness comes from the Greek word *af-ee'-ay-mee*. It means "to send forth, or lay it aside, leave it alone, send it away, or, my favorite, yield it up," which equals a full measure of giving it up to God.

Step Six: *Ought* against *Any*: Ought and Any come from the same Greek word *Ti's*, which means any person, place, or thing. Anything that you dislike or have unforgiveness.

You only must use ingredients 1 and 4. Other elements need to be discarded, or the miracle could be delayed or blocked.

I hope you have a mountain-moving experience!

He is: Elohim Yare
God Most Awesome
Blessings

YOUR FATHER'S CALLING

July 9

"For all the promises of God in Him are yea, and in Him Amen, unto the glory of God by us. Now He which stablisheth us with you in Christ, and hath anointed us, is God".

2 Corinthians 1:20–21

Now, reread this, but this time, insert your name at the beginning and read it out loud: _____ _____ for all the promises in Him are yes! And so be it!

It's okay to personalize your word of God. I'm sure He wants it that way. His answer is yes, and your fulfilled calling in God brings glory to Him. How can your life bring glory to God? Regardless of age, God has a plan for you, and Your delay does not catch him off guard. It will be a more remarkable testimony to God if you take hold of your promise.

"Now He which stablisheth us…"

Paul is speaking about the Holy Spirit, who brought you to Christ; Christ brings you to the Father, and the Father anoints you. "Anoint" in Greek means to furnish what is needed.

You may have a lifetime of skills and abilities stored up in your life experiences, and they will probably all be needed for your task. Ask the Lord: "What do You want me to be in this period of my life for You?" I promise He will answer.

He is: Yotzerenu
Potter
Blessings

FALSE FLAGS

July 10

"But in all things approving ourselves as the ministers of God, in much patience, in afflictions, in necessities, in distresses."

2 Corinthians 6:4

The first word in this sentence is "but." In this context, it means contrast, strikingly different, opposing one another. And with this one word, Paul is opposing the verse before:

"Giving no offense in any thing, that the ministry be not blamed" (2 Corinthians 6:3).

Not giving offense in the ministry, a thing that is judged to be an insult or go against your moral standards in the ministry. But here is the paradox: we approve ourselves.

Have you ever made a mistake, and no one knew, but you beat yourself up over it time and time again? I have; this is a standard (i.e., a flag or a banner in our mind) that we have set against ourselves. I know by doing a live radio broadcast, I have said things that weren't quite correct. For that matter, I have done some things that were blatantly wrong after I became a Christian. In my mind, I hold myself to a very high standard, but I can never live up to the standard I have set, let alone the standard that Jesus set.

We live in a world full of contradictions. I preach forgiveness, but I struggle with forgiveness. I've said these very words: "But Lord, You know what they did to me." At this point, I can only ask Jesus to help me forgive them because I can't. But the one person I struggle with forgiving the most is myself.

Paul goes on to say, in much patience, in afflictions, in necessities, in distresses,

And here, tucked away in this verse, is a unique word that we can easily overlook: necessities.

Necessities are needs that you have, and we need to forgive by necessity to keep the ministry from being blamed.

Then, he follows it with the words "in distresses." How distressful it is when we don't forgive ourselves. We self-*afflict*, and by this, we cause our distress. But Jesus will help us if we ask. He gave us this assurance:

"But my God shall supply all your need according to his riches in glory by Christ Jesus" (Philippians 4:19).

He is: Elohay Selichot
The God Who Is Ready to Forgive
Blessings

BREAK FORTH

July 11

*The Philistines also came and spread themselves in the valley of Rephaim.
And David enquired of the LORD, saying, Shall I go up to the Philistines? wilt thou
deliver them into mine hand? And the LORD said unto David, Go up: for I will
doubtless deliver the Philistines into thine hand.
And David came to Baalperazim, and David smote them there, and said, The
LORD hath broken forth upon mine enemies before me, as the breach of waters.
Therefore he called the name of that place Baalperazim.*

2 Samuel 5:18–20

David was recently anointed as king over Israel, and immediately, the enemy set up an attack. Have you ever noticed that you can achieve something in life, and immediately, there's a new obstacle in your way? Good chance it's the enemy trying to steal your victory.

The enemy's first tactic is to make himself appear more significant than he is. In this case, the Philistines set up their army in *the Valley of Rephaim*, which, interpreted, means *the Valley of Giant*s. It is also the only route the Philistines could take into Jerusalem. But it's the same place where Jonathan and his armor-bearer defeated them. The enemy had to start from a place of defeat. His last defeat was your most recent victory.

Notice King David, after hearing the intel, "David goes straight to the LORD," David is a prophet, and this is why the LORD's name is in all caps; he hears directly from Father God. Father God gives him total assurance concerning his victory. God didn't promote you to fail; in fact, you are looking at the enemy from your victory.

David went up and fought the battle, and I can picture King David directing his army and seeing his men swath through the enemy like a dam's wall breaking. That's why he named it Baalperazim, which means "as the breach of waters."

Get a word from God, a word to go on. Let Him break forth your circumstances.

He is: Jehovah Gibbor Milchamah
Mighty in Battle
Blessings

FRIENDS

July 12

"And the Lord said, Shall I hide from Abraham that thing which I do?"
Genesis 18:17

Of course, this is the famous tent meeting between Abraham and God. God and two of his angels appeared before Abraham, and maybe one was Jesus preincarnate? Some say it was three angels, but the text uses the title LORD in all caps, which translates from the Hebrew word *Yehovah*, which means "God," and indicates that this is the Father God personally.

Why is this important? Because Abraham has become a friend of God, and friends influence friends. God informs Abraham that He is going personally to see for Himself the evil of Sodom and Gomorrah, vs. 21: "I will go down now, and see whether they have done altogether according to the cry of it."

Of course, God already knew what was going on, and He already knew what Abraham would do. But God was looking for someone to intercede on behalf of a wicked city. He came to His friend Abraham for advice. Of course, through Abraham's many miles of travels, God has placed Him here at just this moment; unknown to Abraham, Father God had directed his travels to this very place.

Like your personal prayer time, you may think, "I have to spend some time in prayer," as you start to pray, you may see an image or receive a thought about a person you haven't seen in years. We drift off and think, "I wonder whatever happened to them?"

Did you ever stop to think that God considers you a friend? He's asked the Holy Spirit to have you intercede for that person. When a thought like this happens, take a moment and ask the Holy Spirit, "What do you need me to pray?" Or maybe you know their situation and can intercede on their behalf. What wouldn't you do for a friend? When it comes to Jesus, He gave His life for you, and I'm sure He considers you His friend, a friend that was worth the cost.

He is: Entunchano
The God Who Intercedes
Blessings

BY SHIP OR BY FAITH

July 13

"But not long after there arose against it a tempestuous wind, called: Eu-roc'ly-don."

Acts 27:14

This Bible verse is from the Apostle Paul's journey, in some way, a trip he chose. At this point, he has been in prison for more than two years, then sentenced to sail to Rome for trial. He was placed under the command of a Roman Centurion named Julius.

I'm sure you're familiar with the phrase, "Just when you think it couldn't get any worse." Well, it got worse, with a strong easterly wind that wrecked the ship. But before they set sail, Paul withstood them, telling them that this was going to happen.

In our lives, many times, the Holy Spirit will try and warn us not to do something, and we do it anyway. Then, something terrible happens, on top of all the things we were going through already, and then we think to ourselves, "If only I had listened!"

Paul and 275 other men were cast into the sea that day, but Paul *opposed the storm*!

First, he was bitten by a poisonous viper, with no ill effect. (I'm sure it still hurt.) But then, amazing things began to happen. The island residents started to receive healings when Paul prayed, and for three months, the people housed Paul and his companions. I'm sure that Paul spoke daily to them about Jesus, ministering, and teaching.

None of this would have happened if it weren't for one essential personality trait possessed by Paul: Paul's attitude—something we all need to strive for—*no complaining*.

When you chose Jesus as your Lord, you got the whole package, trials and all, everything designed by the enemy to make you quit serving the Lord. Out of pure hardship and trials, Paul wrote this from his captivity in Rome:

"And we know that all things work together for good to them that love God, to them who are the called according to his purpose" (Romans 8:28).

You can *oppose the storm* with a smile, a good attitude, and the verse from above.

He is: Qeren Yesha
Horn of My Salvation: (Deliverance, Prosperity, Safety, Liberty)
Blessings

YOUR WORD, YOUR LIFE

July 14

"For this reason, holy brothers, called to be partakers of a heavenly calling, consider the Apostle and High Priest of our confession, Christ Jesus".

Hebrews 3:1

I have spent years in sales and attended many sales classes. In sales, you're taught the difference between an open-ended question and a close-ended question. With open-ended questions, you never really know the outcome of the potential answer from a client. There's more than you know. With closed-ended questions, you're getting a "yes" or "no" type answer.

To me, this verse is not closed; it's open-ended, thus giving it more than one meaning. Jesus is the High Priest of our confession as found in:

"That if thou shalt confess with thy mouth the Lord Jesus, and shalt believe in thine heart that God hath raised Him from the dead, thou shalt be saved" (Romans 10:9).

Have you ever considered that Jesus is the High Priest of your confession? A confession of guilt or sin is easy to understand, but what about negative declarations of yourself?

"Your words have been stout against Me, saith the Lord…" (Malachi 3:13)

We need to be careful about the negative words we speak to ourselves, and it can make us our own worst enemy. Things such as "I can't ever get ahead!" or "Everything breaks down on me all the time." You get the point.

Try a week of positive words and see how it goes. Next time you are tempted to say how bad it's going, say something like this instead:

"My God rebukes the devourer for my sake!" (Malachi 3:11)

or

"I can do all things through Christ who strengthens me!" (Phillippians 4:13)

He is: Logos
The Word
Blessings

TRAILS COURSE 101

July 15

Blessed be God, even the Father of our Lord Jesus Christ,
the Father of Mercies, and the God of all comfort;
Who comforteth us in all our tribulation, that we may be able to comfort them
which are in any trouble, by the comfort wherewith we
ourselves are comforted of God.

2 Corinthians 1:3–4

Blessed be God. "Blessed," in this context, means adorable; or an easier way to read is this: "Adorable be our God, also the Father of our Lord Jesus Christ, the Father of compassion, and the God of all comfort."

I think the hidden gem is that the Holy Spirit is also known as the Comforter. This verse implies God Himself directs the Holy Spirit concerning your distress.

He comforts us in all our tribulations or problems so that when we mature as Christians, we can comfort others as well. There was a period in my life where it was just one trial after the other. For years, at one point, it was so hopeless that when I woke up one morning, I couldn't move from the chest down. I was paralyzed by hopelessness. I prayed to Jesus and asked for help, and He strengthened me with hope.

Not long after this experience, a prophetess just out of the blue looked at me. She said: "The reason the Lord allows you to go through so many trials is so that when other people come to you with their problems and ask you for prayer, you will be able to say: 'I know God can deliver you, instead of, "I think He can!"'"

Truthfully, this wasn't the word I wanted to hear; I liked the easy way out. Within the next couple of weeks, I remember three different people just started sharing their problems with me, even in other towns. After telling their stories, I would say to them I've been through that same trial; it was almost word for word what I had been through before.

But when I prayed for them, it was with joy because I knew that the Father of Compassion and Mercies would deliver them.

This trial could be your training for someone extraordinary down the road, and remember:

"Trust in the Lord with thy heart, and lean not to thine own understanding. In all thy ways acknowledge Him, and He shall direct thy paths" (Proverbs 3:5–6).

He is: Theos Pas Paraklesis
The God of All Comfort
Blessings

LOVE, LIBERTY, AND THE CROSS

July 16

*"From henceforth let no man trouble me: for I bear
in my body the marks of the Lord Jesus."*

Galatians 6:17

I think, at this point, Apostle Paul has had enough. Jewish teachers, known as Judiazers, were following Paul. He would establish a church and build them up with the sound doctrine of the New Covenant in Jesus Christ; then, Jewish teachers would show up and try to legalize everyone.

They would teach that you had to be circumcised and you had to follow the teachings of Moses to be a good Christian. Sadly, they were wrong. Paul is so fed-up with this legalism that he lays all the law out in this one crucial verse:

"For all the law is fulfilled in one word, in this; Thou shalt Love thy neighbor as thyself" (Galatians 5:14).

But how is the law fulfilled in this verse? This verse explains it:

"Love worketh no ill to his neighbor: therefore, love is the fulfilling of the law" (Romans 13:10).

Here's the irony: Paul is preaching on *love* and *liberty*. He received 195 lashes to his back, and three times, he was beaten with Rods on his back. Under Mosaic Law, this would have been 117 hits, but the Romans were under no such rule, so it could have been even more, three shipwrecks, in countless perils for his very survival.

Love did not invoke the beatings; it was *liberty*.

"Now the Lord is that Spirit: and where the Spirit of the Lord is, there is Liberty" (2 Corinthians 3:17).

The enemy would send legalism to quench the Spirit of Liberty, and Paul said, "I have the marks to prove my gospel is genuine. I have the experience. All they have is an argument. A man with experience is never at the mercy of a man with an argument."

Now you know why dictators always want to destroy Christianity—because it brings *liberty*, it sets us free from the bondage of sin, and Satan can't stand that.

Love, liberty, and the cross—it's amazing how all three tie together for your salvation.

He is: Or Goyim
Light of the Nations
Blessings

JUDGE, NO JURY

July 17

"And the angels which kept not their first estate, but left their own habitation, he hath reserved in everlasting darkness unto the judgment of the great day."

Jude 1:6

Angels are creations of God, but roughly one-third rebelled against Him, and God cast out of heaven. The angels referred to in Jude 1:6 left their first estate, and these are believed to be the angels mentioned in Genesis 6:1–5. About 200 angels left their angelic state and became human.

According to Genesis, these angels saw that the daughters of men were beautiful and took them as wives. Their children became giants, known as Nephilim, and were known for their wicked deeds. The book of Enoch states that these angels were supposed to intercede on humanity's behalf, but instead, they chose to ravish humankind. Eventually, they asked Enoch to intercede for them, but God gave them eternal damnation. He said, "You were supposed to watch over mankind and intercede on their behalf, but now you want a man to intercede for you?" God sentenced them to live on earth for 500 years before being chained in darkness until the day of judgment. Their children would have the choice to serve God, but if they chose not to live a righteous life, they would become demons and roam the earth until judgment. These are where demons came from human beings, the children of giants who wholly gave themselves over to evil, serving the devil and fallen angels.

Years ago, while on patrol as a police officer, I asked the Lord, "Why do demons have to flee in Your name?" While driving, I had an instant vision. I was pulling up to a burglary in my police unit, and the criminals were running in every direction, fleeing my authority. Because of the name of Jesus, you have the same power. "These signs will accompany those who have believed: in My Name, they will cast out demons, they will speak with new tongues" (Mark 16:17).

Thank God for the name of Jesus!

He is: Shaphat
Judge
Blessings

PURCHASED BY THE CREATOR

July 18

But now thus saith the LORD that created thee, O Jacob, and he that formed thee, O Israel, Fear not: for I have redeemed thee, I have called thee by thy name; thou art mine. When thou passest through the waters, I will be with thee; and through the rivers, they shall not overflow thee: when thou walkest through the fire, thou shalt not be burned; neither shall the flame kindle upon thee.

Isaiah 43:1–2

In the above verse, we see Father God proclaiming an immutable statement about Jacob and Israel. If you recall, Jacob wrestled an angel, and the angel renamed Jacob Israel. Jacob means supplanter, and it refers to governments or rulers, which means to trip up or overthrow. It's what he did to his brother Esau.

The second name is Israel, which means "He will rule as God/Jesus." A symbolic picture of Christ He came and tripped up the nations, taking the authority over governments, and He rules as God.

When Jesus walked on water, the waters did not overflow Him. When He went to hell, the fires could not consume Him.

What does this have to do with our circumstances? Try replacing the names of Jacob and Israel with your first and last name in the scripture and read it out loud. You will feel the sense of comfort and strength needed to get you through today. Can this be relevant? These verses show that all scripture is good and for the edifying:

> *For it is written in the law of Moses, Thou shalt not muzzle the mouth of the ox that treadeth out the corn. Doth God take care for oxen?*
>
> *Or saith he it altogether for our sakes? For our sakes, no doubt, this is written:*

1 Corinthians 9:9–10

God gave us these verses to use in our circumstances, and there's much authority in the written and spoken word; let's continue.

"Fear not." Fear is subtle. It creeps up on you, or it can hit you suddenly. Either way, *fear not*, for God has redeemed you.

"I have redeemed thee," which means that God has repurchased you from slavery or widowhood for a price, and that price was the cost of Jesus.

It's comforting to know that you belong to God. Selah.

He is: Jehovah-Goel
Redeeming God
Blessings

THROUGH HIM

July 19

And he said unto me, My grace is sufficient for thee: for my strength is made perfect in weakness. Most gladly therefore will I rather glory in my infirmities, that the power of Christ may rest upon me.

2 Corinthians 12:9

Jesus reveals to Paul that His strength is made perfect in weakness. Paul goes on to say that he would rather glory in his infirmities. Infirmities originated from the Greek word *astheneia / as-then'-i-ah*; it means "feebleness of body or mind, sickness, or weakness."

I sometimes find myself praying to God for strength when, in fact, I should be praying to God to show His strength in my weakness. When we are young, there seems to be no mountain that we can't climb, and slowly, we start to realize that we can't do everything in one day, that we can't do the entire job by ourselves without help from others.

As you get older, you start to understand that weakness is an opportunity for God to show you who He is. That's why I always end every devotional with the name of God and the word "Blessings."

His names are insights into His character, and by understanding His nature, He can reveal to you who He wants to be for you during trying times in your life. I use "Blessings" instead of "Goodbye" because I want you to *be blessed*, and I want you to possess all the blessings of God!

With this knowledge and through His strength, you will be made strong. Through His strength, you be made glad. Through His strength, you will be able to lift your head.

He is: Rum Rosh
The One Who Lifts My Head
Blessings

GOD GIVES

July 20

And He gave some, apostles; and some, prophets; and some,
evangelists; and some, pastors and teachers;
For the perfecting of the saints, for the work of the ministry,
for the edifying of the body of Christ.

Ephesians 4:11–12

These are the order of the callings in Christ. Jesus starts with the calling of the apostles. Being the most challenging call, it attracts the least number of persons called, and for a good reason. The apostle is an ambassador for Christ. This person should demonstrate the miraculous powers of Christ, for they are sent out as a messenger for God to establish new churches.

The enemy will do everything possible to stop this work. The few apostles that I have met have suffered from extremely harsh conditions on the missionary field, sleeping in chicken coops, beaten and robbed, harshly treated, and dependent on Jesus for their very survival.

Next is the prophet. A more significant number are called, but here is what a true prophet of God goes through. Mostly, they are loners. People don't like to hang around them a lot unless they are successful in the ministry. Often misunderstood, typically, they're not great with other people. When they give prophetic words, you can be sure that people will scream that they're false prophets. The prophetic word makes no sense. They are considered fools by others in the church because God has done away with the office of prophets and apostles, but in the same paragraph, they believe in evangelists, pastors, and teachers.

Next is the evangelist. To me, this was always an elevated position, but many believe it is below the office of pastor, yet that's not how the Bible sees it. To be an evangelist, you will spend hours on the road driving to a church 1000 miles away, preach your heart out, and receive a $50.00 offering— or no offering at all—and out of love for the gospel, you will donate to their ministry. Evangelists quickly learn to trust God for their finances. But they get to sleep in run-down hotels and eat at any restaurant that has a cheap buffet. Loneliness is your closest companion. Sometimes, churches and congregations treat you like gold; others have no etiquette for caring for their guest.

Pastors, well, get ready to have your heart broken time and time again. You will learn how to forgive, and you will learn how to intercede for others. Anytime someone leaves the church, you can be assured it was your fault. You will be constantly asked for money by many people who don't even go to church. People you give to the most will provide the least in return, and your phone will ring at all hours of the night. And then, there's your staff, and your volunteers will all bring their problems to you.

Next but not last is the office of the teacher. Teachers have it made! As I chuckle to myself, to be a teacher in the ministry must be filled with love and an extreme amount of patience. You start a class, and five minutes later, another child arrives, and out of love and concern, you start the course over so they can participate, and then five minutes later, another group of children shows up. Now, a child must go to the restroom, another asks a question, interruption seems to be the theme of the class, time is up, and the parents wonder why their children aren't learning the Bible, which should be taught at home.

They sacrifice their time and some of their lives. Next time you want to shake a hero's hand, start with your pastor.

He is: El Chaiyai
God of My Life
Blessings

RENOVATE YOUR THOUGHTS

July 21

"And be renewed in the spirit of your mind;

And that ye put on the new man, which after God is created in righteousness and true holiness" (Ephesians 4:23–24).

A comparable scripture is:

"And be not conformed to this world: but be ye transformed by the renewing of your mind, that ye may prove what is that good, and acceptable, and perfect, will of God" (Romans 12:2).

Years ago, I was at a men's Bible study; some pastors and other well-known Christian men attended Bible study that evening. A young man new to serving the Lord asked us about this verse. "How do you go about renewing your mind?"

I was much younger than these other Christian men. I sat there and listened to their complex answers; to be honest, I can't recall any of them. I felt like Elihu in the book of Job—too young to give my answer—even though I had been serving the Lord for several years.

As we sat around this table, I could see the look of concern on this young man's facial expression as he was trying to assimilate everything being said. I could tell he was becoming overwhelmed. I noticed another pastor, well respected in the community, was not saying anything either. He looked a little angry at all the answers being given.

Everyone was finished, and confusion reigned. That's when I could take it no more, and the young man was sitting almost directly across from me. I looked at him and said, "To renew your mind, simply read your Bible." Everyone agreed, but it almost seemed like disdain from some of the other men in the room.

Finally, the other pastor, who had remained silent, said: "I want to say this just for the record," he raised his finger and pointed it at me. "I agree with everything that man just said!"

In this day and age, we are so inundated with doctrines from the enemy through media that right and wrong can become a grey area, a fog that dims your understanding.

Renewed means to renovate or even remodel your mind.

Let the Bible and the Holy Spirit be your interior decorator.

He is: Shub Nephesh
Renewer of Life
Blessings

HOW TO ABOUND

July 22

*"But I have all, and abound: I am full, having received of Epaphroditus
the things which were sent from you, an odour of a sweet smell,
a sacrifice acceptable, wellpleasing to God."*

Philippians 4:18

Positionally, this letter is to a group of saved Christians. The Philippian church was founded around 51 AD. St. Luke was the pastor of this church for the first six years. With Luke being the pastor, I'm confident they were doctrinally sound. Paul is writing this letter out of deep gratitude for their offering delivered to him at a high cost. Epaphroditus gave the offering to Paul and almost lost his life during the process.

Paul is enduring hardship for the gospel without complaint, and he has asked no one for help. He worked to supply for his own needs by making prayer shawls and selling them.

I can tell you what has touched Paul's heart so much about this. It's the growth of the church in love.

Some of my children were servers in restaurants, and they would tell me that the most generous tippers were servers from other restaurants. These people worked in the same type of occupation, and because they understood the challenges of serving, they gave more significant tips.

It comes to me as no surprise that St. Luke has raised his church to be generous towards those in need because Luke knew the sacrifice of service. He knew the cost. Maybe Luke even knew the reward.

"Not because I desire a gift: but I desire fruit that may abound to your account" (Philippians 4:17).

Because they have done this, they received fruit to their account. Everyone who sacrificed and gave that day gets a part in this epistle! How many hundreds of millions of people has this letter touched? It's like the best stock investment you could have ever made, and the interest has never stopped.

We can't all be missionaries or pastors, but we can support other ministries, and by doing so, we take part in their reward. Who knows where your fruit will lead on your account?

Jesus does.

He is: Georgos
Gardener
Blessings

PROBLEM-SOLVING

July 23

*"Therefore, brethren, stand fast, and hold the traditions
which ye have been taught, whether by word, or our epistle."*

2 Thessalonians 2:15

In this epistle, Apostle Paul is encouraging his disciples to remain and stand fast in the Lord. He is also setting some people straight in their charity. Unless a man works, he should not eat because people are quitting their day jobs and expecting the church to support them.

Why would people do this? Because they thought the rapture was going to happen at any moment. Now, in this letter, Paul is setting the church straight about timelines. He tells them to stand fast, and this means to be stationary, to persevere. Persevere is a word most Christians don't want to hear. We rather the words *miracle*, *rapture*, and *blessing*.

Paul was letting them know that tough times would come before the return of the Lord and that the "Ap-os-tas-ee'-ah," or the "Falling away," would happen first. *Apostaseeah* means many Christians will give up their faith and probably take the mark of the beast.

But have you ever noticed how many problems Paul dealt with concerning his churches? Indeed, he must have wanted to give up, and he talks about going on to be with the Lord or staying here for our sakes. All his struggles, every church error that needed to be corrected, he wrote in these long letters. How many times did he rest his head in his hands in disbelief?

We can see that he unknowingly was adding to the Old Testament, helping to create the New Testament. He wrote more than half the books!

"Who comforteth us in all our tribulation, that we may be able to comfort them which are in any trouble, by the comfort wherewith we ourselves are comforted of God" (2 Corinthians 1:4).

We have so many problems in our lives to deal with. Maybe God knows your strength, your perseverance, your ability to stand fast and allow Him to be strong on your behalf.

Watch what God can make out of you.

He is: Jehovah Qadash
The Lord Who Sanctifies
Blessings

CHOOSING TO FORGIVE

July 24

"I, even I, am he that blotteth out thy transgressions for mine own sake, and will not remember thy sins. Put me in remembrance: let us plead together: declare thou, that thou mayest be justified."

Isaiah 43:25–26

Father God blots out our sins for His sake. I wish I had His ability to His extent. There have been times when I have spoken to people who severely wronged me (I guess they thought I didn't know what they had done?) Smiling and being as polite as possible, but in my mind, I'm thinking, "Dude! I know what you did!"

I remember a person who was very close to me that hurt me deeply. I prayed and asked God how they could possibly have done this to me. He answered, "They haven't done this to you; they have done it to Me."

Somehow, that helped me to understand that the outward appearance seemed against me, but inwardly, they had committed this sin against God. Knowing this allowed me to think things through from their perspective. They had harbored a very deep unforgiveness towards some people in the church, and their response was self-destruction.

What does this say about us if God forgets our sins for His peace? It says we must forgive and are not allowed to say I can't forget. (Yes, I'm also guilty of refusing to forget.) Forgetting and forgiving, but how? One word: love. "Above all, keep your love for one another constant, for 'love covers a multitude of sins'" (1 Peter 4:8).

Ask Jesus to give you love for that person and place Him in remembrance. I know it's hard, but just maybe God will let you see that person through the eyes of His compassion.

He is: Elohim Shama
The God Who Hears
Blessings

GENERATIONAL FAITH

July 25

"When I call to remembrance the unfeigned faith that is in thee, which dwelt first in thy grandmother Lois, and thy mother Eunice; and I am persuaded that is in thee also."

2 Timothy 1:5

In this letter to his young protégé and pastor, Timothy, Apostle Paul provides a word of encouragement. Paul's command and use of words are superior, reflecting his intellect and holy dispensation in Scripture knowledge. He uses the word as a sword, cutting through to the very heart of any situation. Paul's intelligence, coupled with the anointing of the Holy Spirit, makes him one of the most intelligent men that ever walked the earth.

Let's look at the use of the word unfeigned. Unfeigned originates from the Greek word *an-oo-pok'-ree-tos*. This word originated from another Greek word, *Alpha*, the first letter of the Greek alphabet. It means genuine and sincere. But it is no coincidence that Grandmother Lois's faith, sincerity, and genuineness established her as the Alpha in Timothy's faith.

Interestingly, the lead dog is the Alpha female in a wolf pack. She takes the lead on the hunts or the expeditions, bringing back the meat. Similarly, Grandma Lois brought back the meat of the word, leading Timothy to faith.

We thank God for grandmothers who pray for their children and grandchildren! They can change the course of a family and the eternal destiny of all their lineages. They are staying on their knees or sitting in their rocking chairs, praying for loved ones, and laying up an inheritance for their children's children.

Proverbs 13:22 states, "A good man leaveth an inheritance to his children's children: and the wealth of the sinner is laid up for the just." While we often hear about generational curses, Grandma Lois laid up generations of faith, creating a blueprint for generational faith that her family and others could follow.

You can do the same. God has been around for a long time and has a great memory. He remembers the prayers of His saints.

He is: Atik Yomin
Ancient of Days
Blessings

LIVE FREE

July 26

"For the LORD heareth the poor, and despiseth not his prisoners."

Psalm 69:33

Praise be to our God and our Lord Jesus Christ for such a comforting word as this. There are several different takes on how this verse could be translated. It all comes down to the very last word, the peculiar use of the word prisoners. Some versions change it to read: needy ones or his people in prison. But it's clear that the intended use of this word or implied meaning, according to the root word in the original Hebrew, was *Asiyr' / Aw-sere'*, meaning those who are bound captives or a prisoner.

Paul and Silas indeed could have identified with this scripture when, in the book of Acts chapter 16, they were whipped and severely beaten, then cast into prison for the gospel's sake. But there is a different type of bondage that keeps Christians under a yoke of oppression and servitude with a silent plantation master behind the scenes. It is the plantation of debt. It's easy to get caught up in credit card debt, car notes, and purchasing more houses than we can afford. Being "house poor," people make an excellent income and buy a home more than their budget can handle, expecting it to be a little rough for a couple of years until their finances catch up. They expect to receive a pay raise, and instead, the trap slams shut. If they don't get that raise, the company must give pay reductions to stay in business, which could be a thousand reasons. It's like a trap. Hunters used to catch birds. They would stretch a vast net across two trees that have a natural flight path for birds, and then the unsuspecting bird travels the exact flight path it has taken dozens of times before when suddenly it is caught, or rather snared in the net, the net of the fowler. "Surely he shall deliver thee from the snare of the fowler" (Psalm 91:3). God will deliver you from that, too; you have a promise. Ask God to provide for you, send you help and sound financial advice for the future, and don't limit Him to a single solution. After all, we serve a limitless God.

He is: Jehovah-Jireh
God My Provider
Blessings

NEED HELP?

July 27

*Who can understand his errors? cleanse thou me from secret faults.
Keep back thy servant also from presumptuous sins; let them not have dominion
over me: then shall I be upright, and I shall be innocent
from the great transgression.
Let the words of my mouth, and the meditation of my heart, be acceptable in thy
sight, O LORD, my strength, and my redeemer.*

Psalm 19:12–14

King David had some deep understanding of the way of the Lord, and himself for that matter. One time, I observed someone take communion. Let's politely say they were not walking perfectly with the Lord.

Standing in the back of the church, I was deeply concerned for that person's well-being. I prayed. I forget what I asked, but the Lord spoke to me and said, "Everyone who comes to Me is in sin, Scott."

I was astonished. He didn't even say, 'Except for you, of course.' But we don't always know that we have sinned against the Lord. Knowing that He will cleanse us from our secret faults is good.

Presumptuous sin is a door you are willing to go through; you know better, but you still do it anyway. For instance, I know better than to say negative things about professional athletes, yet I still do it every football season. Here's the good part: you can petition the Lord for your need and ask Him not to let that sin have dominion over you; and why is this important?

> *Wherefore God also gave them up to uncleanness through the lusts of their own hearts. Let your words and your thoughts be acceptable to the Lord, pleasing to Him, repent in your heart, ask for forgiveness, and most important of all, ask for help.*

Romans 1:24

He'll be your Strength and your Redeemer.

He is: El Yeshuati
The God of My Salvation
Blessings

WANT POWER?

July 28

"But God hath chosen the foolish things of this world to confound the wise,
And God hath chosen the weak things of the world to
confound the things which are mighty."

1 Corinthians 1:27

Only an immutable and sovereign God could write something so liberating to humanity. No monarch on earth would think this way. Kings want power and surround their courts with the wisest of the wise. They arm their knights with the best armor they can afford and display their power.

President Roosevelt said, "Speak softly and carry a big stick; you will go far." It was referred to as "Big Stick Diplomacy." President Roosevelt once sent our Navy halfway around the world to make a show of American strength. But God doesn't tend to work that way. In Bible days, if you were a king about to go to battle, sometimes, instead of losing thousands of men in a single battle, the kings would work out an agreement: let's each send out our mightiest man to fight on behalf of our kingdom.

King David, a young boy, stood up against a well-known giant named Goliath. The Hebrews feared Goliath, and for a good reason. Some historians believe that, a few years earlier, when the Philistines were at war with the Hebrews, Goliath, a twelve-foot-tall giant, went on a one-person rampage. Goliath stormed the Hebrew camp singlehandedly and, with his fifteen-plus-pound spear, killed Hebrew soldiers as he ran into the most protected part of the camp. He picked up the ark of the covenant placed on his shoulder and fought his way back out!

When David approached him, Goliath was a mighty man, and he became confounded (angry). David appeared foolish before everyone watched, but David knew God, and Goliath was seeking a more extraordinary reputation. He wanted to become a legend. Unfortunately, the reputation he received was different from what he expected (Samuel 17).

Sometimes, we face a problem that is too big to conquer ourselves, and we feel overwhelmed. Usually, at this stage, the enemy has been beating us down with his words of discouragement. We may even feel too weak to go on. However, this is when God steps in:

"My grace is sufficient for thee: for my strength is made perfect in weakness" (2 Corinthians 12:9))

The Lord told me: "A miracle is something you go through."

He is: Jehovah Gibbor Milchamah
Mighty in Battle
Blessings

BE THE WATER

July 29

"And the Spirit and the bride say, Come. And let him that heareth say, Come. And let him that is athirst come. And whosoever will, let him take the water of life freely."

Revelation 22:17

The great invitation of Jesus Christ and the Spirit is the Holy Spirit. The bride is us, the people. As church members, we welcome those who thirst into our church family. Then, we're given instructions. We who have received Jesus Christ as our Savior will say, "Come."

When I was a child, my friends and I watched "Big Time Wrestling," with stars like the Junk Yard Dog and Big Bad Ernie Ladd. We would imitate the wrestling moves in the living room of my friend's house. In the mayhem of our little matches, one person would go down on the mat, and another would tag his partner. The partner would enter the ring and do a body slam from the fireplace's hearth. It was hilarious and so much fun. After all that hard work, we would have to take a break and get water.

Maybe not quite to that extent, but in the Spirit, it is. When we tell someone about Jesus, we have just tagged the Holy Spirit. After we leave (Honestly, before entering the ring), the Holy Spirit jumps in and takes over the match. He will wrestle with that person on behalf of that person. A wrestling ring that we, as Christians, have all entered. The great "Cage Match" is a battle of the flesh, the opinions of others, and the tactics of the enemy.

The Holy Spirit will tag-team others to witness to that person until that person is so thirsty for the salvation of Christ that they will drink from the *water of life* freely. Don't be afraid to share the gospel of Christ with others; the truth is that when you do, the Holy Spirit will flow through you.

Jump in the ring. When you get tired, tag the Holy Spirit. He always wins the match:

"If any man thirst, let him come unto me and drink."

"He that believeth on me, as the Scripture hath said, out of his belly shall flow rivers of living water" (John 7:37–38).

Jump in the ring! If you get tired, tag the Holy Spirit. He always wins the match.

He is: Maqowr Chay Mayim
Fountain of Living Waters
Blessings

SEASONED WITH GRACE

July 30

*Jesus Christ the same yesterday, and today, and forever.
Be not carried about with diverse doctrines. For it is a good thing that the
heart be established with grace; not with meats, which have not
profited them that have been occupied therein.*

Hebrews 13:8–9

Do you know what it's like to have your heart affected by the grace of the gospel? Jesus stands alone, never changing, willing to sacrifice His life for yours, and He would do it again if it were only you. As I write this, the Holy Spirit told me, "Grace personified," which means Jesus was grace in human form.

We tend to complicate our lives, self-implementing our own rules that don't add anything to enrich ourselves, but instead, they limit the joy and grace we can have as Christians. If I choose not to eat pork because I think it is against the dietary laws of the Old Testament, which no longer apply, how does that help me be a better Christian to you? All my friends love bacon! Bacon doesn't take away from grace or add anything to grace. Grace is a gift from Jesus Christ that affects your heart.

If you have unforgiveness in your heart, this can also affect the grace of your life, binding Christ from forgiving you. Your unforgiveness can hinder His grace towards you. Be established in grace, not dietary doctrines, and it doesn't do you any good regarding the gospel. Legalism doesn't make you any holier.

He is: Jehovah-Tzidkenu
The Lord Our Righteousness
Blessings

DON'T LET THE TRAP FOOL YOU

July 31

Therefore, thou son of man, say unto the children of thy people, The righteousness of the righteous shall not deliver him in the day of his transgression: as for the wickedness of the wicked, he shall not fall thereby in the day that he turneth from his wickedness; neither shall the righteous be able to live for his righteousness in the day that he sinneth.

Ezekiel 33:12

We all need a reminder of the consequences of sin. Many of us think we can escape our corruption because we have lived so well in the past, but God doesn't see it that way. He lets us know that His standard is this: a sinful person who has not known God can receive forgiveness if they turn to Him and ask for forgiveness. However, righteous people will be held accountable for their actions.

That's why it is so sad to see a man of God fall on the day of temptation. The enemy knows this verse and uses temptation to cause mighty men to stumble. If we let him, he'll use it to make us transgress.

What I have noticed over the years is that the enemy will often use a weakness or sin you have previously overcome to tempt you and make you stumble. Guard yourself, and if you are struggling with a secret sin, find a man or woman of God, preferably a pastor or a chaplain with integrity that you can trust. Share the truth with them and ask for prayer.

"Then you will know the truth, and the truth will set you free" (John 8:32).

He is: El Yeshuati
The God of My Salvation
Blessings

HOW CLOSE?

August 1

"And Enoch walked with God: and he was not; for God took him."

Genesis 5:24

Enoch is one of the most mysterious men in the Bible. He was the fifth descendant of Adam, and his name meant "teaching." According to Genesis 5:24, Enoch walked with God so closely that God took him to heaven without experiencing death. Enoch's walk with God exemplifies what God intends for us: to be companions and friends with Him.

Enoch was also a prophet who warned the people before Noah of the coming flood by naming his son Methuselah, which meant "my death shall bring." In addition, Enoch wrote the book of Enoch as a letter to the people of the last days. Moses and the Hebrews carried it out of Egypt along with the book of Job. Jesus and Jude both quoted him.

Enoch will return in the book of Revelation 11:3 as one of the two witnesses. He is before God with Elijah, called "the two olive trees and the two candlesticks standing before the God of the earth."

Enoch's relationship with God was so close that he poured out the knowledge of God, interceded for many, taught the way, explained the truth about sin, and warned of judgment and its consequences. He became a light in the darkness, trying to direct humanity.

Enoch's life teaches us that we are all on the road with God, and how close we walk with Him is up to us. Let us aim to be like Enoch, seeking a close and intimate relationship with God.

In conclusion, Enoch is a fascinating figure in the Bible whose life shows us the importance of walking closely with God. He teaches us that a deep and meaningful relationship with God is possible and that it can profoundly impact our lives and those around us.

He is: Teleiotes Pistis
Finisher of our Faith
Blessings

FAITH IN THE BLOOD

August 2

For all have sinned, and come short of the Glory of God;
Being justified freely by his grace through the redemption that is in Christ Jesus:
Whom God hath set forth to be a propitiation through faith in his blood, to declare
his righteousness for the remission of sins that are past,
through the forbearance of God;

Romans 3:23–25

No one can deny the truth of this passage, except maybe an atheist who doesn't believe in God. But one day, we will all stand before God to be judged.

So, how can we be justified before God? By placing our faith in the blood of Jesus Christ. God's ways are higher than ours, and His thoughts are higher than ours. Long before we fell, He sacrificed blood to atone for our sins.

Back in the day, people sacrificed the blood of animals, but this was like putting our sins on a credit card. The bill would eventually come due. Before Jesus, when a saint died, they went to Abraham's Bosom, a place next to hell. There, they waited for the day when the Messiah would also come and deliver them.

When Christ died on the cross, His blood cried out for forgiveness, unlike Abel's, which cried out for justice. Now, we must cry out in our hearts that we believe in the blood of Jesus and place our faith in it. The sacrifice is now offered in our hearts, which is the perfect place for the perfect sacrifice.

Romans 10:10 says, "For with the heart one believes and is justified, and with the mouth, one confesses and is saved."

When we place our faith in His blood, it brings life to our hearts. We have just received the greatest blood transfusion of all time, with the blood "Type O-So Amazing"! Get an eternal transfusion today.

Believe with your heart that Jesus's blood covers your sins, and confess this prayer out loud:

"Dear heavenly Father, I have sinned and fallen short of Your glory. I place my faith in Your only begotten Son, Jesus Christ. I believe He shed His blood for my sins. In His grace and mercy, I ask for the forgiveness of my sins. I believe Jesus died, and on the third day, He rose again and sat at Your right hand. I renounce the enemy's works and declare that Jesus is the Christ, My Lord and Savior! I dedicate the rest of my life to You. Please come into my heart and fill me with Your presence. Teach me Your ways, Lord God. In the name of Jesus, Amen."

Now, seal your commitment with Christ and tell at least three people that you have accepted Jesus as your Savior.

Matthew 10:32 says, "So everyone who acknowledges me before men, I also will acknowledge before my Father who is in heaven."

He is: El Yeshuati
The God of My Salvation
Blessings

LIFE'S STRUGGLES

August 3

Jesus said unto the Twelve, Will you also go away?
[And do you too desire to leave me?]
Simon Peter answered, Lord to whom shall we go?
You have the words (the message) of eternal life.

John 6:67–68

Life can get complicated, and we face struggles challenging our faith. In John 6, many disciples left Jesus because they did not understand His message. But Simon Peter, speaking for the Twelve, recognized that Jesus had the words of eternal life and chose to stay with Him.

When we face difficult situations, we may ask God, "Why?" and demand an explanation for what is happening. But often, the answer we need is not an explanation but faith. Faith trusts in God even when we don't understand.

I once witnessed my friend Jerome's faith in action when his only son passed away. Despite his deep grief, he did not speak against God but expressed his trust in Him. He recognized that God was all he had left, and his faith in Him strengthened him.

In our struggles, we must hold onto our faith in God, our compassionate God. We may not always understand why things happen, but we can trust His love and goodness.

He is: El Racham
The Compassionate God
Blessings

GOD'S BLUEPRINT

August 4

*And he said, Lord GOD, whereby shall I know that I shall inherit it?
And he said unto him, Take me a heifer of three years old, and a she-goat of three
years old, and a ram of three years old, and a turtledove, and a young pigeon.*

Genesis 15:8–9

In response to Abram's request for a sign, he said, "Lord GOD, whereby shall I know that I shall inherit it?" God replied, "Take Me a heifer of three years old, and a she-goat of three years old, and a ram of three years old, and a turtledove, and a young pigeon." These sacrifices had a significant symbolic meaning, representing different aspects of Abram's relationship with God and the journey of salvation.

The number three, which the three-year-old animals represent, symbolizes integration and harmony. It represents the unity of the Father, the Son, and the Holy Spirit. The heifer represents increased wealth, while the goat represents the curse. The ram symbolizes power and represents Jesus Christ. The turtledove represents innocence and the Holy Spirit, and the young pigeon represents poverty, suggesting the idea of starting life with very little.

By sacrificing these animals, Abram demonstrated his willingness to give everything to God. He placed his trust in God and showed his commitment to following God's plan, laying the blueprint for salvation through the cross. This act of obedience and faithfulness foreshadowed the ultimate sacrifice of Jesus Christ, who would give His life to save humanity from sin and death.

Although Abram laid out his sacrifice, that day, God, looking down from heaven above, saw a different picture lying on the ground. In the dirt, God saw His blueprint for salvation through the cross. Hebrews 10:14 says, "For by that one offering He made forever perfect in the sight of God all those He is making holy." In Hebrews, we see the ultimate significance of this sacrifice. Through Jesus Christ's sacrifice on the cross, God made forever perfect in His sight all those whom He is making holy. God has a blueprint for our lives, and it is to make us holy. We can follow in the footsteps of Abraham by placing our trust in God and committing ourselves to follow His plan for our lives.

"For by that one offering He made forever perfect in the sight of God all those whom He is making holy" (Hebrews 10:14).

Therefore, remember that God has a blueprint for your life, and it is to make you holy.

He is: El OLAM
The Beginning and the End, Strength to the Weary
Blessings

PROPER HELLO

August 5

"Beloved, I wish above all things that thou mayest prosper and be in health, even as thy soul prospereth."

3 John 1:2

What a beautiful greeting! It would be wonderful if we greeted our friends in this way. Sometimes, friends, with their greetings, will almost pronounce a curse on the people they love. John wrote this letter to one of his pastors, Gaius, who was leading a church and having trouble with another pastor, Diotrephes, who held false beliefs. People like Diotrephes can be stressful, and John let Gaius know that he would deal with Diotrephes when he arrived.

Gaius cherished this letter commissioned by the Holy Spirit and penned it by the hand of John. He cared for it and preserved it for posterity. How many times did he think about this letter?

One word in this verse can provoke deep thought: *soul.* But what did the Holy Spirit mean by this? There are two schools of thought. One is that the soul is life, your inner spirit, and the other is that it refers to your conscience, mind, and thoughts.

Let's examine this verse: without your mind, you are dead, and without your spirit, your body is over. Therefore, we need the presence of both.

"And be not conformed to this world: but be ye transformed by the renewing of your mind, that ye may prove what that good, and acceptable, and perfect, will of God is" (Romans 12:2). The more you read your Bible, the more your spirit grows into the truth of God. This self-education will bring you prosperity, which means success.

Training your soul, mind, and spirit with the Holy Spirit is true prosperity.

He is: Jehovah Shalom
The Lord Is Peace
Blessings

GET TO KNOW GOD

August 6

"He that loveth not knoweth not God; for God is love."

1 John 4:8

I have a friend named Jerry. He's gone on to be with the Lord several years ago. Jerry was such a good old guy it would take the whole page to say enough good about him. But Jerry wasn't always such a good ole' boy, and you could tell he used to be one tough character, a fighter. Then, his wife became a Christian, and he finally came around through her dedication to the Lord.

I talked to my pastor about Jerry, and it seemed so unfair that this tough, hard-core man had a personality change and became a tough, old, kind man. Why couldn't I get a personality infusion like that? My pastor said: "Scott, I don't know. Some people change overnight, and others take years." For some, it takes a lot of effort to love people; for others, not so hard.

Psychology is very complex. I remember doing a psychology study, and the very next day, I went to work, and at that time, I was a city bus driver. So many of the passengers had problems. I felt so much empathy for them; I could understand that many people were a product of their environment. Things that other people had done to them along this path called life. Defense mechanisms are implemented to self-protect and stop the subsequent potential pain.

I had an understanding, a day of revelation about people. If you are having trouble walking in love with someone, please pray and ask the Lord to give you knowledge of the actual cause that causes them to be this way.

When you receive this revelation, do not go and share it with others, God is entrusting you to pray for them, and when He can trust you in the little things, He will trust you for more extraordinary things. Intercede for them and ask God to help you love them.

After all, they may be saying the same prayer for you and me.

He is: El Ahavah
The God Who Loves
Blessings

FIREPROOF

August 7

And they shall go forth, and look upon the carcasses of the men that have transgressed against Me: for their worm shall not die, neither shall their fire be quenched; and they shall be an abhorring unto all flesh.

Isaiah 66:24

Not everything in the Bible is pleasant. When this world's time ends, we will all witness the scene described by Isaiah, which is hell. Hell, the second death, is characterized by unquenchable fire, torment from flames and flesh-eating worms, and an eternity separated from God. There is no middle ground; you're either on one side of the flames or the other. Those who have accepted Jesus as their Lord and Savior will not suffer this fate.

I once saw a man on TV who claimed this verse disproved the Bible, questioning how a person could be engulfed in flames while a worm remained unharmed. He believed this verse, which he based his entire eternity, was scientifically impossible.

Relying on a scientific hypothesis with limited knowledge can lead to dire consequences. However, there is scientific evidence supporting this Bible verse. A tiny, resilient creature known as the tardigrade or *water bear* provides such evidence.

The tardigrade, measuring only 0.002 to 0.5 mm in length, can survive temperatures as low as minus 272 degrees Celsius (minus 457 degrees Fahrenheit) and as high as 150 degrees Celsius (302 degrees Fahrenheit). It can live inside a nuclear reactor unharmed and survive without food or water for over thirty years. When exposed to outer space, tardigrades even multiplied!

The tardigrade demonstrates that a worm could indeed dwell in flames without being harmed, proving this verse true. The Bible and science support each other when studied with the right heart.

Don't let a hardened heart place you on the wrong side of the flames. God created you, and He loves His creation. He loves you so much that Jesus came and died on the cross for you, granting you eternal life. The path to salvation is simple:

"For whosoever shall call upon the name of the Lord (Jesus) shall be saved" (Romans 10:13).

Go ahead and call upon Him today. You can even call collect, person to person. He will answer, as He has already paid for the call.

He is: Jehova-Go'el
Redeeming God
Blessings

TO THE FINISH

August 8

Wherefore seeing we also are compassed about with so great a cloud of witnesses, let us lay aside every weight, and the sin which doth so easily beset us, and let us run with patience the race that is set before us, Looking unto Jesus the author and finisher of our faith; who for the joy that was set before him endured the cross, despising the shame, and is set down at the right hand of the throne of God.

Hebrews 12:1–2

Fixing our eyes on Jesus, the pioneer and perfecter of our faith, who, for the joy set before Him, endured the cross, scorning its shame, and sat down at the right hand of the throne of God.

I often think of this verse when I pray. I have a family portrait of my ancestors from over 100 years ago. It's a large black and white photo in an old wooden frame, depicting some sitting, others standing, but no children, only the heads of different families. Though I don't know who they were, when I go to my place of prayer, they seem to be looking at me as if to remind me that they are in heaven, watching me run my race.

Over the years, I've had a few visions and dreams of a heavenly stadium. It resembles an open stadium, similar to an open-air football stadium, with a vast field and grandstands surrounding it. The saints who have gone before us and the angels can look down and see what Christians are doing.

An angel once told me, "I only ever see you in your righteousness!" So, I assume the witnesses can only see us in our righteousness. When we're doing things for the Lord, they highly approve. They are rooting for you to win your race. Your race is not the same as mine. Notice there are no other people mentioned in the race besides you.

I recall attending a high school football game and sitting in the stands. An older man would always run a few miles on the track surrounding the football field, a daily routine he had been doing for years. He ignored the game and the hundreds of people in the stands, focusing on completing his exercise.

For some reason, I have never forgotten that what others thought didn't matter to him. It was his race. No one joined him, and he ran alone. Sometimes, your faith in what Jesus has called you to do will make you feel like you are doing it alone. People may think you've missed it, or "Oh, that's not God."

Once, I told the Lord that I was exhausted. Suddenly, I had a vision: I was a spectator in the stands, watching myself on the track, struggling to finish as if I had run a marathon and had nothing left to give. Jesus ran onto the way, my arm over His shoulder, and carried me to the finish line.

Jesus has authored His plan of faith for your life and will complete what He started. You'll finish your race, even if Jesus must jump out of the stands and carry you across the finish line because you're the joy set before Him. For some, life is a sprint; for others, it's a marathon.

He is: El Roi
The God Who Sees Me
Blessings

WARNING!

August 9

"And he causeth all, both small and great, rich and poor, free and bond, to receive a mark in their right hand, or in their foreheads."

Revelations 13:16

"The Mark of the Beast" may be approaching sooner than people think. It is already being integrated into our culture through vaccinations and mind control. The church has been discussing it for centuries.

There has been so much debate and differing opinions that confusion is the enemy's greatest tactic. Who is this author of confusion? Satan, who doesn't play fair and targets everyone.

Satan is not omnipotent like God. He can control humankind through law and finances.

Let's examine the word "mark." It states people will receive the mark in their right hand or in their foreheads. The keyword is "in," not "on." A tattoo goes on top of the skin, while this mark goes under the skin.

The word "mark" comes from Greek and, in this context, means palisade. A palisade is a post sharpened to a pointed end. Romans used these as defense barriers around their forts and camps. Not understanding what he was seeing, John essentially described a hypodermic needle.

This technology, known as RFID or radio frequency identification, is already here; some people unwittingly accept it. It involves a capsule the size of a grain of rice implanted in the right hand or forehead. These two locations optimize the ability of the battery to recharge.

The widespread acceptance of tattoos in global culture makes it easier for people to embrace this mark. Now, tattoo artists can earn a side income by implanting chips, which could lead people to eternal damnation. There are stories of Christians who have taken the chip and later felt God had abandoned them. After Adam and Eve sinned, Eve uttered these immortal words: "The serpent beguiled me, and I did eat."

Please don't let the enemy deceive you! How can we get by without the chip? God has provided this promise to see us through:

"But my God shall supply all your need according to his riches in glory by Christ Jesus" (Philippians 4:19).

He is: El Moshaah
The God Who Saves
Blessings

ONE IN A MILLION

August 10

And the LORD spake unto Moses face to face, as a man speaketh unto his friend. And he turned again into the camp: but his servant Joshua, the son of Nun, a young man, departed not out of the tabernacle.

Exodus 33:11

The children of Israel had sinned against God, so God instructed Moses to move the Tabernacle to the camp outside because He could no longer dwell within it.

When Moses met God, all the men stood at the door of their tents in honor of Moses. This custom of honoring the man of God took place every morning as Moses walked to the Tabernacle.

However, one man out of a million went with Moses—Joshua, who served as Moses's servant. Joshua faithfully waited for forty days at the foot of Mount Sinai, as close as he could get without being put to death, for the prophet to come down with the word. While Joshua waited, Aaron led the Israelites into pagan worship of a golden calf. Joshua wanted no part in this sin and knew God could care for Moses during those forty days.

No one else went to the Tabernacle door. There's no mention of Aaron, Levites, or anyone else. Joshua's defining quality was his desire to be as close to God as possible, even if it meant being a servant. After just being liberated from Egypt as a slave, Joshua willingly took on the title of servant to be as close to God as he could.

It's almost as if he had read Matthew 11:29 centuries before: "Take my yoke upon you and learn from Me, for I am gentle and humble in heart, and you will find rest for your souls."

Joshua learned from Moses and discovered that a relationship with God comes first. He learned leadership, and when Moses passed away, God knew whom He had trained for the position. The Lord appointed Joshua to lead His people. A Navy Admiral once said, "You can't be a good leader until you have learned to become a good follower."

He is: El Roi
The God Who Sees Me
Blessings

NO DEBATE

August 11

And without controversy great is the mystery of godliness: God was manifest in the flesh, justified in the Spirit, seen of angels, preached unto the Gentiles, believed on in the world, received up into glory.

1 Timothy 3:16

Upon first reading this scripture, it can be a little perplexing as it delves into the deep knowledge of God and who He is. The books of Timothy, written by the Apostle Paul, are pastoral epistles addressing conduct, behavior, and qualifications for positions in the church. In the first sentence of this verse, "And without controversy great is the mystery of godliness," Paul asserts without argument that godliness is a mystery. But why would he write this? Wasn't Paul one of the godliest men to have ever lived?

Paul began pursuing godliness by persecuting the church, torturing and even putting Christians to death, and forcing Christians to recant Christ. He beat people with absolute hatred, thinking he was doing this for God, yet acting against God.

Some people will cut themselves and beat their backs with whips and cords, attempting to attain godliness. Sadly, in a twist of irony, Timothy was killed while trying to stop the ungodly procession of the goddess Diana. He wanted to prevent people from worshiping idols.

"Every way of a man is right in his own eyes: but the LORD pondereth the hearts" (Proverbs 21:2).

We often think we are right but need someone to compare our lives to. It's hard for us to grasp that Jesus is God, but at the same time, knowing that God came to live and die for us should bring peace. He searched for a man to stand in the gap but found no one.

On the road to Damascus, Saul discovered his true identity, left behind his old form of godliness, and embraced a new identity in Christ. He then became the Apostle Paul, an ambassador for Christ, understanding that godliness comes through Jesus Christ.

And how did Jesus instruct us?

Jesus said unto him, Thou shalt love the Lord thy God with all thy heart, and with all thy soul, and with all thy mind. This is the first and great commandment. And the second is like unto it, Thou shalt love thy neighbor as thyself. On these two commandments hang all the law and the prophets.

Matthew 22:37–40

He is: Immanuel
God with Us
Blessings

CHILDLIKE COMPASSION

August 12

At the same time came the disciples unto Jesus, saying,
Who is the greatest in the kingdom of heaven?
And Jesus called a little child unto him, and set him in the midst of them,
And said, Verily I say unto you, Except ye be converted, and become as little
children, ye shall not enter into the kingdom of heaven.
Whosoever therefore shall humble himself as this little child,
the same is greatest in the kingdom of heaven.

Matthew 18:1–5

Honestly, this was one of those answers that perplexed the disciples. They expected to hear Moses, Elijah, and maybe a couple of votes cast for Isaiah. It shows the heart of men. He had just explained to them that He would be crucified and revealed Himself on top of the Mount of Transfiguration. And here are the founders of our faith debating who will be the greatest, like horse jockeys trying to position themselves to win a race. Never mind that Jesus was looking at one of the most painful deaths in human history. Instead of the rebuke they deserved, Jesus showed grace without hesitation by giving this answer. This answer is the total opposite of what we would think. That is often the case with heavenly things.

One time, my wife and I watched a friend's minor child. We brought her to the children's playground and watched her play. Several other children were playing, and when one child fell, got hurt, and began to cry, the parents naturally rushed over. My wife told me, "Now watch; all the other little children will run and gather around to see if the child is okay." As if on cue, every child ran over to the crying child, forming a huddle of concern. I thought of this verse with this moment of silence and childlike compassion. It wasn't about them having fun and playing; it was about the well-being of another child. As the child stopped crying one by one, the children peeled away, going back to their fun. The little girl we cared for remained and was the last child to leave. I've never forgotten the look of concern and relief as she decided the child was okay and went to play again. I wasn't even her parent, but I was proud of our child that day.

You see, we are all in this playground called life.

He is: ABBA
Father
Blessings

THOUGHT CATCHER

August 13

For though we walk in the flesh, we do not war after the flesh:
(For the weapons of our warfare are not carnal, but mighty
through God to the pulling down of strong holds:)
Casting down imaginations, and every high thing that exalteth itself against the
knowledge of God, and bringing into captivity every thought
to the obedience of Christ.

2 Corinthians 10:3–5

Have you ever been so upset with the devil that you wanted to challenge him to a fistfight? Yeah, that's probably not the wisest idea, and if you do, that will cause him to laugh.

One night, as I was sleeping, I heard a voice tell me that I was a liar. It was audible and clear. I thought, *Wait a minute! I'm not a liar!* I woke myself, and next to my bed was a faceless demon clothed like an angel. I was so tired I threw this weak punch at it and fell back into my pillow. The attempted punch did nothing.

But there was another instance where I woke up, and I tried to say "Jesus!" but I was so scared all I could get out was "Je, Je, Je." The fear was so intense I couldn't speak, but I saw the demon take off, knowing that I was trying to say the name of Jesus. Suddenly, the demon was gone so fast it turned into a blur.

The name of Jesus is the weapon, and in the spirit realm, it's a nuclear weapon, and when you use the name of Jesus Christ, those are easy fights in the Spirit. The most challenging battles are in your mind. The enemy knows how to place thoughts, usually things from the past, little things that upset you, in your mind.

The weapon for this fight is captivity—capture this thought and cast it out. I find the best way is the quick way. As soon as you get a terrible thought, cast it down. I might add that's easier said than done. The enemy is very subtle. Once you recognize where this thought comes from, replace it with Scripture, praise God, think about good things, and believe in Jesus. "If you want to be good, think good." Think of His name.

He is: Sar-Shalom
Prince of Peace
Blessings

COURAGE

August 14

"For they loved the praise of men more than the praise of God."
John 12:43

It saddens me to think about this verse. The scenario that positioned John to write this sentence was shortly before Jesus was crucified. Many people believed in Jesus, but because of what others thought or their impact on their positions with the church, they would not openly admit it. It's still this way today. I have been a coward at proclaiming the gospel to others when I had the opportunity to pray for someone or even witness Jesus, and I didn't. Was I just concerned about what people would think or say? The truth is both.

When you accept Jesus Christ as your Lord and Savior, you won't always be greeted with open arms. You'll be talked about and laughed at. But some people lose everything, face total rejection by their families, are shunned from society, and even face death. From an American perspective, our cost is minimal. We have much more religious freedom in this country than in many others. Indeed, it is a privilege to share the Good News.

God will help you share the gospel if you ask Him to give you an opportunity. Trust Him to help you say the right thing when the situation arises. I remember the first time I stepped out in faith to tell someone about Jesus. I was with a good friend at a department store, and I saw this lady shopping. I told my friend I would say to her about Jesus. I had never really done that before. I was so scared I worked up the nerve to approach her, and I said: "Would you like to hear the Good News?" She looked at me, smiled, and said, "Jesus is my Lord and Savior!" It was almost like God planted her!

Years later, I've had so many experiences with God that I talk about Jesus as a friend, the most incredible person I have ever met. I don't need courage because I have the experiences that have provided faith, and faith equals *truth*, and the *truth* will set you free.

Ask the Lord to allow you to minister for Him. It's as simple as asking, "Would you like me to pray with you?" That's all the Holy Spirit needs. What happens after you say "Amen"? *A miracle.*

He is: Jehovah Jireh
The Lord Will Provide
Blessings

BARTIMAEUS

August 15

*And they came to Jericho: and as he went out of Jericho with his disciples and a
great number of people, blind Bartimaeus, the son of Timaeus,
sat by the highway side begging.
And when he heard it was Jesus of Nazareth, he began to cry out,
and say, Jesus, thou Son of David, have mercy on me.
And many charged him that he should hold his peace: but he cried
the more a great deal, Thou Son of David, have mercy on me.
And Jesus stood still, and commanded him to be called. And they called the blind
man, saying unto him, Be of good comfort, rise; he calleth thee.
And he, casting away his garment, rose, and came to Jesus.
And Jesus answered and said unto him, "What wilt thou that I should do unto
thee?" The blind man said unto him, Lord, that I might receive my sight.
And Jesus said unto him, "Go thy way; thy faith hath made thee whole." And
immediately he received his sight, and followed Jesus in the way.*

Mark 10:46–52

There are some fascinating insights into this account of Bartimaeus. First, Jesus arrives in Jericho. Jericho was considered a sinful place; you left the city of peace to travel to Jericho, and it was downward. However, Jesus leads the people upward away from the city of sin to Jerusalem, the city of peace. Jesus always brings you up to a higher level.

Notice how Bartimaeus's identity is known to the public. It seems like everyone knew this beggar by name: blind Bartimaeus, the son of Timaeus. Bartimaeus and Timaeus have the same meaning in Hebrew: foul, polluted, and unclean. Possibly, Timaeus had the same blind condition as Bartimaeus, and culturally, they believed that he was born into sin, a sinner at birth.

He learns it's Jesus of Nazareth; Bartimaeus could relate to the city of Nazareth. Nazareth was considered a lowly and rejected community. One thing for certain: Bartimaeus understood rejection. That's what he identified with. Immediately, he cries out Jesus, thou son of David!

Son of David meant that all the promises given to Abraham and David belonged to Jesus, the true inheritor of the kingdom of God! Only the Messiah had the right and the ability to heal the blind, and there are no recorded healings of the blind or the deaf in the Old Testament. The Messiah could only perform this miracle (Isaiah 35:5).

Many charged him to shut up, and he cried even louder. Imagine your only opportunity to change your life forever, to see, to be able to support yourself to get out of this cursed condition that was passing by. Do you think he was shouting? He was grieving for his healing; I could see this man wailing as if he had just lost someone he loved: "Have mercy on me!"

The enemy tried very hard to prevent his healing with the only weapon he had available, other people, other followers, by ordering him to shut up. You would think that they would be ushering him to Jesus.

He caught the ear of God, and Jesus stood still; you can do this with your prayers, too, when you sincerely cry out from within your heart. Suddenly, Bartimaeus has favor from the crowd because God noticed him; they start to comfort him and begin helping him get to Jesus, God's blessing.

Bartimaeus casts away his garment, a beggar's garment given by the priests that proved he was disabled and legally allowed to beg to support himself. No need for it now; he's getting his eyesight! He's getting his new identity!

Jesus told him, "Go thy way, thy faith hath made thee whole."

Jesus gave him a choice, "Go thy way," and which way did he go?

Jesus healed Bartimaeus, and his name was recorded in the Bible. Mary Magdalene was the only other person healed by Jesus whose name is mentioned. Here is some insight as to why they were named.

After their recoveries, they continued to follow Jesus, as we see in this last portion of the account, and followed Jesus in the way. The way was what the early church was referred to before we were called Christians. After this, there's no mention of Bartimaeus, but this is how he probably would have been known by others, "Bartimaeus, he's in *the Way*." Jump in *the Way*, and God can change your circumstances, too.

He is: Shub Nephesh
Renewer of Life
Blessings

NOBILITY

August 16

Forasmuch as many have taken in hand to set forth in order a declaration
of those things which are most surely believed among us,
Even as they delivered them unto us, which from the beginning
were eyewitnesses, and ministers of the word;
It seemed good to me also, having had perfect understanding of all things from the
very first, to write unto thee in order, most excellent Theophilus
That thou mightest know the certainty of those things,
wherein thou hast been instructed.

Luke 1:1–4

Luke, Matthew, and Mark are synoptic gospels, meaning "seeing the whole together at a glance." They are considered the "human gospel." Luke portrays Jesus Christ as both God and man.

One thing worth knowing is that Luke was not one of the original disciples of Christ. His ministry began with the Apostle Paul. He was educated as a physician, became a historian, a faithful, loyal aide to Paul, and a co-worker with Mark.

Luke is observant, and he seems always to be taking in the gospel, studying and preserving those essential things, and then determining that he needs to write down his knowledge so that others will receive understanding. He talks to others and reads a compilation of firsthand accounts.

He qualifies his book by writing "with perfect understanding." We would say, "I know exactly what I'm talking about." It sounds like a doctor to me. Confident and filled with the Holy Spirit, Luke pens this letter to "most excellent Theophilus."

Again, there's much speculation about who the "most excellent Theophilus" may have been. Someone of nobility, he held a high position, held in high honor to receive the gospel, the Good News, to share it with others. Amazingly, Theophilus means "friend of God."

It sounds to me like he was writing this letter to you: someone of nobility, a child of God, someone held in a high position seated next to Jesus Christ at His right hand, held in high honor so valuable that you were bought with the precious Blood of the Lamb. You are worthy to receive the gospel of the Good News and share it with others.

A most excellent friend of God, enjoy your day!

He is: Immanuel
God with Us
Blessings

YOUR WAYS

August 17

"I will bless the LORD at all times: his praise shall continually be in my mouth."

Psalm 34:1

At this point in his life, David is fleeing from King Saul, who is in hot pursuit of killing him, yet he takes the time to compose this Psalm. The words are so beautiful, pouring out from his heart. But were they pouring out from his circumstances? Before this, in his flight from King Saul, David unbelievably went to the Philistine King of Gath for help, which wasn't the best of ideas. Gath was the very city that Goliath was from, and Goliath was the giant that David killed. Goliath was the king of Gath's prize warrior. Trying to escape, David pretended to be insane. The king said, "I don't need any more madmen," and sent David on his way.

Severe stress can cause you to do the unthinkable. The devil will parade you before your enemies to display his victory or what he thinks will be a victory.

David had a remarkable ability to leave his past behind him. Instead of blaming God for his circumstances, he praised God. Through his prophetic praise, he wrote this verse that has touched countless lives.

Yesterday, I listened to a song that started with these words: "I will bless the Lord." I thought about this momentarily, and a question came to mind: "How can I bless the Lord? I'm just a person." As I thought about this, I asked the Lord, "How can I bless you?" His response was immediate: "Your ways."

He is: El Roi
The God Who Sees Me
Blessings

TASTE TEST

August 18

"O taste and see that the LORD is good: blessed is the man that trusteth in him."

Psalm 34:8

To taste is to experience something, to test something. The tongue is a multi-use organ that allows us to eat, swallow, and communicate with others, and it distinguishes between four familiar tastes: sweet, sour, salty, and bitter.

Psalm 119:103 says, "How sweet are your words to my taste, sweeter than honey to my mouth!"

God's words are indeed sweeter than honey, and God is asking us to taste or experience His word by reading our Bible and asking Him for revelation about Him.

But David deploys another sense in this verse, and it's a sense that God values in us: faith. It's very pleasing to Him. "Blessed is the man that trusteth in him." Another way of experiencing God is to approach Him during your time of need, call on His name, and experience His breakthrough.

Have you ever heard the term that someone has a sixth sense? It's a good thing, and now you can have a sixth sense: trust in God or have faith in God to help you.

Here's the most tasteful thing about God: when you trust Him to help you, you get blessed! Afterward, return to verse one: "I will bless the LORD at all times: his praise shall continually be in my mouth."

"I will bless the LORD at all times: His praise shall continually be in my mouth" (Psalm 34:1).

He is: Jehova-Shammah
The Lord Is There
Blessings

BOTTLED WATER

August 19

"If a man, therefore, purges himself from these things, he shall be a vessel unto honor, sanctified, and profitable for the master's use, and prepared unto every good work."

2 Timothy 2:21

Have you ever marveled at the exceptional ministries that some men have built? We know that they possess loads of charisma and intellect. Frankly, I wish I had half as much charm and intelligence as some of these great generals of the Lord. But we are all vessels made for the Lord's use—some are small, and some are huge—and we all hold the same oil, the oil of the Holy Spirit.

I used to deliver bottled water for a living, and the water bottles came in many different sizes: 16 oz, half-gallon, one-gallon, three-gallon, and five-gallon bottles. Each bottle had its level of difficulty when carrying or moving it to another location. I noticed that some homes in Louisiana had cisterns that held hundreds of gallons of water, and they never moved. The cisterns functioned in their capacity to serve the members of the household.

If you think you are too small to be helpful to the Lord, remember that it's much easier to move a three-gallon bottle than a cistern. Jesus will often place you at the moment where you can give a word of encouragement, a prayer, or a simple act of kindness that He can use to water someone's seed. Your words count, your prayers matter, and they matter to God, who loves to answer them. You have the choice of whether or not you can be a vessel to the Lord, a vessel of honor, prepared unto every good work, and remember it's His water that you pour out when you share His name.

He is: Maqowr Chay Mayim
Fountain of Living Waters
Blessings

SHIELDS

August 20

King Shishak of Egypt conquered Jerusalem and took away all the treasures of the Temple and of the palace, also all of Solomon's gold shields. King Rehoboam replaced them with bronze shields and committed them to the care of the captain of his bodyguard.

2 Chronicles 12:9–10

Inheritance—the passing down of something old, something of great value, maybe wisdom, a pocket watch, some property, or a bank account—is to be valued. King Solomon left great wealth for his son, King Rehoboam, and great teachings in the books of Proverbs, Ecclesiastes, and Solomon's Songs. Sadly, King Rehoboam didn't value all his ancestors had passed down.

When the Hebrews left Egypt, they took all of Egypt's wealth with them, and I can't help but notice that the enemy came and took it all back, plus some interest. But this time, they took the golden shields for tribute payment; symbolically, what did they take?

Gold represents pureness, wealth, and honor. Silver: a silver-headed person is honored in the Bible, and their advice is considered valuable because of their age and wisdom. Bronze represents the power of man, doing it your way. King Rehoboam would have the guard captain take the bronze shields out on special occasions and lock them securely. He did this for two reasons: one, he suddenly valued what little he had; it became more precious to him than the wealth he had possessed before. Secondly, he didn't want to see his defeat whenever he left the palace.

Before, the shining gold shields represented honor and glory, a bright future. He saw the consequences of turning his back on God every time he looked. When he looked at the bronze shields, all he thought about was the darkened past. We all have a past, a regret, something we wish we would have never done. People tend to look at life thinking they can conquer it through their strengths, only to be defeated.

The Good News is Jesus has a new shield just for you. In a vision, I have seen the armor of God. It was beautiful, gold with silver inlay in a beautiful design. Jesus will give you a shield, too; it's called the *shield of faith*.

"Above all, taking the shield of faith, wherewith ye shall be able to quench all the fiery darts of the wicked" (Ephesians 6:16).

This shield never needs to be put in a closet; the more you use it, the more it shines! Be a bright light for Christ.

He is: Jehovah-Magen
Shield
Blessings

WHEN GOD IS SILENT

August 21

"Even though I walk through the darkest valley, I will fear no evil, for you are with me; your rod and your staff, they comfort me."

Psalm 23:4, NIV

There have been times in my life when I faced death, or better stated, death met me. Sometimes, I was terrified; other times, it wasn't until after the event that fear came upon me.

I had a thought the other day, "Life is fear-based when it should be faith-based." We respond out of fear throughout the day. How so? When the alarm goes off, we don't rise in faith; we force ourselves to roll out of bed in fear, subtle and unnoticeable. We fear being late for work, the consequences, and the list goes on.

In my early twenties, waking up in the mornings was so hard it seemed as though I could never get enough sleep. My alarm clock was my mortal enemy, so I renamed it "The Opportunity Clock." When it sounded, I would sit up in bed, simultaneously slap both sides of my face, and say, "Today is going to be a great day, a day of opportunity!"

I needed to wake up and create a positive outlook for the day that lay ahead. I knew the day would be hard, and I had to face it. In some ways, the Holy Spirit is our alarm, our motivation for the day, the weeks, and the months that loom ahead. But what about when God is silent? The verse reads, "Your rod and your staff, they comfort me." What happens when we can't feel the staff?

Imagine you're a sheep, and you fall into a crevice, and the shepherd comes to your aid; instead of crawling down into your circumstances, He takes His staff, reaches the hook end down, and grabs your leg to pull you up.

In the silent times, we need to think about our shepherd. We know He's there. He doesn't have to say anything. He's still there.

Through the long night, we know He's watching. If we were in the flock, we would understand that He may be watching over us at the end of the field or on the higher ground. We know the sun will rise; maybe there was a harsh storm during the night, or perhaps it was cold, but He's still there and knows what we can endure. There's a mist in the pre-nautical twilight. We can faintly see His silhouette, the figure of our protection, and in His hand, we can see the staff and the rod that comforts us.

Without saying anything, He guides us to the next pasture, our next opportunity. He knows your clock is ticking. Sometimes, that sound of opportunity sounds like silence.

He is: Jehovah Rohi
Lord, Our Shepherd and Friend
Blessings

HAPPY BIRTHDAY

August 22

"Buried together with him in baptism, wherein also ye are risen with him through the faith of the operation of God, who has raised him from the dead."

Colossians 2:12

Baptism is a crucial step of faith that signifies our burial with Christ and our resurrection in Him. Although some unbelievers view the Bible as just a book written by man, baptism is a tradition that symbolizes God's existence and love.

For instance, the Hebrews were baptized with Moses as they left Egypt and crossed the Red Sea, demonstrating the importance of baptism as a sign of faith. However, over time, the Jewish people adopted the belief that only new converts to Judaism needed baptism.

Yet, baptism is not just a ritual for new converts. It is a public confession of our faith in Jesus as our Lord and Savior. We are initially drowned briefly during baptism, symbolizing our burial with Christ. When we break the water's surface and take a much-needed breath of air, we suddenly value our life much more.

In addition, baptism represents the circumcision of our past and the beginning of a new life in Christ. By being baptized, we publicly declare that we have died to our old selves and have been born again in Christ.

Attending a baptism is a must-go-to event for our faith and the faith of others. Baptism is a crucial second step of faith after confessing Jesus as our Lord and Savior.

He is: El Yalad
The God Who Gave You Birth
Blessings

GREAT PLEASURE

August 23

"Delight thyself also in the Lord; and He shall give thee the desires of thine heart. Commit thy way unto the Lord; trust also in Him; and He shall bring it to pass."

Psalm 37:4–5

This verse is a promise from Father God to you. It's your first instruction, your potential, your future. But how do you delight yourself in the Lord?

King David's choice of words is fascinating. In this instance, the word "delight" comes from a Greek word called *katatrechō*. It means "to run down from a tower, hasten, and move quickly." Going into the root word, it translates into delight, which, in this case, is a verb, giving it the meaning of action required on your part. That part is: Please someone greatly. From there, it becomes a noun, changing its essence into a great pleasure.

Sometimes, we must humble ourselves and come down from our ivory tower as fast as we can, running as if we see the King approaching from afar, whom we love so much. This action of humility is a verb, which brings us to the noun: A great pleasure in the Lord.

When we do our part, extraordinary things happen, and our desires change. God gives us these desires, which the Holy Spirit places in our hearts. When we commit our ways to the Lord, He gives us the desires of our heart, and He will bring them to pass so that our delight becomes a noun, our great pleasure.

What a wonderful God we serve!

He is: El-HaNe'eman
The God Who Is Faithful
Blessings

WHERE'S YOUR CORNER?

August 24

"And when ye reap the harvest of your land, thou shalt not wholly reap the corners of thy field, neither shalt thou gather the gleanings of thy harvest."

Leviticus 19:9

Rules for harvesting are known as sundry laws, various laws God gives as instructions for living. It was a unique system in which the poor could earn a living by gleaning the fields. In an agricultural society, this provided enough for people to get by.

A farmer was not to strip every last bit of grain from the field. If the head of grain fell to the ground, it would be left for the poor to come and pick up. Neither were they to harvest the corners of the field.

But what are the corners? Some of my family members own olive orchards. My mother's orchard is a rectangle with four corners, but my brother-in-law has his orchard situated so that it has eight corners. How big is the corner? Is the corner just one tree, or is it one side of the tree? I searched the scriptures, searched online, and could not find any real answers to this. I reached out to a Rabbi, and he didn't know either, apparently there is no definitive answer.

I prayed about this, looking for an answer for a couple of weeks. My response was: "The corner is the offering, and the offering is subjective to one's own heart."

Last night, while driving, I came up to a red light, and while waiting, a young lady holding a sign approached my car, asking for help. Initially, I shook my head no, then the Holy Spirit said, "You know I would give it back to you."

I honked my horn, and the lady turned around and came back. I gave her five dollars; she said, "God bless you," and I said the same. Less than two minutes later, I received a text with a picture of a case of bottled water on sale, which was $5.00 off the regular price. We bought this water every other week! I was so happy to get this bargain. And the sale price lasted for a couple of years!

I realized sometimes, the orchard is someone standing on the corner holding a street sign and asking for help. God asked us to help the poor; He never said for us to judge them. After all, He's the reason you're blessed.

He is: Jehovah Jireh
God My Provider
Blessings

YOUR PEDESTAL

August 25

"Sow to yourselves in righteousness, reap in mercy; breakup your fallow ground: for it is time to seek the Lord, till he come and rain righteousness upon you."

Hosea 10:12

Hosea was a prophet of God, serving in the Northern Kingdom from 760 BC to 725 BC. He was known as the "weeping prophet," a heartbroken man serving the Lord at all costs. Hosea was instructed by God to take a wife of whoredom, a prostitute named Gomer.

Obedience can come at a heavy price. In this case, God needed to make an example for His people. He chose Hosea to represent Him and His love for people symbolically. Hosea loved Gomer, but she wasn't faithful; by that, I mean *unfaithful*. At one point, Gomer left him for another man, wound up in debt, and was on the auctioning block to the highest bidder. God told Hosea to go and redeem her; imagine how Gomer felt when she heard the voice of Hosea bidding for her.

Symbolically, Gomer represented the sins of the people. Hosea's broken heart showed God's love for people and willingness to redeem us at any cost.

All sin has one name, and that name is sin, and we have all sinned. Sin will take you farther than you want to go; it will enslave you into its grasp and place you on a unique auction block, a pedestal of our own making.

We've all stood there, but thanks be to God, our Redeemer, standing waiting to place the highest bid at all costs and raising the cross every time the enemy counters with another sin.

But in this auction, we're the ones that call out the winning bid, and the winning bid is "repentance." When you repent, suddenly Jesus becomes the judge, your judge. A judge knows we can never pay the fine in full because we lack the proper payment, and that payment is His blood, and with His blood, He pays the penalty.

Repentance is how you can sow righteousness by breaking your heart's hardened (fallow) ground.

"…for it is time to seek the Lord, till he come and rain righteousness upon you."

He will come.

He is: Jehovah-Tzidkenu
The Lord Our Righteousness
Blessings

GOD MOST AWESOME

August 26

"And it shall come to pass, that whosoever shall call on the name of the Lord shall be delivered."

Joel 2:32

Again, it is one of my favorite sayings: "And it shall come to pass." Remember, it never reads, "it came to stay." "Whosoever shall call" covers a lot of people, and it includes you. The word "call" means to invoke aid, to worship, to testify, to decide, and these are powerful words in God's ears.

We can call on God through worship, praise, and our testimony, the things we've said about God in the past and present. If you have confessed God to be a miracle-working God, you may believe that.

How do you call upon the name of the Lord? Knowing His name is crucial. I place His self-appointed names at the bottom of the devotions because His names reveal His identity.

I had a Jewish friend once who came to me for prayer. Someone unjustly sued her. A landlord intentionally forced her into a breach of contract, and she filed a countersuit to defend herself. She asked me for Scripture she could use for court.

I said, "Read Romans 13; it's about subjection to authority." She asked me to come over to her desk, and it turned out that was the Bible verse she had pulled up on her computer. The look on her face was total astonishment.

The next day, she went to court. The woman who was suing her did not arrive. The judge dismissed her case and awarded my friend $6,000.00 in the countersuit! As she was leaving the building, the landlord was being detained by officers at the metal detector, and the police would not let her through. The landlord was on a merry-go-round, trying to get past security.

When you call out to God, He renders a decision on your behalf.

"For whosoever shall call upon the name of the Lord shall be saved" (Romans 10:11).

He is: Elohim Yare
God Most Awesome
Blessings

SPIRITUAL CHECKING

August 27

"Unto the pure all things are pure: but unto them that are defiled, and unbelieving is nothing pure; but even their mind and conscience is defiled."

Titus 1:15

Titus 1:5 is one of the verses that has always resonated with me; it's interesting to observe how some people who are dishonest in business tend to assume that everyone is corrupt. Unfortunately, sometimes, they project their values onto others, causing unjust accusations. This behavior reminds me of the next verse, "They profess that they know God, but in works they deny Him..." (Titus 1:16). It's like they go to church on Sunday, and then on Monday at work, they're just "one of the guys." Keeping our minds renewed and protected by reading the Bible daily and taking our thoughts captive is crucial. Sin sears our conscience like a hotdog roasting over a fire, but if it gets burned too severely, the devil takes it and throws it in the fire! Therefore, we need to put some armor on our minds and think the best about people, checking our spiritual condition along the way.

He is: Akal Esh
Consuming Fire
Blessings

MAILBOXES

August 28

"And unclean spirits, when they saw him, fell down before him, and cried, saying, Thou art the Son of God. And he straitly charged them that they should not make him known."

Mark 3:11–12

It's a strange form of flattery, but Jesus had none of it. With His authority, He commanded the unclean spirits not to make Him known. Satan was sacrificing his front-line pawns, strategically sending demonically possessed people to attack by yelling, "We know who You are, thou Son of God!" But what was he trying to accomplish? My guess would be pride. Satan tried to puff up Jesus with pride and cause Him to sin. However, Jesus chose the time when He would reveal Himself.

The enemy uses pride to make us all fall, often subtly. Little thoughts can creep in unawares, and then we may notice that we're not hearing from the Lord like we used to. It's time for a pride check.

Once, I spent a considerable amount of time painting my mailbox. I began to notice how all my neighbor's mailboxes needed painting. I thought, *Man, I've got the nicest-looking mailbox in the neighborhood.* The next day, someone ran into my mailbox, breaking all the decorative cast iron off the box. Now I have a shiny mailbox that's missing the bottom half.

The point is Jesus will help us get rid of pride even if we don't ask for His help because He loves us. "The arrogant shall not stand in Thy sight; Thou hatest all workers of iniquity" (Psalm 5:5).

Don't let the enemy place pride in your mailbox. Put a lock on it by being humble because God hates pride.

He is: Sane
The God Who Hates
Blessings

DON'T REJECT—ACCEPT

August 29

*"My people are destroyed for lack of knowledge:
because thou hast rejected knowledge."*

Hosea 4:6

Oh, how the devil has used this to his advantage over the centuries. Of course, this verse targets the nation of Israel and a specific generation.

But how true is this same verse for today? Very accurate in many ways. Healthwise, people have fallen for crazy beliefs in health. People used to think it was very healthy to take mercury. Another common practice is bloodletting, which happens when we stray too far away from the Word of God. The Bible clearly states that life is in the blood:

"For the life of the flesh [is] in the blood: and I have given it to you upon the altar to make an atonement for your souls: for it [is] the blood [that] maketh an atonement for the soul" (Leviticus 17:11).

I've heard it preached that when you are faced with a challenging situation, you should stop and take a break, eat a "ham sammich," and rest for a little bit. Then, you'll gain an understanding on how to solve the problem.

If you need understanding and the project is at a standstill, I suggest you stop and take communion with the Lord. Spend that precious minute with God and ask for understanding. Then, see what happens.

He is: El Deah
The God of All Knowledge
Blessings

LET'S GET RIGHTEOUS

August 30

"For thou, Lord, wilt bless the righteous;
with favor wilt thou compass him as with a shield."

Psalm 5:12

King David prayed this verse as part of a morning prayer. In verse 1 of Psalm 5, David asks God to consider his meditation. In this context, "meditation" has a dual meaning: thoughts and murmurings. Throughout the day, I engage in this practice almost like a whisper, speaking to God under my breath. Nobody can hear what I'm saying (unless I'm deaf and unaware that I'm shouting out loud).

Nonetheless, I'm confident that God hears me. And God hearing us is a profound blessing from a compassionate God who cares about our little murmurings. It is worth noting that this verse requires a qualifying aspect: righteousness.

People often confuse righteousness with holiness. Trying to be holy can lead to frustration and drive one crazy. However, there has only been one genuinely holy person, Jesus Christ. It's impossible to achieve holiness on our own. Nonetheless, we can be righteous: "And be found in him, not having mine own righteousness, which is of the law, but that which is through the faith of Christ, the righteousness which is of God by faith" (Philippians 3:9).

Our righteousness comes through faith in Christ, not our efforts to obey the law. Acts of faith in Christ, such as believing that God hears our prayers, produce righteousness in us.

Believe this: "With favor wilt thou compass him as with a shield." May you have a blessed and favorable day!

He is: Tsaddik
Righteous
Blessings

SUFFERING

August 31

And it came to pass, when Joseph was come unto his brethren, that they stripped Joseph of his coat, the coat of many colors that was on him; and they took him, and cast him into the pit: and the pit was empty, there was no water in it.

Genesis 37:23–24

Rejection doesn't get much more profound than Joseph being thrown down into a pit by his own family and, a couple of hours later, sold into slavery. Rejection can have significant spiritual, emotional, and psychological impacts on a person. How it affects an individual can vary greatly depending on their beliefs, coping mechanisms, and support system.

However, some possible good consequences come from rejection; just ask any famous country singer. But in Joseph's case, his brothers were about to murder him, and then Reuben stepped in and saved his life by having him thrown into the pit, intending to save him later. What would Reuben have been able to do if he had returned and rescued Joseph later that day? Hand him a flask of water and a morsel of bread, and like Moses, send him out into the wilderness. My point is, the trial was happening no matter which way Joseph turned.

You may suffer from rejection as we all have, and you may not know how to turn. It gets to the point where we beg God instead of thanking God. "In everything give thanks: for this is the will of God in Christ Jesus to you-ward" (1 Thessalonians 5:18, KJV).

Some signs that you are suffering from rejection are loss of self-worth, low self-esteem, feeling inadequate, self-doubt, questing God, your belief in Christ, and anger. We have an enemy, and these are emotions that he will employ to bring you to a place of rejection, rejection of Jesus Christ as your Lord and Savior, and even cause you to reject Him as your deliverer. The whole purpose of any trial is to get you to renounce God, get angry, quit, and give up. It's like Satan is filling your cup, a cup of wrath.

I have been fortunate to have suffered through these types of trials. I asked Jesus with a broken heart a couple of times, "Why?" I heard the same answer, "They didn't reject you; they rejected Me." Jesus is well acquainted with rejection; Joseph was a prototype of Christ's suffering and His rejection. Every time someone walks away from Jesus, it's that type of rejection that He suffers once again. It is like a form of worship to the enemy, but to Christ, it is an opportunity for Him to display His grace and His love towards you.

He knows what you have been through and chooses to fill your cup with His blood, the communion of Christ. No matter which way you turn, Jesus has a plan. It may not look or feel like it now, but I know "you will overcome." The actions of others do not determine your value. Jesus Christ determines your value; He laid down His life for you because He determines your worth.

He is: Hesed (   )
O give thanks unto the LORD; for he is good: for his mercy endureth forever.
Blessings

THANKSGIVING

SEVEN AND A HALF

September 1

*And it came to pass, that, while they communed together and reasoned,
Jesus himself drew near, and went with them.
But their eyes were holden that they should not know him.
And he said unto them, "What manner of communications are these
that ye have one to another, as ye walk, and are sad?"*

Luke 24:15–17

After the crucifixion, these two disciples were on a long, lonely hike of seven and a half miles, or so they thought. Most of us read over this scripture without realizing that Jesus is already fulfilling a promise He made back in the book of:

"For where two or three are gathered together in my name, there am I in the midst of them" (Matthew 18:20).

Christ chose to manifest Himself in His physical body to console His disciples. If you are talking about Jesus, when there are two, there are three because Jesus will always be there.

If you continue reading, you will notice that Christ didn't tell them plainly who He was; he began explaining thoroughly from the Scriptures, starting with Moses and all the prophets, everything concerning Himself.

In verses 30–31, Jesus took the bread and blessed it, gave it to them, and their eyes opened, and they knew Him!

Why now? Why after they ate the bread? Because Jesus is the Bread of Life.

"Behold, I stand at the door, and knock: if any man hear my voice, and open the door, I will come in to him, and will sup with him, and he with me" (Revelation 3:20). Jesus keeps His word because He is the Word.

He is: Immanuel
God with Us
Blessings

READY TO FORGIVE

September 2

And to our beloved Apphia, and Archippus our fellow-soldier,
and to the church in thy house:
Grace to you, and peace, from God our Father and the Lord Jesus Christ.
I thank my God, making mention of thee always in my prayers,
Hearing of thy love and faith, which thou hast toward the
Lord Jesus, and toward all saints;

Philemon 1:2–5

Apphia is presumed to be the wife of Philemon and Archippus, his son. Notice that Paul greets them rather than Philemon; in fact, Philemon is mentioned in the very last verse of this letter.

We can gather insights from this epistle seeking forgiveness for a runaway slave named Onesimus. First, Onesimus wasn't running away from slavery; he was running to the gospel. He wanted to remain a servant, but he wanted to serve in another capacity.

Honestly, I believe he wanted to be next to the man of God, and the of anointing on Paul was authentic. Having been around some very anointed men and women of God myself, I can attest to the presence of the Lord. Onesimus wanted that so much that he was willing to serve in a dungeon!

Notice Philemon pastored a church in his home. When anointed to be a pastor, the entire family gets the call.

This letter is about forgiveness, so Paul sees the need to forgive and positions the first two people who've been affected the most. Apphia and Archippus. Mother and son probably had to pick up Onesimus's chores, which perhaps caused some harsh feelings.

But this letter is open-ended. When Paul arrives, he will settle the debt, and there is no mention of him returning to settle up. It's open-ended for a reason.

We are always to be forgiving.

He is: Elohay Selichot
The God Who Is Ready to Forgive
Blessings

290 | Who Is God?

LINE OF FAITH

September 3

"Give us help from trouble: for vain is the help of man. Through God we shall do valiantly: for He it is that shall tread down our enemies."

Psalm 60:11–12

Reading this gives you peace and understanding that God will help you through difficult times. When reading this Psalm from the beginning and relating it to the historical timeline of King David, you feel where it came from and what birthed this Line of Faith.

This Psalm accounts for David's battles and victories found in 2 Samuel chapter 8. But in this chapter, there is no mention of any defeats. King David slams down victory after victory against his enemies, yet he pens this Psalm, saying God has cast us off.

David's armies had a severe setback; in battle, an earthquake allowed the enemy forces to break his front lines. King David writes, "You made us drink from the cup of astonishment" (a cup of suffering).

Through understanding this historical context, we can see the character traits that God cherished so much in King David. Why has the devil prevailed over us?'

Instead, he humbles himself by asking God to give us help and reminding God that he can't win these battles without Him.

Maybe that recent defeat wasn't from the enemy; perhaps it was God stepping back a little. I do know what one cause can be: pride.

Pride comes before the great fall. When things get going well, it's within our nature to start taking credit for what God has done. Pride creeps in slowly, and he pretends to be innocent. If things aren't going well, we must check our attitudes for signs of pride; it can hide in unexpected places. Sometimes, it's just our attitude.

He is: Jehovah-Magen
Shield
Blessings

PUTTING FORTH THE TEST

September 4

Do not believe every spirit, but test the spirits, whether they are of God. Many false prophets have gone out into the world. By this, you know the Spirit of God. Every spirit that confesses that Jesus Christ has come in the flesh is of God. And every spirit that does not confess that Jesus Christ has come in the flesh is not of God. This is the spirit of the Antichrist, which you have heard was coming and is now already in the world.

1 John 4:1-3

Believe not every voice you hear; the devil is a liar, and he will try to deceive you. John continues to posit our faith with the following verse, a guarantee: "For whatever is born of God overcomes the world. And this is the victory that has overcome the world, our faith. Who is he who overcomes the world, but he who believes that Jesus is the Son of God. (1 John 5:4-5).

If the time comes when the enemy tries to deceive you, state these words (the Holy Passcode), "Confess that Jesus Christ has come in the flesh" (1 John 4:2). But make no mistake, the enemy will try to deceive you, he will try and sidestep the answer, or try to make you feel guilty for asking, or even use flattery. Flattery is a tactic he uses to make you think you are righteous and theologically superior. How could he possibly fool you?

Unfortunately, I learned these tactics from the enemy through his deceit. He beat me, fooled me, and battered me down with unbelief. But his mistake was that Jesus recovered me, and because of these experiences and my defeats, you can learn some battle tactics. The last thing he wants is for you to learn how to defeat him.

I had a positive experience of this nature not long ago. I heard the Holy Spirit say, "I have something I want to impart to you." And I wasn't expecting to hear the Lord's voice then, so I asked, "Confess that Jesus Christ has come in the flesh" (1 John 4:2).

The Holy Spirit answered me, saying, "I confess Jesus Christ came in the flesh, and He is your Lord and Savior." It wasn't dramatic. His tone was very polite and professional. But talk about refreshing, knowing that it was, in fact, the Holy Spirit. And His following words blessed me. So, I asked, "Lord can you tell me what you are going to impart to me?"

And He said, "The ability to believe Me."

It pays to know who you are speaking with.

He is: Magen
The Lord is my Shield, my Protector
Blessings

HIS FLOWING

September 5

"And out of the throne proceeded lightnings and thunderings and voices: and there were seven lamps of fire burning before the throne, which are the seven Spirits of God."

Revelations 4:5

As described here, the Throne Room of God is not tranquil. But why is that?

Revelation 4:11 provides some insight: "Thou art worthy, O Lord, to receive glory and honor and power: for thou, hast created all things, and for thy pleasure they are and were created."

God cherishes His creation, and His nature is to give. Everything emanates from Him. He created us for His pleasure, which signifies fellowship and companionship. It might be challenging to comprehend this, but we see a parallel in our world. Successful people often associate with other successful individuals—it's just how society operates. God, in His omnipotence, seeks to commune with us. He desires to spend time with you! Just as a parent enjoys spending time with their children and listening to their perspectives on various topics, even when they possess a more profound understanding, so does God desire fellowship with us.

The seven lamps mentioned in Revelation represent a Menorah, the seven Spirits of God signify the totality of the Holy Spirit, and the seven symbolizes completion.

"And the Spirit of the LORD shall rest upon him, the Spirit of wisdom and understanding, the Spirit of counsel and might, the Spirit of knowledge and of the fear of the LORD" (Isaiah 11:2).

These seven spirits flowed from the Throne of God to one individual, Jesus Christ. All seven rested upon and within Him. What did Jesus do with these Spirits?

And suddenly, there came a sound from heaven as of a mighty rushing wind, and it filled all the house where they were sitting. And there appeared unto them cloven tongues like as of fire, and it sat upon each of them. And they were all filled with the Holy Ghost and began to speak with other tongues, as the Spirit gave them utterance.

Acts 2:2–4

Jesus bestowed gifts upon people; He gave them to you.

He is: Gelah Raz
Revealer of Mysteries
Blessings

YOUR WILDERNESS

September 6

"And He withdrew Himself into the wilderness, and prayed."
Luke 5:16

In modern-day words, Jesus just finished a healing crusade to kick off His ministry. Jesus attracted massive crowds to listen to His teachings and receive desperately needed healing.

Imagine being surrounded by crowds, each pressing closer for a prayer. The sheer quantity of prayer needed is exhausting, not to mention the potential safety concern with such a crowd. I experienced a similar situation in Haiti, albeit on a much smaller scale compared to what Jesus must have encountered. I was in danger of being pressed against my vehicle as people gathered around me. It was a bit "concerning."

Fortunately, before setting out that day, I had arranged for young men to accompany me and assist in distributing rice and milk while I prayed. By God's grace, they ended up providing crowd control. The Holy Spirit had anticipated this need.

In our daily lives, we confront various forms of pressure. Our minds can become overwhelmed by a relentless onslaught of noise and demands. Stress manifests in countless ways, including financial worries, job-related issues, family conflict, or even the habit of biting your fingernails excessively.

Jesus, in one sentence, gave us a strategy for stress relief: find a quiet place to commune with God and spend some uninterrupted time with Him. Ideally, you might retreat to the mountains, but finding a quiet corner in your car for ten minutes of prayer is equally effective. Sometimes, I find solace sitting on the bathtub's edge, immersed in prayer.

The term "wilderness" signifies a solitary place. Remember, no matter where you are, there's a "wilderness" nearby—a place where you can find solitude and connection with God.

He is: Elohim Shama
The God Who Hears
Blessings

SUDDENLY!

September 7

"Surely the Lord God will do nothing, but He revealeth His secret unto His servants the prophets."

Amos 3:7

Do you yearn to uncover a secret? Many individuals believe that God's promise in this scripture has already come to pass, primarily due to a misinterpretation of the following verse: "Charity never faileth: but whether there be prophecies, they shall fail; whether there be tongues, they shall cease; whether there be knowledge, it shall vanish away" (1 Corinthians 13:8).

Charity signifies love, and love will never cease because God embodies love. However, a time will come when Jesus establishes His kingdom on earth. There will be no need for prophecies in this time, as we will understand God's will. Similarly, there will be no need to pray in tongues since we will be in His presence. Words of knowledge are situational, and there won't be a circumstance where God's wisdom isn't available to guide our actions.

The gift of speaking in tongues becomes crucial when praying in the Holy Spirit. Unbeknownst to us, we discuss divine strategies and secure a spiritual legacy for our future generations, such as salvation.

While typing this devotion, the Lord spoke to me and said: "Tell them there will be a *suddenly*!"

He is: Jehovah-Palat
Deliverer
Blessings

WANT TO BE REMEMBERED?

September 8

Then they that feared the Lord spake often to one to another: and the Lord hearkened, and heard it, and a book of remembrance was written before Him for them that feared the Lord, and that thought upon His name.

Malachi 3:16

I asked the Lord this, "What is the Book of Remembrance?" The answer is, "This is the book of all who have done My will."

The Book of Life contains the names of everyone who has accepted Jesus Christ as their Lord and Savior, serving as our passport to heaven.

On the other hand, the Book of Remembrance is dedicated to those who have not only believed in Jesus Christ but also pursued His callings with conviction and passion.

As a youth pastor, I constantly urged teenagers to seek God's purpose. In return, I often received blank stares, reflecting their fear of potentially committing to a life in ministry or, even more daunting, on the mission field.

To help them understand God's callings, I invited a renowned Christian medical doctor to discuss career choices and spiritual callings. He held their attention with a story about a new Mercedes he had purchased. The Lord instructed him to take a different route home as he left the dealership. Ignoring this divine directive, he ended up in a car accident, resulting in his new vehicle's total loss.

In his despair, he wept, grieving the loss of his car but primarily for his failure to heed God's guidance. At that moment, he must have understood that God wasn't trying to prevent him from enjoying his new car but was attempting to spare him the pain of loss.

That is precisely the lesson I wanted to impart to the young people I was mentoring: God's calling isn't a burden but a blessing. If God calls you to a purpose, it is for your benefit as much as His.

And when you fulfill His will, He remembers your deeds. What a profound honor it is to be recognized by God.

He is: Logos
The Word
Blessings

GREAT DEPTHS

September 9

"But I will sacrifice unto thee with the voice of thanksgiving; I will pay that that I have vowed. Salvation is of the LORD."

Jonah 2:9

After three days, Jonah decides to pray. He has spent these days in the belly of a great fish. The word "great" here pertains to the fish's size and age.

In verse 1:17, the LORD had prepared a great fish to swallow up Jonah.

Considering this, it's possible to speculate that this fish was of significant age. The oldest Koi fish alive is Hanako; she was born in 1751 and is now 226 years old!

Jonah's act of disobedience did not surprise God. Jonah had such an intense dislike for the people of Nineveh that he preferred they go to hell. However, God's perspective was different. Jonah's hatred was so fierce that he fled from God, boarded the first ship in the opposite direction, was cast into the sea, and was swallowed by a 'great fish', and only after three days did he decide to pray!

Jonah's stubbornness was noteworthy; strangely, I respect it. But what eventually changed? His attitude. He made a vow and promised God that he would honor it. His vow came from a place of utter anguish and surrender. He tells God, "I will sacrifice with the voice of thanksgiving."

When you find yourself in life's deepest lows, the most brutal form of praise to offer, which requires pushing aside all pride and anger, is a sacrifice of thanksgiving to the Lord. After Jonah's prayer, the Lord spoke to the fish, and it spits Jonah out.

Have you ever pondered whether the fish might have been close to the shore for the last two and a half days?

"And let the peace of God rule in your hearts, to the which also ye are called in one body; and be ye thankful" (Colossians 3:15).

He is: Elohim Shama
The God Who Hears
Blessings

BEING PREPARED

September 10

"Then said the Lord, thou hast had pity on the gourd, for the which thou hast not labored, neither madest it grow; which came up in a night, and perished".

Jonah 4:10

After spending three days in the belly of a sea creature and walking through the streets of Nineveh for another three days, shouting at everyone that they had forty days before God would overthrow the city, Jonah had some issues. He was angry, and he didn't care who knew it.

Jonah climbed a hill to observe the city's destruction and waited. The news of a man being vomited out by a fish, appearing as if he had been slimed on the movie set of Ghostbusters, and walking through their city while proclaiming the imminent arrival of God's judgment caused the people to repent swiftly.

During all this, God took pity on Jonah and grew a gourd overnight to provide shade from the scorching heat of the day. But then God prepared a worm to attack the gourd, followed by a vehement east wind, and the sun beat down on Jonah's head until he fainted.

Jonah became angry about God sending the worm to destroy the gourd because he had grown fond of it. In response, God corrected Jonah, emphasizing that people and animals are far more valuable than a mere gourd. The book ends with Jonah still harboring anger over what hasn't happened.

As you read this historical account, you'll notice the phrase "God prepared" mentioned four times. Each time, a hardship brought Jonah closer to his destiny.

We know what became of Jonah. In 2015, ISIS destroyed Jonah's headstone, a small monument marking his final resting place in the heart of the city of Nineveh.

Jonah spent the remainder of his days in the city of Nineveh, likely teaching the word of God rather than proclaiming judgment.

Now, the question arises: What has God prepared for you?

He is: Jehovah-Goel
Redeeming God
Blessings

ALL THINGS WORK TOGETHER

September 11

Why do the heathen rage, and the people imagine a vain thing?
The kings of the earth set themselves, and the rulers take counsel together, against
the LORD, and against his anointed, saying,
Let us break their bands asunder, and cast away their cords from us.
He that sitteth in the heavens shall laugh: the Lord shall have them in derision.

(Psalm 2:1–4)

Inundation's definition is an overwhelming abundance of people or things, a flood. In this day and age, it's effortless to become inundated with negative news. It's almost like people are in a rage. When you listen with spiritual ears, you hear a plan, subtle words that go against the kingdom of Christ.

The word anointed is from the Hebrew word *MASHIACH*, which means "Christ." It can also refer to the saints of Christ. Let us break their bands asunder is the elimination of MASHIACH. We see this in communist and Islamic countries, where the church is persecuted. For centuries, the enemy of God has worked hard to cause the defeat, but God sits on His throne and laughs.

I heard a pastor tell a story about how he listened to the Holy Spirit laughing, faint at first. Finally, the pastor said: "God, is that You?" and God said, "Yes." The pastor replied, "What are You laughing at?" He said that God said, "The devil. He thinks he's going to win!" The pastor said God's laughter became even louder, and then the pastor began to laugh and laugh.

There is no place you can go where God is not. It must be hard to have a secret meeting when God hears every word spoken.

I've had people plot against me; honestly, it hurts, and I haven't always responded the way I know a Christian should have, but I know that God said:

"And we know that all things work together for good to them that love God, to them who are the called according to his purpose" (Romans 8:28).

For good to them that love God, if you want things to go well, learn to love God. There have been times that all I can say to God is:

"Father, I love You!" And I know that it is enough.

He is: YAHUAH AHAVAH SHALOM
God of Love and Peace
Blessings

LEARN TO COUNT

September 12

"Teach us to number our days and recognize how few they are;
help us to spend them as we should."

Psalm 90:12

This psalm is a psalm that Moses, the man of God, wrote. At this time, he has been wandering in the wilderness with the children of Israel. Israel tested God ten times with unbelief, and the punishment was that this generation must live in the wilderness for forty years and die before the next generation can enter the Promised Land.

We come from dust, and God gives a command for the day that we return to dust. Just like the children of Israel, we all have an appointed time to return. *Teach us to number our days.* I've noticed twice in my life: two different men who were ungodly and wouldn't even give me the time of day. At various times, they each had heart attacks. Afterward, they were so glad to see me, and they valued me. I noticed that they appreciated everything in life, they were grateful to be alive, but I also noticed this about both of them. After a couple of months, they returned to their old ways.

They didn't value their remaining days. If we knew our number, how would we act? Would we appreciate the people placed in our lives, or would we be bitter about how much time we have left? You may notice older people become more loving and kinder because they learn to love. In his last days of life, as the story goes, the Apostle John had to be carried in someone's arms everywhere he went, his body beaten and frail. In the end, he quoted this phrase more often than others, "My little children love one another." When asked why he always said this, he replied, "It is the Lord's command, and if this alone is done, it is enough."

If you love God with all your heart, you will learn to number your days and love your neighbor.

He is: El Yalad
The God Who Gave You Birth
Blessings

MOVING FORWARD

September 13

*"And it came to pass, when the ark was set forward, that Moses said,
Rise up, Lord, and let thine enemies be scattered; and let them
that hate thee flee before thee."*

Numbers 10:35

I love the words: "And it came to pass." The Bible doesn't ever say: "And it came to stay." When the ark was set forward, this means that the ark of God was moving forward. God never backs down. As Christians, we should always be moving forward. Yesterday is behind us, and we can't do anything about the mistakes we made. Apostle Paul was aware of this when he said:

"No, dear brothers and sisters, I have not achieved it, but I focus on this one thing: Forgetting the past and looking forward to what lies ahead" (Philippians 3:13).

It seems, just like us, Paul carried the weight of his past sins. Before he took the surname of Paul, his name was Saul of Tarsus, and Saul was a fierce man. When he became a Christian, the very movement that he was trying to stop, the movement of Christ, moved forward and overtook Saul, scattering his sin and making him a new man, so much so that he decided to change his name.

What was Paul trying to achieve? Christ-likeness, I think, we can only achieve it in small moments, where we bless someone, or when we turn the other cheek, little things like this, little things that cause the enemy to be scattered.

Through the Holy Spirit, the ark of God rests in your heart, and His movements are in your actions.

*He is: Jehovah Uzzi
The Lord My Strength
Blessings*

MORE THAN A CONQUEROR

September 14

"Nay, in all these things we are more than conquerors through him that loved us."

Romans 8:37

It's almost humorous that this verse starts with a negative word: Nay. Except it is in response to some very tragic suffering incurred by fellow Christians long ago.

It reminds me of all the times I have complained to the Lord about challenging situations. Years ago, when our children would get into something, we would sometimes say something like: "No, no, no!" or "I don't think so!"

Romans 8 offsets that when you get low on strategy and victory seems far off, the complaints start to speak out. It's like your Father in heaven says: "No, no, no, I made you more than a conqueror." What's it like to be more than a conqueror? Here's a great example:

A heavyweight prizefighter trains all his life to become the champion.

He takes thousands of hits.

Physical endurance is punishing every day.

Finally, he makes it to the heavyweight championship fight. He fights fifteen rounds and, at the last moment, knocks his opponent out and becomes the champion.

He stands in that ring and lifts the belt above his head in total victory. The promoter hands him a giant check. Then, he goes home and celebrates with his wife, whom he loves and trusts. He signs the back of the check and hands it over to her to take care of, and suddenly, she has become more than a conqueror!

Sometimes, we must be patient while the Master is in the ring…

He is: Jehovah Gibbor Milchamah
Mighty in Battle
Blessings

HOPE IS FUEL

September 15

So, I pray for you Gentiles that God who gives you hope will keep you happy and full of peace as you believe in Him. I pray that God will help you overflow with Hope in him through the Holy Spirit's power within you.

Romans 15:13

Hope is the most fantastic fuel for humankind. However, when spelled out backward, it spells "FEAR." Yes, the opposite of hope is fear. That's why the enemy uses it to steal our hope away. When you have hope, you know it shall come to pass no matter how difficult the situation. It's the hopeless times in life that are the most difficult.

Hopelessness continuously drains you of strength. The great evangelist Smith Wigglesworth, who lived from the 1800s to 1947, observed the very poor, and he said this: "The reason poor people live in such unclean conditions is that they have no hope."

Poverty can rob your strength, and simple chores can become mountains to climb; just doing the laundry can feel like lifting weights. But it's times like these that you can find something to hope for. "These troubles and sufferings of ours are, after all, quite small and won't last very long. Yet this short time of distress will result in God's richest blessing upon us forever and ever!" (2 Corinthians 4:17)

Encourage yourself with hope in the Word. The Word was made flesh and dwelt with mankind; that's Jesus! When you get to your weakest point, get happy because 2 Corinthians 12:10 reminds us: *for when I am weak, then I am strong—the less I have, the more I depend on him.*

He is: Shub Nephesh
Renewer of Life
Blessings

HOPE TIMES 2

September 16

"And Noah went in, and his sons, and his wife, and his sons' wives with him, into the ark, because of the waters of the flood."

Genesis 7:7

I remember my great-grandmother Lillie once wrote me a letter, and she said: "I suppose every generation gets their trial."

When Noah entered the ark, he had an expectation of leaving the ark. He knew the floodwaters would rise, but he had the expected hope that they would recede, and they did.

There are two types of hope in the Hebrew language. Unfortunately, we get the same word for both meanings. Noah had a kind of hope that in Hebrew is called *YAKHAL*, hoping that he could wait upon the LORD to end the storm and that the waters would recede. Hope in the LORD to bring the trial to an end.

The second type of hope is *QAVAH*. It's a feeling or a tension similar to a cord being stretched. Stretch it hard enough, and the cord will break, thus releasing the pressure.

When we hope in the LORD, we remember His past deliverances, and we look back on all the times He saved us from trials, disasters, and even death. He always pulled me through. Maybe what I see as personal failures God sees as victories.

Our generation has come into our flood. We must symbolically enter the ark and see this through, trusting God to bring us to dry ground. It's a test of two hopes.

"And the ark rested in the seventh month, on the seventeenth day of the month, upon the mountains of Ararat" (Genesis 8:4).

Notice the ark was constructed in a valley, and when the storm was over, the floods receded. When it came to rest, it was on top of the mountain. Maybe God is bringing you to a higher level, closer to Him.

He is: Jehovah-Shammah
The Lord Is There
Blessings

MY WEAKNESS

September 17

If I must boast, I will boast of my weakness.
The God and Father of the Lord Yeshua, who is blessed forever,
knows that I am not lying.
In Damascus, the governor under King Aretas was guarding
the city of the Damascenes in order to seize me,
and I was lowered in a basket through a window in the wall and escaped his hands.

2 Corinthians 11:30–33

Boastfulness is something we take pride in that we want to talk about, even shout out to others about how great we are. But Paul chose to boast about his weakness. It's a fantastic turn of events. At this time in Paul's life, the Gentiles want to kill him, and the Christian Jews are terrified of him. I see some profound things in this story.

Why did Paul consider this a weakness? Maybe for the first time in his life, he had to depend on someone else to save his life. He had to get in the basket, give up control, let go of the wall, and let go. Christians have a saying: "Let go and let God."

The symbolism of Paul placed in a basket reminds me of the offering basket we use at church. Made of whicker, we put our offering in the basket and let it go, giving it to God.

At the beginning of his ministry, Paul was placed as an offering in a basket and lowered, even humbled. Lowered into a new calling by God, he had no idea where the rope would set him, no clue what he would become to us, a patriarch in the gospel directing generations of Christians to Christ.

What are you holding on to? What can we let go of that will offer us to Christ? When you let go, I'm sure you will land on solid ground.

He is: Tsur Yisrael
Rock of Israel
Blessings

SHARE THE COMFORT

September 18

Blessed be God, even the Father of our Lord Jesus Christ,
the Father of mercies, and the God of all comfort;
Who comforteth us in all our tribulation, that we may be able to comfort them
which are in any trouble, by the comfort wherewith we
ourselves are comforted of God.

2 Corinthians 1:3–5

Apostle Paul knew how to encourage his followers because he knew who God was: our Comforter. Paul was the ultimate wordsmith. I think that he was probably one of the most intelligent men that ever lived. Notice how he proceeds with this statement by invoking a blessing towards God, then he announces who God is: "Blessed be God, even the Father of our Lord Jesus Christ, the Father of mercies, and the God of all comfort."

After the word "comfort," the priests translated this scripture and placed a semicolon instead of a period or a comma. Semicolons provide a break in the flow, almost like the word in Hebrew: *Selah* (which means: pause and think about that). It clarifies, and then it joins the two thoughts together in connecting ideas, and both concepts have to be a complete sentence.

When we're in Christ Jesus, we cannot separate God from our tribulations, His mercies, and His comfort. The Hebrew letter "Yod" resembles an apostrophe' and it is the letter that represents God, the smallest letter in the Hebrew 'alephabet'. Knowing that Christ Jesus symbolically would be the ultimate use of a semicolon, connecting us with God enabling us to comfort others in their time of need. Now you know why you have gone through tribulations. It's so that you can comfort others with the knowledge of the comfort you have received in the past.

He is: Theos Pas Paraklesis
The God of All Comfort
Blessings

STRENGTH TO THE FAINT

September 19

*"He giveth power to the faint; and to them that
have no might He increaseth strength."*

Isaiah 40:29

Understanding—God has it. When He carried the burden of our sin on the cross, He did this because of two of His many great traits: Love and understanding. He knew we could never defeat sin on our own, and He knows the burden of the sin we carry. Sometimes, we can let our past mistakes weigh us down to the point of weariness or becoming faint, and some Christians refer to these times as being in the wilderness. It's a place of our own making and a place we go when we get down for some of us.

We do not want to pray, like Adam and Eve trying to hide our ways from God. Or we can face another type of faintness, exhaustion, physical, mental, or demonic attacks of the worst kind.

Years ago, I was going through some emotional times, and I felt like a wounded fish in an aquarium filled with piranhas. At every angle, the enemy was applying severe pressure. It felt like every other fish knew I was wounded and would take another painful bite. Then, one morning, I knelt on my knees and could feel my veins bulging in my neck from anger. My face must have been beat red. I told God I couldn't take it anymore and needed His help. At that exact moment, I felt His hand reach inside my chest and gently squeeze my heart. He didn't fill my heart with joy or happiness; He filled it with strength. He strengthened me with the power that He gives to the faint.

Instantly, I went from anger and weakness to confidence. Suddenly, I knew I could get through this. My strength came back, and that's partly what the word "power" means: to give you strength and the ability to get through this.

He is: Rum Rosh
The One Who Lifts My Head
Blessings

THE PRINCIPLE OF TWO

September 20

*"If you have two coats, he replied, give one to the poor.
If you have extra food, give it away to those who are hungry."*

Luke 3:11

In the preceding verse, the people asked John the Baptist, "What shall we do then?" And verse 11 was his answer. The principle of two is two definitions of one answer.

If you continue to read this chapter, you will notice he took one answer and gave two more definitions. The publicans asked, "Master, what shall we do?" The answer was, "Take no more than what was appointed you." The soldiers asked, "What shall we do?" The answer: "Do violence to no man, neither accuse any falsely, and be content with your wages."

How is it that each group received different answers? Three different types of people, three types of sins. The tax collectors took more than they should; the soldiers were brutal and never content with their wages. And the people needed to be more benevolent.

Do you remember the rich young ruler who came to Jesus and said, "What must I do to inherit eternal life? He told Jesus he had kept all the commandments; Jesus said, you lack treasure in heaven give away everything and come follow Me" (Luke 18:18–30).

Like the rich young ruler, the first group had issues with being self-centered, placing their faith in wealth rather than God. In modern terms, when you get new clothes, take the time to sort out your old ones, donate them, and make an offering to your local food bank.

But here is the principle of two: my son was reading his Bible one day when he read this verse (Luke 3:11). The Lord spoke to him and told him these words:

"The Principle of Two, for every dollar you give in the offering, you must match dollar for dollar to your savings."

The Lord doesn't want us broke or destitute. He wants us debt-free so that we can give abundantly.

He is: Jehova-Jireh
My Provider
Blessings

BE A GOOD GARDENER

September 21

"For our people must learn to help all who need their assistance, that their lives will be fruitful."

Titus 3:14

This verse is from the Living Bible, and this translation makes it easier to understand what Paul was conveying to the church. There are two quotes I hang onto in life, and one is by Mother Theresa. While traveling by plane, someone asked her, "How do you do ministry?" She responded, "Find something to give and then give it."

The second quote was by a friend, "It's never convenient to do ministry." By that, he meant that when people need your help, it doesn't just conveniently place itself in your schedule for the day. Usually, it happens after you have worked all day and feel like resting, and then you suddenly get a call.

"Don't forget to do good and to share what you have with those in need, for such sacrifices are very pleasing to him" (Hebrews 13:16).

I'll quote this verse to myself when I don't feel like helping others. Sometimes, I get in a mental rut of feeling used by people. Then, with the proper attitude adjustment, I realized I was planting this seed for Jesus.

He is: Georgos
The Gardener
Blessings

PRAY THE GOOD

September 22

I always thank my God when I mention you in my prayers, because I hear of your love and faith towards the Lord Jesus and for all the saints. I pray that your participation in the faith may become effective through knowing every good thing that is in use for the glory of Christ. For I have great joy and encouragement from your love, because the hearts of the saints have been refreshed through you, brother.

Philemon 1:4–7 (HCSB)

A Good News prayer, a gospel prayer—notice that Paul prays for his friend Philemon from a position of thankfulness. He prays for his good qualities, telling Jesus how good of a person Philemon is.

I think most of us are guilty when it comes to praying for the poor qualities of our friends and family, pointing out to God what we believe to be potentially wrong with them.

From a heart filled with love for his friend, he prays the good qualities to God, and then, as though Paul has promoted Philemon to the Lord, he asks God to grant Philemon the gift of knowing every good thing that is in use for the glory of Christ.

Paul wants Philemon to see the good traits in people and the best qualities in others. I was truly fortunate to study and learn under the teachings of Dr. Sandy Powell; she has this gift of knowing the best qualities in others and making every student feel special. It's love that reflects the qualities of Christ.

Maybe if we pray for the best traits in others, it will help us to have *great joy* and *encouragement*.

He is: Yahweh-Channun
God Is Grace
Blessings

LOGOS / RHEMA

September 23

"In the beginning was the Word, and the Word was with God, and the Word was God. The same was in the beginning with God".

John 1:1–2

And,
"So then faith cometh by hearing, and hearing by the Word of God."

Romans 10:17

In the beginning was the Divine Expression, the Logos of God. Notice that in John 1:1, the Word is capitalized because it is the name of Jesus Christ. When written in the original Greek, they used the word *Logos*, and *Logos* means the Divine Expression (that is, Jesus Christ) or something said, and much more.

When they translated it into English, they translated it into "Word," sometimes capitalized and sometimes not.

In the second verse, Romans 10:17, Paul uses the Greek word *Rhema*, which translates over as "word," which are the spoken words of the Bible or the written words in the Bible. So, we have one word with two possible meanings.

It reveals the magnificent beauty of God's glory, His intellect, and so much more. In Genesis, chapter 1, God spoke the universe into existence using these words: "God said."

"God said" ten times, eight times He referred to the creation, and two times were instructions given to humankind.

So, what's the point behind all this? Jesus's name in heaven was probably Logos before He became flesh. God used the Rhema word to create the world and universe. Jesus became the Logos on earth to speak the Rhema words of God to reconcile His creation and defeat the enemy with His Word so that He can make all things new: Revelation 21:5

"And he that sat upon the throne said, Behold, I make all things new. And he said unto me, Write: for these words are true and faithful."

Now that's Logos.

He is: Logos
The Word
Blessings

HIS TRUTH

September 24

"And the LORD God said unto the woman, What is this that thou hast done? And the woman said, The serpent beguiled me, and I did eat."

Genesis 3:13

On the day of the forbidden fruit, what did we do? We have all partaken of the forbidden fruit, the fruit of temptation. The enemy tempts everyone, and just like Eve, we have all eaten.

There are so many ways the enemy can deceive. Jesus is the way, the truth, and the life; Satan is the father of all lies, quite the contrast. The enemy has so many ways to seduce, and here is one of the worst lies he uses to deceive us: the lies we believe about ourselves.

Sticks and stones will break my bones, but words will never hurt me. Imagine a criminal telling that to the judge right before he passes a sentence. The enemy uses words and subtle thoughts to imprison you, keeping you in a place lower than God intended. He typically does this through others, insults hurled at you in jest, or any other way he can get them into your subconscious.

For years, I would pray and ask God to help me be an eloquent speaker. I constantly compared myself to the great pastors and evangelists I listened to. Then, one day, I prayed this prayer, and the Lord spoke to me: "Who told you weren't an eloquent speaker?"

I thought for a moment and could not think of anyone ever saying that to me, so sheepishly, I said, "The devil?"

"That's right! You're full of My experience and love!"

And that was the end of the conversation; enough said. I had been deceived for years. The next time I preached, I had much more confidence (okay, I confess it was last Sunday).

But you get the point: take out the trash and start seeing yourself as God sees you. He sees you as *more* than a conqueror!

He is: El Roi
The God Who Sees Me
Blessings

A CALL TO BE WITH ME (HOLY SPIRIT)

September 25

"Better is the end of a thing than the beginning thereof: and the patient in spirit is better than the proud in spirit."

Ecclesiastes 7:8

Our nation has so much adversity, trouble, and hatred. Our people scoff at the values that made us free. There is so much violence and hate when you read or watch the news. Place adversity, trouble, and hatred into a funnel, and it dribbles down to bondage. It is all about trying to bind the Holy Spirit, and the Holy Spirit told me, "He wants to be free; it's bondage of Me.

"This is the beginning of a bitter thing, a spiritual battle that Christians must fight on their knees, in it with Me. It's a battle for the light, and the land is going to be free."

Patience is a virtue, and virtue will get you through this. The ability to wait for something without frustration is the opposite of the enemy. He vaunts his pride with chants and violence. Forever roaring like a lion that does not regard the will of humanity, a yearning to be free. However, Jesus gives us that liberty.

A proud spirit got Lucifer kicked out of heaven, and in his pride, he always suffers defeat. That's why, with God, we will win.

He is: Jehovah Gibbor Milchamah
Mighty in Battle
Blessings

NO LIMITS

September 26

"I have seen an end of all perfection: but thy commandment is exceeding broad."

Psalm 119:96

This scripture is one of those verses you can read over and thoroughly not understand and keep on reading. The Psalmist says this: "I have seen a limit to all completion."

"And then you set a boundary for the seas so that they would never again cover the earth" (Psalm 104:9).

Have you ever stood on the beach, looking out at the ocean, and the water level look higher than where you are standing, and wondered why it doesn't just flood over us? Because everything has a boundary, even the oceans. God set a limit to what things can do. A plane can only fly so high, a horse can only run so fast, and we can only live so long, and the earth will have an end, *but thy commandment is exceeding broad.*

"Heaven and earth shall pass away, but my words shall not pass away" (Matthew 24:35).

The Psalmist realized that anything will fail you, but God's word never will, Selah.

He is: El Olam
The Everlasting God, The Eternal God
Blessings

HAPPY FATHER'S DAY

September 27

"He is like a father to us, tender and sympathetic to those who reverence him."

Psalm 103:13)

Webster's dictionary defines the word "reverence" as profound respect mingled with love and awe, as for a holy being. God loves us; in fact, you can't outlove God. As much love as you can muster, He still loves you more. He's a Father to us, loving and compassionate. "Tender" means to take care of any person or thing, and "sympathetic" has an enormous meaning, but I believe He means to suffer with us in our pains.

Psalm 103 describes several attributes of Father God, and the Psalmist calls these "His benefits." Here are some of God's benefits listed:

> *He forgives all our iniquities; He heals our diseases, He redeems our life, He crowns us with Loving-kindness and tender mercies. He satisfies your mouth with good things, He renews your youth like that of an eagle, He executes righteous judgment for the oppressed, He's slow to anger, He casts our sins as far as the east is from the west, He remembers where we came from and where we are going.*
>
> **Psalm 103**

It pays to love your Father.

He is: ABBA
Father
Blessings

YOUR DAY IN COURT

September 28

"Because God does not punish sinners instantly, people feel it is safe to do wrong."

Ecclesiastes 8:11

Does this verse relate to what's going on in the world today? It seems as though people have no regard for God or man and no fear of judgment. I have heard people say this: "If you don't get caught, it's not a crime." But the truth is this: even if you get caught and paid the maximum penalty of human law, you will stand in judgment before God, and if you're not caught, you will stand in judgment before God.

"…their days shall pass away as quickly as shadows because they don't fear God" (Ecclesiastes 8:13).

Their days will end, and when their life is over, it will seem as though it were only five minutes long. People who don't fear God can easily commit a crime, white-collar or blue-collar, with a pen or gun. When a crime goes unpunished, it encourages the criminal to do more. The Broken Window Theory has been around for some time. In the housing projects, a window gets broken, and the management would not repair it because the apartment was empty. The attitude was that they would break it again, and the consequence was more broken windows, causing entire apartment complexes with broken windows. However, subsequent studies have shown that fewer windows would have been broken if the repairs had been done quickly.

So many of these individuals are like broken windows. When you look through the opening, all you see is darkness, an inner abyss of hopelessness. I pity their souls.

He is: Akal Esh
Consuming Fire
Blessings

TRUE DAT

September 29

"And every man that hath this hope in him purifieth himself, even as He is pure."

1 John 3:3

Every man struggles with hope. Hope defines us for who we are. The word hope comes from the Greek translation, *el-pece´*, which means expectation or confidence: faith, hope. People can easily place their hope in the wrong things. Every belief you have is trust-based; someone or a source that you trusted shared some information or taught you on a subject, with or without rationale, you placed your belief (i.e., faith) in the information given.

Here's an example. Take Darwinism. You're constantly inundated with the theory of biological evolution through media. If you trust the person or the program delivering the information, you can easily get deceived into believing this end-time lie.

On the other edge of the sword is the Word of God. Some people find the truth through carefully studying the written word. For others, Jesus finds them. When someone encounters Jesus Christ through a miracle or an answered prayer, they are no longer at the losing end of the debate because "a person with an experience is not at the mercy of someone with an argument." Jesus said in John 8:31–32:

> *Then said Jesus to those Jews which believed on him, If ye continue in my word, then are ye my disciples indeed;*
>
> *And ye shall know the truth, and the truth shall make you free.*

I pray that you will be free and your hope will be placed in Jesus Christ.

He is: Alethinos Theos
True God
Blessings

ONLY GOD COULD

September 30

*"Thou also, son of man, take thee a tile, and lay it before thee,
and portray upon it the city even Jerusalem."*

Ezekiel 4:1

I'll have to paraphrase this devotion because the verses needed are too long, but please open your Bible and read verses 1–7. The Lord tells Ezekiel to take a tile and draw a drawing depicting Jerusalem. Next, He tells Ezekiel to build fortifications around it, simulating a foreign army laying siege against the city.

Then the confusing part comes: God tells Ezekiel that he will lay their iniquity on it. He's going to judge them for their sins. He then commands Ezekiel to lie next to the model city on his left side for 390 days and forty days on his right side. Each day will represent one year of punishment, equaling 430 years. God warns Israel in Leviticus, chapter 26:18: "Then I will punish you seven times."

Israel has just come out of seventy years of captivity, and God, in His mercy, will deduct the seventy years as time served. Deduct seventy years from 430 years, which leaves 360 years of punishment. However, He multiplies the punishment times seven, which equals 2520 years of dispersion.

Here's how to calculate the timeline correctly: you must take 2520 years and multiply it by 365 days, then reconstruct it into years in the Hebrew calendar (a lunar calendar); now, we have 907,200 days.

Okay, are you still with me? Now, we need a starting date. Fortunately, this is a recorded date in history. It is the date that Persian King Cyrus set the Jews free after he conquered the Babylonians: July 23, 537 B.C.

When we add 907,200 to the calendar, we conclude that the judgment ended on a particular day: May 14, 1948.

The day that Israel became a nation!

Seventy years later, on the day of the seventieth-anniversary celebration, May 14, 2018, the United States of America relocated our embassy to Jerusalem, recognizing Jerusalem as the capital of Israel, proving that God is an awesome God and that God keeps His word.

THE LORD WILL CHOOSE A SIGN

October 1

"Therefore, the Lord himself shall give you a sign; Behold, a virgin shall conceive, and bear a son, and shall call his name Immanuel."

Isaiah 7:14

Let me give a bit of the historical background. It started about 250 years before this event when the twelve tribes of Israel split into two different nations: Israel, composed of ten tribes, and the other two tribes were Judah and Benjamin, the two most minor tribes, which comprised the kingdom of Judah. During this period, the king of Judah was evil, and his name was Ahaz.

The kings of Israel allied with their neighboring king of Syria. The two kings decided to attack Judah, kill Ahaz, and replace him with another king, then conscript Ahaz's soldiers into theirs. Ahaz withstands the initial attacks but loses a lot of men. Ahaz learns of the attacks; he and his household go into panic mode, and rightly so. Ahaz formulates a plan; he takes all the gold and holy articles out of the temple and the gold from the treasury and gives it to the king of Assyria. However, Assyria was still an enemy of Israel and Syria as well.

Ahaz wants nothing to do with God, so God sends Isaiah and his son, whose name translates as "a remnant shall return." God tells Isaiah that he will find King Ahaz standing by the Fuller's —or bleaching—pool. It is very symbolic that a wicked man stands by a pool that makes things white. This verse demonstrates God's absolute mercy towards humankind. Previously, Ahaz had offered his son in the fire to the idol Moloch, locked the temple doors, forbade people to make their sacrifices, and built idols under all the big trees.

God told Isaiah this message to King Ahaz: "I'm for you, I'm with you, be quiet, stop worrying, I know their plans, it shall not come to pass. I know these two kings, and within sixty-five years, their kingdoms won't even be there."

God tells Ahaz to ask whatever you want, and I will give it to you. Because Ahaz was a descendant of King David, God promised David that there would always be a descendent of his on the throne. And just like you and me, no matter how wicked Ahaz was, God was reaching out, trying to save his soul. Isaiah tells Ahaz to ask for a sign, and Ahaz replies with this perplexing statement:

"But Ahaz said, I will not ask, neither will I tempt the LORD" (Isaiah 7:12).

What? Suddenly, Ahaz gets holy? Because his heart is hardened just like Pharaoh's centuries before, he has no intention of asking God for anything. Then, Isaiah famously states: "Behold a virgin." The word virgin comes from the Hebrew word: *al-maw'*, which means "a lass, damsel, maid, or virgin."

> *Butter and honey shall he eat, that he may know to refuse the evil and choose the good.*

For before the child shall know to refuse the evil and choose the good, the land that thou abhorrest shall be forsaken of both her kings.

Isaiah 7:15–16

These scriptures are called a double fulfillment. Ahaz died around 716 years before Christ. God is telling King Ahaz a young maid in his household will have a child, name him Immanuel (God is with us), and before being weaned, both the kings he is battling will be dead.

Children back then were weaned around two to four years of age. After this child was born, Ahaz had a sign from God that God was real. God's mercy toward this man was non-stopping. Ahaz had to know that God was real, that he was chasing after all the wrong things, looking for fulfillment. But, unfortunately for King Ahaz, he died at the young age of thirty-six to forty years old. His day of reckoning came. He was considered so evil by the Jews that they would not bury him with the other kings.

Over 700 years later, this prophecy was once again fulfilled a second time (by a virgin).

"Behold, a virgin shall be with child and shall bring forth a son, and they shall call his name Emmanuel, which being interpreted is God with us" (Matthew 1:23).

If you have not yet accepted Jesus as your Lord and Savior, you're like King Ahaz standing by the bleaching field, and Jesus is saying:

"Ask me for a sign, and I will prove that I AM real."

He is: El Yeshuati
The God of My Salvation
Blessings

BURDEN BEARER

October 2

Come unto me, all ye that labor and are heavy laden, and I will give you rest.
Take my yoke upon you, and learn of me; for I am meek and lowly
in heart: and ye shall find rest unto your souls.
For my yoke is easy, and my burden is light.

Matthew 11:28–30

When you read this, how can you think anything other than how much God loves you? On more than one occasion, while praying for people, I have had a vision of Jesus wearing a crown of thorns and placing a yoke upon His shoulders.

If one is not familiar with old-school farming methods, your first thought would be, "Why would I want that?" It was common back in the day to see two horses side by side, one smaller than the other. The stronger horse carried all the burden. The other horse was more for companionship, a friend to walk alongside.

When Jesus asks you to take His yoke, He says, "I will take the burden for you, learn about Me and My ways, and carry your load. You can be My companion, and My ways will give you rest."

It's curious how He says: "My burden is light." Let Jesus take the burden off your shoulders, and He will lighten your load, and in return, at the same time, He will give you another type of light: "I am the Light of the world. So if you follow me, you won't be stumbling through the darkness, for living light will flood your path" (John 8:12).

Please make Him the *light* of your life.

He is: Sar-Shalom
Prince of Peace
Blessings

LORD OPEN OUR EYES

October 3

*Therefore sent he thither horses, and chariots, and a great host:
and they came by night, and compassed the city about.
And when the servant of the man of God was risen early, and gone forth, behold,
an host compassed the city both with horses and chariots. And his servant said
unto him, Alas, my master! how shall we do?
And he answered, Fear not: for they that be with us are more
than they that be with them.*

2 Kings 6:14–16

The Man of God was Elisha; this massive army had come solely for him. Elisha was a prophet (still is) and a great one at that. Israel was at war with the King of Syria; whenever the King of Syria created a battle plan, Elisha would forewarn the King of Israel. It happened several times, so often that the King of Syria thought he had a spy in his court. Then, his officials told him that it was the prophet, Elisha, and that everything the king said in private was being repeated to the king of Israel by Elisha. In response, the king of Syria sent an army to capture Elisha.

Upon the army's arrival, Elisha makes this epic response: "Fear not, for they that be with us are more than they that be with them."

Have you ever felt like the world was against you? That everyone hates you? I have, but let me assure you, the enemy's tactics have never changed; in this case, it was *sudden fear*.

When we look at things in the natural, we can lose sight of what God is doing in the supernatural.

And how did it turn out for Elisha? God blinded the army, and Elisha told them he would help them find the prophet they were seeking. And the entire army held hands as he marched them into the middle of Israel's military, and God opened their eyes. The king of Israel asked, "If he should kill them?" Elisha said: "No, feed them and send them home." After that, they had peace with Syria for years.

In our battle, we need to pray that God would take the blindness off those who wish to destroy. Pray this for your enemy:

"The eyes of your understanding being enlightened; that ye may know what is the hope of his calling, and what the riches of the glory of his inheritance in the saints" (Ephesians 1:18).

God is calling His saints.

He is: Jehovah-Sabaoth
Lord of Hosts
Blessings

GOD LOVES TO GIVE

October 4

"And also, that every man should eat and drink, and enjoy the good of all his labor, it is the gift of God" (Ecclesiastes 3:13). "A laborer's appetite works on his behalf, for his hunger drives him on."

Proverbs 16:26

Have you ever been told that your work doesn't make you who you are? I'm sure there is some truth to that, but the truth is that we tend to place a lot of our self-esteem in our work, especially for men.

For people who like to work, rest is not an option, and they get stir-crazy looking for something to do. Years ago, I heard about a college that hired ten men at top dollar to come and dig a ditch. On the second day, they told them to fill the trench back in and then re-dig the ditch. Most of the men did not show up on the third day, and by the fourth day, they had all quit. Employment has meaning. It means so much that God has gifted it to us. Some people feel they're not doing enough for God if they're not working in a paid ministry. You hear about pastors and evangelists operating in the gifts of God.

A simple thought: If your job is a gift from God, when you work, you are working in your gifting. If you're out of work right now, like so many people, begin to thank God for your next gift so that you can enjoy life, and if you're retired, thank God.

He is: Rum Rosh
The One Who Lifts My Head
Blessings

KEEP CRYING

October 5

The voice of him that crieth in the wilderness, Prepare ye the way of the LORD, make straight in the desert a highway for our God.
Every valley shall be exalted, and every mountain and hill shall be made low: and the crooked shall be made straight, and the rough places plain:
And the glory of the LORD shall be revealed, and all flesh shall see it together: for the mouth of the LORD hath spoken it.

Isaiah 40:3–5

Isaiah prophesied this about 686 years before the birth of John the Baptist. John had a mission to tell people when the first advent of Christ was approaching.

The symbolism attached to this prophecy is awe-inspiring. The wilderness is a dry place, referring to people who have not learned the trueness of God's word.

A highway symbolizes a straight path from your heart to God, through the desert and through the dry times in your life. There are times in a Christian's life when we can ascend to the mountain tops in praise, and then there are times when it feels like you are in a desert place, a dryness from God. I've been there, and you constantly wonder what you have done wrong; the answer is probably nothing.

Next is the valley, and you look at Christians who have ascended to the mountaintop in their ministry, and you wonder, "Why can't I ever make it to the mountaintop?"

It's through humbleness that we reach the top. That's why you were in the dry place. God positions you to attain the humility required to climb the summit.

Every valley shall be exalted, and every mountain and hill shall be made low: and the crooked shall be made straight, and the rough places plain:

Here's a twist:

- Unsaved people who have exalted themselves will be made low.
- The crooked person will be made whole.
- Their rough edges will be smoothed over for the Lord.

I have known some of the toughest people who have gotten saved, and then, that hard inner shell is softened just like a soft-shell blue crab from South Louisiana.

How does this happen? We all have a little of John the Baptist in us, sharing the gospel with others and praying for our loved ones. Your prayers prepare a way for God to reach those loved ones in the wilderness. And like I have said for years, "Your prayers matter."

He is: Elohim Shama
The God Who Hears
Blessings

MODERN DAY SWORDS

October 6

And after him was Eleazar the son of Dodo the Ahohite, one of the three mighty men with David, when they defied the Philistines that were there gathered together to battle, and the men of Israel were gone away:
He arose, and smote the Philistines until his hand was weary, and his hand clave unto the sword: and the LORD wrought a great victory that day;
and the people returned after him only to spoil.

2 Samuel 23:9–10

Eleazar was the second man in King David's trilogy of the three mighty men. King David was an influential leader who believed God could do anything. David was renowned for his great exploits. He killed a bear and lion with his hands and Goliath with a slingshot.

His greatness, his examples, made others believe they could achieve great things, too, and David's anointing carried over to his men. Eleazar single-handedly fought an army and prevailed. Just like King David, he knew God was on his side and wasn't about to give up any real estate to the enemy, even when everyone else fled.

Great leaders inspire people to achieve great things. Our founders of this nation believed they could do great things. They thought they could obtain Liberty from monarchy.

Our weapons have changed to some degree; instead of flintlock rifles and swords, we carry the word of God.

Years ago, I had a vision of myself. I reached down, picked up a rusty sword, held it in my hand, and gazed at it momentarily. That was the end of the vision. I had yet to learn what it meant. But I would occasionally think about it and wonder. Then, over twenty-plus years later, my mother sent me my great-grandmother's Bible from the 1800s. I was sitting at this desk, and my wife came into my office and said, "The Bible your mother sent you came today." When she handed it across my desk, I had a repeat vision, and the Bible suddenly turned into a rusty sword. I can't explain my emotions, but I was shocked.

My great-grandmother Lilly, a genuine lady of God, had a sword and an old King James Bible. God never forgets a prayer; she passed something to me that day. She lived out of a wagon for some of her life, alone in the great prairies. Like Eleazar clutching his sword, she would not release the blade from her hand, and she carried her old King James all her life.

Clutch the word of God as though your life depends on it. Your exploits in prayer can save a soul or maybe even a nation.

He is: Jehovah Gibbor Milchamah
Mighty in Battle
Blessings

HIS EYE IS ON YOU

October 7

"He that is faithful in that which is least is faithful also in much: and he that is unjust in the least is unjust also in much."

Luke 16:10

Stewardship encompasses much more than money, your family, your job, and your ministry. I remember a story about a company vice president who was next in line to be the president. The current president was retiring and favored passing the torch to his successor.

A day before the board of directors was about to vote, the vice president and the current president went to lunch in the company's cafeteria. While sliding their trays along the food buffet, the president noticed that the vice president took a roll and then a little square of butter and hid it under the bread roll. The cost was 0.03 to 0.05 cents for the butter. The VP did not tell her about the butter under the roll when they reached the cashier.

The next day, the board of directors convened and was ready to cast their votes for the VP into his new role as the next company president. As everyone sat at the table, the president entered the room. He informed the board of directors that he did not want this man to replace him. He told the story of what he had witnessed and finished with this statement, "If he can't be trusted in the little things, he can't be trusted in the big things." The board unanimously voted "No."

The VP thought he was saving himself money by stealing a few cents worth of butter but ended up costing himself tens of thousands in salary, perks, and prestige.

The small assignments are sometimes frustrating and can even seem fruitless.

"The eyes of the LORD are in every place, beholding the evil and the good" (Proverbs 15:3).

He is: El ROI
The God Who Sees Me
Blessings

SEE WHAT HAPPENS UNDER THE FIG TREE

October 8

Philip findeth Nathanael, and saith unto him, We have found him, of whom Moses in the law, and the prophets, did write, Jesus of Nazareth, the son of Joseph. And Nathanael said unto him, Can there any good thing come out of Nazareth? Philip saith unto him, Come and see.

John 1:45

I believe this is one of the most misunderstood statements in the Bible. Philip and Nathanael are probably best friends; excitedly, Philip finds his best friend and tells him that he has found the Messiah.

Philip must have been a salesman, because he positioned mankind's need: Moses proclaims a Messiah will come, and is now fulfilled, then proposes the solution by identifying the name of Jesus, son of Joseph. However, Philip used the name of Jesus in Aramaic, Y'shua, the same name as Joshua in the Old Testament, which means "Yahweh is Salvation," and his dad is Joseph from Nazareth.

People tend to place the worst prejudice on Nathanael because he said, "Can any good thing come out of Nazareth?" When I look at this, I see a young man who has spent much time studying the scriptures. He knows that the Messiah must come out of Bethlehem. Naturally, he is very skeptical about this new revelation, and he is not implying that all the people in Nazareth are evil.

However, this is a time of God moving in their lives. John the Baptist has been preaching and preparing the way for Jesus. Then, Jesus removes Nathanael's skepticism with his introduction by saying: "Behold an Israelite indeed, in whom is no guile!"

Catching Nate's attention, the conversation goes like this, "How do you know me?" and Jesus responds, "Before you left, I saw you sitting under the fig tree." Nathanael is a skeptic, but why would this statement instantly change his whole belief system? He immediately responds, "Rabbi, thou art the Son of God; thou art the King of Israel."

I believe that before Phillip approached Nathanael under the fig tree, symbolizing the nation of Israel and a type of covering, Nathanael had probably been praying to God, asking God to show him the Messiah. He's just heard John the Baptist preach, "Make straight the way of the Lord." Nathanael, sitting under the fig tree, was preparing his heart for the arrival of the Messiah; little did he expect Jesus to show up that day. There's no such thing as a coincidence with God, if you are seeking Jesus, don't be surprised when He shows up.

He is: Elohim Shama
The God Who Hears
Blessings

THE MODEL SUFFERER

October 9

Pilate therefore said unto him, Art thou a king then? Jesus answered, Thou sayest that I am a king. To this end was I born, and for this cause came I into the world, that I should bear witness unto the truth. Every one that is of the truth heareth my voice.

John 18:37

Every chapter in the Gospel of John portrays a remarkable aspect of Jesus's character. Chapter 18 Jesus is described as the Model Sufferer. Jesus understood authority. When directly questioned by persons of authority, He answered accordingly but remained silent with those not in authority.

I noticed some attributes of Jesus leading up to this encounter. Jesus didn't yell at Judas for betraying Him; instead, He pitied Him. The officer of the chief priest sucker-punched Jesus, and Jesus took the blow like a boss. How could He have kept His calm temper? One wrong word, and just like Elijah, everyone is consumed by fire.

He stood in court for His life and laid no blame on anyone. He took it in silence, a model for us to follow. And if you know me, you know I haven't always been a model student. But I have often kept my mouth shut and managed to remain silent. We all need to attain a level of trust in the Father. The big battle usually comes a few hours later or the next day. When my pride swells up, I start thinking of how I could have handled the situation in a worldly way.

I dub this: "The consequences of forgiveness." The battle of the mind is where the enemy comes to rob you of your forgiveness, and it's at these moments we have to pray and ask God to bless that person, even prosper that person. Yes, that's hard to pray, especially when we want to see them suffer. But Jesus paid their price, too.

He is: Tsad-deek Eh'-bed
Righteous Servant
Blessings

THERE IS A TIME LIMIT

October 10

"That seeing they may see, and not perceive; and hearing they may hear, and not understand; lest at any time they should be converted, and their sins should be forgiven them."

Mark 4:12

As I read this verse, it suddenly caught my attention. I was like, "Wait! What? Aren't we supposed to be leading everyone to Christ?" Clearly, Jesus states that not everyone will understand the Word of God. I have been thinking about this verse for days now, and subtly, other verses have come to my attention to lend me understanding. Jesus will approach people throughout their lives, and they reject Him. Honestly, it is because they do not want to change their lifestyle.

I remember a man who was a friend of mine. I tried to tell him about the Lord several times over the years and wouldn't hear it. When he became ill, the last time I saw him, I felt like the Lord did not want me to pray with him, like an invisible wall. Sadly, he passed away some months later. After the funeral, I asked the Lord if he had reached heaven. I instantly saw a memory of when I had spoken to him about Jesus twenty years earlier, and he turned his back on me as I was talking and walked off.

After the funeral, I started hearing about some of his life's sins that I was unaware of, but it wasn't the sin. It was the hardening of his heart towards the gospel twenty years earlier. Like Moses and Pharaoh, Pharaoh saw the same miracles from God but refused to yield to God. And we all know how that went.

He is: Elohay Selichot
The God Who Is Ready to Forgive
Blessings

A NIGHT OUT

October 11

For the earth is the Lord's, and the fulness thereof.
If any of them that believe not bid you to a feast, and ye be disposed to go;
whatsoever is set before you, eat, asking no question for conscience sake.

1 Corinthians 10:26–27

As Christians, we can sometimes get hung up over false but well-intended beliefs, thinking it is inappropriate to do things with non-believers.

I used to go hunting with people who were not totally on board with Christianity; it makes me laugh to think about it now. But those guys were rough and not well-spoken, but I loved each of them.

They always gave me the best hunting spots, rooting for me to get a deer. And I rooted for them to be in the best positions to receive God's word. It's hard to shoot a deer while sitting on the stand, praying in tongues.

One time, a couple of the guys fried up a bunch of wild game that was not in season. I thought, *That's nice of them; they must have taken it out of their freezer.* After eating, they told me they had shot it on the way down to the camp. I had enjoyed the meal, but afterward, I had to battle with my conscience. I understand what Paul says about asking no question for conscience's sake.

I wouldn't have touched it if the guys told me that it was a poached game before we ate it. Because it could have caused trouble with them receiving the Lord's message.

But the point is this: if asked out to dinner by non-Christians, if you want to go, go. Enjoy the company and be a light in the darkness.

He is: Or Goyim
Light of the Nations
Blessings

THE PLACE TO BE

October 12

*"The LORD is good, a strong hold in the day of trouble;
and he knoweth them that trust in Him."*

Nahum 1:7

Nahum was a blessed prophet of God. He prophesied against the city of Nineveh, just like Jonah. The difference was that Nahum was about 150 years after Jonah, and twenty years later, the prophecy came to pass with the city's destruction. It was so complete that scholars thought the city with over a million residents was a myth until, in the 1800s, when they discovered ruins.

He penned this verse about the goodness of God while he prophesied about the destruction to come—a forewarning to those who served God that trusting in God would be their safety.

Nahum was from a small town called Elkoshite. In Arabic, it's called Kafr-Nahum, which means: "The Village of Nahum," located on the Northern coast of the Sea of Galilee. Nahum may have founded the city, or he may have been named after it. In the New Testament, it's referred to as Capernaum.

It was the hometown of a famous tax collector named Matthew; the Apostles Peter, Andrew, James, and John, all four gospels mention Capernaum. It was the town Jesus used as His headquarters for His ministry...*a stronghold.*

The Lord is good and can be your stronghold in the day of trouble. You can trust in Him.

He is: Migdal Oz
Strong Tower
Blessings

EVANGELIZING LIKE A DISCIPLE

October 13

"And they went out, and preached that men should repent. And they cast out many devils, and anointed with oil many that were sick, and healed them."

Mark 6:12

Jesus sends out the twelve disciples, telling them to go into every city, preach the gospel, and cast out devils. He also said that if any city were to reject His message, they would shake the dust off their feet on their way out. He told them that it would be more tolerable for Sodom and Gomorrah on the day of judgment than for the people of that city.

The disciples preached repentance, not benefits, not happiness, and other feel-good messages when they came to report back to Jesus, without mentioning any city rejecting their message.

For some reason, when the sick recover and devils get cast out of someone, it gets people's attention. There's more to life than today. There's eternity, and accepting Jesus is the way in. He's called "the way" for a reason, and He will lead you out of sin, eternal death, and the flames of hell into everlasting life. Jesus can renew your life.

He is: Shub Nephesh
Renewer of Life
Blessings

WHAT'S ON YOUR HEART

October 14

So King Shishak of Egypt conquered Jerusalem and took away all the treasures of the Temple and of the palace, also all of Solomon's gold shields. King Rehoboam replaced them with bronze shields and committed them to the care of the captain of his bodyguard.

2 Chronicles 12:9–10

Just five years into his reign, King Rehoboam suffered defeat by the King of Egypt. Rehoboam was the grandson of King David and the son of Solomon. King Solomon had left a very wealthy dynasty for his son to inherit, but all the wealth wouldn't allow God to enter Rehoboams' heart. Because of sin, God forewarned him that he would face judgment and his wealth taken.

Symbolically, gold represents God's glory, His truth, something precious.

Brass represents judgment, hypocrisy, something fake, and man's traditions.

Father God must have grieved at removing His protection from Israel. It was not just about the gold leaving; God's glory went first. Afterward, King Rehoboam made some shields out of brass, something that, when polished enough, can look like gold, well, almost.

People will substitute tradition for God's glory. But there's still a gold shield that every believer can have, and you can find it in: "Above all, taking the shield of faith, wherewith ye shall be able to quench all the fiery darts of the wicked" (Ephesians 6:16).

It shines so much in the Spirit that the enemy can't look at it. Father God wants to protect you with His glory. Now, His glory shines through His Son.

He is: Jehovah-Magen
Shield
Blessings

DRY WATER

October 15

"He said, 'You cried to me in trouble, and I saved you; I answered from Mount Sinai where the thunder hides. I tested your faith at Meribah, when you complained there was no water'."

Psalm 81:7

In Numbers 22, Moses leads the Hebrews out of Egypt with many signs and wonders by God. After all their unbelief, they start to murmur against Moses again, but why?

God has intentionally led these people to a dry place in the wilderness, not to harm them, which they accuse Moses of, but to test them and measure their faith. Father God wants to show them His magnificence, His Son's glory.

God commanded Moses to strike the Rock once, and water would flow from it, enough to quench the thirst of more than two million people and animals.

Harsh situations in this world can close your eyes to the spiritual. With their spiritual eyes covered, they complained against God, and Moses was so angry he struck the Rock twice, and that Rock was Christ.

"for they were drinking from a spiritual rock that followed them, and the Rock was Messiah" (1 Corinthians 10:4).

Because the people had made Moses so mad, he disobeyed God in his anger, and His punishment was that he would not be allowed to set foot in the Promised Land. The sentence seems unfair and excessive that Moses couldn't enter.

You may think you know your pastor. You may think you know all of their burdens, but you don't. They are like invisible burrows carrying a heavy load, the spiritual weight of a thirsty congregation, just following the leading reigns of the Lord, trying to get a dry congregation into the Promised Land and to help them drink from the spiritual waters flowing from Christ.

Don't blame your pastor when the dry trials come; maybe Jesus brought you there so you could drink from a *Spiritual Rock.*

He is: Maqowr Chay Mayim
Fountain of Living Waters
Blessings

THE SOVEREIGN SHEPHERD

October 16

*"And ye my flock, the flock of My pasture, are men,
and I am your ELOHIYM, says ADONAI YAHUAH."*
Ezekiel 34:31, Cepher Bible

This scripture is so beautiful when written with the transliteration of God's original Hebrew names, giving us the true meaning of Father God's identity and His message to us, His flock. I translate the meanings this way: "And you are My flock, the flock of My pasture, you are My men, and I AM your Mighty Creator, saith The Sovereign Controller, The LORD."

We are His sheep, and His pasture is the earth and the fullness thereof. Growing up, we had sheep and goats; the sheep are more to themselves, and the goats are more problematic. But the funny thing about goats is that they will make you laugh with some of the antics they pull.

On the other hand, sheep are always trying to get out of the pasture. Sheep have this unique ability to find the holes in the fence and enter the neighbor's field. At least the ones we had when I was growing up. I spent some time chasing stray sheep and wouldn't say I liked it.

A friend of mine has goats on his property, and he hates them. He tells me how much trouble and extra work they cause, always having to save them from their destruction. He told me they always get their horns caught up in the fence, and they will die if he does not come to the rescue.

Re-read the previous two paragraphs and change the words hated and hate into *loved* and *love*. Now you can understand what Jesus goes through, rescuing the goats and chasing after the lost sheep, except, somehow, He does it with love.

Even though sheep and goats are different, they graze side by side in the same pastures.

If only humankind could do the same.

He is: ADONAI YAHUAH
The Sovereign Controller, The LORD
Blessings

NOT ALL LIGHTS

October 17

*And no wonder, for even Satan masquerades as an angel of light.
It is no great thing therefore if his servants also masquerade as servants of
righteousness. Their end will be according to their deeds.*

2 Corinthians 11:14

Yep, there are many people in the ministry for the wrong reasons. Most go into the ministry with good intentions, then fall into a slight temptation. That temptation happens repeatedly to where their heart hardens, and then, the enemy has them in full-blown sin.

Years ago, I needed a label printed for my personal use. I took the label maker for the ministry and started to type out the tag, and then I had a vision of the Holy Spirit. "He was wearing blue farmer overalls with a straw hat. He held His hand up, and with His finger, He gestured 'No, no.'"

And that was it. I quickly stopped what I was doing. It was such a small thing, and I didn't think it would matter, just a few pennies worth of the Lord's supplies. Now, I know it was a temptation by the enemy.

Now, I buy all the paper, ink, labels, and things like that for the ministry with my funds. We won't be accountable if I need them or my family uses them.

Know your weaknesses and guard yourself before the enemy can take advantage and know the enemy's tactics so that you can recognize his temptations.

In the book *The Art of War* by General Sun Tzu, around 510 B.C., he wrote this:

"If you know the enemy and know yourself, you need not fear the result of a hundred battles. If you know yourself but not the enemy, for every victory gained you will also suffer a defeat. If you know neither the enemy nor yourself, you will succumb in every battle."

The greatest generals know the tactics of their enemies.

He is: Jehovah Gibbor Milchamah
Mighty in Battle
Blessings

SWAY THIS WAY

October 18

Don't join mobs' intent on evil. When on the witness stand, don't be swayed in your testimony by the mood of the majority present, and do not slant your testimony in favor of a man just because he is poor.

Exodus 23:2–3

Every human has an inner desire to be liked and accepted by the crowd. The enemy knows this, but that same crowd can love you today and crucify you tomorrow.

Studies have been done over the years about "mass behavior," or how people react in social groups. Once, I watched a British television program on this. The object of the show was to see if they could get someone to murder another person by pushing them off the rooftop.

Not knowing he was on a reality show, the man was subconsciously conditioned through peer pressure by group behavior. To achieve the end goal, they kept reinforcing him with this sentence, "Whatever the cost, *do it*!"

Throughout the show, they lead him down a dangerous psychological trail that brings him to the rooftop, where they try to persuade him to push an innocent man off the edge to his demise. At the last moment, the man told them he wouldn't do it. I was pulling for him to do the right thing, and he did.

But the show had one more surprise. At the end of the program, they brought out a dozen other people who had pushed the philanthropist over the edge (of course, the philanthropist had a secret harness that kept him from hitting the ground). The grand finale for shock value, and it worked.

If you understand crowd behavior, you know a tactic used by Satan himself.

"Wherefore take unto you the whole armour of God, that ye may be able to withstand in the evil day, and having done all, to stand" (Ephesians 6:13).

He is: El Sela
God My Rock
Blessings

THE LIBERTY OF ABRAHAM

October 19

Now the LORD had said unto Abram, Get thee out of thy country, and from thy kindred, and from thy father's house, unto a land that I will shew thee: And I will make of thee a great nation, and I will bless thee, and make thy name great; and thou shalt be a blessing: And I will bless them that bless thee, and curse him that curseth thee: and in thee shall all families of the earth be blessed.

Genesis 12:1–3

The LORD told Abram to leave his home country and get away from his relatives. But it is essential to understand what he was leaving behind. Abram lived in Ur, aka Babylonia, where Nimrod built the Tower of Babel. God destroyed it and created different kinds of speech to protect humankind, basically from ourselves. Abram probably had looked upon the destroyed temple in his life. For some reason, Abram decided in his heart that he would listen to God.

The Babylonians had some very abusive religious practices, which would have compelled Abram's wife, Sarah, to participate in the worship of Ishtar. Ishtar was the Mother Goddess, a deity of passion, licentiousness, and prostitution. All women were required to officiate at least one service during their lifetime, and Sarah would have been no exception.

While praying with some fellow Christians, I listened to a pastor from Nigeria. As he prayed, I could understand bits and pieces of what he was saying. I asked him if he was praying in tongues or another language. (Everyone laughed at me.) He sheepishly said, "In tongues." I told him that he was praying these words: "The liberty of Abraham." Moments later, the Lord told me to say to him, "He is under the covenant of Abraham."

When Abraham was obedient and left his country, those who went with him obtained the liberty granted to Abraham. Jesus gave us the blessings of Abraham when He died on the cross.

Cursed is everyone that hangeth on a tree:

That the blessing of Abraham might come on the Gentiles through Jesus Christ; that we might receive the promise of the Spirit through faith.

Galatians 3:13–14

If Jesus asks you to lay something down or give something up, like cigarettes, for example, it may liberate you. Or it may liberate someone else, either way…

It's because He loves you.

He is: Yahweh- Channun
God of Grace
Blessings

PRAISE BEFORE PETITIONS

October 20

He is a father to the fatherless; he gives justice to the widows, for he is holy.
He gives families to the lonely, and releases prisoners from jail, singing with joy!
But for rebels there is famine and distress.

Psalm 68:5–6

This Psalm is so wonderful, written for a time of joy. The ark of the covenant was brought to Mount Zion on this day. However, before this point in time, the Philistines had captured the ark, and God had it miraculously returned to the nation of Israel. On the return trip, the Hebrews became fearful of the ark and stored at the home of Obed-Edom.

Some time passed, and David learned how to properly transport the ark with reverence according to the law of the Torah. Now it is being returned, and King David is dancing before the ark's processional with all his heart, and he wrote this Psalm as a memorial to Father God.

Psalm 68 is worthy of study; it is worthy of a whole sermon. But in verses one through six, we can see an insight into prayer. King David starts with praise, the blueprint for worship: "Praise before petitions."

Over the years, I have prayed for single people whom God would give a husband or a wife, and this is the verse I pray.

On one occasion, a distraught mother asked me to pray for her son, who was in jail for manslaughter. I did, and she asked me to visit him, so I went. When I met the young man, he asked me if I was the one who had prayed with his mother, and I said, "Yes." He told me that the district attorney had dropped all charges, and the young man was all smiles.

I've noticed in my life when everything seemed hopeless, that when I prayed and reminded God what He had done for me, the times He saved me, restored me, and remembered me, my confidence in God would surge, my shoulders would lift, and when that happens.

You just found *faith*.

He is: Jehovah Uzzi
The Lord My Strength
Blessings

A ROCK OR PILLOW

October 21

"And he lighted upon a certain place, and tarried there all night, because the sun was set; and he took of the stones of that place, and put them for his pillows, and lay down in that place to sleep."

Genesis 28:11

There is a cost to serving God. Most would look at this verse in Genesis and think about comfort. However, the verse is about Jacob fleeing from his brother Esau after he stole the birthright (allegedly). Jacob had legally traded a bowl of soup for the birthright that Esau had despised, and obeying his mother's command, he pretended to be Esau and obtained the blessing from Isaac.

His blessing starts in a desert and a rock for a pillow, symbolically laying his troubled thoughts upon a stone. Imagine the mental stress he must have suffered for a rock to be a pillow, the last possible choice. Jacob laid his head upon a rock, and God met him in a dream that night. He saw a ladder and angels ascending and descending from heaven to earth.

When you're stressed out, begin to pray. While writing this, I heard the Holy Spirit say three times, "Begin to pray." When you "begin to pray," you'll discover how to use a rock for a pillow and lay your head upon the Rock of our Salvation, Jesus Christ.

"…and that Rock was Christ" (1 Corinthians 10:4).

He is: El Sela
God My Rock
Blessings

FEAR VS FAITH

October 22

"Fear thou not; for I am with thee: be not dismayed; for I am thy God: I will strengthen thee; yea, I will help thee; yea, I will uphold thee with the right hand of my righteousness."

Isaiah 41:10

I've heard it said that fear is faith spelled backward. Fear can sometimes be the uncertainty of events over which we have no control.

The word "dismayed" means to lose your strength or to depress your spirit due to fear. The enemy gives you two types of hypothetical outcomes and thought processes, both of which we can control.

God alludes to different types of fears. There is no universally agreed-upon numerical classification for types of fear, as fear is a complex and subjective emotion and can manifest in various ways. For example, I had to overcome some fears in my life, the fear of public speaking, which intermingles with a common fear that almost everyone deals with:

Autophobia: The fear of rejection, often in social or romantic situations. I overcame the fear of public speaking by facing it, and now I host a Sunday morning radio program that airs across the country. My mother told me, "You can't fear the 'they,' e.g., 'What will they think or what will they say?' The 'theys' don't exist."

The good news is God says, "For I am with thee." Notice He used His name "I am." I am your every need, I am your strength, I am your righteousness.

Faith is the fact, and fear is often hypothetical. The fact is God reassures us that He is with us, that He is our God, will give us strength, help us, and will hold us up with His right hand of righteousness!

Sometimes, we must give it to God because He controls the circumstances.

He is: El-HaNe'eman
The God Who Is Faithful
Blessings

PATIENT WORKOUT

October 23

"Here is the patience of the saints: here are they that keep the commandments of God, and the faith of Jesus."

Revelation 14:12

Have I reached this point in Scripture yet? No, not yet, but one day, someone may read this that has. Nevertheless, it's something we must all exercise when times of testing and trials come. Patience comes from the Greek word *hupomone* (hoop-om-on-ay'). It means cheerful endurance continuance. If you drill down a little farther, the word "endurance" implies the act or instance of bearing suffering, continuing under pain, hardship, or stress.

Jesus knew things in life would not always be easy; many things require us to lift the weight of patience. People and circumstances can give us a real workout sometimes. It hurts when you lift weights, but the burning feeling in your muscles makes it seem worth it when finished.

It's the same accomplishment as enduring a set of circumstances that you did not think you could go through. Jesus is just like your spotter, standing behind you, encouraging you to lift just one more time because He can see the benefit of the pain when all you can feel is the pain. When it's over (you), the weightlifter, you're all smiles, but I think Jesus wants us to be all smiles while working out. Jesus knows when your last rep will be.

He is: Jehova Uzzi
The Lord My Strength
Blessings

TREASURE HUNTING

October 24

*"Again, the kingdom of heaven is like unto treasure hid in a field; the which
when a man hath found, he hideth, and for joy thereof goeth and
selleth all that he hath, and buyeth that field".*

Matthew 13:44

Have you ever wondered why a man would find a treasure and then hide it in the field? And why would he immediately sell everything he had to buy that field? Why not just take the treasure home?

Because he knew there was more treasure hidden in the field. The treasure is Jesus Christ, and the field is your Bible. For some people, when they accept Jesus Christ as Lord and Savior, it costs them everything. The cost in some cultures can be exclusion from your family and possibly even your life.

Once you become a Christian, there is much more. There's a relationship with Jesus, the baptism of the Holy Spirit, the spiritual blessings, the fruits of the Spirit. "But the fruit of the Spirit is love, joy, peace, longsuffering, gentleness, goodness, faith, Meekness, temperance: against such, there is no law" (Galatians 5:22–23).

When people accept Jesus as their Lord and Savior, they seem to get these blessings/fruits right off as if the fruit of the Spirit was lying on top of the ground, but others like me have to dig to get the fruit. Try digging through pride to find humility. It's like digging through granite sometimes.

No matter what your circumstance is in life, I assure you the Bible has the answer. If you dig into the Word of God, you will discover what He planted for you.

He is: Georgos
The Gardner
Blessings

THE PARABLE OF THE PERSISTENT

October 25

And he spake a parable unto them to this end,
that men ought always to pray, and not to faint;
Saying, There was in a city a judge, which feared not God, neither regarded man:
And there was a widow in that city; and she came unto him, saying,
Avenge me of mine adversary.
And he would not for a while: but afterward he said within himself,
Though I fear not God, nor regard man;
Yet because this widow troubleth me, I will avenge her,
lest by her continual coming she weary me.
And the Lord said, Hear what the unjust judge saith.
And shall not God avenge his own elect, which cry day and night
unto him, though he bear long with them?
I tell you that he will avenge them speedily. Nevertheless, when
the Son of man cometh, shall he find faith on the earth?

Luke 18:1–8

Like an instruction manual for your car, this parable explains how to keep your check engine light off, pray, and then pray some more and not *faint*. The word faint means "to fail" or "be weak." Sometimes, like "now-times," we need to push through the victory with constant prayer.

Notice that the widow never named her adversary or what happened. The enemy is like an unknown adversary in our lives, with different types of principalities and stumbling blocks placed before us. Things block God's blessings, and we wonder what happened. Or what did I do wrong? But in the widow's case, she knew who and what. She persisted and persevered with the judge by being relentless. I always have this picture of a little old Jewish lady banging on the door in the middle of the night and yelling at an upstairs window, demanding justice.

The next thing I noticed was that the judge knew her. He knew the situation and the adversary. Frankly, he did not care about justice, and she didn't have the money for a customary bribe. The judge had no incentive to help. Finally, he has had enough and is wearied by the perpetual complaint. He decides to act on her behalf. He gave no thought to her adversary; after all, the adversary wasn't bothering him.

And shall not God avenge His own elect? The word "elect" means favorite. As a child of God, you are His favorite. I have heard testimonies of people who have met Jesus, and they said that when He looks into your eyes, He has a specific love that is only for you because you are His elect, His favorite.

Jesus asks, "Will I find faith on earth when I return?" Your faith is like a mustard seed in this universe, a needle in a haystack that only God can see. Jesus is checking to see if you have faith. Maybe the question is: "Will He find faith in you?"

He is: Shaphat
Judge
Blessings

THANKFULNESS

October 26

*"And let the peace of God rule in your hearts, to the which
also ye are called in one body; and be ye thankful."*

Colossians 3:15

As I meditated on Colossians 3:15, the Holy Spirit told me, "This is a complicated piece of industry." A quick dictionary visit revealed that "industry" can mean *cleverness*. It's almost as if the Holy Spirit is playfully weaving these words together, inviting us to explore their deeper meaning.

This verse presents us with a choice: to allow peace or fear to reign in our hearts. Yet, the message takes a profound turn with the phrase, "to the which also ye are called in one body." Here, the Spirit reminds us that we are not isolated individuals but a unified body in Christ. This collective unity is a powerful source of protection, capable of saving, shielding, and even healing. This interplay of language and spiritual insight underscores the complexity and richness of the message. It challenges us to delve deeper, recognizing the cleverly placed words as an invitation to explore the depths of God's wisdom and guidance.

Furthermore, being called in one body speaks to the strength and solidarity we find in our shared faith. It paints a vivid picture of a community bound by love and devotion, offering a sanctuary of safety and healing for all who belong.

Don't go to people who are all stressed out when under tremendous stress. In the past, I have gone to my pastors, representing the head of the body, for prayer or counsel. I am thankful to have such Spirit-filled advisors to help me through the hard times. I've also had Jesus tell me to "thank Him for…" and then He states my need. I haven't even asked Him for help, and He is telling me to thank Him for an answered prayer. Being thankful is a sense of being impressed by the kindness received. If you are thankful before the need is met, that is called faith, and afterward, it is called gratitude. God is very kind, and He is generous in so many ways. There is always something we can find to give Him thanks for.

He is: Adonai Tov
The Lord Is Good
Blessings

STAND STRONG

October 27

*"Watch ye, stand fast in the faith, quit you like men, be strong.
Let all your things be done with charity."*
1 Corinthians 16:13–14

Christians are to be on the lookout for false teachers in Christ. With modern-day media, we are inundated with teachers who mislead with false doctrines—teaching people what they want to hear.

I was invited to a church service that had an evangelist speaking. He first told everyone to close their eyes so that he could see whose unbelief of his gift would keep their eyes open. That raised a red flag in my mind, and I just stared directly into his eyes.

He used some gimmicks, and he kept a close eye on me. Afterward, he started praying for people, so I went up for prayer, and he kept skipping over me. I noticed that he was prophesying the same four blessings over everyone.

After the service, I asked the Lord if he was for real, and immediately, the Holy Spirit showed me a vision of an usher walking by with a basket full of offerings. The envelopes were sticking out of the basket, and I knew then that he was fake.

Quit comes from the Hebrew word *andrizomai*, which means "acting manly, followed by being strong." Let all your things be done in love.

Strong Christians observe, trust in the word, and are strong in love because love is *strong*.

He is: Elohim Ahavah
The God Who Loves
Blessings

WE GET TO

October 28

"For by grace are ye saved through faith; and that not of yourselves: it is the gift of God: Not of works, lest any man should boast."

Ephesians 2:8–9

Salvation is a gift from God. Christianity is the only religion on earth that does not require work to get into heaven. Why? If God based my eternity on how much I pray or how much piety I can achieve, it would make the cross useless.

There are false religions that require you to do certain things to obtain salvation, a point system that guarantees you an eternal position in heaven—the more points, the better the mansion.

Saved by grace and not by works. Although your works are recorded in heaven, they won't get you to heaven. So, what motivates me to do things for the Lord? I know one day I will see Jesus face to face. I don't want to say I didn't do anything to help save others. Wouldn't you sound the alarm if the building you were in caught fire? Many, many people are facing the fire of eternity. If you share Jesus with someone and they accept Jesus as their Savior, you have covered many sins and saved them from eternal life.

But it's not I who leads someone to Jesus Christ; it's the Holy Spirit. Next time you see someone go up to the altar to accept Jesus, think how much work the Holy Spirit put into that person's soul. Oh! That God would use us as a vessel to share His love and salvation with others! With some religions, you've *got* to share certain things. True Christians *get* to share certain things. One letter makes all the difference between "got" and "get" to. *Gotters* do it out of legalism, and *getters* do it out of love.

He is: Yahweh Channum
God of Grace
Blessings

STANDING IN THE POCKET

October 29

Whosoever cometh to me, and heareth my sayings, and doeth them, I will shew you to whom he is like: He is like a man which built an house, and digged deep, and laid the foundation on a rock: and when the flood arose, the stream beat vehemently upon that house, and could not shake it: for it was founded upon a rock.

Luke 6:47–48

I watched an NFL football game. During the game, the quarterback made a touchdown pass to a wide receiver that was open in the end zone. He was so wide open that the next closest defender seemed to be on the other side of the field. I said to everyone in the room, "I could have made that pass!" The quarterback was standing with all authority in the pocket with all the time in the world, and he confidently threw the touchdown.

The next day, I watched the game replay and thought about what I had said. Honestly, I could never have made that pass because I never had the self-discipline to go through all the training and endurance that man has endured to be in that particular moment.

Jesus said that whoever comes to Him and learns and then does what He has taught will be able to stand when the flood comes. Notice He didn't say, "If the flood comes." He said, "When the flood comes." Many new Christians want to stand in the pocket without going to training camp. A Navy Admiral once said, "You can't be a good leader until you have learned how to be a good follower." The key to withstanding the flood is learning to follow Christ's gospel. Hearing the sayings and doing what He said is the key to building a solid foundation. Build your foundation on a rock and be sure that Jesus is the Rock.

He is: El Sela
God My Rock
Blessings

HARD HARVEST

October 30

"Let both grow together until the harvest: and in the time of harvest, I will say to the reapers, Gather ye together first the tares, and bind them in bundles to burn them: but gather the wheat into my barn."

Matthew 3:30

We live in a time where the wheat and the tares are being revealed, coming to maturity.

In the early stages of growing, wheat and tares look the same, but there is a difference: the grass blades of the tares are thinner (Maybe that's why we have so many overweight Christians?). When fully developed, you can distinguish between a full-fruited seed of the wheat and the thinner fruit seed of the tare. The tare seeds are poisonous if eaten, but they have other uses. By law, the Romans forbid the two seeds to be planted near each other because of the potential for contamination.

We see a maturation process these days, but it seems as though the tares are choking out the wheat. But wheat stands a little taller than a tare and bears much more fruit. There is one utterly unique spiritual fact about tares, and it's not that the blades are similar and look pretty much the same. The fantastic spiritual fact is that tares can suddenly transform into wheat! At any moment, that person you have given up on can become a born-again Christian! I pray that there will be much more wheat than tares. The nice thing about grace is that you choose which blade you want to be.

He is: Elohay Selichot
The God Who Is Ready to Forgive
Blessings

REAL FACE TIME

October 31

If my people, which are called by my name, shall humble themselves, and pray, and seek my face, and turn from their wicked ways; then will I hear from heaven, and will forgive their sin, and will heal their land.

2 Chronicles 7:14

I used to play on a church softball team. Our pastor, an excellent coach, would occasionally yell out, "Attitude check!" Unanimously, the team would shout back, "Jesus is Lord!"

Our nations, our people, need an attitude check. Just like my coach yelling, "Attitude check!" Jesus's name calls out to us, seeking us to humble ourselves before the Lord. Now's the time to pray like never before, being in a spiritual war. It seems like we are living off the prayers of our nation's founders, but the question is, what prayers will our children live off of?

And seek My face: what does it mean to seek God's face? "Face" comes from the Hebrew word *panyim* (*paw-neem*). It has many applications, particularly the *face*, which is the part that turns.

Have you ever had a friend walk by, and you called out their name, and they turned to look at you? Hopefully, when they recognized you, they smiled. Imagine they were angry with you about something; they looked at you for a second or two and then smiled; now you know you have been forgiven. If it's your parents, you get your allowance back. If it's God, we get our nation back. Heaven is far from here, but God's not deaf and is undoubtedly alive, and He hears your prayers, and your prayers matter.

He is: Elohim Shama
The God Who Hears
Blessings

AMAZING ANSWER

November 1

And John calling unto him two of his disciples sent them to Jesus, saying,
Art thou He that should come? or look we for another?
When the men were come unto him, they said, John Baptist hath sent us unto thee,
saying, Art thou He that should come? or look we for another?
And in that same hour He cured many of their infirmities and plagues,
and of evil spirits; and unto many that were blind He gave sight.

Luke 7:19–21

John has been confined in King Herod's prison, but was John secretly reaching out to Jesus asking for help? Many people of that era thought Christ would come as a conquering king and set up His kingdom here on earth. If that happened, would He come and rescue John? Instead, because of John's question, Jesus goes and heals hundreds of people, casting out demons and curing plagues, *and unto many that were blind, He gave sight.*

Why did Jesus answer John in this manner? The book of Isaiah may reveal it to us: "Then the eyes of the blind shall be opened, and the ears of the deaf shall be unstopped" (Isaiah 35:5).

This Bible prophecy was reserved for the Messiah and no one else. There is no other record of a blind person healed in the Old Testament. Even the Pharisees knew this, the one sure sign that Jesus was the Messiah. John received his answer, and maybe it wasn't the hoped-for response. Because John sought the truth about Jesus, that day, people were healed from infirmities of evil spirits, and blind people recovered their sight and changed their lives.

Jesus's answer to John's question was to perform miracles. But it was more than that; it was a blueprint for explaining the Messiah to others. Jesus's disciples applied it, performed miracles and healings, and then preached who Jesus was. That is the blueprint for leading others to the Lord.

When we seek Jesus, there is no telling how many lives we can change.

He is: Christos Theos
Messiah of God
Blessings

LIVING COMPASSION

November 2

Now when he came nigh to the gate of the city, behold, there was a dead man carried out, the only son of his mother, and she was a widow: and much people of the city was with her. And when the Lord saw her, he had compassion on her, and said unto her, Weep not.

Luke 7:12–13

Jesus raised the widow's son. What stands out to me is the direction of Jesus's compassion—not directing His compassion at the deceased son. While everyone else was mourning and weeping for the dead, Jesus had compassion for the living.

"Blessed are those who mourn, for they shall be comforted" (Matthew 5:4).

Jesus not only said this, but He also lived it. He was the Comforter to the widow. But what about the son? This account uses the term lad, which designates the son to be under forty years of age and most likely younger than Jesus. It's important because he was the widow's only form of support. Jesus shows compassion for the mother, not the son.

When someone passes, it's understandable to mourn for a while. When Moses died, the Hebrews seemed as though they were never going to stop mourning; at thirty days, God spoke this to Joshua: "Moses, my servant is dead; now therefore arise, go over this Jordan" (Joshua 1:2).

The Jordan River was a natural barrier that kept the people from reaching their Promised Land. The death of a friend or relative can become a spiritual Jordan that holds us back from life.

You can carry their memory, but you still need to cross over.

He is: Shub Nephesh
Renewer of Life
Blessings

DARK LIGHT

November 3

"Take heed therefore that the light which is in thee be not darkness."
Luke 11:35

This statement by Jesus seems like an impossibility. How can a person have dark light? Take your modern-day light bulbs; there is a wide variety of choices. For example, you have the spotlight that wants to illuminate one area. Some preachers only preach about sin. It's like they burn a hole in the podium.

Christmas lights blink on and off, dazzling the spectator with an array of cute little lights, like people who pretend to be Christians when they need your help. When I was younger, this used to confuse me. I would be around people, and they would act holy or say the appropriate Bible verse when convenient. They do this to appear pious.

Next, we have the dimmer light turned down low to conserve energy; it only lights up when needed. Carnal Christians are good at this; they show up in church on Sunday all lit up and then are dimmed back down on Monday.

But, the light above that Jesus is talking about is the worst kind of light, the stage light. Ministers are preaching a weakened gospel to win YouTube followers. Jesus spoke about the Pharisees and Sadducee's evil doctrine, based on self-gain Old Testament net-worth.

I speak a lot about Jesus, but the one thing I fear the most is standing in judgment for the people I have misled; that's my greatest fear, or worse yet, the people I have offended (carnally) that may have caused them to turn away from Jesus. Remember, your motives reveal your light.

He is: Shaphat
Judge
Blessings

WE CHOOSE

November 4

*"Then shall the dust return to the earth as it was:
and the spirit shall return unto God who gave it."*

Ecclesiastes 12:7

There is no profit in the dust. Ultimately, the only profitable things are what you have laid up in the Spirit. Keep in mind that some things do not exist. One is a belief that there will be no judgment and that you no longer exist after death.

When I first became a Christian, I asked my friend, Charles, "How atheists could believe nothing after death?"

He said, "Look over there. There's no tree. It's not there. That's the way they think."

You can believe there is nothing after death because we can't see it from where we stand, but it is still there. God, in His infinite wisdom, gave us free will, a free will to believe, and a free will to make a choice:

"I have set before you life or death, blessing or curse. Oh, that you would choose life" (Deuteronomy 30:19).

How do we choose life? Simple:

> *That if thou shalt confess with thy mouth the Lord Jesus, and shalt believe in thine heart that God hath raised him from the dead, thou shalt be saved.*
>
> *For with the heart, man believeth unto righteousness; and with the mouth confession is made unto salvation.*
>
> **Romans 10:9–10**

We choose what we believe.

He is: El Yalad
The God Who Gave You Birth
Blessings

FOR THE LOVE OF RUTH

November 5

And Ruth said, Intreat me not to leave thee, or to return from following after thee: for whither thou goest, I will go; and where thou lodgest, I will lodge: thy people shall be my people, and thy God my God:

Ruth 1:16

Ruth was Naomi's daughter-in-law. Now, Ruth is clinging to her mother-in-law, asking her not to force her to leave. The bond between them is inseparable. Their hardship was the cement to their love for one another. Naomi's husband had died, and her two sons also passed. Ruth was married to one of the sons and Orpah to the other.

Out of poverty, Orpah decided to go back to her people. But Ruth had a love that believed, and she loved Naomi so much that she believed Naomi's faith in God. Naomi loved them so much that she was willing to give up her family so that they could survive.

God loved her so much that He saw her cry, and He became her God.

Ruth's desperate cry of devotion was so powerful that the Lord placed her in a place of redemption—a threshing mill at the feet of Boaz. Ruth married Boaz, and Boaz had a son named Obed, and their grandson was named Jessie, and his son was David the King.

The love of God can bring you places you never thought possible.

He is: Jehovah-Goel
Redeeming God
Blessings

FARMING DONE RIGHT

November 6

Plant the good seeds of righteousness, and you will reap a crop of my love; plow the hard ground of your hearts, for now is the time to seek the Lord, that he may come and shower salvation upon you.

Hosea 10:12

Farmers have unique insight into Scriptures like this, the knowledge of what good seed is, and how hard it can be to plow some types of ground. But what are the good seeds of righteousness? Righteousness is simply this: The state of acceptance of God.

"...even so, might grace reign through righteousness unto eternal life by Jesus Christ our Lord" (Romans 5:21).

You planted seeds of righteousness when you decided to accept Jesus as your Lord and Savior. To do this, you first had to plow through the hard ground of your heart, removing seeds of unforgiveness, bitterness, and sin.

When reading this verse in Hosea, it almost seems it was written in reverse, but the seed you have already received has been the testimonies or the words that God had dropped into your life long before you accepted Him as your Savior. Words people spoke to you that caught your attention and made you think about eternal life.

"...for now is the time to seek the Lord, that he may come and shower salvation upon you." "A shower of salvation." Now, that sounds refreshing.

He is: El Yeshuati
The God of My Salvation
Blessings

HIT THE MARK

November 7

And the apostles said unto the Lord, Increase our faith.
And the Lord said, If ye had faith as a grain of mustard seed, ye might say unto this sycamine tree, Be thou plucked up by the root, and be thou planted in the sea; and it should obey you.

Luke 17:5–6

"Increase our faith." An unusual request from the apostles. They have just listened to Jesus teach the parables of *The Dishonest Steward*, *The Law and the Kingdom of God*, *Divorce and Remarriage*, *The Rich Man and Lazarus*, and *Temptations to Sin*. *Temptations to Sin* was the preceding scriptures 17:1–4 about forgiveness.

Jesus tells them to forgive seven times in a day if someone trespassed against them. Trespass comes from the Greek word *ham-ar-tan-o*, meaning "to miss the mark."

We all *miss the mark* when it comes to other people, and even when it comes to forgiving ourselves, the apostles were asking for faith to forgive.

Here is Jesus's immediate response:

> *And the Lord said, If ye had faith as a grain of mustard seed, ye might say unto this sycamine tree, Be thou plucked up by the root, and be thou planted in the sea; and it should obey you.*

Luke 17:6

A sycamine tree is known for its root system; the roots spread out probably about twice the size of the tree, making it nearly impossible to remove. Unforgiveness, like the roots of a sycamine tree, can grow deep into your heart, choking out the life of your spirit. Be quick to forgive. Forgive before it becomes a sapling that takes root. After you have forgiven, you'll probably have to forgive again.

He is: Elohay Selichot
The God Who Is Ready to Forgive
Blessings

KEEP YOUR SEED DRY

November 8

*And the Lord said, Simon, Simon, behold, Satan hath
desired to have you, that he may sift you as wheat:
But I have prayed for thee, that thy faith fail not: and when
thou art converted, strengthen thy brethren.*

Luke 22:31–32

Imagine yourself as Peter sitting here, excited about eating a Passover meal with Jesus. He's administered communion and announced that the one about to betray Him is seated at the table. The twelve apostles begin to self-examine and then get into this evil argument about which one will be the greatest. Satan was in the room and sowed a seed, a thought that started the discord. Isn't it ironic that the discussion is about being the greatest? After all, that got him kicked out of heaven trying to be the greatest and usurping God.

Which apostle do you think brought up the topic of 'who would be the greatest? Let's assume it was Judas. Then, Jesus takes command of the room and explains how leadership works in the kingdom of heaven, and it is by being a servant.

Jesus looks directly into Peter's eyes and speaks about Satan's desire to sift Peter as wheat. Interesting choice of words. Wheat is sifted after the harvest and before Passover. This stage is the most critical part of the harvest. In the last weeks of the wheat harvest, if the wheat becomes wet, it will turn into leaven/yeast, which is not allowed for the Passover feast. Then, Jesus reveals Satan's plan to turn Peter's faith away, and Peter, like a true man, "machos up," saying that will never happen. But Jesus had a plan. He knew what the enemy would do to Peter, and Jesus prayed for protection for Peter's faith that it would not fail and that when converted, he would strengthen his brethren.

Sometimes, our actions fail; the works of the flesh can bring us to a place where we need repentance. Peter left and mourned for his betrayal, but he still had a seed of faith. The tears of repentance can keep your harvest dry or from becoming leaven.

Peter recovered because of Jesus's prayer, but the unfortunate part is that Jesus had also prayed for Judas. Pray that if you should fail, your seed of faith will recover.

He is: Entunchano
The God Who Intercedes
Blessings

A ROCK WITHOUT SIN

November 9

"He is the Rock, his work is perfect: for all his ways are judgment: a God of truth and without iniquity, just and right is He."

Deuteronomy 32:4

This verse shows us some of the fantastic attributes of God, who He is, and an insight into His awesomeness. A rock, for some, is a hiding place, a place of comfort, a place to run for protection; at least, it is for Christians. But to others, it's a place of judgment.

Rock comes from the Hebrew word *Tsur*: a cliff, a boulder, an adversary. How many people have decided to fight against Jesus and make Him their adversary? He is "The Rock of our Salvation," the very being that can save your eternity, and yet, they choose to oppose Him.

Have you ever punched a rock? It doesn't sound too pleasant. But fight against it they will; they will fight against Christ right until they walk off the cliff of eternity for no return.

I had a vision of someone I knew, a Christian that turned against God. He was standing at the edge of a cliff and willingly dove off the cliff. He went headfirst into the dark abyss.

The Holy Spirit showed me this so I would see the destruction that he willingly did to himself, knowing the word of God.

It's better to fall on the stone than have the weighty judgment of God fall on you.

"And whosoever shall fall on this stone shall be broken: but on whomsoever, it shall fall, it will grind him to powder" (Matthew 21:44).

He is: El Tsuri
The Rock
Blessings

CONTINUOUS FRUIT

November 10

Ye have not chosen me, but I have chosen you, and ordained you, that ye should go and bring forth fruit, and that your fruit should remain: that whatsoever ye shall ask of the Father in my name, he may give it you.

John 15:16

Knowing that Jesus has picked you to be on His team is comforting. One of the reasons He chose you is because you have something to offer that no one else has: your special uniqueness.

I watched a man on TV who developed a fruit tree that yields forty different kinds of fruit. It takes him nine years to graft all the other fruit-bearing trees onto a single tree. He brought his tree to the local growers and nurseries. No one could see the benefit of having such a tree. They said it would be too hard to harvest.

But he saw the benefits: a tree that produces different fruits all through the summer, and when it blossoms in the spring, it is so beautiful with all the varieties of flowers. And that's what Jesus sees in you, something unique that others may not see or understand, a fruit that He can harvest year-round.

Continuous fruit is something that remains long after we leave this earth. Things like people we have testified to, church buildings that we helped labor to build, ministries, and missionaries that we supported are the things that remain. Things that keep sending fruit to heaven long after our arrival. The key is asking God to show you good ground to plant your seed, like passive income, pray for places to sow that bear repetitive fruit.

He is: Georgos
The Gardener
Blessings

WINNING EDGE

November 11

And he said unto me, My grace is sufficient for thee: for my strength is made perfect in weakness. Most gladly therefore will I rather glory in my infirmities, that the power of Christ may rest upon me.

2 Corinthians 12:9

As I began to type, these words came to me: "The Winning Edge." Kingdom principles are not always the way we would perceive them to be. We think strength to win, but Jesus needs us to get out of the way so He can become strong on our behalf. Imagine the frustration this must cause the devil. He throws everything he has at you. To him, you're down for the count, no physical strength to call upon, you're weak, and suddenly, Jesus is strong on your behalf.

How many times in your life has Jesus come through at the last possible moment? He has for me multiple times. Never has He failed, and He won't fail you now.

I have noticed that we always seem to wonder *why*. I asked Jesus once, "Why isn't my prayer being answered?" As soon as I asked, the Holy Spirit immediately said: "Why? That's why!" *Why* was my unbelief, and if unbelief has a second name, it's probably "Why." There's no compromise with Christ. Your weakness is His: Winning Edge, it's a Promise.

He is: Lo Shanah
Unchanging
Blessings

ECONOMICS

November 12

In the sweat of thy face shalt thou eat bread, till thou return unto the ground; for out of it wast thou taken: for dust thou art, and unto dust shalt thou return. Probably one of the best-known Bible verses globally, every culture has heard of the curse, but was it?

Genesis 3:19

Probably one of the best-known Bible verses globally. Every culture has heard of the curse. But was it? God knew the consequences of Adam and Eve's sin, and this situation was desperate. We can see how serious the problem was in the following verse, 3:22: "Lest he put forth his hand, and take also of the tree of life, and eat, and live forever:"

God had to remove Adam and Eve from the garden and station a cherubim with a flaming sword to keep humankind out. Scholars believe the commandment was issued urgently because the writers did not place a period (.) after the word *forever*, indicating the speed at which they had to leave.

Father God knew there was only one way to redeem us: through His Son's blood and death. By having mankind sweat to make a living, He created a world economy. All crops are harvested with sweat equity in one way or another.

There are two other mentions of sweat in the Bible. Ezekiel 44:18 forbids the priests from wearing wool inside the temple to prevent sweat in God's presence. You can also find it in one other place: "And being in agony, he prayed more earnestly, and his sweat was as it were great drops of blood falling down to the ground" (Luke 22:44).

When Jesus sweated blood into the ground, He was preparing for a harvest, plowing drops of blood as though it were seeds of salvation for the redemption of humanity. When you accept Jesus as your Lord and Savior, you have become one of the fruits of the costliest crops in world history.

He is: Georgos
The Gardener
Blessings

GOD THE AVENGER!

November 13

Moreover, I make a decree what ye shall do to the elders of these Jews for the building of this house of God: that of the king's goods, even of the tribute beyond the river, forthwith expenses be given unto these men, that they be not hindered.

Ezra 6:8

The book of Ezra serves as a historical account of the temple's construction. After enduring seventy years of captivity, they received a royal decree from King Cyrus instructing them to return to Jerusalem and begin rebuilding the temple. Knowing that their adversaries would attempt to thwart the project, they did manage to halt it temporarily.

Their tactic involved employing individuals who were once adversaries, posing as friends but harboring ulterior motives, all in an attempt to infiltrate the temple's construction. Zerubbabel swiftly dismissed them, declaring, "You have no part with us."

Undeterred, their adversaries pursued legal action, petitioning King Artaxerxes of Persia to halt the project, and successfully managed to halt the rebuild. Some Jewish leaders swiftly intervened with force and, using their authority, issued a stern decree.

Yet, the prophets, Haggai and Zechariah, played a pivotal role. They prophesied that the rebuilding must persist, and so it did.

Upon the return of the regional governors, they vehemently demanded an immediate halt to the project. The Jewish community, unwavering in their purpose, refused and continued their labor. Once again, adversaries sought legal recourse, but this time, King Darius held sway. Darius meticulously examined King Cyrus's decree and comprehended the authority at play. This understanding led him to request the prayers of the priests and Jewish people for himself and his sons.

The remarkable aspect of this verse lies in the extraordinary edict issued by King Darius. He mandated that the adversaries of the temple shoulder the financial burden and provide all necessary resources for its reconstruction, underscoring the task's urgency. Furthermore, he offered an incentive for their support of the Jewish endeavor, cautioning that any disruption would result in their own dwellings being dismantled, with the materials repurposed for the construction of gallows from which they would be hanged.

When you face hindrance, God can turn the situation around overnight! He has the power to transform the resources of your adversary to your advantage. As we look forward to the imminent reconstruction of the third Temple, the enemy will likely attempt to obstruct it once again. But keep a watchful eye on what God can accomplish!

He is: El Nathan Neqamah
The God Who Avenges Me
Blessings

HOPE DEFERRED

November 14

"Hope that is deferred makes the heart sick, but a desire fulfilled is a tree of life."
Proverbs 13:12

Let's look at some words here to get into the meaning. Hope does not mean to Wish. Hope is to be patient, stay, trust, and wait. *Hope* means that we are patiently expecting. What are we expecting? For the desired outcome, please do not hope for a bad result for someone else.

Deferred, to sound, to prolong, develop, continue, scatter, to *stretch out*. To sound means to take a line and drop it over the side of a boat and see how deep the water is, to measure the depths of the water. *Stretch out*: Why would God stretch out your expectancy? So that He can see your heart. *The heart* is used widely to describe feelings, the will, and even intellect, the center of anything: your emotions, will, strength, understanding, wisdom, and mind. *Sick*: to be rubbed, worn, or polished, to be weak or afflicted; to grieve, to be sorry, or to be wounded. *Desire*: A longing, a delight, desire, exceedingly pleasant.

"Delight thyself also in the LORD; and he shall give thee the desires of thine heart" (Psalm 37:4).

Applying this verse, we can better understand Proverbs 13:12. By combining these two verses for an expectation. When God gives you the desires of your heart, this has a dual usage.

First, He places that desire in your heart. Second, He gives you that desire.

So why would God give you a desire and then allow it to be delayed? Remember the word *sick*, to be rubbed or worn (or polished)? While typing this, I saw a vision of the Holy Spirit polishing a vessel. What I interpret this to mean is that God wants to see the true beauty of your heart, not as we negatively think, that He is trying to uncover the wickedness of your heart, but the beauty. People never polish a vessel to see the damage but to reveal the beauty, *Selah*.

He is: Yahuah Tsidqenu
The Lord Our Righteousness
Blessings

THE BRONZE SERPENT

November 15

And the people spoke against God and against Moses: "Why have you brought us up out of Egypt to die in the wilderness? For there is no food and no water, and our soul loathes this worthless bread."
So, the Lord sent fiery serpents among the people; and many of the people of Israel died.
Therefore, the people of Israel came to Moses and said: "We have sinned, for we have spoken against the Lord and against you; pray to the Lord that He take away the serpents from us." So, Moses prayed for the people.
Then the Lord said to Moses, "Make a fiery serpent, and set it on a pole; and it shall be that everyone who is bitten, when he looks at it, shall live."
Therefore, the people of Israel came to Moses and said: "We have sinned, for we have spoken against the Lord and against you; pray to the Lord that He take away the serpents from us." So, Moses prayed for the people.
Then the Lord said to Moses, "Make a fiery serpent, and set it on a pole; and it shall be that everyone who is bitten, when he looks at it, shall live."

Numbers 21:5–8

When the Hebrews came out of Egypt, they brought out a lot of treasure. But, unfortunately, they brought with them a lot of mental bondage, a different type of heavy baggage that they carried with them wherever they went, the luggage of complaints.

Four hundred years of harsh circumstances have caused generations of complainers. Misery can be comforting if you allow it, a constant companion of gloom and doom. Many Christians never get past this stage. After they get saved, they complain about how things used to be, not learning to leave the past behind.

God saw to it that these people would get past their constant complaining. Instead of being thankful for what they had, they complained about what they had. What if they had rejoiced? Notice God didn't remove the fiery serpents. He had Moses build a pole and place a bronze serpent on a pole. Those bitten by a snake had to look to the bronze serpent for healing. The bronze serpent represented Jesus Christ.

"And as Moses lifted up the serpent in the wilderness, so must the son of man be lifted up" (John 3:14).

By looking at the serpent, it acknowledged the need for healing, for a Savior. They were also looking at their sin. Remarkably, modern-day medicine makes snake anti-venom out of its venom, and they use the serpent symbol on a pole as a medical standard, Selah.

"If we confess our sins, He is faithful and just to forgive us our sins and to cleanse us from all unrighteousness" (1 John 1:9).

There has been a time or two that I have sinned. And I know inside me that I must confess that sin out loud to the Lord like I must look at the pole, the cross. I don't want to admit it, but I know I must. It makes you never want to do it again. I get up and leave that baggage behind. Like the baggage handlers at the airport, they throw your old bags onto a cart, and you never see your bags again until you sin, then it's off to baggage claim. That's why I travel light. Let Jesus lighten your luggage today.

He is: Jehovah-Palat
Deliverer
Blessings

ONE MORE DAY

November 16

*Therefore, we do not lose heart, even though our outward man
is perishing, yet the inward man is being renewed day by day.
For our light affliction, which is but for a moment, is working for
us a far more exceeding and eternal weight of glory.*

2 Corinthians 4:16–17

These two verses are from the letter to the church at Corinth in Greece. It was also known as "the city of sin." It looks like an island off the southern part of Greece connected by a small strip of land, and it was a very wealthy city back in the day, a party town, you could call it. They had a temple with 1000 prostitutes who would walk out every evening to apply their trade.

Paul is addressing the local Christians and encouraging them not to lose heart and give up. It reminds me of modern-day America, television, and social media. Not a day goes by that the enemy doesn't throw temptation your way. For Christians, this can be an affliction to our soul.

Sometimes, you may think you can't take any more adversity. At this very moment, while typing this devotion, the Lord told me, "I have a message I must get out."

How can tragedy bring God glory? Consider the passing of a loved one; this pain is but for a moment, possibly for the remainder of your life, to others a moment, a twinkling in time, but your response will be for their eternity.

In those moments when you feel like you've hit rock bottom, when your spirit feels too weary to rise, remember this: let your response bring glory to God. Reach out to Jesus and ask Him to renew your inner being to restore your spirit.

Years ago, I borrowed someone's boat to go hunting. When we woke up the following day, my friend called me loudly, "Scott! Come see! The boat sunk!" Everyone in the camp was looking at me. I walked over to the camp door just in time to see the bow go underwater, and the boat had sunk. My friend excitedly said: "What are we going to do?" I replied: "I'm going to eat breakfast. You hungry?"

He was very perplexed at my response. However, as I saw it, the boat wouldn't get any wetter, but my bacon would get cold. I hadn't even had a cup of coffee yet. It was just too early in the morning to have a tragedy.

We ate our breakfast and, a little while later, pulled the boat up onto dry land, dried everything out, and went hunting. When I returned it to the owner, I told him what happened, and he said, "Oh! I forgot to tell you it has a slow leak. It's sunk on me twice. Did you get it running okay?" Everything was good.

When tragedy hits, you're the "Christian book" others will read. Believe me, they look at the fine print. It'll be better tomorrow, the next day, or even today.

He is: El Racham
The Compassionate God
Blessings

BLESSINGS

November 17

God is not a man, that He should lie, nor a son of man, that He should repent. Has He said, and will He not do? Or has He spoken, and will He not make good? Behold I have received a command to Bless, He has Blessed and I cannot reverse it.

Numbers 23:19–20

A prophesied blessing proclaimed to the children of Israel, but it has come in a very unusual way. The king of Moab, Balak, had hired Balaam, a false prophet, to curse Israel. But God, through Balaam, ended up blessing Israel instead.

Sometimes, seeing what God is doing on our behalf can be challenging. This blessing took place in the mountains above the encampments of Israel, where Moses had positioned the Hebrews in a very orderly fashion designed by God. Each of the twelve tribes of Israel had their own designated areas.

King Balak had set himself on top of a mountain called "The Field of Zophim," which means "the field of watchers." Moses and the Israelites had no clue this meeting was taking place, high above their position, above their place of habitation. When King Balak and Balaam looked down from "the field of watchers," what did they see? Thousands of tents with more than two million people in the formation of a cross.

They tried to pronounce a curse on the cross, but the cross brought the blessing, which is forever. Remember the blessing of the cross when you feel as though you are down in the desert.

"For we wrestle not against flesh and blood, but against principalities, against powers, against the rulers of the darkness of this world, against spiritual wickedness in high places" (Ephesians 6:12).

When the enemy tries to tell you how defeated you are, remember all the devil can see is the cross.

He is: El Elyon
Most High God
Blessings

THE GOD WHO LOVES

November 18

"But the fruit of the Spirit is Love, Joy, Peace, Patience, Kindness, Goodness, Faithfulness, Gentleness, Self-Control; against such things there is no law."

Galatians 5:22–23

This verse is one of the loveliest scriptures in the Bible and probably one of the hardest to live. As a younger Christian, I would attend church and marvel at some of our members' outstanding attributes. I would think how our pastor is so intelligent and his wife was the most joyful. Our assistant pastor had so much patience with people; his wife was and still is one of the most self-disciplined people I have ever met. Another man carried himself with so much integrity, another was so kind, some were so good and gentlemen and women of great character.

I would often think, "If only I could carry myself like them, I would take everyone's best quality and put it into myself." I did this to myself for years. To this day, I still see the best qualities in people; maybe it's a gift from God. I know that God is very merciful, and He knows our thoughts. One day, while driving along, it hit me! If I had all those attributes, I would be Jesus!

Age does have some benefits. As I've gotten older, I have realized that these are fruits we all possess if we receive the Holy Spirit. I may only sometimes display them on my outer character all the time, but as needed. When someone does you wrong, *self-control* is required. Smiling and saying "hello" to someone equals kindness. When a link pulls you into an inappropriate website and you immediately click out, that is faithfulness. Be gentle to your animals and your spouse. Kindness doesn't stop at five o'clock when you get off work.

You see, *there is no law against love*, or a time clock.

He is: Elohim Ahavah
The God Who Loves
Blessings

THE GOD OF MY SALVATION

November 19

"This is good and pleases God our Savior, who wants all men to be saved and to come to a knowledge of the Truth."

1 Timothy 2:3–4

This verse manifests the goodness of Jesus Christ. It pleases Him to see people accept the truth, and the truth is He wants all men to come to this truth.

A few days ago, a Muslim man told me he had been reading the Bible I had given him. He said it was easy to understand, and he was reading it to his daughter every night.

You see, he is coming to the knowledge of the *truth*. I shared this with him, and he listened. The Koran mentions Jesus twenty-six times in their writings. I told him about a man who had studied the world's religions, seeking the truth.

One day, while reading an Eastern religion, he noticed it referenced the Bible. Then, he realized that in every faith he had studied quoted the Bible to substantiate their credibility.

If you go to a job interview, HR will want professional references from others. For a reference to be valid, it must come from a higher source. Someone who was more credible or had authority over you in the past to validate or endorse you.

So, if all the religions reflect the Bible, they are trying to get credibility from a Higher Source. Unfortunately for them, Jesus does not endorse other beliefs: "Jesus said unto him, I AM the Way, the Truth, and the Life; no one comes unto the Father, but by Me" (John 14:6).

He is: El Yeshuati
The God of My Salvation
Blessings

LORD OF VICTORY AND MIRACLES

November 20

"The effectual fervent prayer of a righteous man availeth much."
James 5:16

I took this verse out of my original Bible that I bought back in 1982, taking it off the shelf just now, welled up memories of an old friend my first bible. I remember when the meaning of this verse hit me with its intensity back in 1993 (?) when my dad was diagnosed with cancer.

Things were so different back then. There was no such thing as cell phones; you couldn't just hop on the internet and find a church in another state. My dad was in California, and I was living in Louisiana. I asked the Lord what to do, and when I opened my Bible, it fell to this verse: *The effectual fervent prayer of a righteous man availeth much.*

I sank to my knees and prayed for my dad's salvation. He wasn't saved, and now, suddenly, he was lying in a hospital bed, dying of cancer. I asked God to please save my dad.

I knew I had to get a pastor to go over there and pray with him, so I picked up the house phone and dialed information for the state of California. I received an operator and pleaded with him my cause, and he said, "We're not supposed to do this." (Risking his job to help me). "I know of a church in Yuba City, California, that is Pentecostal, I think?" I said, "That will work!" He gave me the number, and I called. A man with a deep, solid voice answered the phone, and he was the pastor. I told him what was going on. I was grasping at anything that could help. Overwhelmed with emotions, I began to cry, and the man said he would make a trip to Chico to see my dad.

Imagine this: a phone call from over 2,000 miles away to Yuba City, CA. Yuba City is fifty-four miles from Chico. How many churches could have possibly been in between?

My dad used to be a police officer, turned into a carpenter, and was known for doing excellent work. He loved to barter with people for materials and always got the best end of the deal. People would laugh while losing money, but it was okay. It was Bob.

The pastor wore a blue carpenter shirt and jeans when he walked into the room. He might have even had sawdust on his jeans. My dad loved him! He told my dad that when he got out of the hospital, he would have to work on his new church, and by the way, he wasn't about to pay my dad for his labor! Finally, Bob was out bartered! They prayed together, and my dad had a new appreciation for Christians.

I spoke with my stepmother a few days later, and she told me this story. She said a young male nurse cared for my dad in the hospital. She said, "My dad really liked this young man and got along great. He talked with my dad about the Lord."

A few days later, she stepped into an elevator with the young man, and he asked her, "Do you have a son that lives in Louisiana?" My stepmother said, "Well, yes, I have a stepson." He replied, "He

372 | Who Is God?

called my dad and asked him if he would come here and pray for Bob!"

My dad did not recover from his cancer. However, he did accept Jesus as his Lord and Savior before he died. I visited him before he passed. I walked by his room and overheard him say, "I guess God would forgive you?" A young lady had called him asking if it would be okay to have an abortion. He was new in the Lord and did not know, so I sat down next to him and whispered the answers to her questions. This young lady had so much respect for my dad that she listened to his counsel. After my dad died, her baby boy was born, and she named him Robert, after my dad.

A young pastor did the funeral, and he gave an altar call at the end. And two people accepted Jesus as their Savior, one of them my life long best friend Jerome. To God be the glory!

He is: Jehovah Nissi
Lord of Victory and Miracles
Blessings

THE POWER OF BELIEF

November 21

For from the first making of the world, those things of God which the eye is unable to see, that is, His eternal Power and existence, are fully made clear, He having given the knowledge of them through the things which He has made, so that men have no reason for wrongdoing:

Romans 1:20 (BBE)

Have you ever been asked by someone to do something you are very skilled at? And then they ask again if you can do it, even while you're working on their request. Your first thought is, "I'm working on your request; it will slow me down to explain it." They need to learn that you are very knowledgeable in your trade. Worrisome people will drive you crazy if you let them. You will think they don't trust you, but mostly, it is a lack of belief in themselves.

I'm guilty of this with God, trying to explain how to handle my circumstances—the power of belief over my affairs. Knowing your adversary helps. In this case, our adversary would be called *circumstance*. Circumstance means a condition or fact that affects a situation. Or the way something happens: the specific details of an event. An event or situation that you cannot control.

The Holy Spirit told me how to handle circumstances:

"Here's the solution: Get down on your knees and pray to get rid of iniquity." Iniquity means sin, but this brings it into a different category. I had just finished praying, and the Holy Spirit had already revealed what I needed to repent from. He also said, "You're being pressured from all sides."

Iniquity means gross injustice, wickedness, a wicked act or thing, sin:

"…those things of God which the eye is unable to see."

When evil abounds, and bad things keep happening, realize it is the enemy. Yesterday, a lady told me, "Do you really know my name?" She said, "It's before the world began," and gave me this crazy look as if to intimidate me. It was a manifestation of a demonic spirit. I just silently prayed, "Do you know my name? I'm a blood-washed Christian operating in the power of the blood, and you will respect me and shut up! In the name of Jesus." She relaxed and was suddenly a very kind person.

These are the "things" that we are unable to see. But here's where it gets good. "…His Power, the blood of Jesus, is fully made clear to the things which we cannot see." So demons know the authority of Jesus!

When I first became a Christian, I was a police officer. While driving in my patrol car, I asked the Lord, "Why do demons have to obey your name?" Immediately, I saw a vision of myself in my patrol car driving towards a crime scene and the perps running away.

There's law in the Spirit, and demons know that if they stick around after invoking authority in the name of Jesus, they can face dire consequences.

"…He having given the knowledge of them through the things which He has made." We are the things He has made, and He has given us the knowledge of how to use His name so that men have no reason for wrongdoing.

Remember Flip Wilson? He was a funny comedian back in the day. Just typing his name makes me smile. He had a line that us oldsters will remember: "The devil made me do it!" Well, that won't stand on the day of judgment.

He is: Jehovah Palat
Lord Deliverer
Blessings

LORD WHO PROVIDES

November 22

"Now Faith is the substance of things hoped for, the evidence of things not seen."

Hebrews 11:1

I love this powerful verse. Let's take a look and break it down a bit. The very first word is like an opening to an action film! "NOW!" So when does *faith* start? Now! What is faith? Faith is a moral conviction or the truthfulness of God.

Substance means concrete, essence, confidence, and person.

Hope is to expect, not wish.

Evidence is proof.

Let's read this with a little more understanding:

Right Now! Faith is my firm moral conviction in the concrete Truthfulness of God that the things expected to come will come, the proof and confidence of things not seen.

In Romans 1:20, His invisible attributes—His eternal power and His divine nature—have been clearly seen ever since the creation of the world, being understood through the things that have been made. So people are without excuse.

Even though we don't see God working on our behalf, we can rest assured that He is. Even though people have said that Jesus will not return, we can rest assured that He will. *...His eternal power and existence are fully made clear.* We know without a doubt that Jesus has risen from the dead: "He is not here, but is risen!" (Luke 24:6)

Now, the rest of this chapter is called "The Hall of Faith." It goes on to explain how people endured so much hardship based on the promises of God. They all did their parts in a universal play scripted for your win.

More extraordinary things can be hoped for if you trust and look for God.

He is: Jehovah Jireh
Lord Who Provides
Blessings

ADVOCATE

November 23

*"Then said Thomas, which is called Didymus, unto his fellow disciples.
Let us also go, that we may die with Him."*

St. John 11:31

I've always admired Thomas. Over the years, I have often heard criticism against him, but he doesn't deserve it. I feel hurt when people talk about the disciples demeaningly, as if somehow we would have said or done the correct thing.

The devil labeled Thomas as "Doubting Thomas." You see, this is a tactic the enemy uses to belittle the true nature of Thomas. In this instance, Thomas was a pessimist, anticipating an evil outcome if they went to Judah with Jesus.

Things were getting hot as far as the desire of the Pharisees to kill Jesus, and the disciples knew they were likely to suffer the same fate. It's almost like they are tired of the criticism and the painful words that the respected people of the community are saying about them. Notice none of the other disciples interjected to go along with Jesus; instead, they tried to talk Him out of it. Maybe Jesus was looking for that intercessor to stand in the gap. Jesus's friend Lazarus was dead and needed help, and Jesus was going.

Then, Thomas negatively said, "Let us also go that we may die with Him." An amazing thing happened; none of the other disciples argued. They all just went; they went because they had respect for Thomas.

Has anyone ever asked you to pray for them, to stand in the gap, and you thought, "I don't think God can do that? That's not the right thing to ask for." I know I have. There have been times when I thought, "There is no way God can answer this prayer." Not only did He answer, but He answered big!

Sometimes, He doesn't need your Faith; He needs your Words. Jesus went on to raise Lazarus from the dead, and I'm sure many people have accepted Jesus as their Savior to this day because of this notable miracle.

Thomas went on to martyrdom in Chennai, India, and that's more than three thousand miles from Jerusalem. One of my pastors met a Christian there who was a direct descendant of St. Thomas's ministry. Her Christian ancestors had accepted Jesus, and she could trace her faith back to Thomas! Thomas traveled farther than the rest and still had a lasting reward.

"But he said unto them, Except I shall see in his hands the print of the nails, and put my finger into the print of the nails, and thrust my hand into his side, I will not believe" (John 20:25).

Interestingly, all the other disciples had said the exact same words, but no one noticed that. Thomas was later martyred with a spear thrust through his side.

"Then saith he to Thomas, Reach hither thy finger, and behold my hands; and reach hither thy hand, and thrust it into my side: and be not faithless, but believing" (John 20:27).

Jesus revealed Himself to Thomas in a special way because Thomas was a leader. And how did this magnificent leader respond? By exclaiming, "My Lord and my God!"

He is: Parakletos
Advocate
Blessings

THE LORD'S PRAYER

November 24

After this manner, therefore, pray ye: Our Father which art in heaven,
Hallowed be thy Name.
Thy kingdom come. Thy will be done on earth as it is in heaven.
Give us this day our daily bread.
And forgive us our debts, as we forgive our debtors.
And lead us not into temptation but deliver us from evil:
For thine is the kingdom and the power, and the Glory, forever.
Amen

St. Matthew 6:9–13

Jesus made it so easy for us to pray. I encourage you to pray for at least thirty minutes a day. I've had people tell me that they run out of words within a few minutes. So here's how you can fill your prayer time by turning this prayer into praise.

I will take the meanings of the words from the Greek translation:

Our Father which art in heaven

Our means company, us, we, you, and me, but this includes Jesus, the Holy Spirit, and Angels. You are not alone! You have a prayer team in the house ready to praise God from the start.

Father which art in heaven

Place God as our Father in reverence, and where is He positioned? Some texts translate the word heaven to heavens, which sets God above us in the third heaven—a place of prominence.

Hallowed be thy Name.

Hallowed: to revere that is with Great respect.

Now, here's where you can start to get into the praise aspect of God's name. To start praising God's name, "Hallowed be thy Name! Glory be thy Name! Holiness be thy Name! Righteousness be thy Name! Strong Tower be thy Name! Deliverer be thy Name! August be thy Name!"

August means respected, impressive, distinguished, eminent, hallowed, illustrious, prestigious, celebrated, honored, acclaimed, esteemed, exalted.

You establish God's character in your mind and heart by praising Him. Say this for ten minutes, easy. Occasionally, I have to push myself past praising the name of God.

...Thy kingdom come. Thy will be done on earth as it is in heaven.

I used to relate this to the book of Revelations, thinking that God's will would take place after the return of Jesus, and it does, but where is the kingdom now?

"Neither shall they say, Lo here! Or, lo there! For, behold, the kingdom of God is within you" (Luke 17:21). God's kingdom is within you! So by praying this, you're saying, "Your will be done in me!" By now, you should be dancing!

Give us this day our daily bread. Thank God He provides our bread for sustenance, but wait! We have established that His will should be in us. How will we know His will if He doesn't speak to us? So what is *bread*?

"And Jesus said unto them, I AM the bread of Life: he that cometh unto me shall never hunger; and he that believeth on Me shall never thirst" (John 6:35). Jesus is the Bread of Life, and it's evident that He is not talking about natural food. A side note: people were not allowed to say the words I AM, because that is the name of God given to Moses. Saying it was punishable by death. Every time Jesus said, "I AM," He said, "I AM GOD."

...And forgive us our debts as we forgive our debtors. Forgive: To send, to go; to send forth, forsake, lay aside, leave, let, omit, put (send) away, remit, suffer, yield up. I like the last part to yield up. Periodically, I experience a letdown when I suddenly have to switch gears and ask for forgiveness. Why? And why here? We're really getting into the praise at this point. I think it is a reminder of how bad sin is.

Imagine in the Old Testament when you had to take a baby lamb out of your flock and bring it to the temple, walking for miles and carrying it—then sacrificing it. The thought makes me cringe.

However, it coincides with the verse before: Jesus is the Bread of Life. So if God can do this for you, you can do this for Him, and I don't mean sacrificing a lamb; I mean sacrifice and forgive by releasing your sin of unforgiveness towards others and forgiving yourself.

Now we can rejoice in that we are forgiven!

...And lead us not into temptation but deliver us from evil: Oh, Hallelujah! Now, we've been delivered from the evil trap of unforgiveness! He's already answering your prayers!

...For thine is the kingdom and the power, and the Glory, forever. Oh, happy days are here again! Who's the kingdom? You are! You're God's forever! You're His kingdom and under the authority of His power and glory forever! Time to start saying "Thank You, Lord!"

Finally, *Amen* means: So be it.

He is: Jehovah-Tzidkenu
The Lord Our Righteousness
Blessings

HOW BEAUTIFUL

November 25

How beautiful upon the mountains are the feet of him that bringeth good tidings, that publish peace; that bringeth good tidings of good, that publisheth salvation; that saith unto Zion, Thy God reigneth!

Isaiah 52:7

Have you ever watched one of those movies where they're climbing a mountain with all this equipment? Their shoes are so important. They use more of a rubber-type boot or tennis shoe at lower altitudes to climb the rocks. But when they get higher, they use crampons, metal spikes you attach to your shoes.

That equipment can be costly, and it should be; your life depends on it. Jesus knows the cost of this equipment for the Christian climber. That's why He gave us the most valuable mountain climbing shoes the universe could know.

"And your feet shod with the preparation of the Gospel of Peace" (Ephesians 6:15).

You can't reach the summit without it. It seems like a simple statement to walk on the mountain tops until you've tried it. Not long ago, while in prayer one morning, the Holy Spirit said to me, "Those gospel shoes you have on belong to Jesus."

I thought, *Okay?* I ended up thinking about it all day. Later that night, I asked the Holy Spirit to explain it. Immediately, I saw a vision of Jesus walking, and He lifted His robe and revealed to me His sandals. The key words were "…they belong to Jesus." The gospel belongs to Jesus, the Good News. Your duty is to share it, to keep walking in it.

Jesus is the Word, and the gospel means the Good News. When we tell others about Jesus and that He has a plan for their life: "For I know the Thoughts, I think concerning you, said the Lord, thoughts of peace, and not of evil, to give you the end that you wait for" (Jeremiah 29:11).

And Romans 10:13: For whosoever shall call upon the Lord shall be saved. By telling others about salvation, you are wearing the gospel shoes, and with these shoes, you can reach the top of the summit.

He is: El Moshaah
The God Who Saves
Blessings

NO BETS ALLOWED

November 26

"And the devil that deceived them was cast into the lake of fire and brimstone, where the beast and the false prophet are, and shall be tormented day and night for ever and ever."

Revelation 20:10

I may not have all the answers, but I know we win in the end. A friend told me that professional wrestling was the only sport in Las Vegas that you couldn't bet on because the outcomes of the wrestling matches were pre-determined. I don't see any bets being placed on the return of Jesus Christ either, and you wouldn't want to be around to collect afterward.

On one occasion, I was making a delivery to a record store and would have to go through this dark room to get to the back shop. I had had an experience on a previous delivery that made me think there was a demon in that room.

On this trip, I heard a voice speak to me. It was so smooth, and it began to tell me that I had no future. That I was a failure. Suddenly, I pulled myself out of the thought and exclaimed, "I have no future? You're the one that's going to the lake of fire!" (Or something like that.)

Then, I was overcome by this sense of sorrow and grief that wanted me to feel pity for it. Truthfully, that shocked me. But believe me, don't feel sorry for it. That same demon does not pity you.

We may not always win every battle we face in this life, or circumstances may not go how we want, but we have a guarantee we win in the end.

God guarantees victory through Jesus.

He is: Jehovah Gibbor Milchamah
Mighty in Battle
Blessings

FOLLOW THE CLOUD

November 27

"And when the cloud was taken up from the tabernacle, then after that the sons of Israel journeyed, and in the place where the cloud abode, there the sons of Israel pitched their tents."

Numbers 9:17

This scripture talks about Moses and the Israelites in the wilderness. A cloud was over the Tabernacle during the day. On occasions, God would move them to a different location. It was to give the land a rest from the estimated two million people and as a training lesson in obedience.

It's easy to connect the cloud being the Spirit of God. We don't know how often or how long in between the movements of the cloud, but we know it moved, and the people went with it. If you stayed behind, you would dry up and die in the desert sun. And if churches don't move with the Spirit, they will dry up too.

The Holy Spirit still moves today. My old pastor used to say, "The message never changes, but the method of delivery does." I have some books on John Wesley, founder of the Methodists, and Peter Cartwright, the famous circuit rider preacher. Riding horses and building churches was a rugged lifestyle. And it was the most effective method of delivery for that day.

But times have changed, and so does the method of delivery. Churches will die rather than move with the Holy Spirit. I understand and respect tradition. But if the Holy Spirit goes this way, I plan on following. I see people with tattoos and men with earrings leading worship. Rappers that look like they just got out of prison rapping for the Lord, with lyrics that heal wounded hearts and people respond.

"To the weak I became as weak, that I might gain the weak; I am made all things to everyone, that I might by all means save some" (1 Corinthians 9:21).

I remember a story years ago about a church in Florida that wanted to start reaching out to the younger generations. The service was packed, and a young man came in wearing flip-flops, shorts, a T-shirt, and a baseball cap. The congregation was shocked that someone dressed like this would show up to church. He was late, so everyone noticed him. There were no open seats in the church that day, so he walked down the steps close to the front seats, sat down on the first step in the middle of the aisle, and started listening to the pastor.

The pious church members were shocked. How could he? Then, one of the church elders came to the same entrance door in the church. He was well respected and in his late eighties or early nineties. He had a walker and slowly started going down the aisle. Everyone was thinking, "Mr. Elder will teach him a lesson!" They said you could hear the walker's squeak and shuffle of his feet as he slowly approached the young man. The tension mounted, waiting to see how he would straighten this boy out. When he finally reached the young man, he slowly sat down next to him and listened to the sermon with him. You see, the elder was following the cloud, and the Holy Spirit was doing something new, an answer to their prayers.

Everyone learned a lesson in evangelism that day. And the wisdom of love and being all things to all people. We may not understand the next generation, but God does, and all He wants us to do is have a little understanding and love.

He is: Elohim Ahavah
The God Who Loves
Blessings

PLANT YOUR CROSS

November 28

"Be sober, be vigilant; Because your adversary the devil, as a roaring lion, walketh about, seeking whom he may devour."

1 Peter 5:8

Notice this scripture doesn't say, "He is a roaring lion." It says, "He acts like a roaring lion." He will use people to intimidate you every chance he gets.

Recently, the Lord told me to return to Detroit and plant a cross at the Packard car plant. The Packard plant went out of business more than sixty-five years ago. A wealthy real estate tycoon from Peru purchased it. Before my wife and I left, the Lord told me He would provide me with a cross.

When we arrived at the building where the Lord wanted me to be, a security guard immediately approached us and forcefully told me I was absolutely not allowed to enter the property. However, this building is not legally owned by the tycoon. The city of Detroit said it was not part of the purchase. The security guard warned me that it was their property and "Do not cross this line."

Well, one obstacle in front of us and, like a roaring lion, trying to hinder our assignment. Now, I needed a cross, and we were running out of time. I went to the lumber and department stores, but we couldn't find a cross.

Then, a man named Packard Al called me. He was a rugged old Christian living in an abandoned warehouse at the plant (directly behind the building I needed). He was waiting for us to arrive. I explained to him our dilemma about not being able to buy a cross. He told us to come over, and he would build one.

We found two pieces of cedarwood stained red when we arrived at his home (?). With all the rusted old metal, the two boards were so out of place that it was like they were waiting for us.

We fashioned a cross, and as we put it together, I thought, *This is going to be way too tall.* I told Mr. Packard Al what the security guard had told us. We were not allowed on the property. He said the parcel was city property, and they could not stop us from going on it. He was very sure of himself and confident in his authority, and he knew they had no power over this piece of land.

So, from the back entrance, we walked onto the property, trusting in Al's authority. In full view of the three security guards, they were not too happy about our presence there. They became vocal but did not approach us.

We needed a way to stand the cross up, and it was all pavement. A year earlier, the Lord told me to build an altar on this site and consecrate the land for the Lord. As I looked for the altar made from rocks, I couldn't find it. But Al noticed a sinkhole about the size of a basketball under a piece of plywood. When I looked down, it was the rocks from the altar! They had sunk and created the perfect hole for our cross-through pavement!

The cross perfectly slipped into that sinkhole, and it was just the right height! We slid the plywood against it to hold it into position. Seventy-five feet away, I could hear the security guard saying, "What are they doing!" But they wouldn't approach us. We poured olive oil on the cross and prayed, consecrating this ground as holy for the Lord.

Packard Al walked ten feet over when we finished and pointed to some painted gravel. He told us this was a marker that the Satanists used; it gave them a coded message into which building to go for their rituals. He had observed them on occasions entering the plant late at night.

Here is the symbolism: The real estate tycoon claims legal land ownership. The security guards enforce the disputed claim with verbal threats of fear. Packard Al knew his authority; more importantly, he knew their lack of power. We walked with Al, placing faith in his authority, and took back what the enemy had taken from the Lord.

The following day, as my wife was praying, she felt we hadn't done enough, and the Lord spoke to her and said, "I provided the cross, and I provided the hole." She knew then that the symbolism in the Spirit was where the battle occurred.

God has plans for that property, and He has plans for you.

He is: Jehovah Jireh
God My Provider
Blessings

In Memory of Al (Detroit) Hill (Packard Al)

TIE A KNOT

November 29

*"For I will contend with him who contends with you.
And I will save your children."*

Isaiah 49:25

I love this verse, and it's simple and straight to the point. When everything seems to be going against you, this is an excellent verse to hang on to.

I remember a poster with a quote by Thomas Jefferson. It was a picture of a kitten hanging onto the end of a rope with one paw, and the caption said: "When you reach the end of your rope, tie a knot and hang on!"

This verse is a lifeline of promise for you. And as a bonus, God said He would save your children, too! I have a prayer shawl called a tallit. I often use it when I pray; it has a sense of comfort, and it has this verse on the bottom corner of the tallit. It's a daily reminder that God will save my children and somehow get me through the trials of life.

The one who contends with you is the enemy.

"For we wrestle not against flesh and blood, but against principalities, against powers, against the rulers of the darkness of the world, against spiritual wickedness in high places" (Ephesians 6:2).

Sometimes, we need to use God's word to tie a knot for us to hang on.

He is: Jehovah-Go'el"
Redeeming God"
Blessings

DO YOU NEED A PICK-ME-UP?

November 30

"In the year that king Uzziah died I saw also the Lord sitting upon a throne, high and lifted up, and His train filled the temple."

Isaiah 6:1

King Uzziah was a righteous king who served well in his office for the Lord until pride took him down. Isaiah was a member of the royal family; Uzziah was his nephew. I'm sure Isaiah was grieving the loss of a great king and family member.

Matthew Henry believed that Isaiah was contemplating quitting his ministry. Isaiah was exhausted, commissioned by God to speak of things to come. Society has never unpunished a prophet; every word and action is under scrutiny.

I'm sure Isaiah saw the smirks, the heads that shook in disbelief, the quiet scoffs, and he heard the bitter words. Rejection combined with grief can make you want off this planet.

God saw this and knew that Isaiah needed a pick-me-up. But when God lifts you, He goes

all out! Isaiah needed to know that even though the king had died, God was still on the Throne! Isaiah needed some victory in life, and God revealed His Throne to him.

When kings defeated another kingdom, I read that they would take a portion of the defeated king's royal robe and attach it to the bottom hem of their royal robe. This was called the train, and God's train filled the temple! Isaiah witnessed God's many victories. Defeat wasn't in the room, only the wins.

I recently had a vision of a train (locomotive) stopping. It was very long, and as I stood there looking at the train, I could feel the power of the engines. I knew Jesus was showing me this regarding His train filling the temple. Our congregation at church felt the presence of God entering the worship service. Our praise and worship had brought God into our sanctuary, and He paused with all His power. Then, the train powered up to pull away. The railroad tracks in front of the railroad tracks signify God's plans, set on rails going to a specific destination. What God decides will be done.

If you need a "pick-me-up," start praising God. I know it can be hard to stir yourself up sometimes. But as you begin to praise Him, his presence will fill you up. He's a good, good God!

He is: Shub Nephesh
Renewer of Life
Blessings

I THIRST

December 1

*"There cometh a woman of Samaria to draw water:
Jesus saith unto her, Give me to drink."*

John 4:7

An appointed time, does Jesus just happen to get here at this exact moment by coincidence? No, this encounter was commissioned by God, and the timing was through the Holy Spirit.

Notice that Jesus didn't say, "Good afternoon, could you spare some water?" There's a reason why He said, "Give me to drink." Let's look at another verse a couple of chapters ahead:

"It is the spirit that quickeneth; the flesh profiteth nothing: the words that I speak unto you, they are spirit, and they are life" (John 6:63). Jesus spoke these words about Himself when He said, "the words that I speak unto you, they are spirit and life."

When I first read this, I was at verse 4:7 and skipped to verse 6:63. After I read this, I realized everything Jesus said was words from the spirit. As I continued reading, I read Jesus's words from the spirit side and flipped back to John 4:7: "Jesus saith unto her, Give me to drink."

I paused and gave deep thought. What was the spirit saying? What would the Holy Spirit thirst for? How could He thirst? Then, the Holy Spirit spoke to me and said, "I thirst for righteousness!"

Wow! Righteousness is the reconciliation of man with God. The Holy Spirit wants you justified with God through Jesus! But we see this statement again in John 19:28: "After this, Jesus knowing that all things were now accomplished, that the Scripture might be fulfilled, saith, I thirst."

The last words Jesus spoke before His death on the cross: "I thirst." It was code for I want humankind to be righteous with God, *Selah.*

And how did humankind respond? They shoved a sponge with vinegar to quench His thirst.

He is: Jehovah-Tzidkenu
The Lord Our Righteousness
Blessings

PETITION AND REASON

December 2

"Shew me a token for good; that they which hate me may see it, and be ashamed: because thou, LORD, hast holpen me, and comforted me."

Psalm 86:17

Psalm 86 is unique because it is more of a prayer than a song. David petitions God and then backs it up with a reason as to why God should answer his prayer. In this Psalm, he makes 13 prayer requests with explanations, and verse 17 is his last request.

I love this verse. When David made all the petitions and all the reasons why God should help him, he said this, "Make me look good on your behalf, embarrass those who had fought against me, because LORD, that is who you are, you had always helped me and comforted me when I was down."

Miracles and trials are confidence builders. You can always look back and realize that God has helped you through then all. Then, you can have confidence to remind God that He has helped you in the past, but mostly, remind yourself.

He is: Theos Pas Paraklesis
The God of All Comfort
Blessings

RECORD HEAT

December 3

But the day of the Lord will come as a thief in the night; in the which the heavens shall pass away with a great noise, and the elements shall melt with fervent heat, the earth also and the works that are therein shall be burned up.

2 Peter 3:10

How loud do you think it will be when God removes the heavens? Everything will go through the fire, and fire removes all the excess.

I mentioned to a friend once that I didn't want to mark a book up, and he laughed and said, "It really doesn't matter. It's all going to be burned to ash one day anyway."

Although there are books that I still value too much to write in, that is an excellent way to look at things.

"Things." They can get a hold of you if you let them, and after a few years, you can have so much stuff that it just gets overbearing.

Works for the Lord will also be placed in the fire, and what is left over will be your reward. I listened to a lady who had a vision of this prophecy. She said a famous evangelist had all his books placed on a fire pit by an angel, and the books burned to ashes with no reward.

She said there were thirty-five books, and he did not get a reward because he wrote them with the wrong motives. One day, an angel will place our motives and works into the fire.

He is: Akal Esh
Consuming Fire
Blessings

FAITH IS BELIEVING

December 4

"For therein is the righteousness of God revealed from faith to faith: as it is written, The just shall live by faith."

Romans 1:17

Upon reading Romans 1:17, Martin Luther experienced a profound revelation that would shape the course of Christian history. He described it as if the gates of heaven had been opened, a moment that marked the beginning of his journey toward a deeper understanding of justification by faith. This revelation revealed that salvation is received through faith, not works; it changed his life. I asked my pastor once, "Why is faith so important?" He laughed and said, "I don't know. I just know God is really big on faith."

"But without faith it is impossible to please him: for he that cometh to God must believe that he is, and that he is a rewarder of them that diligently seek him" (Hebrews 11:6).

Understanding the concept of free will and God's desire for reciprocal love makes it evident that He grants us the freedom to choose whether or not to reciprocate this affection. So, how can one cultivate a genuine love for God? The path lies in trust. Trust is a sentiment nurtured through seeking Him in His written word, a journey that, when undertaken, brings with it a promise of both spiritual reward and the fulfillment of our deepest desires through faith.

Accomplish your reward by faith.

He is: El-Yeshuati
The God of My Salvation
Blessings

THE SHEPHERD INSTRUCTS

December 5

*And moreover, because the preacher was wise, he still taught the people knowledge; yea, he gave good heed, and sought out,
and set in order many proverbs.
The preacher sought to find out acceptable words: and that
which was written was upright, even words of truth.
The words of the wise are as goads, and as nails fastened by the masters of
assemblies, which are given from one shepherd.*

Ecclesiastes 12:9–11

God wants you to be in a good church family where you can learn His ways because His ways work better than ours. When a preacher's sermon pertains to you, they will prod you (goad you) and even cut through you sometimes. The wise will nail the words to their heart and apply the teachings in everyday life.

I once prayed for a man, and the Lord told me: "Increased productivity." As his eyes began to tear, I asked him, "What is going on?" He told me he had gotten two women pregnant at the same time.

I understood what the word meant; he had to work more to provide. Then, the Lord told me: "Tell him to find a church so that I can admonish him." I had to look up the definition of admonish, which means to warn or firmly reprimand. I'm sure God wanted to do something miraculous, but the man's actions had consequences, and God was willing to help him work through the repercussions by teaching him the right way.

If he had nailed God's words to his heart earlier in life, he could have kept five people out of poverty. I don't know what happened to the man, but I know that if he obeyed the word, God would help him.

He is: Jehovah-Makkeh
The Lord Who Disciplines You
Blessings

BE SHARP

December 6

"Iron sharpeneth iron; so a man sharpeneth the countenance of his friend."

Proverbs 27:17

There are some curious attributes regarding this scripture. When you accept Jesus Christ as your Lord and Savior, you humble yourself and fall on the stone of salvation, which is Jesus Christ.

"And whosoever shall fall on this stone shall be broken: but on whomsoever it shall fall, it will grind him to powder" (Matthew 21:44).

Now, here's the curious attribute: when a butcher sharpens a knife, they use a sharpening stone, which microscopically takes the knife's edge down to what looks like the teeth of a saw. Under the microscope, you can see the roughness of the blade, each little "tooth" pointing from side to side.

After they have worked it over with the stone, the butcher will take a steal-honing rod and swipe the knife downwards on each side of the blade, which smooths the teeth and creates uniformity, all the little teeth facing the same direction.

Embracing the challenges and discomforts that may arise during your time at church is an integral part of the spiritual journey. There are moments when the pastor's words may feel uncannily personal, resonating with experiences you thought were known only to you. Yet, this is by design, for Jesus calls His followers to confront themselves, aligning their hearts and minds in the same direction. Within the church family, you find yourself surrounded by others who, like you, are being honed and refined by their faith. It is here that Jesus places you, knowing that through this collective growth and mutual support, you will find strength, purpose, and a deeper connection with Him. Jesus places you in a church body for sharpening.

He is: El Sela
God My Rock
Blessings

KING ME

December 7

*"It is the glory of God to conceal a thing:
but the honour of kings is to search out a matter."*

Proverbs 25:2

This verse has stuck in my head for years. I used to think it pertained to a person's sin or past crimes and that God, by His grace, conceals it. For whatever reason, the authors of King James elected to translate the Hebrew word *daw-bawr* over to the English word thing. Maybe it wasn't the best choice of words, and that's what it means: *word.*

We better understand what Father God is saying by searching out the text. God has elected to conceal His words in the text of the Bible. Solomon wrote in Ecclesiastes 12:10, "The preacher sought to find out acceptable words: and that which was written was upright, even words of truth."

When you study the Bible and discover words and meanings for yourself, it's to your honor. Have you ever been around someone who wants to tell you about a revelation they received from the Lord while reading the Bible? They are excited and usually full of joy, wanting to share their new insights with you. Take your throne, and you can be a king when you study your Bible.

He is: Gelah Raz
Revealer of Mysteries
Blessings

YESTERDAY PAST

December 8

And now art thou cursed from the earth, which hath opened
her mouth to receive thy brother's blood from thy hand;
When thou tillest the ground, it shall not henceforth yield unto thee
her strength; a fugitive and a vagabond shalt thou be in the earth.
And Cain said unto the LORD, My punishment is greater than I can bear.

Genesis 4:11–13

Cain receives punishment from God, or does he? I've considered this Bible passage over the years, and one thing seemed perplexing. If Cain was cursed and made a vagabond, how is it three verses later he builds a city and names it after his son Enoch?

In Webster's dictionary, a vagabond strolls about and wanders from place to place, such a lazy person without a place to settle, a wanderer.

But vagabond in Hebrew has a different meaning. It comes from the Hebrew word nood; it does mean to wander and flee, but it also means to bemoan, express grief over to lament, and to mourn.

Cain expresses no concern over the earth, cursing him by making him till the ground harder. His concern is being a vagabond and that men would kill him. He's facing a life of torment for what he did to his brother. God was letting Cain know the consequences of his actions, which would be guilt for life. To protect Cain, God sealed his forehead with a mark of protection.

When we sin, the enemy does his best to ensure we never forget it. But we have an advocate, Jesus Christ, crowned with thorns and beaten over His head with a reed. The reed was a symbol of grace, symbolically taking the guilt of our sin. Cain's mark was temporary, like credit card debt, and Jesus was the payment in full.

"Forgetting what is behind and straining toward what is ahead..." (Philippians 3:1)

He is: Elohay-Selichot
The God Who Is Ready to Forgive
Blessings

WHO'S ON STAFF?

December 9

And it came to pass, when Moses held up his hand, that Israel prevailed:
and when he let down his hand, Amalek prevailed.
But Moses' hands were heavy, and they took a stone and put it under him, and he
sat thereon; and Aaron and Hur stayed up his hands, the one on the one side, and
the other on the other side; and his hands were steady
until the going down of the sun.

Exodus 17:11–12

Amalek, known as the Amalekites, were direct descendants of Esau. It seems as though Esau's deep resentment and hatred for his brother Jacob carried down through his descendants, even to this day. And Esau was a direct descendant of Abraham, and the Amalekites knew what God told Abraham in Genesis 12:3: "I will bless those who bless you, and I will curse those who curse you." As it turns out, this nation no longer exists.

Unlike when God Himself delivered the Hebrews from the pharaoh's army by drowning them in the Red Sea, the Israelites had to fight this battle themselves. Moses placed himself on top of a mountain behind the battle so his army could see him. As he lifts his staff, which he held over the Red Sea, he stands as an intercessor for his nation. Imagine the consequences if Israel would have lost; the entire people would have suffered genocide.

As Moses's arms weakened, two more intercessors joined in and shared in the pain.

I am so grateful for the intercessors I have in my life, people who have shared in my pain and prayed me through to victory repeatedly.

It's like they pray for a *banner* over me, and that banner is God.

"And Moses built an altar, and called the name of it Jehovahnissi" (Exodus 17:15).

He is: Jehovah-Nissi
The Lord My Banner
Blessings

STRONGER THAN WIND

December 10

"Ye are of God, little children, and have overcome them: because greater is he that is in you, than he that is in the world."

1 John 4:4

It's a beautiful thing to belong to God, and sometimes we forget that, through Jesus Christ, we're contending with a defeated adversary. Jesus spoke of having "faith like that of a small child."

The good news is that if Jesus is your Lord, you're already a child of God. Now, the challenge lies in cultivating childlike faith. Many adults need help with this. I recall a story from years ago, during a severe drought, likely in the 1930s or '40s.

The farming community decided to gather and pray for rain. The town gathered a large crowd. Pastors preached, and fervent prayers filled the air. As the meeting concluded, amidst the dispersing crowd, a little girl with childlike faith unfurled an umbrella over her head. She remained, patiently waiting for God to send the rain, fully expecting victory.

Because of her faith, the rain came.

Another noteworthy point is the word "them," which derives from the Greek word *autos*, meaning "a baffling wind." Remember, when you're in spiritual combat, the enemy is usually just blowing hot air.

Don't be afraid to open your umbrella.

He is: El Haggadol
The Great God
Blessings

A POOR PROMISE

December 11

"I will also leave in the midst of thee an afflicted and poor people, and they shall trust in the name of the LORD."

Zephaniah 3:12

This verse brings out some emotions when you meditate upon it for a while because it reveals the kindness of a loving God who looks at your heart and not your circumstances.

Zephaniah was the great-great-grandson of King Hezekiah (a righteous king who loved the Lord). Zephaniah felt it necessary to prove his royal genealogy, which makes his rebukes of the royalty more significant.

He was prophesying to specific groups of people, those in idolatry and pagan worship. Letting them know that judgment is coming, which includes death and captivity. But God leaves this promise that some afflicted and poor will remain because they trusted in Him.

The definition of "afflicted" is depressed in mind or circumstances, *humble.*

The definition of "poor" is weaker, lean, or needy.

By embracing affliction as a form of humility, we acknowledge our impending judgment for our actions while recognizing our inherent neediness. "Blessed are the poor (needy) in spirit, for theirs is the kingdom of the heavens" (Matthew 5:3).

When your spirit, afflicted and poor, yearns to trust in God, you position yourself to inherit His promises.

He is: Jehovah-Palat
Deliver
Blessings

LIVE THE SALT-FREE LIFE

December 12

"Remember Lot's wife."

Luke 17:32

Jesus quoted this verse referring to His second coming. We can find Lot's wife in Genesis 19, and God is about to destroy Sodom & Gomorrah. Angels instructed Lot and his wife not to look back as they fled the city. However, Lot's wife looked back as the destruction took place, and she became a pillar of salt. On the side of a mountain near this location is a pillar of salt that resembles a woman, and it is called Lot's wife.

Why did she turn and look back? Was she looking at the destruction? Or was she looking back at her past? Lot lingered until morning; he did not want to leave his stuff behind, and the angels forced him to leave. Was she looking back for the stuff she left behind?

Stuff, we have so much of it. It can be property or things from our past. I've listened to Christians talk about how bad they were before they accepted Jesus as their Savior. Sometimes, it seems like a competition to see who was worse.

Some pride swells up as they talk about their sinful pasts. Sometimes, sharing your testimony is good, and there is a time to leave your past behind and not look back.

When you look back, you're bound to stumble.

He is: El Yeshuati
The God of My Salvation
Blessings

LEARNING TO LOVE

December 13

"But as it is written, Eye hath not seen, nor ear heard, neither have entered into the heart of man, the things which God hath prepared for them that love him."

1 Corinthians 2:9

Apostle Paul wrote this epistle to the Corinthian church. It started as a scathing letter rebuking them for their pride and their divisions in doctrine. Corinth was a central commercial hub for commerce, and it had two harbors that allowed trade into Asia: Spain, Italy, and Egypt. The population consisted of 220,000 free people and about 400,000 enslaved people.

It was also known for the famous temple of the goddess Aphrodite, the goddess of love. Temple prostitution consisted of as many as 1000 prostitutes applying their trade every evening, walking out of the temple down a long walkway.

The temptations were great. In the modern-day, I can see some correlations as we live in a time where sin is easy to fall into; one click of the mouse and you can be in the sin of pornography.

After the reprimand, the Apostle Paul wanted us to see that the wait would be worth it. Waiting upon the Lord brings great rewards. Here, he is also alluring us into a relationship with the Holy Spirit that will reveal Christ's secret mysteries. The keywords are: *for them that love him.*

The Holy Spirit will show you the love of the Trinity, and like a small child develops a love for their parents, you will learn to love Him too.

He is: Elohim Ahavah
The God Who Loves
Blessings

HAVE A BATTLE PLAN

December 14

"And Asa did that which was good and right in the eyes of the LORD his God."

2 Chronicles 14:2

This should be our goal in life, that when our race is done, people will say "___ ___ did that which was good and right in the eyes of the LORD his God."

Asa's understanding of God's ways didn't emerge overnight. It was forged through personal study, dedicated prayer, and a profound grasp of the Ten Commandments. Asa arrived at his kingship already equipped with a plan, having long cultivated leadership skills and nurtured a steadfast faith.

His economic strategy was simple yet profound: trust in the Lord and purge the land of evil. In return, God granted respite from adversaries, bestowing peace upon the kingdom.

However, a day came when Asa faced the Ethiopians, encroaching upon his realm. He meticulously devised a battle plan, positioning his warriors for the impending clash. He humbly implored God's aid before his men and the Almighty, offering an emotional plea: "Help us, O Lord our God; for we rest on thee, and in thy name, we go against this multitude."

"And Asa did that which was good and right in the eyes of the LORD his God" did you observe the use of double words? "good and right," and "The LORD his God." This stylistic device, known as a pleonasm, underscores the inseparable union of goodness and righteousness. "The LORD, our God" reinforces the personal connection Asa held with the divine.

Remember, just as God was with Asa, He will be with you too.

He is: Yahuah Elohayu
The Lord His God
Blessings

DIVINE INSTRUCTION

December 15

"I will instruct you and teach you in the way you should go;
I will counsel you and watch over you."

Psalm 32:8

We often come to places in life where we don't know which way or how to respond to a situation. This promise assures us that God knows the way. Over the years, I have been in situations where I didn't know which way to turn. Stress can cause so much confusion. I've noticed it can build up or hit you like a freight train; either way, it's not from God.

His solution will come if you ask and know how to wait. Once, I was in a job interview, and it was going very well. Suddenly, the interviewer asked, "If you were a cartoon character, who would you be?"

By design, this question was intended to throw me off balance and to see how I would react to such an awkward question, and it did. I hadn't watched a cartoon in years, and suddenly, this voice said, "Elmer Fudd!" I knew this wasn't me, and it certainly wasn't God. As the eternal seconds ticked by and the two men sat staring at me, I held my composure while this battle engaged in my mind. Again, I heard "Elmer Fudd!" shout at me, and I thought I am not saying Elmer Fudd! It happened a third time. I thought, Lord, I need help.

Then, I remembered that my oldest son used to watch this cartoon as a child. I said, "What's the name of that cartoon where the cars turn into robots?" They looked at each other and came up with the transformers. I asked, "The robot that led the good guys, what was his name?" They said, "Optimus Prime?" Then, I said, "I would be Optimus Prime." The two men looked at each other and said, "Man, that's a good answer." Inside, I knew that the Holy Spirit had bailed me out. God sees you as a leader, not as a foolish cartoon character.

He promises to watch over and instruct you. How awesome is that?

He is: Gelah Raz
Revealer of Mysteries
Blessings

REVEALER OF MYSTERIES

December 16

For My thoughts are not your thoughts, nor are your ways My ways," says the Lord. "For as the heavens are higher than the earth, so are My ways higher than your ways, And My thoughts higher than your thoughts.

Isaiah 55:8–9

The world is very complex, and sometimes you ask: "Why?" You've been through more than enough, but enough won't stop. One time during ministry, a man came up to me for prayer, and the Lord very clearly said: "He is blessed with the circumstances of life!"

The man didn't say a word. Moments later, I looked over, and he was sitting in a chair with tears streaming down his face.

I remember a story of a company transporting a type of live codfish from the East Coast to the West Coast for restaurants to sell. This codfish was delicious to eat on the East Coast, but by the time it made it to the West Coast, the fish didn't taste the same. The fish were too relaxed in the fish tanks and just enjoyed the ride, causing the meat to be mushy.

The company devised a strategy to keep the fish healthy along the trip. They started placing sea catfish in the tanks along with the codfish. Turns out the sea catfish are natural enemies to the cod. This constant battle kept the cod firm during the trip. They tasted good when they arrived in time for dinner on the West Coast.

We want our lives to sail without struggles, but what would we be in God's eyes? Just a person that served God as long as everything went well. Offer your life up as a sacrifice of praise when things go well, rejoice when things aren't going so well, and trust in God that He is knowledgeable. This will work out to your good.

"So shall My word be that goes forth from My mouth, it shall not return to me void, but it shall accomplish what I please, and it shall prosper in the thing for which I sent it" (Isaiah 55:11).

He is: Gelah Raz
Revealer of Mysteries
Blessings

BUILD ON THE ROCK

December 17

Therefore, whoever hears these sayings of Mine, and does them, I will liken him to a wise man who built his house on the rock; "and the rain descended, the floods came, and the winds blew and beat on that house; and it did not fall, for it was founded on the rock. "But everyone who hears these sayings of Mine, and does not do them, will be like a foolish man who built his house on the sand: "and the rains came, and the winds blew and beat on that house, and it fell, and great was its fall."

Matthew 7:24–27

I lived in South Louisiana for several years. Believe me, I can relate to this verse in the natural and spiritual. Thunderhead clouds would roll off the Gulf of Mexico with furious winds that the locals call "squalls."

The good thing about a squall is that they come and go pretty fast, with lots of rain, lightning, thunder, and wind. You knew they would pass so that you could hold on for a while, but the problem was you never really knew how long a storm would last.

Then, there is the hurricane, a whole different level of storm, stronger winds, tornadoes, and much more rain. Before modern technology, people didn't know when the eye of the storm was passing over. The eye is a round hole in the middle of the cloud. While in the middle of the eye, people would venture out too far away from safety, thinking the storm had passed, and then out of nowhere, the storm would slam them again with its peak intensity. Imagine winds of zero mph, and then suddenly, 125 mph wind hits you; a stick could kill you.

One night, when I first became a Christian, I had a dream (a night vision). I was walking down a beach, and there was this Antebellum-style house. The front columns were starting to fall, and the foundation was breaking. I looked at the home, and the Lord spoke to me and said, "Scott, why are the columns falling on this house?" I pointed behind the house and said, "Lord, it's because they did not go far enough back and build on a solid foundation." That was the end of that dream when I woke up. Even though I had never studied dream interpretations, I knew the meaning: something terrible was coming my way, and bad things did happen.

Always remember the enemy cannot sustain an attack against you forever. You may have your arms wrapped around a tree, waiting for the storm to pass, but it will pass. Unless, of course, you are one of those storm chasers, but that's a whole other devotion.

"But He said to them, 'Why are you so fearful, O you of little faith?' Then He arose and rebuked the winds and the sea, and there was a great calm" (Matthew 8:26).

He is: El Sela
God My Rock
Blessings

PREDESTINATION

December 18

For whom the Lord knew He also predestined to be conformed to the image of His Son, that He might be the firstborn among many brethren.
Moreover, whom He predestined, these He also called; whom He called; these He also justified; these He also justified, these He also glorified.

Romans 8:29–30

Predestination: this word is only found six times in the Bible, and it comes from the Greek word *Proorizo*, which means "to decide beforehand." It reminds me of an old joke: "Look up the word 'predestine' in the dictionary, and your picture will be next to it."

Everyone has a predestination from God. Before the foundation of the world, His destiny for you was to accept Jesus Christ as your Lord and Savior. Once you accept Jesus as your Lord and Savior, He starts working to conform you *to His image*, the image of Jesus.

But now O Lord,

You are our Father;

We are the clay, and You our potter;

And all we are the work of Your hand.

Isaiah 64:8

The word "image" is powerful, implying that we are made in His likeness. I believe this to mean His character.

I just had a vision of Jesus stepping in front of me in the Spirit. If He stands in front of you, the enemy cannot see you. You're His likeness in the Spirit. If the enemy cannot see through Jesus, he can't see you. He only sees Christ. And if he can only see Jesus Christ, it's as if he can only see the power of the King!

"Nay, in all things we are more than conquerors, through Him that Loved us!" (Romans 8:37)

You have a lot more authority than you know.

He is: Jehova-Magen
God Our Shield
Blessings

THE GOD WHO SAVES

December 19

"I called on the Lord in my distress.
The Lord answered me and set me in a broad place."

Psalm 118:5

While visiting family in California, I did my morning Bible study as I looked towards Stoney Creek. I couldn't see the creek from there because the woods were so thick. It reminded me of when I was a young boy. We used to play in those woods all day and night, running up and down the pathways that we knew so well. I never once got lost. I even remembered helping another boy out of the woods who was utterly lost and scared. I heard him crying out for help. I walked him to a place and pointed him down the right path. The path eventually led back to the city, the broad place, safety.

I remember thinking, "How could he have been so lost and close to the correct path?"

"For the ways of a man are before the Lord. And He ponders all his paths" (Proverbs 5:21).

God will allow you to run around in the woods following whatever path you want, and I use the word will because you have free will, a choice:

"Then the Lord knows how to deliver the godly out of temptations and to reserve the unjust under punishment for the day of judgment for the day of punishment" (2 Peter 2:9).

If that young boy had not cried out for help, I would have walked past him that day. He was so close to salvation. However, silence would have stranded him. People remain silent for various reasons; pride is probably the number one reason.

After I placed the young man on the correct path, he had to do his part. He had to stay on the path to get back to town. It makes me laugh to think about it. He had to pass along a way with a ditch on one side and a hot wire fence on the other, with little room for error. I can tell you that hot wire fence zapped my friends and me. I don't remember falling into the ditch, but the ditch was evident, and the hot wire was hard to see. Same with sin, it looks like a good thing to grab, until it grabs you. I want to pose this question: how do you avoid the pitfalls in life?

"Be diligent in presenting yourself approved to God, a worker who does not need to be ashamed, rightly dividing the word of truth" (2 Timothy 2:15).

Not being ashamed is something we all strive to achieve. *It is rightly dividing the word of truth.* Spend time reading the Bible daily, and it will come alive and become your living word. It will become your friend that helps you stay on the right path.

He is: El Moshaah
The God Who Saves
Blessings

THE GREAT WHITE THRONE JUDGEMENT

December 20

Then I saw a great white throne and Him who sat on it, from whose face the earth and the heaven fled away. And there was found no place for them.
And I saw the dead, small and great, standing before God and books were opened. And another book was opened, which is the Book of Life, and the dead were judged according to their works, by the things which were written in the books.
The sea gave up the dead who were in it, and Death and Hades delivered up the dead who were in them. And they were judged, each one according to his works. Then Death and Hades were cast into the lake of fire. This is the second death, And anyone not found written in the Book of Life was cast into the lake of fire.

Revelation 20:11–15

The Great White Throne Judgement: not everything in the Bible is pretty; it's just true. This judgment takes place after the 1000-year reign of Jesus Christ, known as the millennial reign of Christ. Time-wise, we don't really know anything more than that. Satan is loosed from the pit after 1000 years. Once again, he tries to overthrow the nations and Christ. It may take hundreds or just a few years, but men will again turn against God. After this uprising comes, we will all stand and witness The Great White Throne Judgment.

"…from whose face the earth and the heaven fled away. And there was found no place for them."

Almost like in a movie scene, all expanse will open up, no corners to hide in, no shadow of darkness, everyone's deeds will be exposed, good and bad. Suppose your name isn't in the Book of Life; the lake of fire is where you will be forever. No one will rejoice; in fact, there will be much weeping and many tears.

If your name is in the Lamb's Book of Life, you will see this prophecy fulfilled:

"And God shall wipe away every tear from their eyes; there shall be no more death, sorrow, or crying, no more pain, for the former things have passed away" (Revelation 21:4).

Sadly, I can almost see someone scoff and say: "I don't believe those things, huh!" Sorry, friend, it's true whether you believe it or not. "Write, for these words are true and faithful" (Revelation 21:5).

But here's your hope, your salvation, your way out of the lake of fire: "Jesus, who delivers us from the wrath to come" (1 Thessalonians 1:10). The same person who would be your judge wants to be your Deliverer. All you have to do is ask before it's too late. Deliver comes from the Greek word *rhuomai*, meaning "to save or rescue, release, buyback, or set free." It also has an eschatological meaning (eschatological relates to the ultimate destination of mankind): Jesus rescues the sinner from the day of wrath.

Please take the life ring that Jesus has to offer.

He is: Jehovah-Palat
Deliverer
Blessings

THE LORD YOUR GOD

December 21

As ye have therefore received Christ Jesus the Lord, so walk ye in Him. Rooted and built up in Him, and established in the faith, as ye have been taught, abounding therein with thanksgiving. Beware lest any man spoil you through philosophy and vain deceit, after the tradition of men, after the rudiments of the world, and not after Christ. For in him dwells all the fullness of Godhead bodily. And ye are complete in him, which is the head of all principality and power.

Colossians 2:6–10

You can see the actual depth of what Paul is saying to the Colossians. I'll paraphrase some here: As ye have therefore received the Divine Anointed Messiah, the Divine Jesus our Lord, so walk ye in Him.

By using a Hebrew concordance, we can amplify the names of God to try and understand His character. Applying this, we can walk in Jesus, not just alongside Jesus. Paul explains the authority you have in Christ.

Rooted and built up in him: In a world where we only see the trees for their topside appearance, God wants you to look at your roots in Him. The roots hold every tree up in Him. …and established in the faith, as ye have been taught, abounding therein with thanksgiving.

Established refers to your roots of belief in Christ or your foundation. There is a theory called "The First Learned Experience." The view is that the first time you hear something about a particular subject, this will be your baseline for your beliefs about that subject, in other words, a "bias." If someone tells you a more accurate explanation, you will judge their explanation from your original baseline, no matter how wrong the first explanation was.

So here is the point of all that: you want to be the first person to explain the truth about love to your child, the truth about sexual relations outside of marriage, the truth about how much God loves them. Don't let the world establish a root in your children, a basis of unbelief; teach them your faith, and be "thankful to God." Sometimes, it's hard to be thankful in a challenging circumstance, but maybe God is pruning you so that your roots will grow to hold up your character because character builds hope.

Beware lest any man spoil you through philosophy and vain deceit, after the tradition of men, after the rudiments of the world, and not after Christ.

Everyone has a belief system, a philosophy of some sort, good or bad, right or wrong. Some are rooted in the television.

For in him dwells all the fullness of Godhead bodily. And ye are complete in him, which is the head of all principality and power.

In Jesus is all the fullness of the Father, the Son, and the Holy Spirit, and you. This is why you have authority over spiritual authorities in high places because you are in Him!

He is: Yahuah Elohaykem
The Lord Your God
Blessings

THE LORD IS GOOD

December 22

"But My servant Caleb, because he has a different spirit in him and has followed me fully, I will bring into the land where he went, and his descendants shall inherit it."

Numbers 14:24

Numbers 14:24 mentions God's servant, Caleb, who possessed a unique spirit and wholeheartedly followed God. Because of this, God promised to lead him into the land he and Joshua had explored forty-five years earlier when Moses sent forth the twelve spies. Because of Caleb's faithfulness, he and his descendants will inherit a sizable territory.

It's worth noting that Caleb's background is quite distinctive. He was born into the tribe of Judah. Still, his family wasn't originally counted among the twelve tribes of Israel, as we learn from Joshua 14:14, which identifies him as "Caleb, the son of Jephunneh the Kenizzite."

After the twelve spies returned, ten spies filled the Israelites with doubt and unbelief. The next day, the Israelites were afraid of the giants in the land; they wanted to go back to Egypt, and some were talking about stoning Moses and Arron. As the people complained and rebelled against God and Moses, Caleb and Joshua responded. They rushed into the crowd and tore their clothes in repentance and anguish, trying to encourage the people with faith. They knew there would be repercussions from God and went out amongst the people, trying to calm them down and yelling, "Let us go up at once and take the possession, for we are well able to overcome it!" Risking their own lives to protect *the priest*, *the prophet*, and *God's promise*. Notice they were trying to get the people to fight now! Before fear compromised the promise.

What insights can we glean from this pivotal moment in history?

1. Sometimes, leaders need to exercise discernment in how much information they share, especially in situations where the details might be overwhelming.

2. Moses should have met with the men separately, not before the congregation, and ordered them to refrain from speaking of their observations.

3. Taking prompt action, as exemplified by Caleb and Joshua, can help prevent potential obstacles and negative conversations as Caleb and Joshua did. Sometimes, when you receive direction from God, strap your amour on and head out to the battle before the enemy places a stumbling block in your path.

4. Caleb had a different spirit, a spirit of faith. Faith, in essence, is the antithesis of fear. Consider the forty years in the wilderness: God provided for their every need. Caleb recognized God's presence and chose to trust in Him. By placing his belief in God, he exercised his spirit. Conversely, others forget the promise and let fear guide them. You have the same capacity for the spirit that Caleb embodied, a 'can-do

attitude,' and it all starts with your mindset. Embracing faith means acknowledging God's power and provision, even in the face of adversity or uncertainty. It's a transformative perspective that empowers you to overcome challenges with confidence and assurance

5. Caleb's family was grafted into the branches of the Hebrews, and so are you if you have received Jesus Christ as your Lord and Savior:

"And if some of the branches were broken off, and you being a wild olive tree, were grafted in among them, and with them became a partaker of the root and fatness of the olive tree" (Romans 11:17).

Caleb and Joshua entered the Promised Land, and at age eighty-five, when everyone else wanted to quit fighting, Caleb stood up and said, "I have a promise: I will go to the mountains and fight the giants!" He did just that and took the promise God had given him forty-five years earlier. He took all the land of Hebron, the high, rugged mountains the giants lived in, and the cities. Now, Caleb had become one of God's generals, a general in battle and a general in faith.

The Lord told me: "Audacity in the Spirit is for posterity," which means that acts of boldness in the Holy Spirit are recorded for all future generations to see. Ask God for your inheritance; it's waiting there for you.

He is: Adonai Tov
The Lord Is Good
Blessings

HE'S A GOOD, GOOD GOD

December 23

Eye has not seen, nor ear heard, nor have entered into the heart of man the things which God has prepared for those who love Him. But God has revealed them to us through His Spirit, or the Spirit searches all things, yes, the deep things of God.

1 Corinthians 2:9–10

I love this verse, and I think about it often. It is an endless promise from God. As far as your eye can see, you have still not seen the good things God has promised for you. The farthest distance you can hear, you have more to listen to, but listen to what? See what?

I've noticed that God is a teacher; He loves to teach, and He loves for you to ask Him questions. It amazes me that if I ask about a subject, He will get the answer to me.

The Bible is the best textbook ever written, but the splendor in how He can teach you is astonishing. Once for three weeks, the Lord asked me to go to the front of the church for prayer at the end of each service. I have always preferred not to be the person up front or doing the public speaking, so going up for prayer took a lot of effort.

Every service, the pastor preached on something I had been going through. The third week came around, and the Holy Spirit asked me to go to the altar for prayer again. I told the Lord, "I will, but please don't ask me to go up for prayer again, not a fourth time, please!"

Our pastor was gone, and his wife, Sister Nell, did the sermon that day. As usual, I sat in the back row. She began by announcing the name of the sermon: "Peter Walks on Water." I fell forward in my seat and said out loud, "No, not this message, Lord!" The man next to me just looked at me in bewilderment.

And then the moment came that I knew she was going to say: "If anyone wants to get out of the boat and walk on water for the Lord, come up here for prayer." It was a relatively large church, and you could have heard a pin drop; it was so quiet no one moved, not even a mouse. I think I saw a mouse, and he was frozen motionless in total fear of what the Lord was about to do, and it was my reflection! I pushed myself up and walked forward. I could feel every eye in the building looking at me, pressing their thoughts into my low self-esteem. As she prayed for me, I didn't hear a word she said because I feared being in front of everyone. It must have been a great prayer because I heard the congregation cheering and clapping.

When she finished, I walked in the opposite direction so I wouldn't see anyone looking at me. Then, this little old Cajun lady, Miss Eula, said, "Obedience! God told me you were obedient!" God was looking for Obedience so that He could teach me to trust In Him. Later on, this little old Cajun lady gave me this word two times from the Lord: Eye has not seen, nor ear heard, nor have entered into the heart of man the things which God has prepared for those who love Him.

That was more than twenty years ago. Miss Eula has gone on to be with the Lord, but I will never forget those words spoken with the beautiful Cajun accent.

Never could I have envisioned the expansive journey of my ministry—from Scott Coy Prophetic Ministries, Prayer Stop, and Prayer Stop on the Air radio program to obtaining my Chaplain's license and achieving ordination. Most profoundly, I've been blessed with the precious gift of praying for others. Through these endeavors, I've discovered the profound purpose God has woven into my life, time and again, by enabling me to uplift and support those in need. Indeed, He is a God of boundless goodness!

He is: Shub Nephesh
Renewer of Life
Blessings

UNCHANGING GOD

December 24

"But the fruit of the Spirit is love, joy, peace, patience, kindness, goodness, faithfulness, gentleness, self-control, against such there is no law."

Galatians 5:22–23

The other day, I watched a newscast, and the lawmakers were voting. I contemplated the news broadcast and could not get it out of my mind. Today, while studying this verse, it dawned on me.

As a nation, there isn't a clear answer to how many laws we currently have on the books. I did see where 40,000 laws were added in one day, January 2012.

But no laws can be formed against the Spirit of God. However, there is a tax, "a love tax," I guess you could call it when you go get your marriage license. But love is legal, and joy is a gift you give yourself, peace is a gift from God, patience is learned, kindness is something you do, goodness comes from your thoughts, faithfulness substantiates who you are, gentleness is power under control, that's why it is followed up by self-control. *Against such, there is no law; legislators* can't make that illegal. God's word still stands.

He is: Lo Shanah
Unchanging
Blessings

MERRY CHRISTMAS

December 25

And, lo, the angel of the Lord came upon them, and the glory
of the Lord shone round about them: and they were sore afraid.
And the angel said unto them, Fear not: for, behold,
I bring you good tidings of great joy, which shall be to all people.
For unto you is born this day in the city of David a Saviour,
which is Christ the Lord.
And this shall be a sign unto you; Ye shall find the babe
wrapped in swaddling clothes, lying in a manger.
And suddenly there was with the angel a multitude of the
heavenly host praising God, and saying,
Glory to God in the highest, and on earth peace, goodwill toward men.

Luke 2:9–14

You know Jesus is no longer a baby; sometimes, we must remember that. However, this was the ultimate act of humility, and nothing can compare to it, except maybe the cross. In the Hebrew alphebet (not the alphabet), the tenth letter in the alphebet is called *Yod*, or YOOD, and it's the smallest letter in the alphebet. It looks like a curved apostrophe ('). Every letter in the Hebrew language has a meaning and a numerical number associated with it.

Over 500 years ago, the rabbis explained that the Yod is the universe's smallest point. When you put your pen to paper, the initial touch is called a YOD. And YOD represents God. God is infinite, and our universe is finite. God had to contract Himself to become finite and create the universe, and this is called the "Concept of Contraction," which gives us the smallest point in the universe, a Yod.

While explaining this on one of my radio programs, live on the air, I had a vision of an embryo and realized it was Jesus in the shape of a YOD!

Jesus gave everything He had to save our souls—the ultimate act of YOD.

He is: Elohim
Mighty Creator
Blessings

GOD IS LISTENING . . .

December 26

"Then the Lord gave Israel a deliverer, so that they escaped from under the hand of the Syrians; and the Children of Israel dwelt in their tents as before."

2 Kings 13:5

Second Kings 13:5 recounted that the Lord provided Israel with a rescuer, enabling them to break free from the grip of the Syrians. Consequently, the children of Israel could resume their customary way of life, dwelling in their tents as they had done previously.

Before this event, King Jehoahaz, who had erred in the eyes of the Lord, fervently implored God for deliverance from the Syrian oppression. In the preceding verse, it is recorded that his supplication was heard, as stated in verse four, "The Lord listened."

It gets complicated with the dual kingdoms of Judah and Israel existing simultaneously. They were family but enemies, two domains from the same household. A divided house and big brother Israel was in defeat.

King Jehoahaz had turned his back on God all his life and time as the ruling king. But at the end of his days, he asks God for help. It took him a long time to run out of options. Everything under the ruler was exhausted except for the power of a broken heart.

If a contrite heart is all you've got, give it to God, and God will take it and create a victory, a way where there seems to be no way. Notice God sent a deliverer; scholars believe his son Jehoash conquered Syria.

But in our lives, God sent His Son Jesus. I feel like God left the identity of the deliverer unnamed, unseen, working on Jehoahaz's behalf, just like the Holy Spirit will work on your behalf when you cry out to the Son for help.

How complicated things are in your life and how far down you've gone doesn't matter. God can do it! Sadly, Israel did not turn from their sins after God had saved them. Please don't make that mistake. Be thankful. Ask Him how to remove the sinful desires from your life that cause your defeat.

He is: Elohim Shama
The God Who Hears
Blessings

FROM OLD TO NEW

December 27

And he took bread, and gave thanks, and brake it, and gave unto them, saying,
This is my body which is given for you: this do in remembrance of me.
Likewise also the cup after supper, saying, This cup is the
New Testament in my blood, which is shed for you.
But, behold, the hand of him that betrayeth me is with me on the table.
And truly the Son of man goeth, as it was determined:
but woe unto that man by whom he is betrayed!

Luke 22:19–20

Known as "The Lord's Supper," Jesus explains His previous statements in John 6:53:

"Then Jesus said unto them, Verily, verily, I say unto you, Except ye eat the flesh of the Son of man, and drink his blood, ye have no life in you."

Many of the disciples left when He said this, and they said, "This is a hard saying; who can believe this?" These were the same seventy that Jesus had sent out in His name to heal the nation. Now they have deserted Him. But it was a fulfilling prophecy about scattering the sheep found in Ezekiel.

When we take communion, we take Christ's body and His blood to remember Him. Here's an additional fantastic aspect concerning communion:

"This cup is the New Testament in my blood..." (Luke 22:19)

Have you ever considered what Jesus meant when He said the New Testament? They had just finished the Passover Supper, which represented the deliverance of the Hebrews out of Egypt when they crossed the Red Sea.

When Jesus died on the cross, He passed from death to life. And now Jesus has instituted the New Testament, His will, and Testament, by taking of His body and His blood in Holy Communion.

When a will is enforced, all the legal rights go to the person inheriting the will, all the belongings. When you partake in communion, you receive all the legal rights to the New Testament! The New Testament is in you! Along with all the power and authority that goes with it, you have the power of Jesus Christ! Selah.

He is: Jehovah Qadesh:
The Lord Who Sanctifies
Blessings

ANOINTING OIL

December 28

"And they cast out many devils, and anointed with oil many that were sick, and healed them."

Mark 6:13

Where did the anointing of oil for the sick begin? Christians pray for one another, and they'll break out the oil, but most people need to learn the significance behind using oil. Some people believe it represents the anointing of the Holy Spirit. Let's go back in history and see if we can figure this out.

In Exodus 30:22, God gives Moses instructions on how to make holy anointing oil, and this oil was not to be replicated for anyone other than the priests. If someone made and used it, they would be cut off from Israel.

Aaron and his sons were anointed with this oil, and the other priests were consecrating them for the ministry. Tradition has it that the oil in the lampstand never ran dry. God miraculously kept the lamp burning for centuries. But this also signifies that the anointing never departed once the priests became consecrated with oil.

"For the gifts and calling of God are without repentance" (Romans 11:29).

You should receive your healing when anointed and prayed over by a priest or an elder. Once healed, the anointing for that healing should not end. Keep your recovery. I've seen this before: Christians will get healed for a few days, and then it comes back, but you have a promise.

Priests used oil for sacred ceremonies, consecration, anointing furniture, medicinal purposes, perfumes, and anointing the dead. We see the anointing of Jesus was at Bethany before His crucifixion.

"There came unto him a woman having an alabaster box of very precious ointment, and poured it on his head, as he sat at meat" (Matthew 26:7).

I have used olive oil several times to anoint houses for homeowners, mine included. You can often feel the peace enter the home and sense the presence of a demonic spirit leaving. I was instructed once by the Holy Spirit to build an altar at the Packard car plant in Detroit and anoint it with oil, consecrating the land for God's use.

It's not the oil that heals; it's the power of God's word by your act of faith or action of consecration. You open the door for God to do a mighty miracle.

He is: Jehovah-Rapha
The Lord Who Heals
Blessings

YOUR MISSION

December 29

By faith Moses, when he was come to years,
refused to be called the son of Pharaoh's daughter;
Choosing rather to suffer affliction with the people of God,
than to enjoy the pleasures of sin for a season;
Esteeming the reproach of Christ greater riches than the treasures
in Egypt: for he had respect unto the recompense of the reward.

Hebrews 11:24–26

We can learn much from Moses's humility; he walked away from it all. Moses was living in the lap of luxury. When he decided to defend his people by killing an Egyptian, the Hebrews turned against him, and he fled into the wilderness, but God called this faith. Moses knew there would be consequences if he started helping the Hebrews. He probably expected them to come slower.

He chose to suffer affliction rather than enjoy the treasures of Egypt. I know some Christians that have given up much to serve the Lord. Someone told me that he was praying for a missionary. He prayed, "Lord, they have given everything up for You." And he told me that the Lord spoke to him and said, "You have no idea how much they gave up!" We both know that the person would have succeeded in business and marriage. Instead, they chose to serve God and the afflictions of being in his missionary service.

If you can, find a missionary that you can support. Every dollar you donate can help save a soul. Even $20.00 a month goes a long way, and they need it. It costs a missionary about $30,000.00 a year to operate overseas. So, your help is essential, and when things get financially tight, don't stop giving to them because missions are the first thing most Christians will cut from their budget.

Moses became a missionary to his people, a deliverer. You can send a missionary to your people. Once a person gets saved, they become your brothers and sisters; our people are the sons and daughters of Jesus Christ, the Deliverer.

He is: Jehovah-Palat
Deliverer
Blessings

SWIMMING LESSON

December 30

*And he saw them toiling in rowing; for the wind was contrary unto them: and
about the fourth watch of the night he cometh unto them,
walking upon the sea, and would have passed by them.
But when they saw him walking upon the sea, they supposed
it had been a spirit, and cried out:
For they all saw him, and were troubled. And immediately he talked with them,
and saith unto them, Be of good cheer: it is I; be not afraid.
And he went up unto them into the ship; and the wind ceased: and they were sore
amazed in themselves beyond measure, and wondered.
For they considered not the miracle of the loaves: for their heart was hardened.*

Mark 6:48–52

The Gospel of Mark: It is apparent that Mark is an intriguing man. We can find him in the book of Acts 12:12 after Peter was released from prison by an angel: "And when he had considered the thing, he came to the house of Mary, the mother of John, whose surname was Mark, where many were gathered together praying."

Scholars also believe that Mark was possibly the young man in the Garden of Gethsemane on the night of Jesus's arrest. "And there followed him a certain young man, having a linen cloth cast about his naked body; and the young men laid hold on him: And he left the linen cloth, and fled from them naked" (Mark 14:51–52).

It's also possible that he was the rich young man in Mark 10:17–27 whom Jesus looked on with love and told him to give up all his possessions and come follow Him.

He was also a cousin to Barnabas in the book of Acts and was the focal point of great contention between Paul and Barnabas. He went to Rome with Peter and stayed with Peter while he was in prison. Peter used Mark to interpret from Hebrew into Greek, writing the account of Jesus Christ as dictated by Peter, called *The Gospel* according to St. Mark.

This brings us back to Jesus walking on water. Did you observe that in the Gospel of Mark, Peter is not mentioned trying to walk on water? I find it curious that Peter did not share this with Mark. Peter told Mark about getting rebuked by the Lord and shared the details about getting corrected by God at the transfiguration, but he did not share his failed attempt to walk on water.

When we read Matthew's account, we see Peter getting scolded by Jesus for not having enough faith: "And immediately Jesus stretched forth his hand, and caught him, and said unto him, O thou of little faith, wherefore didst thou doubt?" (Matthew 14:31)

Of all the things he shared, why not this? I have been offshore in the ocean, and I can tell you firsthand that a six-foot swell is violent when in the water, especially in a storm with the fierceness of the wind.

After the resurrection, we see Peter was an excellent swimmer when he dove into the water without thought and swam to meet Jesus. However, when Peter began to sink, fear consumed him. He suddenly realizes his situation and cries out to Jesus to save him.

I think Peter looked at this as a personal failure, something too hurtful to share. We all have disappointments and hurts that are too painful to reveal, especially in the best-selling book in history. Peter was harder on himself than the Lord was. But his failure did not stop him. Selah.

He is: Rum Rosh
The One Who Lifts My Head
Blessings

NEW YEAR'S RESOLUTION

December 31

And there shall come forth a rod out of the stem of Jesse,
and a Branch shall grow out of his roots:
And the spirit of the LORD shall rest upon him, the spirit of wisdom and
understanding, the spirit of counsel and might, the spirit of
knowledge and of the fear of the LORD;
And shall make him of quick understanding in the fear of the LORD: and he shall
not judge after the sight of his eyes, neither reprove after the hearing of his ears:
But with righteousness shall he judge the poor, and reprove with equity for the
meek of the earth: and he shall smite the earth with the rod of his mouth, and with
the breath of his lips shall he slay the wicked.

Isaiah 11:1–4

This prophecy is about Jesus and how God would establish His character. It is so touching and humbling. Jesse was King David's father, not known for his wealth and a humble family at the time. The stump represents the remnants of this royal family by the time Jesus was born. We see how poor Joseph and Mary were. King David set aside much wealth and material to build the temple; his son Solomon was the wealthiest man then. Joseph and Mary were descendants of this royal family brought down to a carpenter and a promise.

Jesus would be the twig that came out of the roots, leaving a little shoot of life to a royal dynasty. But the twig has become the rod that will judge the world, a strong branch that will never break.

The Holy Spirit shall descend upon Him, giving Him these qualities:

A Spirit of wisdom and insight,

A Spirit of counsel and Valor,

A Spirit of devotion and reverence for the Lord.

A promise from God, a word written in stone that could not break. But the next verse strikes my heart because it is our part: *He shall sense the truth by His reverence for the Lord.*

Reverence: if we operate in reverence before the Lord, we should be able to sense the truth! If you want to see the truth in someone, be reverent before the Lord. He will give you an understanding of the situation that guides their life. Operate in understanding to help better a broken life. Purpose within yourself to be reverent towards the Lord this year. A New Year's resolution worth keeping.

He is: El Elyon
God Most High
Blessings

ABOUT THE AUTHOR

Chaplain Coy founded Scott Coy Prophetic Ministries and formerly hosted the weekly radio program "Prayer Stop on the Air," which broadcasted throughout multiple states. For years, every Saturday, he set up signs on the side of the road called "Prayer Stop," drive-up prayer trusting in Zechariah 4:6: "Not by might, nor by power, but by My Spirit, saith the Lord of Hosts." Since accepting Jesus in 1983, he's witnessed the faithfulness of God and the miraculous miracles of Christ. He was ordained and graduated as a chaplain through Powerhouse Ministries and continues his studies in psychology and biblical studies at Point University.

Please visit our website at: **www.chaplaincoy.com**.

PRAYER OF SALVATION

"…—continue to work out your salvation with fear and trembling." And, "For he says, 'In the time of my favor I heard you, and in the day of salvation I helped you.' I tell you, now is the time of God's favor, now is the day of salvation."

2 Corinthians 6:2 and Philippians 2:12 (NIV)

My dear friend, accepting Jesus Christ as your LORD is between you and Jesus; no one can do it for you, and no one can stop you. There is no greater joy than when someone repents and asks Jesus for forgiveness. There is no better day than today; you have no promise of tomorrow. I invite you to pray this prayer, ask the Holy Spirit to guide you to a church where you can belong and ask the pastor to baptize you in the Name of the Father, the Son, and the Holy Spirit. Please, with your heart, pray:

"LORD Jesus, humbly, I come before You, and I confess that I have sinned, Jesus; I believe You were crucified on the cross for my salvation; I believe You are LORD and that You have been resurrected from the dead and that You conquered sin. I ask You to please forgive me of all my sin, I plead the blood of Jesus Christ upon my sins and ask for forgiveness. LORD, I ask that You bring me into relationship with the Father and the Holy Spirit and You. Thank You, Jesus, for my redemption, Amen."

Congratulations! Welcome to the family!

Signature:_____   Signed on: _____

BIBLIOGRAPHY

Thompson, A. F., Beale, A., & King, P. (2011). *The Divinity Code to Understanding Your Dreams and Visions*. Destiny Image.

Milton Keynes UK
Ingram Content Group UK Ltd.
UKHW050827270524
443319UK00015B/760